RESIDENTIAL CARE

The Research Reviewed

Literature Surveys commissioned by
the Independent Review of Residential Care

Chaired by Gillian Wagner, OBE, Ph D

Edited by

IAN SINCLAIR

LONDON
HER MAJESTY'S STATIONERY OFFICE

ISBN 0 11 701063 4

Contents

Preface

In his introductory chapter Professor Roy Parker writes, 'No informed conclusion about the future of residential care can be reached without some understanding and appreciation of those forces which have shaped its history'. Understanding the past illuminates the present and ensures that recommendations for the future are more soundly based.

As a committee, charged with the task of reviewing residential care and the range of services given in statutory, voluntary and private residential establishments within the personal social services in England and Wales, we have been very fortunate. Thanks to the timely advice given by Mr Peter Barclay, chairman of the Barclay committee, we were able to commission these research reviews. It may indeed be the first time that a committee such as ours has had the advantage of specially commissioned reviews becoming available to it in time to influence its thinking. We are extremely grateful to all those who undertook the work for the speed with which they produced their papers.

The research has provided us with the necessary background knowledge as well as giving us a deeper understanding of how and why present day problems which afflict the residential sector have arisen; why there are general unease and low staff morale; why the negative image of residential care remains so deeply engraved on the public psyche. It has provided us with a baseline from which to start our deliberations.

We have been enabled to stand back and consider the whole spectrum of residential services from the historical perspective through to the present day. Instead of simply building on the past, making adjustments to a system where, in the main, decisions have been made for people by others, we came to understand the importance of reversing that legacy. If people are put first and given the opportunity to make a positive choice, be it to remain in the community, to opt for a form of sheltered housing or, if they so wish, to choose to go into residential care, we believe, in time, the whole climate within the residential sector could change. Enabling people to make a positive choice will seldom be either simple or straightforward and we deal, in part I of the Report on Residential Care, with some of the complex issues that need to be addressed.

Other evidence, most notably the personal letters we received, also helped to influence our thinking, but the fact that the research reviews are published as a separate volume as part II of the Report into Residential Care indicates their importance, not only to the committee, but to a wider public. They will be of interest to all those who want to understand how economic, political and moral forces have contributed to the history and development of present day residential services.

The research volume is divided into three sections, the first of which deals with the historical background to residential care; the second part surveys current provision for different groups and the third deals with costs. The authors of the different reviews agreed on the general ground they would cover, but remained free to develop the main themes in their own way. Their reviews are included as they were presented to the committee, with minimal changes designed, for example, to ensure consistent referencing, although even in this respect some allowance has been made for individual style.

We are particularly grateful to Dr Ian Sinclair under whose direction the volume took shape and to Professor Roy Parker who agreed to write the historical introduction after the reviews were completed. We are also grateful to the Joseph Rowntree Memorial Trust for financial help.

GILLIAN WAGNER

December 6th 1987

An Historical Background to Residential Care

R A Parker

Department of Social Administration,
University of Bristol

CONTENTS

An Historical Background to Residential Care

1 Introduction

No informed conclusion about the future of residential care can be reached without paying careful attention to the kinds of external changes that are likely to determine its scale and character. That, in turn, cannot be done satisfactorily without some understanding and appreciation of those forces that have shaped its history. The most important of these are located within prevailing social and economic structures. Most of the thoughtful explanations for the proliferation of institutions in this country during the nineteenth century have approached the question in this way.[1] Although they have emphasised different aspects, they have tended to assume that all institutions had enough in common for it to be possible to derive general propositions about their significance and development. The issue of social control has occupied a central position in these formulations.[2] Institutions such as the workhouse, the prison and the asylum are interpreted as responses on the part of the State to the collapse of traditional forms of social regulation. That collapse occurred as a result of 'the advent of a mature capitalist economy'[3] which demanded new forms of occupational discipline but which also made the labouring classes wholly dependent upon wages in an economy increasingly prone to periods of recession. These changes were also accompanied by growing industrialisation and urbanisation, both of which led to the concentration of labour and crowded settlement. Disaffection was, therefore, also concentrated. In the context of such upheaval, the prospect of disorder and the spread of pauperism assumed alarming proportions.

The emergence of the institution, it is argued, has to be seen within that context. Take, for instance, the workhouse system that emerged after 1834.[4] The idea that lay behind it was simple enough. If the conditions for the receipt of relief could be made both stringent and abhorrent then only those in genuine and desperate need would apply; but those conditions could not be imposed except in the controlled space of an institution. This offered the added advantage that those who were admitted could also be trained in the habits of industry and obedience.

[3]

Since much of the assumed threat from a disorderly under-class arose because of their idleness the workhouse had a double value: either it forced the unwilling to find work or, by admitting them, it brought them under an alternative discipline.

Considerable insight has been gained by linking the growth of institutions to the profound transformations that occurred in the nineteenth-century economy. Nor is there any doubt that the desire to control or alter behaviour was a salient feature of most institutional provision. Nonetheless, the ways in which this was attempted varied considerably, as did the level of success. Some control simply took the form of incarceration; some was sought through education, training or treatment, and some through religious exhortation. Other mechanisms of control were less obvious. For example, there were establishments (like asylums) which, by accepting people whose behaviour could not be readily controlled, enabled other institutions (like workhouses) to operate disciplined regimes. Whatever its character, any form of residential segregation increases opportunities for control, as can be seen from the importance attached to barrack-living in the evolution of the army and navy.

Control was (and is) a remarkably complicated thread running through the history of institutions and if we are to understand its significance it is necessary to appreciate that complexity. How, for example, does one assess the impact of the history of institutions upon the view that, at all costs, the admission of an elderly relative to an institution must be avoided? How far has the sense of an obligation to care for such a relative been intensified by the long and sorry history of poor law provision? Or how does one gauge the contribution of institutions to the more general processes of informal social control when, for instance, a child in care could say in 1977: 'I always used to be threatened with being put away in a home where they're always nasty to you. That's the general impression everyone outside has'.[5]

It is also crucial to consider the availability at different times of forms of control other than the institution; for example, the existence of a modern police force, compulsory education, medication, contraception or debt. Likewise, the way in which the problems of social regulation are perceived varies according to a range of other changes, not least in whose perceptions come to prevail. All societies face the need for a measure of both formal and informal social control, but they assume different forms and are experienced differently. Variations also occur within countries as social, economic and political conditions alter. If we assume that institutions contribute to the network of control then that contribution is likely to change as other contributions change.

The idea of social control undoubtedly offers a valuable basis for interpreting the history of institutions; the danger is that it leads to such a preoccupation with the similarities between establishments that the

significance of variations and divergencies is either overlooked or discounted. We need to understand the nature of these differences as much
as we need to understand the structure of similarities. Likewise, just as
we need to identify the reasons why institutions gained or lost support
as remedies for social ills, so we also need to explain why, once
established, some survived in the face of their objective failure to
achieve their aims.

The emphasis upon control has helped to explain the existence of
institutions: it has done much less to explain their scale. In this respect
other factors have assumed a greater importance; demographic change
especially.[6] If the population is divided in groups by age and marital
status it is plain that their rates for care in residential institutions have
always varied dramatically. The table below sets out, for example, the
highest and lowest rates for 1931 and 1971.

**Residential Care Rates (including hospitals) per 10,000 of the Relevant Population,
England and Wales, 1931 and 1971[7]**

1931		1971	
Highest		**Highest**	
Single men, 65 and over:	1,955	Single men, 65 and over:	1,419
Single men, 45–64:	957	Single women, 65 and over:	1,094
Single women, 65 and over:	640	Widowed and divorced men, 65	
Widowed and divorced men, 65		and over:	787
and over:	501	Widowed and divorced women,	
Single women, 45–64:	404	65 and over:	666
		Single women, 45–64:	468
Lowest		**Lowest**	
Married men, 15–44:	52	Married men, 15–44:	37
Married women, 15–44:	57	Married women, 45–64:	43
Married women, 45–64:	76	Married women, 15–44:	47
Married men, 45–64:	81	Married men, 45–64:	49
Widowed and divorced women,		Women under 15:	49
15–44:	85		
Rate for all men	147	**Rate for all men**	118
Rate for all women	122	**Rate for all women**	145
Overall rate	134	**Overall rate**	132

Clearly, changes in the population structure that alter the number in
the 'high risk' categories will have a substantial influence on the
demand for residential places (however that demand be expressed)
unless the factors that predispose these groups to high 'in care' rates
change. It will be seen from the table that in the period 1931–71 the only
categories that experienced any pronounced upward movement in their
rate of residential care were single elderly women (a rise of 70 per cent);
widowed and divorced elderly men (up by 57 per cent), and widowed
and divorced elderly women (an increase of 12 per cent). Where there

have been considerable increases in the total population in each of these groups the implications for the scale of residential care are obvious: even when there is a reduction in 'in care' rates the overall growth in numbers may still be large enough to sustain or increase the pressure on residential places. Thus, the inter-relationships between the rate of residential care for different groups and the size of the total population in these groups is a crucial factor that enlarges or reduces demand. As a result of some of these demographic changes the last 50 years have seen a shift in the balance of residential care towards the elderly and hence towards less custodial arrangements.

The changing relationship between residential care and other social services has also been of immense significance to the course of its history. After 1908 the gradual introduction of a social security system that was separate from the poor law began to disentangle residential care from destitution, a process that was substantially completed in 1948. The importance of this development can hardly be over-estimated. Other changes, such as the transfer of poor law responsibilities from boards of guardians to local authorities in 1930 also created a new environment for a large section of residential care, not least as the poor law medical services began to be absorbed into the local authority health services. Finally, again in 1948, all hospital services were removed from the poor law jurisdiction. The first major development in social work recruitment and training occurred in child care after the war. The new child care officers were seen in many respects as boarding-out officers whose principal task was to find and supervise foster homes and thereby reduce dependence upon residential homes. Indeed, as the new social work profession expanded into other fields as well it took with it a strong orientation towards care solutions other than those in residential settings.

Rising costs imparted a powerful impetus to the search for alternatives to residential care; but, it should be noted that it was running costs rather than capital costs which caused most concern. Running costs climbed not simply because of the growing expense of operating old and run-down buildings but because expenditure on salaries rose. Of course, improved standards and smaller units meant better staffing ratios, and more staff were needed as it became unacceptable (as well as impracticable) to use residents to assist with the running of homes. The most fundamental reason for the increase in staff costs, however, was demographic in origin. There were fewer single women who depended upon residential homes for their accommodation and vocation. The Williams committee, reporting in 1967, probably recorded the end of an era when it noted that: 'two-thirds of people at present employed in residential homes are single women and one-third of all staff are over 50 years of age'.[8] The vast pool of women without children that had partly been created by the terrible loss of men during the

1914–18 war was drying up and, as these women retired, they themselves were transformed from a care solution to a care problem. Even in 1967 all but seven per cent of the staff in the residential homes that the Williams' enquiry surveyed were resident. With the disappearance of the mature single woman it became impossible to sustain that tradition. Non-residential arrangements for staff grew rapidly and with them the work took on a more contractual character—the length of the working day became defined and marked by the shift system. More part-time staff were recruited as well as more men, and the turnover of staff became both a new expense and a new source of disruption. The residential home can no longer rely upon the availability of single women, squeezed out of the housing market by their status and ready to dedicate a lifetime's work to the care of others. In historical terms this must be one of the most notable changes in the environment within which residential care has evolved.

Finally, it is important to recognise the ways in which the environment of ideas changed. One powerful nineteenth-century conviction, born of middle-class prosperity, self confidence and optimism, was that behaviour could be altered and improved. This might be achieved through systems of coercion and inducement but quite as readily, and probably better, by training and treatment. Scull, for example, has pointed out that the idea that lunacy could be treated (and therefore cured) won influential support for the asylum movement.[9] Poor law officials (especially the inspectorate) believed that the cycle of pauperism could be broken by giving the children in their Homes the right education and training, and the charitable societies certainly believed that by example and religious upbringing children could be saved from a lifetime of degradation. However, these ideas of corrigibility were accompanied by the firm belief that success in these ventures could only be realised by the exercise of careful control. Experts, instructors or administrators could not ensure the desired changes by occasional contact with an individual in an unregulated environment. An all-embracing influence was required, much as in the boarding school tradition. Given such notions it is hardly surprising that the institution came to be seen as the key to reformation.

The twentieth century ushered in new and more cautious ideas. Some had begun to argue, with the aid of social enquiries,[10] that institutional life, especially for children, was positively detrimental, and in an increasing number of children's homes education was separated from care. Furthermore, as a larger proportion of the institutional population became aged both the incentive and the need to change behaviours were reduced. In any case, the hospitals had begun to monopolise curative optimism, leaving a whole class of chronic cases to be dealt with elsewhere. Other things happened too: the fervour of evangelicalism began to wane; a sense of psychological determinism started to spread with the advent of Freudian theories,[11] and the belief in the inevitability of human and economic progress was seriously challenged by the 1914–18 war and by the inter-war depression. It is interesting that the general impression of residential care in these years is one of inertia.

It is impossible to explore fully the changing web of ideas within which the role and nature of institutions have evolved. Nonetheless, as with some of the other broad influences that have been touched upon they must be taken into account in any historical analysis, for they too are the products of particular social and economic structures.

The sections that follow endeavour to elaborate the general approach that has been followed in this introduction. It has rested upon the assumptions that:

(a) we are more likely to understand the history of institutions by looking away from them and towards what is happening in the wider society;

(b) that it is crucial to examine continuities as well as changes, and

(c) that the history of institutions in this country has been dominated by destitution, madness and criminality. Of all the people enumerated as inmates of institutions in 1901 (including hospitals of all kinds) 55 per cent were in workhouses or other poor law establishments; 24 per cent lived in lunatic asylums, and 10 per cent were prisoners.[12]

2 The Persistent Image

The idea of institutional life has always been viewed with repugnance by a broad section of the population. This attitude has persisted despite many changes and improvements and although now it may be weakening, it nevertheless continues to be influential. Its survival has been assured by at least four forms of reinforcement: the deliberate cultivation of a repellent image; reported cases of the abuse of inmates; the enforced association and routine of institutional life, and the compulsion often associated with entry as well as with subsequent detention.

As we have seen, the management of destitution, and to a lesser extent madness and criminality, has dominated the history of institutions in this country. In this, the aim of the poor law was as much to affect the beliefs, attitudes and behaviour of working-class people generally as it was to discipline or provide for those who received its out-door relief or entered its institutions. 'The poor law', wrote Rose, 'was an ever-present symbol to the...poor of the fate to which their poverty might condemn them'.[13] The workhouse was at once the most visible and most impressive manifestation of that symbol. The similarities to the penal system are obvious. A common factor was the belief in the need for deterrence, not primarily aimed at those who were incarcerated but at the far greater number who were assumed to threaten to overwhelm the available resources or to disturb a precarious social order. However great the commitment to reformation and humane treatment, a regime fulfilling such deterrent purposes is constrained to preserve the evidence of severity, discipline and deprivation if it is both to be feared and supported by those outside.[14]

Although the workhouse occupied such a central position in the history of the rise of the institution, comparatively few people passed through its doors. For example, in the peak year of 1871, after a prolonged period of economic depression, about a million people were getting poor relief in England and Wales: that was 4.6 per cent of the population. Most of these recipients were being paid out-door relief; only 150,000, or 0.6 per cent of the population, were in poor law institutions, a third of them children under sixteen.[15] If, as seems likely, this reflected the success of the workhouse as a deterrent, it also reflected the success of the poor law system as a whole in restricting the scale of its relief payments. The moralistic and inquisitorial manner in which relieving officers or the committees conducted their inquiries made any approach to the poor law a step to be avoided if at all possible. Uncertainty about the outcome of an application doubtless played its part as well. Given the laws of settlement (at least in England and Wales) recent arrivals in an area might well find that relief involved being returned to their union of settlement and, of course, it might also be linked with the offer of the House. We do not know how many people, after having applied, refused to accept relief on these terms.

Thus fear and hatred of the workhouse have to be set within the context of poor law administration as a whole. Nonetheless, the workhouse represented the ultimate sanction. The fact that comparatively few people came to be admitted did not detract from the power of its negative image, an image that was sustained by the accounts that circulated about the harsh treatment and the separation of families that admission entailed. The success of 'less eligibility' in deterring the able bodied and others from seeking relief relied heavily upon the currency of such images. Newspapers, songs and gossip, as well as orchestrated campaigns for the abolition or reform of the system, all lent support to the deliberate attempts that were made to ensure that entry to a workhouse was widely regarded as an awful fate.

Of course, the dread of the workhouse felt by the poor was not simply the product of hearsay and rumour or of exaggerated horrors. Well-documented accounts of ill-treatment, victimisation, humiliation and appalling living conditions are to be found at all periods, even though views about what is excessive and intolerable have changed. Furthermore, what commissions and inquiries reported was certainly only a fraction of what was suffered in asylums, boarding schools, training ships and children's homes, as well as in workhouses and prisons. Such accounts stretch at least from the massive report produced by the committee that investigated the Andover Union and its scandals in 1846[16] to the series of inquiries into cruelty against patients in hospitals for the mentally handicapped that were conducted in the 1970s.[17] The extremes were never part of any deliberate policy; indeed, central authorities were at pains to advocate and legislate for fair and reasonable treatment. In their eyes the scandals that from time to time erupted were usually attributable to a combination of the inadequate nature of their power to control what happened locally; cruel or ignorant staff; or brutal, incompetent and weak leadership. They were seen as deplorable deviations caused by the perversity of human nature and therefore as departures from good practice that were difficult to prevent. What was less often acknowledged was that such incidents were also symptomatic of the contemporary rationales of institutions (of deterrence, punishment or reformation) or of the gap that existed between benign aims (like treatment or care) and the resources that were made available. Whether institutions were set up as cost-cutting initiatives (as were the workhouses, at least after 1834) or whether they were under-funded for the more elevated purposes that they were intended to serve, the common result was an unwillingness or inability to appoint and train sufficient staff of the right calibre.

Whether or not the reality of life in an institution accorded wholly with its popular image, what was certain was that it entailed associating with strangers in intimate surroundings and worse, the probability of thereby becoming a member of a stigmatised group. Townsend captured the essence of the first element when he described what he considered to be an inherent disadvantage of residential homes for old people:

> Individuals from diverse localities and backgrounds are brought together under one roof and are expected to share most of the events of daily life. Staff are employed and a common routine is established. The resulting 'community' is in many ways an artificial one because it does not consist of people...who are linked by a network of family, occupational and neighbour ties and whose relationships are reinforced by the reciprocation of services.[18]

Half a century before, Charles Booth had stated his belief 'that the respectable aged were deterred from entering the workhouse because they might be herded with disreputable characters'.[19] Despite the desire on the part of many administrators to separate the deserving from the undeserving and the reputable from the disreputable, the reality of institutional life has been one of enforced and uncertain association. Choice of associates has been limited and escape from the disruptive, distressing or frightening behaviour of other people well-nigh impossible.

Furthermore, the separation, often at moments of crisis, from those who were most cherished and best known was always painful, not least because it left the new inmate without established support or dependable allies. The prospect of entry to a residential establishment touches a deep-seated fear of being inescapably cast alone and defenceless amongst strangers, especially strangers whose codes are unknown but assumed to be disturbingly different from one's own. Such a basic social and psychological component of human fearfulness has played its part in sustaining the widespread negative image of institutions; but when many of the strangers who lived in them were believed to be, and indeed frequently were, members of some of the most stigmatised groups in society the fear of association took on an added dimension.

The distinction repeatedly drawn between the deserving and the undeserving in both official and charitable quarters was undoubtedly also made by members of the working class. The Royal Commission on the Aged Poor in 1895 concluded that although there was a widespread dislike among the poor of entering the workhouse they nonetheless regarded it as suitable for wastrels and ne'er-do-wells and, indeed, as much better than they deserved.[20] Strong conventions existed to ensure the retention of an identity distinctively separate from the 'rough' or under-class. For many working-class people admission to a workhouse (or even the need to apply for out-door relief) threatened the painstakingly constructed and carefully maintained differentiation from that level. Perhaps the most significant achievement of the poor law was to have provided and confirmed the lowest stratum of the many that existed within the working class. As Roberts recalls in his personal account of life in a Salford slum during the first quarter of this century: 'the workhouse paupers hardly registered as human beings at all'.[21] They were at the bottom of a carefully graded heap and provided the means by which others, however lowly, could elevate their status. Thus, it was not simply a fear of associating with strangers that created the widespread aversion to institutions but also the fear that entry would result in a loss of status and self-respect as one became reclassified by association. This was an important weapon in the armoury of deterrence clearly revealed in the reaction of the 1895 commissioners to the proposal, made by a number of their witnesses, that in order to protect the aged but respectable poor from having to mix with objectionable people almshouses should be provided instead.[22] This was considered to be unwise since it would discourage individuals from making adequate provision for their old age as well as weaken the resolve of sons and daughters to provide for their aged parents in their own homes.

Echoes of concerns about disagreeable associations are still to be heard today, albeit in the modified forms of the distaste that the elderly express for having to live alongside those who are mentally infirm; in what children in care say about being assumed to have been 'in trouble' if they live in a children's home, and in the way in which many parents of mentally handicapped children react to their offspring being placed residentially with those whose handicaps are obviously more severe.[23] The issues of classification, the debasement of status and stigma by association have all been enduring themes in the history of institutional provision. The fact that proportionately few people have entered residential care has made it that much more likely that those who do (or who have to stay) come to be regarded—and regard themselves—as a defeated and outcast group.

The negative image of institutions has undoubtedly been reinforced by the processes of legal compulsion that have preceded much admission. Until 1930 the doors of public institutions for the treatment of the mentally disordered were closed to all but people certified as 'a lunatic, an idiot or a person of unsound mind' and ordered to be detained for care and treatment by a judicial authority. Such a requirement imposed a stigma additional to any that was associated with being in an asylum. Not only was admission dependent upon certification, but the order for commitment carried with it the prospect of its irrevocability. De-certification and release were not easily obtained. Under these circumstances it is understandable that admission was frequently deferred for as long as possible. As a result, patients were liable to arrive on the wards in particularly distressed states and without the benefit of any earlier intervention that might have mitigated their condition. Visitors to the asylums therefore saw patients in states of crisis as well as many others suffering from the adverse effects of their long residence. Moreover, many mentally handicapped people were certified and admitted alongside the mentally ill.[24] All these things tended to reinforce prevailing stereotypes about the uniform character of madness. Indeed, the lack of understanding about the difference between mental illness and mental handicap was superimposed upon the widespread popular assumption that mental afflictions were hereditary in nature. This made the act of certification an additionally distressing event. Relatives were upset by the public confirmation of mental weakness in the family and could feel stigmatised by their membership. In that sense certification was often experienced as a matter of family shame.

Over and above this, in the great majority of cases, certification also led to the stigma of pauperism. Unless the certified person could pay, or be paid for, as a private patient, the costs of confinement and treatment had to be borne by the poor law up until 1930. Many inmates therefore became certified paupers as well as certified lunatics. For many families this would have been their first encounter with the poor law, although there was also a steady stream of entrants to the asylums who were already in receipt of out-door relief or who came from the work-houses. Indeed, certification as a means of establishing eligibility for admission to an asylum (re-named mental hospitals after 1930) at public expense was 'equivalent to the order for the admission of a pauper to a workhouse, and to the order and medical certificate which were required until...1948 for the admission of any patient, except in an emergency, to a poor law hospital'.[25] Where it differed was that it was also an authority for the detention of the patient, whether in an asylum, workhouse or elsewhere. Even though it was possible for patients to enter a mental hospital on a voluntary basis after 1930, this relaxation did not extend to the so-called mentally defective. From 1913 until the reforms of 1957 nobody could be admitted to a public mental deficiency institution without certification and the parallel authority for confinement.[26]

The statistics assembled by the Royal Commission on the Law Relating to Mental Illness and Mental Deficiency (1954–7) show how extensive the elements of compulsion and detention remained in spite of the growing use of voluntary admission to mental hospitals. Although only 18 per cent of patients received into mental hospitals in 1955 were certified, about 70 per cent of all patients in hospital at the end of the year fell into that category. This was because many of them had been there a long time but also because, being detained, this population accumulated. Thus, there were some 105,000 certified patients in mental hospitals in England and Wales in 1955. Added to these were a further 58,000 in mental deficiency hospitals, making a total of 163,000 certified and detained patients—more than double the number at the turn of the century.[27] Although the 1959 Mental Health Act eliminated the traditional use of certification, the long-term certified patients from the earlier period remained in the hospitals for some time and arrangements were continued for compulsory admission and detention under certain circumstances.

Compulsion combined with detention was not the only disquieting aspect of admission to an institution. By the end of the nineteenth century there were various laws that enabled authorities to detain those who had originally been admitted to institutions on a voluntary basis. This had been a longstanding option for boards of guardians. For example, where families were admitted to the workhouse parents could not discharge themselves unless they took their children with them and guardians could seek to have inmates certified and thus reallocated to a detained class. Moreover, in the late nineteenth century several measures were introduced that enabled organisations to retain children (who were mostly in their institutions) against the wishes of their parents. In 1889 boards of guardians were enabled by administrative procedures to assume parental rights and duties over children in their care until they were sixteen.[28] There was other legislation of a similar kind. Under the Custody of Children Act, 1891 not only guardians but any person or institution could acquire custody of a child in place of the parents if they had been looking after that child at their expense and the parents could not reimburse them. This was largely the outcome of intensive pressure by Barnardo but it enabled any voluntary children's society to prevent children being returned to poor parents who were not considered to be fit persons. In the same year the Reformatory and Industrial Schools Act also made it more difficult for parents to have their children back after the term of their detention had expired. Managers, under certain provisions, could override parental wishes about what should happen to a boy or girl upon discharge. This was considered to be especially valuable in arranging their emigration or employment well away from detrimental parental influences.[29]

These are but examples: the important point is that there were circumstances in which admission to an institution on a voluntary basis could lead to compulsory detention which might also be accompanied by transfer to a different regime. Few people would understand the legal niceties but many would be aware that simply being in an institution could lead to steps being taken to prevent you leaving. It is difficult to assess, at different times, the full extent of compulsion and detention as correlates of institutional life; but it has been considerable. If, for example, one takes the figures in the 1931 Census, then of all the recorded inmate population (including those in prisons and hospitals but not in boarding schools) about 45 per cent would have been subject to compulsory detention.[30] Although that proportion had probably fallen to some 10 per cent by the time of the 1981 Census (mainly as a result of the abandonment of certification and an ageing population) the idea of residential establishments as places where people are confined against their will lingers on; not least, perhaps, because in practice many residents have little or no alternative. Legal compulsion may have been replaced, especially amongst the aged, by the compulsion of their circumstances. The historical association of commitment to an institution with being either mad or bad dies hard and has certainly contributed to the unfavourable view of residential provision. How could it be otherwise if one needed to be compelled to enter and stopped from leaving?

Thus, the negative image of residential establishments that has embedded itself in popular consciousness has been, and continues to be, important. Certainly it has contributed to the widespread support enjoyed by policies for the reduction of residential care in favour of community-based alternatives. Yet, although the image persists it may be weakening. If it is, that could have far-reaching implications for the future. In order to assess this likelihood we need to ask what it is that has sustained these images despite the formal abolition of the poor law in 1948, the reforming mental health legislation of 1959, substantial improvements in physical standards, as well as the use of smaller units and greater flexibility in the arrangements for admission and discharge. One obvious answer is that these changes have not been sufficient to alter basic attitudes. For example, after 1948 about four hundred public assistance institutions were redistributed and renamed.[31] Some became hospitals within the national health service, others were used jointly by the health services and the local authorities whilst the rest were inherited by the new local welfare and children's departments. These legacies not only comprised the old and readily identified public assistance buildings but, in many cases, their largely untrained staff as well, the longest serving of whom had had a lifetime's association with poor law traditions and practices. Both the buildings and the staff took a long time to replace and, in the meantime, comparatively little was done by way of improvement or training. For example, as a prelude to his study of institutions and homes for the elderly, Townsend obtained information from local authorities in England and Wales about the number and type of residential institutions that they operated in 1958. Of nearly 3,000 establishments 11 per cent were former public assistance institutions; but 80 per cent of the homes with more than 100 residents fell into that category so that these large buildings housed a quarter of all the residents.[32] It is not simply that large, old and inadequate buildings remained (and have remained) but that, however upgraded, renamed or refurbished, they retain the hallmarks of the poor law in their appearance and design and in people's minds, especially in the minds of those old enough to remember the pre-war years—about 20 per cent of today's population. However, that generation will be succeeded by another with no direct recollections of the era of deterrence and humiliation that these buildings stood for. If standards are further improved and especially if the autonomy of residents is better pre-served, then a new public may come to hold a more positive view of residential care. Much will then turn on the intensity of the needs that residential services are seen as capable of meeting and on the extent to which the related demands are met. These issues are considered in the last section.

3 Variation and Divergence

Much of the negative view of institutions has been encouraged by their dominant features and by processes of generalisation that have taken little account of the variation between them. In her study of the work-house system Crowther warns that although 'the historian may observe...institutions from a distance and note remarkable similarities between them...under the microscope the differences are equally striking'.[33] That contention has been borne out by a series of detailed local studies of the poor law that have shown notable divergences in policies and in workhouse regimes in various parts of the country. For example, Digby's reseach into the operation of the poor law in Norfolk drew attention to the fact that although arrangements differed in detail from place to place 'they were characterised generally by a humane consideration for old people's needs'. In general, she continued, 'the Norfolk guardians maintained a benign administration of indoor relief to old people, and one that mitigated as much as possible the conditions in a union workhouse that had been designed for the able-bodied, as well as the elderly, pauper'. By contrast, she found that 'most Norfolk guardians were indifferent about the medical arrangements in the workhouse'. The provision of sufficient trained nurses was the weakest point. Finally, she drew the conclusion that

> After reviewing the available evidence, it would appear that the Norfolk poor law administrators' treatment of the poor was far more humane than the stereotyped views of the 'grinders of the poor' might have led one to suppose, and that *this humanity was most marked in relation to indoor paupers* (emphasis added).[34]

This is not to say that the living conditions in such workhouses would pass muster today or that even by contemporary middle-class standards they were satisfactory; but set against the prevailing poverty of much working-class life, against the major alternatives available and against widespread criticism, they were surprisingly good—especially for the elderly. In Norfolk, as elsewhere, many elderly couples were able to live together in their own room and in some workhouses there were separate cottages available in the grounds. Indeed, after 1885 guardians were obliged by the Local Government Board to allow elderly couples in workhouses to stay together if they were both over 60 and if only one of them was of that age they were permitted to do so. Yet there were undoubtedly unions, especially in urban areas, where the regimes for all continued to be harsh and degrading. This may have been because of the poor calibre and unsympathetic approach of the masters and matrons or their collusion with careless and insensitive guardians. Certainly, it is important to pay close attention to the composition of the boards and, as several commentators have argued, the election of women and representatives of labour as guardians, particularly from the 1890s onwards, may have done much to ensure the more sympathetic treatment of certain groups such as unmarried mothers.[35] Nevertheless, these changes in the membership of boards of guardians also coincided with other important changes in both economic conditions and social policy which led to the workhouses (and their successors the public assistance institutions) containing mainly elderly people who were there chiefly because they needed to be cared for and only secondly because they were destitute. Most notable amongst the social policy changes was the introduction and gradual improvement of old age pensions after 1908 and the development of separate facilities for the younger mentally disordered.

Labour market factors had always played an important part in determining the mixture and numbers of workhouse inmates and, thereby, influencing the regimes that were adopted. As a rule the crucial factor was the way in which guardians responded to the administration of out-door relief, especially for the able-bodied. Where this was generous and the orders prohibiting or limiting such payments ignored or circumvented then the number of the able-bodied in the workhouses was small. Where contrary policies were pursued and indoor relief for the able-bodied was the general rule their numbers in the workhouses rose and this tended to create generally sterner regimes for all inmates. Typically, attitudes towards the payment of out-door relief reflected the size of the local problem of unemployment or the pattern of casual labour. As the 1895 Royal Commission on the Aged Poor pointed out, 'the practice as to giving outdoor relief varies very widely in different unions, the general tendency being to greater strictness in the more crowded urban unions where the amount of pauperism to be dealt with is largest'.[36] Where guardians felt in danger of being inundated by demands for relief the 'test of the house' was more likely to be applied as a means of preventing a flood of demand.

However, such reactions were by no means universal. They were mediated by various other factors; for instance, by the availability of charitable relief for the unemployed; by the opportunities for women and children to contribute to the household income and, not least, by the particular nature of the local labour market. Digby, for instance, points out that in Norfolk

> The farmer-guardians...were reluctant to send married men of good character to the workhouse, both because of the high cost of relieving them there with their families, and because of the inconvenience which they faced as employers in retrieving them when the weather improved and ploughing or sowing needed to be quickly put in hand.[37]

This observation not only illustrates labour market influences upon guardians' attitudes towards the relief of the able-bodied but also the fact that much out-door relief fell short of the minimum necessary for subsistence without recourse to supplementation from other sources. It underlines the contradiction that ran through so much of the poor law administration. Although the workhouses were used as a deterrent mechanism to keep down relief expenditure in general, if that relief had to be provided then it was often thought preferable to grant out-door relief since it was less expensive than supporting a family in a work-house. Furthermore, whereas the level of out-door relief could always be reduced it was more difficult to lower the unit costs in a workhouse run according to the regulations, for example with respect to minimum diets.

By the inter-war years mass unemployment dealt the final blow to policies for relieving those without work in the workhouses. Neither the guardians nor (after 1930) the local authority public assistance committees were equipped, either financially or administratively, to deal with problems of destitution on such a vast and frequently concentrated scale. The Unemployment Act of 1934 transferred responsibility for the relief of the unemployed to central government in the shape of the Unemployment Assistance Board. It signalled a significant turning point in the role of the poor law; a change that was finally completed in 1948 with the virtual separation of responsibilities for the payment of relief (national assistance and now supplementary benefit) from the provision of residential care. The financial rationale for deterrent policies in poor law institutions thus largely disappeared. Ironically the 1980s have witnessed the appearance of a new relationship between residential care and the receipt of assistance in the form of the board and lodging allowances paid by the supplementary benefits system to the elderly in the increasing number of private residential homes.[38] Subtler and more acceptable policies than deterrence will have to be found if, as seems to be the government's intention, a brake is to be applied to the rapid growth of public expenditure that this has entailed; but that runs ahead of the history.

Not only have there been differences between institutions but also within them. Different categories of inmate might well experience markedly different treatment. That was to be expected where children, the sick or the old were separated; but the process often went further than this if the buildings allowed it and was based more clearly upon the imposition of a crude moral calculus, a calculus that too often ensured that unmarried mothers in particular were dealt with in shameful and humiliating ways. Yet they were not the only ones to be subjected to moral discrimination. The special report of the 1909 Royal Commission on the Poor Laws on its hundreds of visits to poor law and charitable institutions provides a rich source of illustration. In describing a provincial workhouse, for instance, it is explained with satisfaction that its outstanding feature was 'the classification of the aged inmates according to character, each class having separate accommodation and being entirely separate from the others'. A list of special privileges enjoyed by the group was then given, followed by an explanation of the grounds upon which the classification was made. 'The qualifications necessary to obtain these privileges are good character, twenty years' residence in the union area, freedom from any connection with crime and having not previously received relief.' The qualifications for membership of the second class were ten years' residence and a slightly less unblemished character. No special accommodation or extras were allowed to the third class who slept and ate with the generality of the inmates and were only allowed half a day's leave a fortnight in contrast to the virtual freedom to come and go as they pleased enjoyed by those in the first class. Should inmates in the upper class misbehave, however, they could be demoted to a lower class and this, the commissioners were told, proved to be 'a very effective method of enforcing discipline'.[39]

The important lesson to be learned from this example is that all institutions are (and continue to be) complicated social arrangements that, either by design or choice, are experienced differently by different groups and individuals. Furthermore, just as institutions have served the aim of regulating the behaviour of those outside their walls, so they have been operated in ways that were thought to secure internal discipline and smooth running.

The commissioners of 1909 did visit and describe some apparently excellent institutions, both public and charitable; so did the Curtis Committee that reported on the care of children in 1946.[40] Nonetheless, just as in Townsend's 1958 study,[41] the predominant picture in all such enquiries was of establishments that failed to meet the physical, social or psychological needs of their residents. That being so, it is not surprising that the existence of some good provision made little impact upon the generally negative view of institutions: there was simply not enough of it. The best estimate that could be made was that institutional life would be a wretched and sad experience exacerbated by the problems of social readjustment and the unlikelihood of an early departure.

Nonetheless, some variations were substantial enough to become divergencies and pronounced enough to remove parts of the system from the opprobrium and stigma that institutions usually attracted. The hospitals are the best example. They occupy a strategic position in the recent history of institutional care, not only because of their growing importance but because of the many repercussions that this change has had upon other forms of institutional provision. These consequences have followed in particular from the enhancement of the status of hospitals as centres of scientific medicine and professional advancement. Yet the rise of the hospital only dates from the latter part of the nineteenth century. Throughout most of that century 'illness of any kind was mainly endured at home'.[42] Sick people were constrained to enter institutions because they were destitute, homeless or lacked anyone to look after them; and, more often than not, they went to the workhouse. As Pinker has pointed out, 'in 1861 there were roughly 900 institutions for the physically ill in England and Wales, but 650 of these were ordinary workhouses'.[43] Resort to an institution in time of illness was closely linked with poverty and pauperism.

Once started, the late-Victorian expansion of hospital provision proceeded apace. The number of beds in institutions classed as hospitals rose dramatically, and at a faster rate than the growth of the population. In the sixty years between 1861 and 1921 the number of beds in voluntary hospitals increased from 15,000 to 57,000. A hospital service also emerged within the poor law and by 1921 their infirmaries provided some 37,000 beds quite separate from the workhouses. In addition, local authorities with public health responsibilities began to build hospitals for infectious diseases—popularly known as the fever hospitals. By 1921 there were 48,000 beds in such hospitals (although they were rarely fully occupied).[44]

Despite these developments the sick wards of the workhouses continued to play a prominent part in provision for the physically ill. In 1921 they supplied 85,000 beds, or 37 per cent of the available accommodation. Thus, taken together with the infirmaries this meant that the poor law still accounted for over half of the country's 'hospital' places. By then, however, the infirmaries were regarded quite differently from other parts of the poor law. Far from aversion or fear of stigmatisation a wide cross-section of the public was actively seeking the services they offered. This had not been the original intention or expectation. The development of poor law infirmaries was part of an initiative to reduce out-door relief, a quest that began in earnest in the 1870s and lasted, in one guise or another, well into the twentieth century. The payment of out-door medical relief represented a serious obstacle: only 'the creation of a chain of infirmaries would make it possible to abolish all outdoor relief'.[45] Furthermore, the availability of separate infirmaries would permit the pauper sick to be removed from the general workhouses and this, in its turn, would make it possible 'to restore due discipline amongst the able-bodied'.[46] Beyond that it was believed in official quarters that because of an enduring association with the poor law all but the truly necessitous sick would be deterred from seeking admission to the new infirmaries.

The infirmaries, however, did not develop along these lines. There were three main reasons for this. First, important changes followed the appointment of medical superintendents rather than lay administrators (as in the workhouses) and also from employing more doctors. The desire to enhance and uphold professional standards could not be readily separated from the better treatment of patients. Secondly, the infirmaries were unable to use able-bodied inmates for nursing and other sick ward duties. Outside staff had to be recruited, especially nurses; and this occurred at a time when the 'nursing revolution' had already begun to raise nursing standards and expectations. Thirdly, as the treatment offered in the infirmaries improved so many who were not paupers sought and obtained admission. 'It was no longer necessary', Abel-Smith concluded, 'to drive patients into these institutions; on the contrary, the problem was to ration these limited facilities amongst the different types of patients seeking care'.[47] The selections made by the superintendents and their medical staff favoured the acute sick. These were the cases whose treatment conferred professional prestige. They were also the kinds of conditions that doctors had been trained to treat and which opened the way for the infirmaries to participate in medical and nursing education.

These developments in the infirmaries were similar to what was happening in the voluntary hospitals: the combined results had major implications for the role of the workhouse in the care of the sick. In as much as the expanding hospital system concentrated its resources upon the acute sick, so it became increasingly likely that the chronic cases would be retained in or discharged to, the sick wards of the work-houses. They were consigned thereby to a still stigmatised part of the poor law and to a system that, even by the turn of the century, still relied upon pauper inmates as attendants and nurses in many places.

The Local Government Act, 1929, vested poor law responsibilities in the hands of the counties and county boroughs working through their newly formed public assistance committees. The Act also permitted the local authorities to transfer poor law 'hospital' facilities to their health services or to reclassify other poor law establishments as hospitals.[48] Progress was uneven, but by the outbreak of war the contribution of the poor law to the institutional care of the sick had been substantially reduced as more and more facilities became part of local health administrations. However, these transfers were selective. The poor law facilities that the local authorities were willing to redesignate as hospitals were predominantly the best developed. That usually meant the infirmaries catering for acute cases. The establishments dealing with the chronic sick (by then called public assistance institutions) mostly remained within the poor law. It is reasonable to conclude, therefore, that one of the results of the gathering momentum of the 'hospital movement' was to leave large numbers of the chronically ill and elderly infirm stranded in low-standard, under-funded and stigmatised public assistance institutions. Their care in these establishments remained largely untouched by the combined impact of scientific medicine and professional aspiration, a combination that had effectively raised the status, and hence the public acceptability, of hospital treatment.

The substantial separation of hospital care from the stigma of pauperism had been achieved well before the creation of the national health service and the dismantling of the poor law administration in the early post-war years. This disassociation has been important in shaping public attitudes to different forms of residential care: by and large that which is considered to be necessary on medical grounds has been more favourably regarded than that which is not. Hence, both the classifi-cation of people's conditions and the designation of institutions has been influential in modifying attitudes. Notwithstanding that, the process of re-designation such as occurred in the 1930s and 1940s did not, as we have seen, transform old public assistance institutions into desirable hospitals. Both the buildings and popular terminology outlasted the changes. However, the general conclusion remains: when institutions are considered to provide medical treatment they are more likely to be well regarded than when they are not. Neither the patients nor their relatives are held to have failed: admission is, or is portrayed as being, a matter of professional judgement unaffected by questions of social merit or family responsibility. Yet the issue of classification lingers on in the demarcation disputes that arise between health services, social services and housing in deciding whether a dependent person's principal need is for treatment, nursing, care or accommodation.

The high esteem in which most parts of the hospital system are held is closely related to their success in repair and restoration. The hospitals that do not share in that esteem are usually those that deal with chronic illness. Yet it is not merely the ability of the acute sector to offer (or to offer the prospect of) cure that invests it with status; it is also, one suspects, that it is seen as purposeful. Where institutions fail to be purposeful for the individual it is hardly likely that they will command respect or be seen to provide anything but a last-resort service. Unfortunately, the hospital example suggests that as it becomes more possible to offer positive and valued services through developments in science, technology, skill and insight, so those groups that are not considered to be able to profit from such help become increasingly separated from the mainstream of improvement; and that has been particularly so in the case of residential care even though there have been (and continue to be) exceptions contrived through charismatic leadership or high levels of dedication.

4   The Components of Demand

Unlike the poor law and the prison, deterrence was not an explicit feature of the history of other kinds of institutions. For instance, Scull has argued that the remarkable growth in the use of asylums was attributable to the encouragement of demand.[49] That was because, first, the emerging profession of psychiatry had good reason to welcome more patients. Its future was closely associated with the scale of development and with the idea of expert practice in hospital-like settings. Moreover, it became increasingly involved in the process of certification that created the flow of admissions. Secondly, the asylums prospered because they met certain organisational needs within the poor law: in particular, since workhouses needed to maintain order amongst their inmates they had an interest in expelling those who, because of their

derangement, threatened to subvert the aims of a well-run establishment. The asylum, through the machinery of certification, provided a
means of achieving this but, more importantly, it also offered a means
of preventing the admission of lunatics to workhouses in the first place.
It is difficult to asssess the scale of such diversions but they certainly
occurred and provided one rationale for the asylums, a rationale located
within workhouse regimes whose primary purpose was to impose com-
pliance, discipline and labour upon those who entered. The third
impetus for growth lay, Scull has argued, in the fact that the county
asylum became an acceptable solution to the problems faced by
working-class families in looking after (or tolerating) relatives whose
behaviour severely strained their emotional, practical and financial
resources. If one accepts this view then a significant part of the demand
that fed the expansion of the asylum system was initiated within
families. Some commentators, like Walton, are dubious about this interpretation. He reminds us, for example, that in the middle decades of the
nineteenth century at least, the elderly formed only a small proportion
of admissions.[50]

The issue of the part played by families in despatching their kin to
institutional care is liable to be overlooked; yet in the opinion of his-
torians like Ignatieff, the working-class family played an active, rather
than a passive part, in the history of institutional development.[51] The
process of presenting people for certification must have begun at home,
at work or in the community, and the most likely of those settings was
the home. How else can a rise in the asylum population from 3 per
10,000 of the total population at the beginning of the nineteenth century
to 30 per 10,000 at the end, and to 40 by 1931, be fully explained?[52]
Crowther has noted that although 'the poor were suspicious of institutions [they] nevertheless supported them: new hospital beds were
filled as soon as possible; pressure on asylums and charitable homes
continued to grow. Even the workhouse,' she adds, 'responded to this
new belief in institutional care'.[53] There was clearly a tension between
the dislike of institutions and the weight of problems to which they
offered a potential solution. Nobody wanted to go into an institution but
not every relative found it possible to keep their dependent kin,
especially so it seems, the mentally disordered and the aged.

Anderson's study of family structure in nineteenth-century
Lancashire suggests some of the complex considerations that may have
informed such decisions.[54] The general conclusion he reaches is that
despite all the pressures to which kinship networks were exposed in the
upheavals of that century they nevertheless survived relatively intact.
What sustained them was a strong element of calculation. In poor
families living on low incomes and constantly under the threat of economic crisis, the offer of help had to be based upon the careful assessment
of its implications. Reciprocity was at a premium. Short-term commit-

ments to assistance were safer than long-term ones and the restriction of help to a small number of relatives preferable to making it available to several. The emphasis was upon riding out crises rather than establishing permanent supportive responsibilities. For example, childless widows were more likely to be 'taken in' by relatives than those with numerous children. The elderly were more readily accepted into the household if they were able to look after children, do some housework or earn a little money. The conclusion from Anderson's evidence is that those who possessed few reciprocal resources, those who had failed to fulfil their side of the implicit reciprocal bargains, or those whose dependencies were likely to be progressive and prolonged were in danger of being excluded from these systems of mutual aid. By definition, the other group that was liable to be excluded from these reciprocal solutions contained those who lacked close relatives. The censuses of institutional populations make this increasingly plain, especially as the population ages. As Donnison and Ungerson show in their review of the census data from 1911 to 1961, the highest rate for institutional care in England and Wales was (with a slight variation in 1951) amongst elderly single, widowed or divorced men, followed by elderly single, widowed or divorced women.[55] There were, of course, more elderly women than men in residential care at all the dates (although that would not have been the case earlier in the nineteenth century[56]) because there were more elderly women in the population. The fact that the 'risk' rate for elderly single, widowed or divorced men has been (and is) significantly higher than for women may have something to do with Anderson's theory of 'usefulness' in the home or, more possibly, it reflects the greater lifetime responsibility that women take for maintaining and nurturing the network within which ties of recriprocity are forged.

The kind of evidence produced by studies like Anderson's suggests that negative attitudes towards institutions may have been overridden when the cost to those having to care for and support their dependent kin was considered to be too great. Stated quite simply, the level of demand for institutional care seems to have been (and may continue to be) a function of (a) the acceptability of that care as perceived by relatives; (b) the costs which they consider they and their family bear in continuing to look after the dependent or disruptive member, and (c) the number of dependent people without close relatives.

This formulation leaves at least one important dimension out of account; namely, the historical role of institutions in campaigns of rescue. Some organisations actively sought their inmates and some of the most energetic and effective advocates of institutional rescue were to be found amongst those who were concerned with charitable provision for children. Indeed, the second half of the last century saw a veritable patchwork of industrial schools, reformatories, orphanages and training homes being established by numerous voluntary societies. For example, by the mid 1880s there were over 130 industrial schools in Britain, mostly run by voluntary societies, and holding some 18,000 children.[57] Twenty-five years earlier there had hardly been any.

The rescue movement was driven forward by a mixture of motives and incentives that may be broadly characterised as social insecurity; missionary zeal, and economic opportunity. The spectre of impending social upheaval was never far distant from the expressions of concern about this or that social problem or from the solutions that were proposed. It was widely believed that traditional forms of social control and discipline amongst the labouring classes had disappeared or had been seriously weakened. Vagrancy, prostitution, drunkenness, destitution and the enlargement of the 'residuum' provided compelling evidence. So too did the children of the poor. The crowded towns testified to the fact as children, singly or in marauding groups, roamed, begged, stole and suffered, to all intents and purposes free from any hint of parental supervision. There were several reasons why concern about such things should have intensified in the 1850s and 1860s, but amongst these the economic changes that were redefining the position of the child were paramount.[58]

The character and level of demand for child labour was altering. On the one hand technical advances had made certain kinds of child labour permanently redundant, whilst on the other the legal restrictions imposed upon the nature and conditions of children's employment had begun to have their effect. Deep troughs of periodic economic depression accentuated the impact of these changes. Fewer children and young people found work to do and those of poverty-stricken parents, or whose parents were dead, looked to obtain what they could by the exercise of their wits on the city streets. By the 1850s and 1860s far fewer children were subject to the harsh discipline of work; but they had yet to be brought under the disciplines of compulsory education. By contrast, their parents continued to be drawn into the increasingly constraining discipline and vicissitudes of wage labour. It was hardly surprising that the structure of control over the children of the poor seemed to be in imminent danger of collapse.

There were, therefore, good reasons for the mounting disquiet about the condition and behaviour of the children of the urban poor. Yet it was the future as much as the present that worried the established classes, and in that their fears about the reproductive capacity of the under-class played an important part.[59] Unless something was done to prevent it then their social, moral or physical defects would be multiplied and spread. However, the cycle of depravation might be broken, so it was argued, by a combination of training and moral education; and this was more likely to succeed with malleable children than with their hardened and incorrigible parents. Just as it came to be considered necessary to control the productive urges of mental defectives through the close supervision facilitated by institutional detention, so the safeguarding of children from a future of pauperism, immorality or crime could be achieved by interposing a *cordon sanitaire* between them and the corrupting influences of their parents and surroundings. Yet the children's institution promised more than this, for it also protected the community from the depredations of ill-disciplined youngsters whilst they remained under supervision for the lengthy spells that were considered essential if training were to have a lasting effect. The confidence that this could be done derived largely from missionary zeal and the reformative optimism that accompanied it.

A belief in the value of education as a means of breaking the habit of pauperism was already established in the policies of the central poor law authorities if not in the practices of local boards of guardians.[60] Poor law education was to produce independent, well-disciplined and useful workers who would have neither the need nor the desire to rely upon relief. The motives of those who set up the new charitable homes and orphanages in the second half of the last century were both similar and different. They too believed in the power of education and training in the battle against habitual pauperism but they were also convinced that this battle could not be won unless children were saved from the contaminating influences of the poor law system itself. Over and above this, however, was the passionate evangelicalism that inspired many of the philanthropists, a religious fervour that led them to confront evil head-on and to wrestle for the eternal souls of those whose lives it had invaded. What better and more hopeful cause than child-rescue? And what better means or more appropriate way of taking up that cause than by providing a self-contained and dedicated institution that offered shelter, protection and regular training alongside religious instruction?

It would be misleading, however, to portray the surge of interest in providing homes for children outside the poor law as the outcome of narrow religious fervour. There was also genuine compassion for the child suffering homelessness, neglect, malnutrition or exploitation. Indeed, faced with the appalling conditions under which many children lived and with virtually no means of effecting any improvement in them, an ordered and controllable residential home must have appeared to be the obvious way to provide help. The only other alternatives were emergency schemes (like soup kitchens or night shelters) that made no lasting impact, or money, which was believed to submerge the recipients deeper in the evil of pauper dependence.

However, neither the desire to ensure spiritual salvation for the child nor compassion could have been translated into the solution of the residential home without the financial means of doing so. There were at least three factors that created a conducive economic environment. The first of these was the availability of the 'new wealth' and the popularity of charitable giving as an expression of piety. Appeals of all kinds in the national and religious press found ready respondents. Furthermore, revivalist networks were both strong and extensive whilst the traditional churches benefited from a parochial system that could be used to attract donations. Innocent but endangered children made an obvious appeal as did the idea of the rescuing home. Buildings provided tangible evidence of something achieved and of the gift given. Land and buildings were often obtained freely or cheaply from wealthy supporters. Even so, homes were expensive to establish and to keep open; charitable donations were rarely sufficient or sufficiently reliable.

What helped to overcome this problem was the readiness of both local and central government to pay for children to be looked after in these homes. Boards of guardians, and later public assistance committees, placed children with the voluntary societies for various reasons. Sometimes it was reckoned to be cheaper; sometimes it was seen as a means of weaning adolescent youngsters away from dependence on the poor law, and sometimes the guardians sent children to the voluntary homes because they were unwilling or unable to conform with the growing range of central government regulations about how poor law children should be cared for (for example, after 1870 they were required to ensure that children were brought up in the religion of their birth and after 1913 that no child over the age of two should be accommodated in a workhouse). Although they were often at pains to disguise the fact, the voluntary children's societies relied heavily upon a supply of poor law children. For example, by the turn of the century a fifth of the children looked after by the Waifs and Strays Society and by the National Children's Homes were paid for by the poor law, and three-quarters of those provided for by the principal Catholic agencies.[61]

The largest sector of voluntary residential child care provision was for many years the industrial schools. Central government, especially the Home Office, played a vital role in financing their activities as well as those of the reformatories. Indeed, an increasingly large proportion of the revenue for these ventures was obtained in this way. By the last days of the voluntary approved schools in 1973 virtually all their income was derived from public sources. The reasons why the Home Office was willing to offer a *per capita* subsidy were complex. Partly the department shared many of the concerns about juvenile disorder that preoccupied the founders of the industrial schools and reformatories; but the initial willingness of central government to assist the voluntary organisations was also a reflection of the undeveloped nature of local government, superimposed upon a deep suspicion of boards of guardians, over whose activities the Home Office exercised no control. Once begun, of course, this arrangement for payments proved difficult to control or modify since the supply of children was determined by independent decisions and the schools had every incentive to admit as many as possible and to keep them as long as they could. Although it grew increasingly uneasy about the mounting costs and triviality of the grounds upon which children were committed to industrial schools, the Home Office found it well-nigh impossible to withdraw or reduce its commitment.

The final cluster of factors in the economic equation is less clear but nonetheless important. Once established, the various institutions for children and young people could minimise their running costs in two ways. Homes (but less so the industrial schools) were often staffed by dedicated but poorly paid women. Sometimes they were unpaid, as were Barnardo's housemothers at the outset,[62] and as were members of religious orders. As well as this, older children, especially in the work-shops and gardens, could contribute to the cost of their own mainten-ance. They could also be used as auxiliary staff, especially the girls who worked in the laundries, kitchens or nurseries. Such practices could be readily defended as valuable industrial training. Children did much of the housework whilst boys in industrial schools could be employed in building extensions or making adaptations. As well as having their own internal economies, some of the larger homes also had arrangements with other institutions: industrial schools for girls were known to take in the laundry from nearby industrial schools for boys, whilst they, in their turn, mended the girls' footwear. Of course, the use of inmate labour was not peculiar to the voluntary sector but the particular emphasis upon the value of industrial training for children provided a powerful rationale.

All these considerations help to explain the establishment and viability of voluntary children's institutions. They do not fully account for the demand that sustained them and, in many instances, led to their expansion. Poor law referrals were one source and compulsion another. The Industrial Schools Acts (beginning in 1859) enabled magistrates to commit children until they were 16—usually for minor thefts, begging, vagrancy and later, with the introduction of compulsory education, for not attending school. Exactly how children, many of them very young, were brought to the court's notice is rarely clear, but it was by no means only by the actions of the police: bible women; home visitors; relieving officers and truancy officers all played their part—and sometimes the parents too. After 1889, it was also possible for courts to commit children who had been subjected to cruel treatment to the care of a 'fit person', and these fit persons were often the principal voluntary children's organisations.

By and large, however, children did not come to the homes (as dis-tinct from the industrial schools) via the compulsory route. Many of the religious organisations had local committees or subscribing members, some of whom might take it upon themselves to refer poor children (especially those from large families, or with widowed or unmarried mothers). Sometimes, as with the Waifs and Strays Society, a system of financial sponsorship existed. Although many of the children in the voluntary homes came from the most crowded urban areas, a surprising number were also drawn from small country towns, spas and rural areas. There is some case material to show that local ladies were responsible for encouraging, persuading and occasionally paying poor parents to place their children with the agencies.[63]

Barnardo in particular popularised the image of the self-referred child; especially the London homeless, hungry and ragged. Their plight readily evoked sympathy and compassion. Undoubtedly there were such children who were offered or who sought the comfort of the home. Yet although self-referral may have been important in the early days there is little evidence to suggest that it continued to be anything but a minor factor.

The likelihood that, for a variety of reasons, parents brought their children to the voluntary societies themselves (or, at least, took the initiative in getting somebody else to do so) is less well documented and has been less thoroughly investigated. The circumstances of such applications were, of course, closely associated with poverty and the particular social and economic dilemmas that mothers faced. Their treatment (or expected treatment) by the poor law shaped their attitude towards the charitable societies. For example, although widows were likely to receive out-door relief, deserted wives and especially unmarried mothers were not. More often than not they and their children would be offered the workhouse or, in order to avoid the payment of out-door relief, the relieving officer might offer to take the older children into institutional care leaving mothers to manage the care of the younger ones as best they could whilst they worked. The admission of a child to a voluntary society avoided many of these unwelcome possibilities; it evaded the stigma of pauperism, and allowed mothers to keep or obtain paid work. Since so much of this was in residential domestic service or related occupations where children were not accepted, mothers who took such work were obliged to find permanent care for their offspring rather than the readily available daily childminding to be found in working-class communities. Perhaps one of the most ironic possibilities is that widespread domestic service (maids, nurses and governesses) may have enabled the middle and upper classes to keep their dependent relatives at home whilst forcing more of the dependants of the women whom they employed into institutional care, as well as increasing the likelihood that they, in their turn, would finish their lives in the same way. Even in 1958 Townsend found that a large number of the elderly women in the homes he studied had spent lifetimes as domestic servants.[64]

Of course, there was often a difference in what mothers (it was usually mothers) wanted from voluntary care for their children outside the poor law and what the agencies wanted to provide. The former were anxious to retain contact and to be able to recover their children when their circumstances improved—typically upon marriage or remarriage or when the children were old enough to contribute to the household income. What the agencies usually wanted was the ability to strengthen the religious, moral and practical capacities of the children in their care; and for this it was considered necessary to exercise uninterrupted and long-term responsibility. The severely restrictive rules about contact and communication between children and their parents that some societies imposed (and that seem to have lasted well into the twentieth century) bear witness to the belief that a child's well-being was best secured and assured by keeping parental influences to a minimum.

Thus, a mixture of interests and procedures propelled children towards the voluntary children's societies. Since children tended to remain in care for long periods the problem of an ever-growing institutional population had to be faced if admissions were to continue. This was one of the key pressures for growth; but there were limits to the extent and speed with which expansion could occur. Emigration was one solution, boarding-out another. Yet, at least in the case of boarding-out, there was only modest development. Even when children were placed in foster homes many of the societies recalled them to the homes from eight years of age onwards (even from settled foster homes) in order to train them for subsequent employment or to ensure and consolidate the religious component in their upbringing during the years of vulnerability. The residential homes' populations were swollen for this reason and, of course, by those children who had to be readmitted when their foster home placement broke down.

The growth in the charitable children's home (as well as the voluntary industrial school) must be related to social and economic forces that operated upon both supply and demand and which existed mainly outside the institutions. As the pattern of these forces changed so did the place of the voluntary children's home. Changes in policies and practices were, however, slow to occur since it proved exceedingly difficult to abandon the centrality of residential care in favour of other forms of activity, especially for the smaller societies. The number of homes and children involved were considerable. By 1946, in England and Wales, there were some 11,000 children in approved schools plus another 20,000 in voluntary children's homes (about a fifth of whom were paid for by public assistance committees). There were about the same number in homes provided by public authorities.[65] Hence the voluntary sector accounted for well over half of all residential child care places. It was not easy to replace such a large and longstanding system: it was difficult to redeploy or train the staff; it was hard to redirect the current of charitable support and to create new sources, and it was difficult to break free from the legacy of ideas whose history was embodied in the physical existence of buildings. Fortunately for the survival of the voluntary sector the pace of change in the public sector, to which it was irrevocably tied, was also slow; and for similar reasons.

These two examples, drawn from the history of the asylums and the voluntary children's homes, provide further evidence of the complexity of the factors that shaped the evolution of residential care. However, four issues might be emphasised. The first is the need to understand and acknowledge the circumstances in which families resorted to the use of institutions. We know comparatively little about what influenced these decisions, although a family's composition (especially lone parenthood) and the place of its members in the labour market appear to have been of great importance. A second feature of these examples is the significant part played in the growth and survival of institutional provision by those whose professional or philanthropic interests it served. The more extensive the institutional systems became the more significant these interests became. The third discernible theme in the illustrations is the absence, unacceptability or stunted development of any other formal solutions to the problems that institutions were assumed to address. This reflected the rudimentary nature of community-based welfare services until the last few decades; indeed, it was not until the 1950s that a profession of social work began to emerge that based its identity partly upon the fact that it did not work within institutions. Finally, it is important to recognise that the methods by which institutions were financed had a profound bearing upon the course of their development.

5 The Future

What has the history of residential care to suggest about the factors that may shape its future? It is generally assumed that the major determinant will be an expanding emphasis on community care. That will certainly be important but the success with which it can be pursued will be affected by many structural forces and not simply by policy commitment or even special resources: these are necessary but not sufficient conditions. Furthermore, the questions of quality and acceptability are as pertinent for community care as they are for residential care.

The chapters that follow consider these issues and deal with recent and current situations in depth. An historical perspective enables us to leap-frog forward and consider some of the more general themes that need to be taken into account if the interweaving futures of community care and residential care are to be assessed. Six topics suggest themselves although, of course, others could readily be added. However, this selection serves to indicate an approach to thinking about the future that may add an extra dimension to the present debate.

Purposes for other systems

The historical examples have shown how important it is to see residential care as part of a wider system of services. The relationship of the workhouses to the asylums has been noted, as has the evolution of the hospital to the character of poor law institutions. It would certainly have been enlightening to have looked at the way in which the industrial schools and reformatories related to the prisons and, in the inter-war years, to have traced the impact elsewhere of a growing convalescent and nursing home sector (it catered for 26,000 patients in 1921 and 33,000 by 1931).[66] Residential homes provide accommodation as well as care so that when the housing problem improves or worsens they are likely to feel the repercussions—albeit the residential sector assumes the thinly disguised form of bed and breakfast hotels or lodging houses. Yet the importance of such connections goes beyond residential care alone; there are flows between residential and non-residential services and both the volume and speed of these have considerable significance. Indeed, the whole question of the duration of a person's stay in residential care is more likely to be affected by external than by internal circumstances. In large residential populations like the elderly, small changes in the average length of residence can have magnified consequences for the level of demand.

The structure of interests

We have seen the way in which the pattern of professional interests has helped to shape the fortunes of residential care and the different parts that have been played by, say, doctors and social workers. It has also been clear that the existence of a strong and developing residential sector tended to create interests in its continuity, whether these interests were those of founders, supporters or other organisations. What this review has not been able to do is to chart the historical pattern of commercial interests in residential care, partly because what development there was has not been systematically recorded; most of the time it was assumed to be peripheral. There are a few indicators that tend to confirm that view. The 1891 and 1901 censuses, for example, classified private 'asylums' separately; they accounted for four per cent and six per cent of the total places available in the respective years.[67] However, it is plain that private enterprise is likely to be the single biggest new factor shaping both the supply and the demand for residential care in the foreseeable future. These interests now become important and the manner in which they proliferate, become powerful or form alliances (for example, with professional groups) will open a fresh chapter in the history of residential care.

Financing

Obviously, the structure of financial support for residential care has been of the utmost significance in the past, especially support from public sources. The voluntarily-run reformatories and industrial schools would simply not have been established without such assistance. The modern counterparts are local authority funded services and the board and lodging allowances paid by the supplementary benefits system; but other sources are important too and may not have been sufficiently recognised. The capacity of many groups (certainly not all) to pay for residential care is increasing. How far that capacity will be translated into effective demand remains to be seen. Take the elderly as an example. We have an unprecedented situation in which something like two-thirds of all people over 65 own their house outright, unencumbered by a mortgage (at the turn of the century fewer than five per cent of houses were owner-occupied). The proportion may well rise. So far the value of such property has not systematically been converted into purchasing power, except when the elderly person sells upon moving in with a relative or upon entering a home. New schemes for realising the value of a house in other ways are already available and may well become more popular. If this happens, and the character of residential care for the elderly changes (for example, sheltered housing combined with a 'next-stage' home on the same site), then a positive demand of considerable size may be created. What seems fairly sure is that developments are passing out of the public arena to the private and, apart from the late eighteenth and early nineteenth-century private mad-houses, we have little historical experience of where such a change might lead.

Women and the labour market

Both residential care and community care rely (and have relied) heavily upon the labour of women. We have seen how dependent the residential sector was upon the large pool of single women, many of whom found in residential work the solution to the problem of securing accommodation in a housing market geared to families and to the purchasing power of men. Much of today's residential care is still undertaken by women but on a non-resident and, more often, part-time basis as well. It is not well paid and were better opportunities to be offered elsewhere in the labour market that supply might well decline. Future trends in part-time work throughout the labour market could have profound implications for the development of residential care. Changes in the market for female labour are having, and will continue to have, equally far-reaching consequences for the major alternative to residential care. Women's willingness and ability to care for dependent relatives at home is, to a greater or lesser degree, a function of their involvement in paid work. The future of residential care may be best assessed by the careful analysis of how that involvement is likely to develop according to age, family composition and household income. Certainly neither community care nor residential care would remain unaffected by a marked shift from part-time to full-time work or an increased rate of participation in paid employment within specific age ranges (for example, 45–64 years).

Standards and images

This review devoted considerable attention to the image of residential care and suggested some of the ways in which it might change in light of its history. As destitution, madness and crime have become less pronounced features, it is possible that the image will become less negative. Moreover, in the past the institutional solution was predominantly a solution for the poor. If the middle classes increasingly resort to residential care (with the emergence of the private market) that too may modify the image. Similarly, how residential care is described and perceived may make a difference. We have noted the more favourable view taken of that which is seen as falling under a medical designation, and there is evidence that an emphasis upon it as housing also alters the image.[68] However, the most powerful impact upon the public image may occur as a result of improvement in the standards provided. Paradoxically that is most likely to be achieved if the amount of provision contracts—but that could then herald renewed growth.

Demography

It is plain that changes in demographic structure have, and will continue to have, a profound bearing upon the scale and character of residential provision. The more obvious trends have been noted already. However, there are other aspects of current and future demographic development that should be taken into account as well. Take, for example, the issue of the differential rates of mortality as between men and women. If there is a spouse, we know that they are the person most likely to care for a dependent person at home. It may follow, therefore, that were the life expectancies of men and women in old age to become more equal the demand for residential care would fall. There would be fewer widows and a larger pool of husbands; but who became the carers and who the cared-for would depend in part upon differences in the morbidity within each group. Detailed analyses of this kind will add to our understanding of the vitally important relationship between demographic change and the future of residential care.

Notes and References

1 Amongst a rich literature that, to different extents, approaches the issue in this way, see: Skull, A. T. (1979), *Museums of Madness: the Social Organisation of Insanity in Nineteenth Century England*, Allen Lane; Crowther, M. A. (1983), *The Workhouse System, 1834–1929: The History of an English Social Institution*, Methuen; Ignatieff, M. (1978), *A Just Measure of Pain: the Penitentiary in the Industrial Revolution, 1750–1850*, Macmillan, or Mellett, D. J. (1982), *The Prerogative of Asylumdom: Social, Cultural and Administrative Aspects of the Institutional Treatment of the Insane in Nineteenth Century Britain*, Garland Publishing. For a useful review of different theoretical approaches to the study of institutions see, Jones, K. and Fowles, A. J. (1984), *Ideas on Institutions: Analysing the Literature on Long-term Care and Custody*, Routledge and Kegan Paul, as well as Jones, K. (1967), 'The development of institutional care' in Association of Social Workers, *New Thinking about Institutional Care*, ASW.

2 For an excellent review and critique see Mayer, J. A. (1983), 'Notes towards a working definition of social control in historical analysis' in Cohen, S. and Scull, A. T. (eds), *Social Control and the State*, Robertson, as well as Higgins, J. (1980), 'Social control theories of social policy', *Journal of Social Policy*, 9, 1, pp. 1–23.

3 Scull, A. T. (1979), *op. cit.* p. 30.

4 See Brundage, A. (1978), *The Making of the New Poor Law, 1832–39*, Hutchinson.

5 Reported in Page, R. and Clark, G. A. (eds) (1977), *Who Cares?* National Children's Bureau, p. 16.

6 For valuable essays on several demographic issues see, Barker, T. and Drake, M. (eds) (1982), *Population and Society in Britain, 1850–1980*, Batsford.

7 Figures for 1931 from Donnison, D. V. and Ungerson, C. (1968), 'Trends in residential care, 1911–1961', *Social and Economic Administration*, 2(2), p. 79; and from Office of Population Censuses and Surveys (1974), *Non-Private Households in 1971*; tables 7 and 9. It is difficult to make similar calculations from the 1981 Census but for a review of the evidence see, Pearce, D. (1983), 'Population in communal establishments', *Population Trends*, 33, Autumn, HMSO.

8 Report of the Committee of Enquiry set up by the National Council of Social Service (1967), *Caring for People: Staffing Residential Homes*, Allen and Unwin, p. 122.

9 Scull, A. T. (1979), *op. cit.*

10 See, for example, Nassau Senior, Jane (1874), 'Report on the education of girls in pauper schools', *Annual Report of the Local Government Board for 1873–4*, c. 1071; appendix, p. 311.

11 In many ways these find particularly forceful expression in Bowlby, J. (1951), *Maternal Care and Mental Health*, monograph series, no. 2, World Health Organisation.

12 Sanders, W. (1903), *A Digest of the Census of England and Wales, 1901*, Layton; calculated from table, p. 64.

13 Rose, M. E. (ed.) (1985), *The Poor and the City: the English Poor Law in its Urban Context, 1834–1914*, Leicester University Press, p. 3.

14 See Ignatieff, M. (1983), 'Total institutions and working classes: a review essay', *History Workshop Journal*, 15.

15 Registrar General (1873), *Digest of the English Census of 1871*, p. 13.

16 *The Report of the Select Committee on the Andover Union* (1846), HC 663 I and II, HMSO. See also Anstruther, I. (1973), *The Scandal of the Andover Workhouse*, Bles, London, for a discussion of the role of *The Times* in using the official report to further the campaign against the poor law.

17 For example, Department of Health and Social Security (1969), *Report of the Committee of Inquiry into Allegations of Ill-Treatment of Patients and other Irregularities at the Ely Hospital, Cardiff*, Cmnd. 3975, HMSO; and DHSS (1971), *Report of the Farleigh Hospital Committee of Inquiry*, Cmnd. 4557, HMSO.

18 Townsend, P. (1962), *The Last Refuge: A Survey of Residential Institutions and Homes for the Aged in England and Wales*, Routledge and Kegan Paul, p. 435.

19 Quoted in Crowther, M. A. (1981), *The Workhouse System, 1834–1929; the History of an English Social Institution*, Methuen, p. 84.

20 *Report of the Royal Commission on the Aged Poor* (1895), vol. 1, c. 7684, HMSO, para. 97, p. xxxi.

21 Roberts, R. (1971), *The Classic Slum: Salford Life in the First Quarter of the Century*, Manchester University Press, p. 8.

22 *Report of the Royal Commission on The Aged Poor* (1895); *op, cit.* para. 128, p. xxxviii.

23 Page R. and Clark G. A. (1977), *op. cit.*; another child in care explains that 'When you go to a new place before you've got your foot in the door they say "Hey, what are you in for?"...they came to me and said "What you done wrong?" Because, you know, they look upon it [a children's home] as a detention centre'.

24 For a general review and account of these issues see the *Report of the Royal Commission on Lunacy and Mental Disorder* (1926), Cmd. 2700, HMSO, pp. 15–30.

25 *Report of the Royal Commission on the Law Relating to Mental Illness and Mental Deficiency, 1954–57* (1957), Cmnd. 169, HMSO; pp. 62–3.

26 For discussion and details see Board of Control (1929), *Report of the Mental Deficiency Committee*, HMSO, part 1.

27 *Report of the Royal Commission* (1957), *op. cit.* p. 318.

28 This provision continues to the present day in the form of section 3 of the *Child Care Act, 1980*.

29 For a further discussion of some of these issues see, Parker, R. A. (1986), 'Child care: the roots of a dilemma', *Political Quarterly*, 57 (3).

30 Estimated from Registrar General (1934), *General Report of the Census, 1931*, HMSO table 16, p. 118.

31 See, *Report of the Ministry of Health for the Year Ended 31 March, 1949* (1949), Cmd. 7910, HMSO, p. 370.

32 Townsend, P. (1962), *op. cit.* pp. 42–4.

33 Crowther, M. A. (1981), *op. cit.* p. 67.

34 Digby, A. (1978), *Pauper Palaces* Routledge and Kegan Paul, p. 177.

35 For an interesting biographical account see Linklater, A. (1980). *An Unhusbanded Life: Charlotte Despard: Suffragette, Socialist and Sinn Feiner*, Hutchinson; she was for some time a member of the Lambeth board of guardians.

36 *Report of the Royal Commission* (1895), *op. cit.* p. xix.

37 Digby, A. (1978), *op. cit.* p. 145.

38 See Parker, R. A. (1987), *The Elderly and Residential Care*, Gower, ch. 11 and 12.

39 Royal Commission on the Poor Laws and Relief of Distress (1909), Appendix vol. XXVIII, *Report of Visits to Poor Law and Charitable Institutions and to Meetings of Local Authorities in the United Kingdom*, Cd. 4974, HMSO, p. 45.

40 *Report of the Care of Children Committee* (1946), Cmd. 6922, HMSO.

41 Townsend, P. (1962), *op. cit.*

42 Abel-Smith, B. (1964), *The Hospitals, 1800–1948*, Heinemann, p. 2.

43 Pinker, R. A. (1966), *English Hospital Statistics, 1861–1938*, Heinemann, p. 56.

44 Pinker, R. A. (1966), *op. cit.* See also Ayers, M. A. (1971), *England's First State Hospitals and the Metropolitan Asylums Board, 1867–1930*, Wellcome Institute of the History of Medicine.

45 Abel-Smith, B. (1964), *op. cit.* p. 85.

46 *Ibid.*, p. 86.

47 *Ibid.*, p. 215.

48 For fuller details of the changes see, Ministry of Health (1929, 1930, 1931, 1932), *On the State of the Public Health: the Annual Report of the Chief Medical Officer of Health* for 1928, 1929, 1930 and 1931, HMSO.

49 Scull, A. T. (1979), *op. cit.*

50 Walton, J. K. (1985), 'Casting out and bringing back in Victorian England. Pauper lunatics, 1840–70' in Bynum, W. F., Porter, R. and Shepherd, M. (eds), *The Anatomy of Madness: Essays in the History of Psychiatry, vol 2*. Tavistock, p. 135.

51 Ignatieff, M. (1983), *op. cit*.

52 Figures from Scull, A. T. (1979) *op. cit*. and Registrar General (1934), *op. cit*.

53 Crowther, M. A. (1983), *op. cit*. p. 66.

54 Anderson, M. (1971), *Family Structure in Nineteenth Century Lancashire*, Cambridge University Press.

55 Donnison, D. V. and Ungerson, C. (1968), *op. cit*.

56 Rates of mortality were much more equal as between men and women earlier in the nineteenth century.

57 *Twenty-Seventh Report of the Inspector...Reformatory and Industrial Schools* (1884), c. 4147, Eyre and Spottiswoode.

58 See Musgrove, F. (1966), *The Family, Education and Society*, Routledge and Kegan Paul (he maintained that 'the establishment of elementary schools in the nineteenth century was a gigantic street cleaning device', p. 129); Cruikshank, M. (1981), *Children and Industry*, Manchester University Press; Hurt, J. S. (1979), *Elementary Schooling and the Working Classes, 1860–1918*, Routledge and Kegan Paul, and (translated from the French) Meyer, P. (1983) *The Child and the State: the Intervention of the State in Family Life*, Cambridge University Press and Editions de la Maison des Sciences de l'Homme.

59 See, MacNicol, J. (1987), 'In pursuit of the underclass', *Journal of Social Policy*, 16, 3, pp. 293–318.

60 For an account of this movement see, Finer, S. E. (1952), *The Life and Times of Sir Edwin Chadwick*, Methuen.

61 Proportions calculated from the various annual reports of the Societies.

62 See, Rose, J. (1987), *For the Sake of the Children: Inside Dr Barnardo's: 120 Years of Caring for Children*, Hodder and Stoughton, ch. 4.

63 From my ongoing research on Home Office and Ministry of Health class archives, Public Record Office.

64 Townsend, P. (1962), *op. cit*. p. 55.

65 *Report of the Care of Children Committee* (1946), *op. cit*. pp. 12 and 18.

66 See Registrar General (1924, 1934), *Census Reports* 1921 and 1931; tables on Institutional Population (Inmates), England and Wales.

67 See Registrar General (1904, 1914), *Census Reports* 1891 and 1901; tables on Institutional Population (Inmates), England and Wales.

68 See for example, Harris Research Centre (1984), *Britons Observed* (for the *Observer*) which shows clear public preference for sheltered housing as a solution to the care of the dependent elderly.

Residential Care
Common Issues in the Client Reviews

Ian Sinclair

National Institute for Social Work

CONTENTS

Common Issues in the Client Reviews

1 Introduction

The various kinds of residential care differ in their purposes, excellences and failings; in the end each has to be evaluated separately. Nevertheless trainers, administrators and theorists have all at times found it useful to consider residential care as a whole. Policies which affect one branch of residential care often affect others similarly: hypotheses which have been found to hold true of one set of units may well hold true of others: and most forms of residential care raise similar ethical dilemmas over the competing demands of the individual and the group. By bringing together the six reviews of research into different aspects of residential care which were prepared for the Wagner committee, this book should encourage the identification of such common themes.

This introductory chapter provides background material for four key questions which the reader may wish to bear in mind in reading the book:

What is residential care?

Why should it be provided?

How should it be delivered?

What policies will promote its proper development?

Answers to these four questions are linked, so that decisions about the nature and purpose of residential care determine many of the issues that have to be considered by those administering and providing it.

Most of the following material is drawn from the five client group reviews. (The review on costs already provides an overview of its subject). The evidence cited is fully referenced in the reviews and further referencing has been avoided.

2   What is Residential Care?

Any discussion of residential care might be expected to start with its definition. Unfortunately no definition has been agreed, but at the minimum, residential care involves the provision of both accommodation and care on the same site. The Registered Homes Act 1984, for example, defines a Residential Care Home as 'an establishment which provides or is intended to provide, whether for reward or not, residential accommodation with both board and personal care for persons in need of personal care by reason of old age, disablement, past or present dependence on alcohol or drugs, or past or present mental disorder'.

This definition while adequate for its particular purposes excludes most residential care for children but ostensibly includes certain kinds of care given by families, hospitals and prisons. Further criteria are required to distinguish the residential home or unit. The providers must be public bodies or voluntary or private agencies; families are not normally considered to provide residential care for their members. Moreover, the primary purpose of residential units must be to provide care which includes an element of communal living for an administratively defined group. Thus units whose primary purpose is commonly thought to be educational, medical or penal (eg public schools, hospitals or prisons) are not considered in detail in the reviews. Nor are those which cater for very small numbers (eg foster homes, supported lodgings) or which have no element of communal living (eg much sheltered housing).

These criteria leave grey areas. Is residential care to be distinguished from institutional care, as it is by Dorothy Atkinson? Do landladies give residential care if they contract to provide supported accommodation to four or more mentally ill people? Is the 'cluster' associated with a 'core' unit for the mentally handicapped to be considered part of residential care? What about sheltered housing combined with heavy domiciliary services and a common place to meet? Are residential schools for the delicate or for children with educational and behavioural difficulties part of residential care? Given that care has commonly been held to include 'social treatment' (for example, in therapeutic communities for the young), what distinguishes social treatment from psychiatric treatment?

Some of these dilemmas of definition have arisen from changes in the nature of residential care itself. In the past it has generally been clear where community care stopped and residential care began. Inevitably, these reviews of past research observe these traditional boundaries. They concentrate on the hostels, homes and residential schools which have always been seen as providing residential care. At the same time, they suggest that the boundaries of residential care are being redrawn or blurred. 'Core and cluster' homes and 'heavy sheltered housing' provide examples of developments which seem to straddle residential and community care. Whether provisions of these kinds are included within the definition of residential care is a matter for decisions which are inevitably somewhat arbitrary. What is essential is that such provisions should be considered in policy discussions concerned with residential care. Thus, what the reviews make clear is that, however it is defined, residential care needs to be considered not as a segregated form of provision but in the context of the policies and services related to it.

3 The Purposes of Residential Care

Given that residential care has to be seen as part of a network of services, what particular purposes does it or should it serve?

The variety of possible purposes is well illustrated by the reviews. Residential homes can provide short-term care to relieve relatives or to shelter children at risk, or give a holiday to a disabled person who needs one. They can provide long-term shelter for a variety of groups, but in doing so they may be aiming to allow for ordinary development in the case of the young or to give older groups the opportunity to live as normal a life as possible. They may set out to assess, treat, train or educate the young, teach skills to the mentally handicapped, provide care, attention and even nursing care for the frail elderly, prepare children for foster care or adolescents for independence and make sure that those in care do not lose touch with their families and roots. Less benignly perhaps, they may 'control the disruptive and punish the recalcitrant.'

As the reviews make clear, the groups involved with residential care—residents, staff, potential residents, relatives, professionals, politicians, parent bodies and the general public—differ over the value they attach to these possible aims and the ways these are pursued. The reviews illustrate the resulting conflicts of view, which seem to affect the processes of admission and the details of residential life. Diana Leat, for example, comments on the dilemmas associated with the uncertain goals of residential care for the physically handicapped:

> If homes are not about care and control or reform but about care and development what are the rights and duties of residents? Do residents have the right, for example, to refuse medication, to put themselves at risk in dangerous situations or, more mundanely, to get drunk occasionally or often.

It may well be that the residents hold one view on these matters, and staff, relatives and the general public another. For these reasons it may be useful to classify the various purposes of residential care according to whose interests they serve.

In the first place, the possible conflict between the interests of residents and others highlights the crucial question of how far the aims of residential care serve society in general, having to do with social control and in particular with removing residents from the community. It is apparent from the reviews that residential care deals with some of the most difficult, deprived and dependent individuals in client groups already marked out by these characteristics. The use of residential care to segregate these individuals is suggested by phrases scattered throughout the reviews. The titles 'Put Away' and 'Last Refuge' suggest that the purpose of a residential admission may be to remove an individual from the social world inhabited by the rest of us. So too does the concept of 'social death' introduced by Miller and Gwynne in their discussion of life in residential homes for the disabled which is cited by Diana Leat.

The view that the purpose of residential care is to segregate is further emphasised by discussions of the symbolic role of residential units. Jane Gibbons, for example, quotes Scull's argument that asylums provide a 'culturally legitimate alternative' for the 'awkward and unwanted'. In this respect residential care may legitimate an uneasy deed. Difficult but vulnerable people are removed from ordinary society but to care or treatment rather than punishment. Although the ostensible aim may be to help individuals, a latent purpose may be to relieve those who are troubled by them.

This symbolic role of residential care may be justified by reference to the characters and responsibilities of residents. Roy Parker, for example, comments that 'the image of Observation and Assessment Centres may contribute to the redefinition of problems in ways which make them more amenable to solution; suggesting that because children need to be observed, tested and assessed the problem lies mainly with them.' Yet it should also be recognised that the effects of such redefinitions are not necessarily to the residents' disadvantage. Units whose purpose might have been simply to punish and contain may come to embrace the more positive aims of training, therapy and rehabilitation.

A different kind of purpose for residential care is to provide a service for a wider welfare system. As an example of such a 'systemic function', Roy Parker cites the role of children's homes in acting as a buffer stock for the foster care system, sheltering children before they are placed in foster homes or after a placement has broken down. Such systemic functions may be overtly acknowledged, as is the role played by assessment centres in serving the courts. They can also be deduced from the behaviour of a system, for example from the rise in the number of adolescents receiving youth custody orders which has accompanied the fall in the number of CHEs. Their importance is further illustrated by the efforts of doctors to ensure that elderly people can be discharged from hospitals to old people's homes rather than blocking a bed for social reasons, and by the debate over whether the reduction in beds in psychiatric hospitals has led to a rise in the prison population.

The purposes of residential care may also be defined by the relatives of the residents. The reviews for the mentally ill, physically handicapped and elderly each stress the major burdens borne by relatives caring for very dependent adults. Most, it seems, would prefer to continue caring although the level of domiciliary services they receive is typically very low. Even where elderly people are admitted to residential care, they are usually visited by relatives. The parents of children in care seem to prefer care in children's homes to fostering partly because it makes visiting easier. Nevertheless the reluctance or inability of relatives to care and their need for relief provides a reason for admission to long term care for all client groups and for the growing use of short-term or respite care.

The most obvious group with an interest in residential care consists of those who have already entered it or might do so in the future. Whereas relatives, professionals and the general public may sometimes have reasons for wanting individuals removed to residential care, this aim is not necessarily shared by the potential residents themselves. Little research attention appears to have been paid to the views of children in care, or of residents in homes for the mentally handicapped or mentally ill. However research in the field of the elderly and physically handicapped suggests that while a few of them wish to go into residential homes, most of those who do become residents do so, at best reluctantly, and at worst against their will. Yet at the same time most elderly residents would no doubt endorse the aims of homes to provide them with a secure and comfortable life. And as some of the evidence to the Wagner Committee made clear, some children may prefer residential care to the potential strains and complex demands of foster care.

So far this discussion has emphasised the variety in the purposes pursued by residential care and in the interests it serves. It follows that particular kinds of residential care have to be evaluated against particular purposes and that it is wise to consider the interests of all the groups involved. Questions, however, arise about what can be achieved by residential care and which groups benefit from what kinds of care. It is to these issues that we turn next.

4 Care Regimes and their Effects

The arguments for residential care usually rely on demonstrating some kind of need, for example, for asylum or emergency shelter. Needs, however, can almost always be met in more than one way. Traditional residential institutions provided a form of total care in which as many of the residents' needs as possible were met under the same roof and in accordance with the same plan. There is, however, no necessity for needs to be met in this way. Dorothy Atkinson, for example, organises her discussion of residential care for the mentally handicapped around the concept of a residential service which 'aims to cater for the personal, social and accommodation needs of individual people'. On her analysis the different elements of residential care would be supplied to clients according to their individual needs rather than on the basis that they were resident in a residential unit.

Taken together the research reviews make severe criticisms of traditional residential care, and even of much of the care that is currently provided. The main lines of criticism are:

(a) An unbiased description of residential institutions suggests that they are not places in which the residents can be expected to live normal or reasonable lives. Examples of such criticisms are provided by Townsend's account of old people's homes published in 1962 and Pauline Morris's account of long-stay hospitals for the mentally handicapped published in 1969.

(b) Few people want to go into residential care. The elderly generally wish to avoid it if they possibly can. Some physically handicapped adults see it as a desirable step towards independence and some mentally ill people prefer certain types of residential care to permanent hospitalisation. However, there is no evidence that any group is enthusiastic about the idea.

(c) Traditional forms of residential care have proved ineffective. In particular they do not reform delinquents and in the fields of mental handicap and mental illness they are probably less effective than smaller, community based institutions in developing the skills required for normal living.

(d) Residential care is usually more costly than possibly superior community provision catering for a similar clientele.

These arguments against residential care cannot be easily dismissed, if only because some of them appear to be based on essential characteristics of residential care and others on well replicated findings. Residential care for children, for example, faces inherent problems in terms of the number of staff to whom children may have to relate, their turnover, and the virtual requirement that the child must leave by 18. Moreover there is now abundant evidence that although residential institutions may have a dramatic effect on the delinquent behaviour of those in them, they can have only a marginal effect on the delinquent behaviour of those who have left. The two points are related since both seem to reflect the influence of the immediate environment on delinquent behaviour. Furthermore these unavoidable difficulties are accompanied by evidence of lack of privacy for children in homes, and high rates of unemployment among former children in care. Similarly the evidence of reluctant residents and unstimulating regimes summarised in the review of care for the elderly in local authority homes has been provided from the 1960s to the early 1980s. It is hard to believe that there has been a dramatic change since. Bleddyn Davies' and Martin Knapp's discussion suggests that for most elderly and young clients 'community' alternatives such as fostering and intensive domiciliary care schemes are likely to be cheaper and in the case of the elderly at least more effective. Much can be done with the £1,000 or so a week it apparently costs to keep children in some observation and assessment centres.

Despite these considerations the research based arguments against residential care are not conclusive. In the first place the arguments are based in part on research completed a long time ago and on kinds of institution that are generally agreed to have had their day. As Roy Parker points out, there has been a drastic reduction in the number of children under five in residential care. He comments that 'since much of the early and influential research which charted the ill-effects of residential living was based upon the experiences of this younger age group, its direct relevance for residential care today becomes less significant.' Similarly there have been radical improvements in the fabric at least of old people's homes since Townsend did his research and it would be wrong to condemn residential care as a whole on the basis of descriptions of the large psychiatric and mental handicap hospitals which are now being run down.

More importantly perhaps the attacks on residential care ignore some of its advantages. These include:

Robustness. Residential care ensures that certain needs (for example, for shelter, food, surveillance and pocket money) are at least minimally met. Such needs are often only met in the community through complex arrangements which include a number of individuals and agencies, and are liable to break down. While residential care may not provide a 'normal' life for residents, the alternative to it may be neither 'normal' nor safe.

Benefits to relatives. The reviews on the elderly produce evidence that the mental health of caring relatives may benefit from the removal of an elderly confused person to residential care. Roy Parker cites evidence that parents may prefer residential care for their children to foster care and were more likely to keep in touch with children in care who were not fostered. There may well be similar benefits for relatives concerned with other client groups.

Benefits to the 'welfare system'. Residential care almost by definition relieves hard pressed domiciliary services, helps to clear hospital beds, and acts as a staging post or buffer stock for other parts of the welfare system.

Finally there is abundant evidence of major variations in the quality of residential care, and the reasons for them are beginning to be understood. Life in residential units for children, for example, varies with the ideology of the unit, the degree of 'autonomy' of the staff, and the behaviour and attitude of the staff themselves. The existence of these variations raises questions about what should count as 'good care' but criteria for this can be partly established through evidence from surveys of resident opinion—the elderly, for example, value comfort, control over their lives, and access to their relatives and to the activities they themselves enjoy.

The evidence that all is not well with residential care and of the possibilities for improvement has led to new thinking about how residential care should be provided and to innovations such as the classic Brooklands experiment in the 1950s. Just as Victorian institutions for different client groups had a strong family resemblance to each other, so there are a number of common themes in new thinking about residential care for different client groups. These relate to:

Size. New homes or hostels are much smaller than traditional institutions, although their average size varies between the different sectors.

Isolation. Whereas traditional institutions were isolated from the community, new homes or hostels are supposed to be located inconspicuously within it.

Service integration. New forms of institution are supposed to be linked to a network of community services for which indeed they may provide the focal point.

Differentiated provision. Whereas traditional institutions made essentially the same provision for all their residents, newer forms of residential care may consist of a combination of hostel, staffed or unstaffed group homes, unsupported accommodation of various kinds and foster care, all serviced by the same multidisciplinary team. It may be particularly important to distinguish between needs for accommodation and for care.

Normalisation. Living closer to the community residents may be more likely to live normal lives. Staff too may be more likely to live off the job and have a comparatively normal existence.

Individualisation. Individuals should be treated as individuals rather than subjected to 'block treatment'.

These principles apply both to the way a system of services should be provided and to the running of particular residential units. The ideas behind them are exemplified in very different kinds of unit and seem themselves to have diverse origins. For example, efforts to treat residents as individuals could include the individual programme planning discussed by Dorothy Atkinson, the need for sympathy and individual understanding discussed in the child care review, and the advocacy by some researchers of the residential flatlet for old people.

It is apparent from the reviews that some or all of these principles are being tried out with all the main client groups, with the possible exception of the adult physically handicapped where the evidence is very scanty. Different elements in the ideas are stressed in different sectors of care. In the care of the elderly they provide support for the 'residential flatlet', a convergence between sheltered housing and residential care; in the care of the mentally ill and mentally handicapped they are seen in 'core and cluster' provision and in the use of residential care as a springboard to and back-up for a wide variety of more or less sheltered accommodation; in the children's field they are seen in family centres—the use of small local residential units as adjuncts to services for disturbed families.

As already pointed out, such approaches blur the traditional lines between residential and community care. It is a moot point whether unstaffed group homes or foster care supported by residential staff or a complex of 'residential flatlets' should be seen as part of a residential or a community service. The provision of ordinary accommodation for the mentally ill and mentally handicapped backed by intensive and flexible domiciliary services would not normally be seen as residential care, although this may now be used as an alternative form of residential care for these groups.

Yet for all their diffuseness the ideas have a coherence that does not stem simply from their opposition to the traditional institution described by Goffman. If residents are to be treated as individuals with the right to normal lives, they may be expected to live in ordinary neighbourhoods, use services because they need them rather than because they are in a particular place, and remain in contact with their relatives and friends. From these principles one can deduce the need for small, local units and differentiated service provision.

The research reported in the reviews provides support for some elements in this new thinking. The comments of elderly residents suggest that most would prefer an environment more like sheltered housing than a residential home. Initial research on hospital hostels and group homes suggests that from the point of view of the mentally handicapped and mentally ill these have a number of advantages, including the opportunity to practise normal activities such as shopping. The mentally ill at least seem to prefer such places to the hospitals from which they entered them. The provision of residential accommodation close to a resident's previous address encourages outside contacts, at least among the physically handicapped. And although there does not seem to be conclusive evidence that small units are better than large ones, evidence already cited suggests that staff autonomy, which should be a feature of small units, is associated with better staff performance.

A key issue is whether the new approach to residential care with its emphasis on integration with the community is more effective than the old one with its emphasis on segregation. The earlier approach was partly based on the idea that relearning was best undertaken away from the stresses and corrupting influences of the community. The difficulty was that the impact of the institution while powerful was limited to what went on within its walls. It followed that institutions were most likely to be effective at preventing delinquency if they provided a total break from the past (Approved Schools which prepared their charges for the Merchant Navy had unusually low reconviction rates). The new approach provides the possibility (not one so far explored in research) that small hostels supporting unstaffed accommodation in their neighbourhood might overcome the difficulty of maintaining changes in a resident's behaviour after discharge. For example, a difficult teenager who was able to keep a job and friends made while in a home and received continuing support from the staff might have a better chance than one discharged on his eighteenth birthday without such support.

Unfortunately the evidence in favour of the new approach is not conclusive. The approach is logical in the light of the evidence and some of its prototypes have been positively evaluated. There is as yet no proof that it would work well when widely applied. It is apparent from the review of care for the mentally handicapped that small hostels have their difficulties. They may not readily gain community acceptance, they may contain too many residents for these to integrate easily with the local community and their single rooms may prove to be 'isolating cells'. They may be in effect mini-institutions. As for group homes, these too may suffer from lack of community acceptance and clashes of personality between the residents. Jane Gibbons reports similar difficulties with group homes for the mentally ill, while also noting the evidence in favour of them. She concludes that 'the available research cannot tell us with any certainty what forms of residential care work best for what kinds of people.'

More generally the reviews provide little evidence of the effect of applying the new ideas to the organisation of a set of services as opposed to an individual unit. Dorothy Atkinson usefully discusses the principles which should underly the provision of a residential service but the nearest thing to hard evidence in favour of such principles comes in Bleddyn Davies' and Martin Knapp's discussion of the Kent Community Care project, which was designed to provide an alternative to residential admissions rather than to include residential care as one of its components.

In addition to lacking conclusive evidence in their favour new forms of residential care may fail to resolve or may even exacerbate some of the traditional problems of residential institutions. These include:

Cost. Some, although not all, of the new forms of residential care are very expensive (for example, hospital hostels may cost twice as much per bed as a psychiatric ward, whereas unstaffed group homes are relatively cheap.)

Variation between units. Residential homes and schools in the children's field vary greatly in the quality of care they provide and the behaviour and happiness of those in them. In small hostels these variations probably stem largely from the behaviour and cohesion of the staff. The development of a system of residential care based on small units will require developments in the selection, training and support of staff and in the monitoring of units.

Selection of residents. Both Dorothy Atkinson and Jane Gibbons report disagreements in the literature over the degree to which very demanding clients should be accepted in small community based units. The elderly mentally infirm and very disturbed or disruptive teenagers may raise similar issues. So for different reasons may very small groups of clients who require specialist resources (eg the blind-deaf).

Resource centre role. The new model of residential care emphasises the role of residential units as part of a network of resources. However, the increasing use of old people's homes to provide day care and short term relief care has brought problems for staff, residents and other users. Mental handicap hostels have been said to have difficulty in satisfactorily combining their provision of short-term care with their other roles. Children's homes which provide facilities for the local community are apparently more impersonal than other homes and the practice is unwelcome to some residents. A report by the Social Services Inspectorate suggests that staff in children's homes may find it difficult to combine community and residential roles.

For the Wagner committee part of the importance of the new model of care lies in its practical consequences. The reviews contain much evidence of the vital importance of staff for any attempts to improve residential care or change its nature. Staff will certainly be equally, if not more, important in any new approach to residential care. Furthermore if they are to work inside and outside small residential units their train-ing will need to be close to that of fieldworkers, partly because they will be undertaking fieldwork tasks and partly, perhaps, to provide them with a reasonable career structure.

As pointed out above, there are also implications for staff support and quality assurance. In this respect the task seems formidable. Ian Sinclair, for example, found that depending on the staff in charge the proportion of probationers in boys' probation hostels who absconded or committed offences varied from 14 per cent to 78 per cent. The rates varied as much over time within hostels as between them, and the variations persisted despite the existence of management committees, regular visits by the former Childrens' Inspectorate and contact between probation officers and individual probationers. The formal mechanisms for ensuring uniformly high standards in, say, private old people's homes are not as strong as those examined in Sinclair's study and must be suspected of being ineffective.

More significantly, perhaps, the new approach for all its lack of precision seems to run counter to past visions of residential care. There is less talk of therapy or love and more talk of normal life and service provision. There seems to be little place in the model for the therapeutic community, the village community or the training institution and only a limited and disputed place for the isolated haven or asylum. The shift-working professional running a small unit and supporting a network of provisions outside it may have little in common with the housemother in the voluntary family group home whose husband goes out to work. As far as the research evidence goes, such provisions may still have value for some clients (trade-training, for example, used to be valued by some delinquents). The assertion that past models of care have no value remains unproven.

5 The Policy Context

In the new approach to residential care, residential units are seen as integral to community care rather than as antithetical to it. However, even a cursory reading of the reviews shows that community care means different things to different people. When Dorothy Atkinson writes that 'the move from hospitals to community care is finally under way' she is including under the heading of 'community care' care in local authority homes and hostels. Ian Sinclair, however, contrasts care in local authority homes for the elderly with care in the community by domiciliary services. However they define this concept, the reviews agree on the importance of community care policies for residential care and on the lack of total success there has been in implementing them.

Focuses for this concern are provided by the low level of domiciliary services available for many physically handicapped adults and frail elderly people, by the related failure of home help provision to grow in line with the increase in the numbers of very old people, and by the growth in the numbers of old people in residential care resulting from the increase in private provision. In the fields of mental illness and mental handicap there is anxiety about the slow progress made in decanting long-stay patients from hospital and about whether community care has not simply meant a net loss of resources for this group. In the children's field there is concern about the diversion of adolescents to prison, detention centres and youth custody. There appears to be no firm evidence on how many children are maintained for too long in grossly unsatisfactory family circumstances.

The reasons for these difficulties fall into three main groups. The first has to do with the problems of developing a plan for an integrated set of residential and community services and then co-ordinating and regulating its implementation. Segregated residential provision may be undesirable but it is administratively tidy. One authority is responsible for providing for the residents food, accommodation, employment and recreation. By contrast community care requires adequate provision on the part of separate bodies responsible for accommodation, income maintenance, employment and so on. The problems which ensue may relate to:

Lack of planning yardsticks. There is no consensus on the criteria of need for residential care, how many people meet these criteria, what kind of residential care would meet their needs and the effect on the volume of need of increases in other services.

The co-ordination of different authorities. Community care involves the statutory, private and voluntary sectors, central government and local authorities, and organisations with concerns ranging from health to housing and education to social security. The bodies involved have differing objectives, professional traditions, planning cycles and geographical areas of responsibility. Attempts to co-ordinate these bodies cost time and are fraught with difficulty.

Regulating the growth of the private sector. The development of this sector poses problems for planners since it concentrates resources on particular authorities and areas within them which may not be the 'neediest', is not planned in relation to other services and naturally responds to market forces rather than planners' guidelines.

The second main group of difficulties in implementing community care concerns finance. Jane Gibbons notes that all forms of residential provision for the mentally ill except hospitals rely heavily on social security to underpin them. She also comments on the need for public finance to enable mentally ill people who cannot compete in the open market for ordinary housing to gain access to it. More generally, Diana Leat comments that her review may be 'interpreted as suggesting the limited change which guidance and/or legislation alone may effect and the much greater change produced by allocation of additional resources or by changes in the funding regulations.' Particular issues raised by the reviews include:

The operation of the social security system, in particular the 'perverse incentives' whereby an individual may receive more public resources by entering residential care than by remaining outside it, and the probable unsuitability of the social fund for certain kinds of long term financial support.

The divorce between funding and organisational responsibility. For example, social services are seen as having the prime responsibility for providing alternatives to hospital care for the mentally handicapped while the money to fund this lies with the health service. Statutory authorities would often find it easier to balance their budgets if they ensured that dependent or deviant people who might be seen as their responsibility are handled by other agencies.

Some reviews suggest the additional difficulty that adequate community care for all is likely to be very expensive. As Ian Sinclair and Diana Leat point out, the level of services for the elderly and physically handicapped is very low and few public resources are available for relieving their carers. Increased resources for these groups are unlikely to be devoted solely to those who would otherwise have entered residential care. Potential residents cannot be identified with precision in advance of an application. Moreover it would be inequitable to provide resources for old people who were not very independent or whose carers were reluctant to look after them, but deny services to those with fierce independence or devoted carers. For these reasons, the numbers of people likely to receive an enhanced level of community services under a policy of full community care would be much greater than the numbers now in institutions. The likely result would be an increase in costs.

A third set of difficulties identified in the reviews relate to the problems of developing community care policies. Given that geographical areas differ greatly in their inheritance of services, these problems must also vary across the country. Nevertheless, in all areas there must be the costs of retraining staff and running community and institutional services in parallel as the latter are phased out. Because of its costs there is a danger that community care policy will diminish rather than improve the quality of care for disadvantaged groups. A few showpiece community care programmes may be swamped with demand or attract clients for whom they were not intended (as seems, according to Davies and Knapp, to have occurred with intermediate treatment). Services to the many may suffer through the need to concentrate resources on the severely disadvantaged few. Resources may be taken from institutional care without being transferred to community care or it may be impossible to recruit the required staff such as occupational therapists or community psychiatric nurses. Residential care may linger on under a kind of planning blight and the morale of residential staff may suffer.

These problems in developing residential care are compounded by uncertainties about effectiveness and future demand. Some of the key questions about residential care (for example, over the relative merits of fostering as against residential provision) have not been resolved. When there is evidence that one form of provision (eg hospital hostels) is superior to another (eg long-stay wards) it is uncertain whether the superiority would be maintained if the provision was greatly expanded. And the needs that exist today (for example, to cater for long-stay patients discharged from psychiatric hospitals) may differ from those of tomorrow (eg when those who would have become psychiatric patients are maintained in the community). Thus there is a danger that today's mistaken assumptions will be encapsulated in tomorrow's bricks and mortar.

The reviews, notably that by Davies and Knapp, discuss a number of measures which might help those responsible for policy to overcome these problems. These vary from tax incentives and the use of planning procedures to regulate the growth of provision in the private sector to changes in social security and joint finance, or arrangements whereby the relevant agencies can be involved in planning and monitoring services in a given area. Others have discussed the merits of separating hotel and care costs for the purpose of funding, and the possible virtues of creating area managers responsible for all community care for particular client groups. Particular attention should perhaps be paid to Davies' and Knapp's discussion of the potential of case managers acting as co-ordinators of the diverse services required for successful community care.

Whatever the merits of their various proposals, the reviews make it abundantly clear that residential care cannot finally be viewed as an island entire of itself. From the point of view of policy, it is intimately affected by policies on housing, social security, and the mixed economy of welfare as well as by the other health, social and educational services which surround it.

6 In Conclusion

This introduction has suggested three groups of issues which the reader may wish to bear in mind in reading the reviews:

The variety of interests served by the residential care system and the low priority often given to those of the residents.

The emergence of a new approach to residential care, the practical implications of developing this approach (particularly those that have to do with staff) and the degree to which it should supersede earlier ones.

The need to set policies on residential care in the context of a wider set of policies if they are to be successful.

Research cannot resolve these issues. Much fundamental research has yet to be done. Many of the new ideas have not yet been tested by research. Some of the systems involved are extremely complex, more appropriate subject matter, perhaps, for the historian than the social scientist. And in the last analysis, the fundamental issues of residential care are matters of value rather than fact. Nevertheless, the material covered in these reviews encapsulates at the least a great deal of hard-earned experience. It is hoped that all those involved with residential care will find it of interest.

Residential Care for Children

R A Parker

with the assistance of the
Dartington Social Research Unit

Department of Social Administration
University of Bristol

CONTENTS

Residential Care for Children

Preamble

The review of research upon which this commentary is based concentrates on two interrelated themes: the functions of residential care for children and its quality. The presentation is organised with three considerations in mind. First, that most of the research evidence should be as up-to-date as possible. Secondly, that wherever feasible, the results should be compared with practical alternatives. Thirdly, that the exercise should assist in formulating the future role that residential care is to play in child care.

It is necessary at the outset, however, to provide a brief account of the scale and nature of residential child care and to identify some of the most important trends. This is the purpose of the introduction.

Part 1   Introduction: Numbers and Trends

1   The Overall Picture in England and Wales

Residential care for children is provided by many agencies and organisations. It is difficult to estimate its exact extent since there are problems of definition, overlap, age categories and missing data. In what follows boarding education, other than in special schools, is excluded, as the Committee suggested; but a separate short report on the subject has been prepared by the Dartington Social Research Unit so that this area is not overlooked.

In 1970 Peter Moss endeavoured to determine the number of children who lived in residential facilities. He arrived at an overall figure of 235,850.[1] This included children in non-specialist boarding-schools and ordinary hospitals without whom the total falls to about 80,000. He divided residential establishments into several broad types. Table 1 sets out these categories and the number of children (sometimes under 18, sometimes under 19) included in each. I have tried to bring Moss's figures up to date.

Table 1 The Number of Children 0 to 18 (or 19) in Residential Care in England and Wales, 1970 and 1984–5

	Moss 1970	Up-date 1984–5
1. Children in Homes Provided by Local Authorities and Voluntary Organisations for Children in Care or on Remand	40,902	22,979
2. Children in Special Schools for the Handicapped	21,417	25,500†
3. Children in Residential Provision for the Mentally Handicapped or Mentally Ill	13,979	3,200†
4. Children in Borstals (Youth Custody) or Detention Centres, etc. (estimated population under 18)	2,420*	9,000†
5. Children in Mother and Baby Homes (Babies excluded)	630	250†
	79,348	60,929

Notes:
*This figure is too low. It should be at least 5,000.
†Estimate

From these 'best estimates' it is plain that there has been an overall reduction in the number of children in residential care but that the pattern is uneven. The number in local authority and voluntary homes has fallen markedly, as has the number in hospitals and homes for the mentally handicapped and mentally ill (mostly the mentally handicapped). On the other hand, the number in penal establishments has risen.

Since there is a separate report on the mentally handicapped what follows concentrates on some of the finer detail of the numbers and the trends in three of Moss's categories: the local authority and voluntary residential establishments; the special boarding schools, and the penal sector.

2 Local Authority and Voluntary Homes, mainly for Children in Care

i The Nurseries

The post-war years have witnessed a dramatic reduction in the number of young children in residential nurseries. In the early 1950s upwards of 5,000 children were looked after in these establishments, or about 40 per cent of all children in care under school age. By 1960 the figure had fallen to 3,500, representing some 30 per cent of the under-fives in care. Ten years later the figures were down to 2,500 and 18 per cent respectively. In 1984 there were exactly 100 children in residential nurseries in England, or about 1 per cent of those in care under school age. Six authorities accounted for 70 per cent of this small handful of children.[2]

This dramatic downward trend has been reflected in the voluntary and private sectors as well. In 1958 (when the first national figures were published) 2,300 of the under-fives who were looked after by voluntary societies were in residential nurseries, or 55 per cent of that age band in their care. By 1970, although the number had fallen to 1,600, the proportion had risen to 62 per cent. 1981 was the last year in which any children looked after by the voluntary societies were recorded as being in residential nurseries. Figures for the private sector are only available for the years 1958–61, but during this period the number of young children in private residential nurseries declined from 1,300 to 500.[3]

Although nowadays virtually no young children live in residential nurseries that is not to say that they are not looked after in homes. The Personal Social Services Research Unit (PSSRU) survey, for instance, found that almost two per cent of all the children in the homes that they studied (in all three sectors) were under five. Of these, about three-quarters were in 'ordinary' community homes and most of the remainder in homes for the mentally and physically handicapped.[4] In their 1984 national survey of homes the DHSS social services inspectorate found that about one per cent of the residents were under five.[5] Berridge's smaller study of 'ordinary' children's homes undertaken in 1981–2 noted a higher proportion—eight per cent;[6] but, as already indicated, the majority of pre-school children who are in residential homes are in such establishments. They are substantially under-represented in all other kinds of homes. This is hardly surprising as many of these are specifically for older children. Looked at differently, however, there were 329 children under five and in care in all kinds of residential homes in England at the end of March, 1984:[7] that was four per cent of all those of this age in care.

This downward trend is one of the most significant changes in residential care for children and is only marginally the result of the reduction in the number of under-fives in care. Since much of the early and influential research which charted the ill-effects of residential living was based upon the experiences of this younger age group its direct relevance for residential child care today becomes less significant.

ii 'Ordinary' Children's Homes
The national statistics divide homes into those accommodating twelve or fewer children and those which accommodate more. The smaller 'family group homes' were popular until the mid-70s. Indeed, over the preceding twenty years the number of children so accommodated in the local authority sector grew from about 3,500 to over 10,000 or, as a

proportion of all those in care and in residential homes from nine per
cent to 24 per cent. Despite the reduction in the number of 'in care'
children in residential establishments by 1984, about a quarter of them
remain in these smaller homes.[8]

Slightly fewer children than this were in the larger local authority
homes in 1984, but the history of these establishments has been
different. In the mid-50s some 14,000 children (or 34 per cent of all those
in residential care) lived in such homes; the number fell steadily to 7,250
(or 19 per cent) by 1970, then surged to over 10,000 in 1976 (24 per cent)
but has since fallen back to a little over 5,000, although that remains the
same proportion of all those residentially accommodated. Table 2 sets
out these data for 'ordinary' children's homes, both small and large, for
selected dates.

Table 2   Children in the Care of Local Authorities in England and Wales Accommodated
in Small and Large 'Ordinary' Children's Homes at Selected Dates: Percentages are of
All Children in Care in Residential Establishments[9]

	Children in Small Family Group Homes		Children in Homes for Twelve or More		Total	
	No.	%	No.	%	No.	%
1954	3,645	9	13,874	34	17,519	43
1964	6,355	18	8,357	23	14,712	41
1974	9,775	23	9,020	22	18,795	45
1984	5,417	25	5,118	24	10,535	49

Hence, although the balance between large and small local authority
children's homes has changed over the last thirty years their combined
importance in the array of different residential facilities remains much
the same. Unfortunately, we do not have information about the changing age structure in these homes over the same period. However, the
PSSRU survey of homes in 1983 found that in the local authority sector
11 per cent of the children were under 10; 17 per cent were aged from
10 to 12; 44 per cent from 13 to 15 and 27 per cent were 16 and over.[10]

The voluntary societies now provide far fewer residential care places
of all kinds. At the beginning of the 1950s there were probably about
25,000 children in the whole range of voluntary homes (excluding the
voluntary approved schools); in 1984 there were 3,000 (excluding the
voluntary community homes with education (CHEs)).

The voluntary sector homes mainly look after children who are in
local authority care on a fee basis but they include others as well. In 1984
local authorities sponsored 82 per cent of the children in 'ordinary'
voluntary homes; the percentage being higher in the smaller homes. As
can be seen from table 3, the voluntary societies have consistently
provided proportionately more of their places in larger homes than the

local authorities, but more of the children they care for in residential establishments are in 'ordinary' children's homes, although this is less true than it was as they now give greater emphasis to specialist provision. According to the PSSRU survey the voluntary children's homes care for rather younger children than those in the local authority sector.[11]

Table 3 Children in Voluntary 'Ordinary' Homes in England and Wales: Selected Dates[12]

	Children in Small Family Group Homes		Children in Homes for Twelve or More		Total	
	No.	% of all in Vol. Resid. Care	No.	% of all in Vol. Resid. Care	No.	% of all in Vol. Resid. Care
1964	753	5	8,831	65	9,584	70
1974	724	4	5,366	66	6,090	75
1984	656	19	1,500	43	2,156	62

iii Observation and Assessment Centres
It is not easy to trace the trends in the provision of Observation and Assessment centres (O and A) because the descriptions of the various establishments have changed. Today's O and A centres perform tasks which were previously undertaken by reception centres, remand homes and classifying approved schools. It is difficult, therefore, to assemble long-term data. However, the term 'O and A' has been generally applied since 1974. At the end of March that year there were 4,800 children in local authority centres. By 1984 the figure had fallen to 3,250 (no O and A facilities are provided by the voluntary sector). Nonetheless, it is important to note that this number accounted for 15 per cent of all children in care and in residential establishments: almost exactly the same proportion as were accommodated in CHEs. O and A provisions are a significant residential facility, although they are the most expensive.[13]

iv Community Homes with Education and the Former Approved Schools
Accepting that CHEs and approved schools may be considered as a similar form of residential care then the reduction in their importance since the 1950s can be seen from table 4. If those in approved schools are treated as if they were in care, then, in 1952, the approved schools accommodated 26 per cent of all children who were in care and living in residential establishments whereas the comparable figure for CHEs in 1984, as we have seen, was 15 per cent.

Table 4   Number of Children in Approved Schools and CHEs, England and Wales, 1952–1984; Selected Years[14]

1952	9,079	
1957	6,953	
1962	8,488	Approved Schools
1967	8,213	
1972	6,727	
1977	6,400	
1982	4,500	CHEs (rounded figures)
1984	3,600	

The voluntary organisations now provide only some 500 CHE places but, as the PSSRU survey indicated, these homes were somewhat smaller than those run by the local authorities (a mean size of 40 compared with 49).[15] The survey also showed that two-thirds of the children in all types of CHEs were between 13 and 15 years old. The proportion of older children was about the same as in other community homes.

v Private Children's Homes

Peter Moss did not include private (for profit) children's homes in his 1970 survey. Even now information about the number of children in such homes is sparse and rather unreliable. The DHSS estimated that in 1981 there were 2,500 children who were in local authority care and placed in private homes.[16] In 1984 there were 3,869 children in care returned as living in 'other' accommodation which included private children's homes. On the basis of a postal survey of 71 private homes in 1981 Berridge considered these figures to be too high. He put the overall number at less than 1,000 and also argued that the evidence suggested that the number was declining.[17]

The PSSRU sample survey included 18 private homes, accommodating some 238 children. It also covered 538 local authority and voluntary homes looking after 7,377 children.[18] This was about 50 per cent of the total number of children so accommodated in England and Wales in 1983. If, therefore, the private sector was represented in the same proportion then Berridge's figures would appear to be about right. However, a good deal turns upon definition and classification.

3   Children in Boarding Special Schools and LEA Boarding Homes

Unlike the trends in residential care which have been considered so far the trend in special boarding education was steadily upward until the late 70s. Since then there has been a decline. However, the pattern is different in the different sectors and for children with different kinds of handicap. Thus, the sharpest fall has been in the maintained sector; negligible changes have occurred in the voluntary and private spheres. Furthermore, whereas there has been a noticeable reduction in the number of children with physical and sensory handicaps in boarding special schools, there has been a marked and continuing increase in those classified as maladjusted (redesignated children with emotional and behavioural difficulty as a result of the 1981 Education Act). Their number rose from 4,000 in 1962 to 12,500 in 1983; as a proportion of all children in boarding special schools in England and Wales that is from 16 per cent to 44 per cent. In the private sector the maladjusted constitute about 60 per cent of all pupils in such schools; in maintained schools the figure is 45 per cent and in the voluntary ones 21 per cent. Almost all the 400 or so children in LEA boarding homes are classified as maladjusted.

These trends are seen in table 5, although it must be emphasised that changes in definitions, the transfer of children formerly classed as 'ineducable' from health to education services and the differences between the school returns and the LEA pupil returns make it difficult to ensure comparability. What is important, however, is the new predominance of the maladjusted (now those with emotional and behavioural difficulties) in these schools and the substantial reduction in the number of almost all the other handicapping conditions. The extent of the shift to day special schools appears to vary according to the class of handicap.

Table 5 Pupils Resident in Boarding Special Schools and LEA Boarding Homes, England and Wales or England; Selected Dates[19]

	Maintained Schools		Non-Maintained (Voluntary)		Independent (Essentially Private)		LEA Boarding Homes		Total	
	No.	% Maladj.	No.	% Maladj.	No.	% Maladj.	No.	% Maladj.	No.	% Maladj.
1962	12,881	8	8,299	8	3,016	56	917	77	25,113	16
1965	13,503	9	7,908	10	3,348	57	970	78	25,729	18
1970	14,512	15	7,890	12	4,540	65	867	82	27,809	24
1975	18,216	17	7,671	14	6,589	57	628	80	33,104	26
1979*	18,663	22	6,782	18	7,477	59	492	85	33,414	31
1983*	15,053	45	5,454	21	7,293	60	338	93	28,138	44

*England only

There are, of course, also children in 'hospital schools', some of whom would be long-term patients. Definitions and overlaps are difficult to deal with in this group but the total was probably about 4,000 in 1983.

4 Children and Young People in Penal Establishments

There are two ways of obtaining a picture of the number and distribution of children and young people in penal establishments. First, by
reference to the sentences passed and, secondly, by consulting the average daily prison population figures. Table 6 sets out the number of
young people under 17 sentenced to youth custody (formerly Borstal)
and to detention centres over the last ten years. Until recently, numbers
have risen steadily in both. The increase in youth custody appears to be
levelling out whereas sentences to detention centres are declining.
Overall, however, the proportion of all those sentenced for indictable
offences who go to these forms of custody has remained unchanged at
11 per cent.

Table 6   Young People under 17 Sentenced to Periods in Youth Custody (Borstal) and
Detention Centres, 1975–85; England and Wales[20]

	Borstal/Youth Custody 000s	Detention Centres 000s	Total 000s	% of All Sentences
1975	1.7	4.3	6.0	9
1977	1.8	5.2	7.0	10
1979	1.7	5.3	7.0	11
1981	1.8	6.0	7.8	11
1983	1.9	4.8	6.7	11
1985	2.0	4.0	6.0	11

What is important to note in all these figures is the use of custodial
sentences as a proportion of all sentences within the relevant age
groups. Amongst 14–17 year-old males found guilty of indictable
offences the proportion sentenced to youth custody (Borstal) has risen
from about three per cent throughout the 70s to four per cent in 1985.
After an increase in the earlier 80s the proportion receiving detention
centre orders has settled at about eight per cent, similar to the rate in
the mid-70s.

What is of interest is to see the steady reduction in the proportion
of juvenile offenders who are dealt with by the imposition of care
orders. This has fallen from 6 per cent for all sentenced boys of 14–17
in 1975 to 2 per cent in 1985 and for girls the drop has been more
marked; from 10 per cent to 3 per cent. The same has held true for those
of 10–14 years of age. Of all those of this age group who were sentenced
in 1975, 12 per cent were committed to local authority care on a care
order; by 1985 the proportion had fallen to 4 per cent.

Although the percentages are small in all these changes it must be
borne in mind that because such large numbers are sentenced a shift of
one or two per cent in the pattern of disposal has considerable
repercussions.

The Prison Department statistics provide figures for the average daily prison population by age group at the end of June each year; these also give some indication of trends. Unfortunately, the seventeen-year-olds cannot be separately identified so, in order to gain a fuller picture, the data in table 7 cover the age band 14–20.

Table 7 Average Daily Populations, 14–20 Year-Olds, in all Prison Department Establishments, 1973–83: England and Wales[21]

	Borstal/Youth Custody Centres	Detention Centres	Remand Centres	Prisons	Total
1973	5,307	1,527	1,537	1,141	8,371
1975	6,006	1,850	1,892	1,565	11,313
1977	5,798	1,786	1,830	1,453	10,867
1979	5,464	1,903	1,855	2,040	11,262
1981	5,674	2,167	2,104	1,792	11,737
1983	5,848	1,767	1,974	2,901	12,490
1985	7,029	1,426	2,527	1,811	12,793

5 Summary

Thus, excluding those children in state and private ordinary boarding schools and in non-psychiatric hospitals, there were probably some 65,000 living in residential care in England and Wales at any one time in 1985. That is a rate of about 5.4 per 1,000 of the population under 18. In 1970 Peter Moss's figures suggested a rate of about 6.0 per 1,000. A good deal of the reduction in the number of children in residential care has been achieved, of course, as a result of the reduction in the overall child population. The peak in the population under 18 was reached in 1972 when it stood at some 14¼ million. In 1985 it was about 12 million. Nonetheless, as the rates indicate, there have been real reductions in the use of residential care, although the pattern is divergent. The biggest falls have occurred in local authority and voluntary child care services (encouraged by the greater use of foster care and returning committed children 'home on trial') and in services for the mentally handicapped. The changes in boarding special education have been less pronounced and different for those with emotional and behavioural difficulties (formerly the maladjusted) as compared with all other categories of handicap. The use of penal placements for those under 17 remains steady. It is probably rising for 17-year-olds.

If we are concerned with *all* residential care for those under 18 then the interconnections between these trends and organisations must be borne in mind.

Part 2   The Functions of Residential Care for Children

Various commentators have classified residential care according to the purposes it serves.[22] However, few have distinguished between the functions that it fulfils for the wider welfare system and those for individual children.[23] Yet the distinction is vitally important in considering the future of residential care.

1 The Wider Welfare System

Residential facilities serve many purposes beyond their primary aims. Some of these purposes are recognised and some are not. Each establishment, and each class of establishment, will fulfil several of these wider functions. Some of them will be compatible and some will not. Some will contribute to the well-being of individual children and some will detract from it. Four examples will illustrate the complexity.

i Maintenance Functions—Residential Care and Foster Care

There are three principal ways in which children in the care of local authorities are looked after: by being placed in foster homes, in residential homes or by being allowed to be with their parents or relatives 'home on trial'. The way in which these three sub-systems relate to each other is of the utmost importance in understanding each of them separately and to planning in general: take the way in which residential child care serves the more favoured provision of foster care.

It is clear from a number of studies that when a foster home breaks down another one is not always immediately available. As a result many of the children are admitted (or re-admitted) to residential homes. For example, in Berridge's study of twenty children's homes a third of all the children had experienced a breakdown in a foster placement which had been planned to be long-term.[24] In his more recent study of foster home breakdowns in a London borough and a county authority he found that 70 per cent of all children who had been removed from their short-term foster homes were placed in a residential setting, and that this happened in the cases of 75 per cent of those placements which were intended to have been long-term.[25] Only a fifth to a quarter of both groups was transferred to new foster homes and hardly any returned to their parents or other relatives, clearly indicating that fostering breakdowns do not lead to the reunification of families, even amongst the short-term placements. This is confirmed by the provisional findings of my study of children who have been placed 'home on trial'.[26]

The fact that most children who have to leave their foster homes prematurely are then admitted to residential homes is substantiated by other research. In the Dartington study of a cohort of 450 children who entered care in several authorities it was found that 26 per cent of those who were placed initially in foster homes and who remained in care for at least six months were in residential homes six months later. By contrast only 13 per cent of those who started in residential care were, by six months, living in foster homes. Only a quarter of all the foster placements which broke down in this study were followed by direct transfer to another foster home.[27] Two Scottish studies provide evidence of a similar kind. One was conducted in Strathclyde in 1975 and looked specifically at the number of children who were in community homes (but not list D schools or voluntary establishments) as a result of fostering or adoption disruptions. On one particular day it was found that such children comprised 11 per cent of the total homes' population.[28] The other Scottish study was also completed in 1975 and examined a census of children in residential establishments in south east Scotland. Twenty-one per cent of them had been in foster homes previously (although not necessarily immediately before their admission). The fraction was similar for all age groups.[29]

Of course, the proportion of children in different kinds of residential establishments who enter from a previous placement in an adoptive or foster home may vary considerably. For example, a study of an observation and assessment centre in Hampshire in 1976 found that only six per cent of the admissions came from such placements.[30] In the same year a larger study of such centres in the south west planning region looked at the experiences of some 800 children who were assessed and discharged from nine different establishments. Seven per cent of them had been in local authority foster homes within the previous year; a further two per cent had been in private foster homes.[31]

In the light of the available evidence, therefore, it appears that ordinary children's homes are the main destinations for children who have been removed from foster homes. If the availability of places in such homes is reduced, and if the need for foster home placement continues at its existing level, then several things are likely to follow.

One is that authorities will have to create and maintain a larger pool of foster parents who are ready and willing to deal with such cases. Given the upset and trauma associated with a child having to move, more foster parents would be needed who could provide the skilful help required in the post-disruption period. The difficulties are exacerbated because many removals occur precipitately and without plans having been made to deal with such an eventuality.[32] Alternatively, the accommodation of about the same number of children in children's homes after their removal from foster homes may continue to be achieved, even though there are fewer places, if the number of children who are admitted for other reasons declines. There is another way in which, in general, a smaller number of places in residential homes can accommodate the same number of children (or more): that is by shortening the average length of stay. However, the consequences of a more rapid turnover have attracted little attention.

The precise relationship between residential care and foster care depends heavily upon the rate at which new placements have to be found for children who have to leave foster homes. Early studies produced 'failure' rates of between 40 and 50 per cent amongst long-term placements.[33] In their most recent study, Berridge and Cleaver also found a breakdown rate of 40 per cent amongst the long-term placements in their county authority but only 15 per cent in the London borough.[34] A study undertaken in South Devon in 1980–1 found (depending upon which definition was used) that between 40 and 50 per cent of foster home placements eventually broke down.[35] The recent District Audit report on child care in eight authorities also attempted to establish breakdown rates and concluded that they spread from 28 per cent to 41 per cent.[36] A small study in Stockport in 1981 put the figure at 21 per cent,[37] but an enquiry a year later in Avon emerged with a rate of only five per cent.[38]

There is some evidence that lower levels of breakdown occur amongst placements that are intended to be short-term, and this is certainly borne out in the Berridge and Cleaver study. Looking at placements that were designed to last up to eight weeks he discovered that only ten per cent of them required premature removal; but many continued unexpectedly beyond eight weeks. Of these, 24 per cent ended in some form of crisis that necessitated the child being placed elsewhere. Overall the rate of breakdown was 19 per cent.[39]

The differences in reported 'failure' rates obviously owe something to differences in definition. As much might depend upon other factors such as the characteristics of the children involved (we know, for example, that older children are less likely to be successfully placed), the overall level of fostering, or the way in which departments organise their fostering and adoption work. Few studies unravel these issues, although Berridge and Cleaver found that the different degrees of specialisation did not help to explain the wide variation in the results in their two study authorities.[40]

Whatever the local differences and whatever the complexities of definition it is plain that in most authorities there is a fairly high rate of foster home breakdown. It would be reasonable, on the basis of the evidence available, to put this at 20 per cent a year for all kinds of foster placements. If that is so and if, as Berridge's study and the Dartington cohort study suggest, 75 per cent of these children are then accommodated in children's homes, it is possible to devise an equation which gives some indication of the number of residential care places that are required to support present policies for the promotion of foster care. For instance, with some 38,000 of the children in care in England and Wales in 1984 in foster homes 7,600 might be expected to break down in a year and some 5,700 of them would need to be found residential accommodation. If, say, they stayed in that accommodation on average for six months then each place could be used twice in a year. This gives 2,850 children's homes' places a year which would be needed to facilitate that level of fostering. Given that there were 20,000 residential places in use in England and Wales by local authorities in 1984 (excluding special education) then it could be concluded that about 14 per cent of them were occupied by children from foster care that had ended prematurely.

Whether or not the figures and assumptions in this illustrative example are exactly right they serve to draw attention to the relationship between foster care and residential care in a way that is relevant to planning. If, for instance, the number of children in foster homes in England were to be increased to 40,000 and the failure rate were to rise to 25 per cent a year as a result, then 3,750 back-up places in children's homes would be required if all the other assumptions remained the same—or about 900 more places. This demonstrates the significance for residential care of quite small changes in the breakdown rate, or in the total number of children in foster homes, or both.

Warwickshire, with 89 per cent of its children in care recorded as boarded-out in 1983 (having closed most of its homes), is often held to show that foster care can be expanded dramatically without the fall-back provision of residential care.[41] It needs to be noted, however, that the actual figure was 84 per cent if an unadjusted total in care is used and that this had dropped to 75 per cent by 1984. Although the total number in care in Warwickshire had fallen by three per cent during these two years (to 566) there were fifteen more children in residential care and an additional 37 in 'other' accommodation—mostly 'home on trial'. These figures raise two possible questions. Firstly, how long can a high level of foster care be maintained without residential backing? Secondly, how far can, or should, 'home on trial' be used as a substitute for residential care? Much may depend upon the child's age and upon the reasons for their admission to care. For instance, such a policy may be feasible for offenders or those who are committed to care for not attending school, but not for children who were the victims of neglect or abuse. The study of the Sandwell decision in 1980 to withdraw all its children from CHEs provides some interesting evidence. Most of the children who were removed were boys and offenders. When they were withdrawn about three-quarters went back to their families. None was placed in a foster home.[42]

For purposes of residential care planning it is crucial to be able to monitor:

(1) trends in the breakdown rates in foster homes;

(2) the proportion of the children involved who can be (or who, it is thought, should be) re-placed in other foster homes;

(3) whether, as rates of fostering rise they are accompanied by an increasing risk of disruption (it should be noted that the Audit Commission found no significant correlation between the two in its study[43]);

(4) how long children who are placed in residential care after a foster home breakdown stay there before moving on to a new non-residential placement, and

(5) the extent to which placements other than another foster home or residential care (such as 'home on trial') are being used when children have to be moved from a foster home.

So far, the relationship between residential care and foster care has been examined in terms of the admission to homes of children who have to be moved from foster homes. There is, however, the flow in the opposite direction also to be taken into account. In his children's homes study, for example, Berridge found that 35 per cent of the children were being prepared for placement in a foster home.[44] In my study of the success and failure of long-term foster homes, which was conducted some twenty-five years ago, I discovered that 79 per cent of the foster children had previously lived in a residential home.[45] Furthermore, the success rate for those who had been in residential care for a comparatively short period was almost as high as for those who were placed directly in foster homes, either from their own homes or from other foster homes. This did not hold true for those who had spent more than two years in residential care. However, I suggested that the fact of a child having been in a home prior to a foster home placement could be advantageous in at least two respects. First, that it was likely that more information was available about the child and, secondly, that for some children a period in residential care could provide a valuable breathing space between either their own homes and a foster home or between one foster home and the next. Berridge and Cleaver's recent study of foster care also found that 'an interlude in the more territorially neutral environment of a children's home before living with another family seems beneficial'. Indeed, periods of under one year in a home before placement were significantly more likely to be associated with success than either direct placements or longer periods in residential care.[46]

The role which residential care plays in preparing children for foster homes has become more explicit in recent years. The Social Services

Inspectorate's recent report on community homes identified five pre-fostering units amongst the 149 homes that were visited.[47] However, other community homes performed this role alongside their other work, although it should be noted that comparatively few children leave observation and assessment centres or CHEs for foster homes. For instance, the South West Regional Planning Committee's study of observation and assessment centres in the mid-1970s found that in only 11 per cent of the cases was a foster home recommended and that in only eight per cent was it actually achieved.[48] Moreover, children destined for foster homes were amongst those who had to wait longest in the centres (as were those for whom residential special education was being sought). In the Portsmouth study of an observation and assessment centre only three children out of 60 were recommended for foster care and only one actually left for a foster home.[49] These findings suggest that the main outward flow between residential care and foster care is from 'ordinary' community homes.

Thus, the evidence indicates a close relationship between certain parts of the residential child care system and foster care. It is obviously inappropriate, therefore, to regard them as exclusive options. In general, and as time passes for individual children, there is a good deal of interdependence. Both the Dartington cohort study[50] and the Sheffield study of the experiences of children, parents and social workers[51] found that between 70 and 80 per cent of the children they studied had spent some part of their time in care in residential homes, albeit that many of them experienced other forms of care as well, both before and afterwards. Seen from the child's viewpoint residential care and foster care are often sequential episodes in a string of different placements.

ii Multiple Functions—Observation and Assessment Centres

Observation and assessment (O and A) centres for children in care perform various functions for the wider child care system which go beyond assessment and allocation.[52] They contain and control the disruptive; they punish the recalcitrant; they provide transitional care between placements; they supply shelter in emergencies (such as after place of safety orders have been made); they receive children into care; they offer a decision-making forum for professionals; they act as gatekeepers to certain specialist services and provide somewhere for children to wait until an appropriate placement is available.

The two main studies of O and A centres have already been mentioned. Both were conducted in 1976: one in the south west regional planning area included twelve establishments and the other, in Portsmouth, dealt with a single centre. The larger study established that only 54 per cent of the 1,484 children who had been discharged in the year 1975–6 had been subject to an assessment.[53] Unfortunately, there was little information about the differences between the assessed and the unassessed group. However, it was clear that boys were significantly more likely to be assessed than girls, presumably because more of them were offenders for whom court reports were required. Certainly, nearly a quarter of all admissions were on remand or subject to interim care orders (86 per cent of them boys) and court reports would have been required in most of these cases. Another five per cent were subject to place of safety orders (two-thirds of them girls) and reports for the court would be needed for them as well. Thus, at least 30 per cent of the admissions were serving purposes connected with court procedures. This largely accounts for the fact that two-thirds of all the children admitted were in the 12–15 age band. Children being assessed spent an average of 15 weeks in the o and a centres whereas for those who were not assessed this fell to just over four weeks, emphasising the temporary and emergency functions which the centres fulfil. The predominance of the young adolescent boy population in these establishments may also help to explain why, of the assessed children (there was no information on the others) a third were placed in CHEs although only four per cent were recommended for secure provision. Overall, two-thirds of the assessed children were discharged to residential establishments, about a fifth went home and only a few were placed in foster homes.

The Portsmouth study was more detailed but included fewer children.[54] It covered the year 1973–4 (with some additional information for 1975). Fifty-four per cent of the children admitted were referred by the social services department. Another quarter were classed as emergencies of one kind or another (the majority being absconders from elsewhere) and 12 per cent were on remand or subject to an interim care order. One in ten, it should be noted, were admitted principally because they were excluded from school and if one adds to them the cases where truanting was given as the main social reason (rather than the legal reason) for admission then the proportion of 'education' problems amounted to a third. Thus, as well as the courts the schools were also responsible for channelling children into the o and a centres, either directly or indirectly.

A third and similar study of o and a centres was conducted by the Wessex Regional Children's Planning Committee at about the same time.[55] In almost all respects it reflected the main findings of the other two studies, particularly the close relationship of these units to the juvenile court system, a relationship which was similar to that of remand homes and classifying approved schools before the changes introduced by the 1969 Children and Young Persons Act.

Unfortunately, there is rather sparse information about today's o and a centres. As we have seen, the number of children in care in England and Wales who are accommodated in these facilities at the end of March each year has fallen from 5,000 (five per cent) in 1976 to 3,250 (four per cent) in 1984;[56] but these figures should be treated with some caution since a proportion of the children placed in O and A centres are not in care—for instance, those subject to place of safety orders. However, we do know something about the legal status of the 3,000 children in O and A centres, and in care, in England in 1984 (table 8).

Table 8 The Legal Status of Children in Care in England who Were Accommodated in O and A Centres, as at 31.3.84

	No.	%
Remanded (or detained)	320	10
Subject to an Interim Care Order	144	5
Committed to Care on a full Care Order on the grounds of:		
Neglect or abuse	230	8
Beyond control	37	1
In moral danger	211	7
Non-attendance at school	186	6
Offending	651	22
Matrimonial proceedings	98	3
Other	74	3
Not subject to a Care Order, admitted under sect. 2, 1980 Child Care Act	1,029	35
	2,980	100

The study of the child care provisions in eight social services departments in England and Wales which was undertaken in 1980 by the management consultants Arthur Andersen for the Audit Commission provided some additional information. In particular they reported that external factors played an important part in determining the use of the centres. Two influences especially were noted. They found that 'in most of the regions...the authorities are constrained to provide a formal residential assessment on each child considered...to require placement in a Community Home with Education. In most cases this is a formal Children's Regional Planning Committee policy whilst in others it is the result of individual CHEs' unwillingness to provide places for children without formal residential assessment'. This betrays marked similarities to the way in which the former approved school system worked. The second important external influence was exercised by the courts which 'expected that some children remanded to care for reports should be subject to a period of containment'.[57] Where, as in one authority, three-quarters of the children placed in O and A centres fell into this category a substantial majority of them were discharged home and only one in eight went on to a CHE. Furthermore, the fact that in one of the eight authorities no children were accommodated in O and A centres raised doubts about the real strength or unavoidability of these external pressures. Since then, of course, the CHE system has contracted and most children's regional planning committees have been disbanded. These changes may have served to erode the legacy of the old classifying schools in favour of some of the other functions that have been noted. Indeed, a recognition of the diverse and changing functions fulfilled by o and a centres is reflected in the variety of names now given to them.

We know how children committed to care on remand in England at the end of March, 1984 were accommodated: 48 per cent were in o and a centres; 12 per cent were in youth custody or prison establishments; 10 per cent in CHEs; another 10 per cent at home 'in charge of parents or relatives'; eight per cent were placed in children's homes and four per cent in foster homes. The remainder were scattered amongst a wide variety of other settings.[58] Hence, o and a centres played an important part in dealing with children who were remanded to care by the courts; but, as we shall see, others were not remanded to care and found themselves in remand centres or prisons pending a court's final decision. The level of o and a provision, therefore, may have a significant part to play in protecting young people from remand in prison department establishments.

Thus, the evidence that is available about the activities of o and a centres confirms the variety of functions which they fulfil, many of which, directly or indirectly, resolve (at least for the time being) problems that arise elsewhere in the child care system and, further afield, in the courts and in the schools. Furthermore, the image of o and a centres may contribute to the redefinition of problems in ways which appear to make them more amenable to solution; suggesting that because children need to be observed, tested and assessed the problem lies mainly with them.

iii Extended Functions—Residential Care and Non-Residential Services

Children's homes have changed and continue to change, not least because of developments in day care services. Some of these are now provided on or from the premises. The PSSRU survey offers the most up-to-date information about the scale of these activities. Overall, in the public, voluntary and private sectors, about one in four homes in 1983 claimed to be supplying some form of day care. Amongst local authority homes the proportion varied from around a half in CHEs, observation and assessment centres and homes for the mentally and physically handicapped to 17 per cent in community homes and to less than five per cent in hostels. The voluntary sector was broadly similar but the private homes generally provided less day care.[59]

The survey found that the variety of day care services offered in conjunction with residential care was considerable. It included after-school and holiday provision for younger school children; non-residential assessment; the education of those who were excluded from school; after-care support for former residents; behaviour programmes for the mentally handicapped and the preparation of food for the meals-on-wheels service. Not all the services were for children.

The expanded role of residential establishments is not restricted to the provision of traditional day care services. In some areas the opportunity created by the 1969 Children and Young Persons Act for local authorities to provide residential accommodation for children who are not in care has been used to incorporate a residential component in some intermediate treatment schemes.[60]

The integration of residential services and non-residential programmes in these ways make the future of residential care more difficult to determine. For instance, with half the CHEs in the PSSRU survey now offering some form of day care it may become more difficult to close them. Indeed, the development of day care could be regarded as something of an insurance policy for residential care, and one which is by no means restricted to the public sector.

There is another way in which homes appear to be diversifying their activities. Staff in half the homes included in the PSSRU survey were reported by the heads to be undertaking 'social work or related tasks with clients outside the home'.[61] Two tasks in particular were mentioned. Twenty-eight per cent of the homes had some staff working with the children's families and in 20 per cent of them staff were used to support or supervise current foster home placements or to visit and train prospective foster parents.

Of course, in some homes only one member of staff may be engaged in these extra-mural duties so that the scale of the activities should not be exaggerated. Nevertheless, if the accounts of heads of homes are accurate the contribution of children's homes to the range of local day care and field services has grown and may well continue to do so. Even if some of the reports from heads of homes reflect aspirations rather than achievements it still suggests that these are the directions in which homes are likely to travel. However, it may not be an entirely trouble-free journey.

The report of the DHSS inspectorate found that where residential care staff undertook extra-mural work it was often accompanied by a degree of confusion about the roles they should play. It was not always clear how what they did was to be integrated with (or distinguished from) what was done by field social workers; for example, in respect of pre-fostering work.[62] An earlier DHSS Social Work Service report on residential homes in London also sounded a cautionary note, for although 'in most homes the staff maintained contact with the children's schools and teachers and...attended parents' meetings... most homes appeared to have little involvement in the local community'. It was also noted that 'a number of authorities have not yet accepted that when a child is in residential care it can be more convenient and effective for the residential social worker to adopt a more widely co-ordinating role'. Furthermore, in discussing the fairly common use of 'key workers' the London report pointed out that 'in a number of cases the role...was confined to the residential establishment, work with the family and community agencies being seen as the field social workers' domain alone'.[63]

The difference between residential care staff being involved in 'day care' or in extra-mural social work on behalf of children who are resident is not always clear. Despite that, both kinds of developments suggest that homes will be less narrowly concerned with residential care in the future and, to that extent, they will serve a wider range of purposes within and beyond the child care system. The notion of residential facilities as 'resource centres' is already part of the conventional wisdom. Furthermore, some centres which previously only offered day care now include a number of temporary residential places—for respite or for emergencies.

iv Control Functions—Residential Provision for Young People in Penal Establishments

So far the examples of the functions that residential provision fulfils for other systems have been drawn from the work of social services departments. If, instead, we look at young people in penal establishments it is possible to consider these connections from a different perspective.

The prison service provides a large sector of residential provision for adolescents and offers the majority of secure places for young people under the age of 17. Boys over the age of 14 can be sentenced to periods in detention centres and boys and girls over the age of 15 can go to youth custody establishments, formerly called Borstals. It is also possible for young people over the age of 15 to be remanded in custody, either in remand centres or in adult prisons. The vast majority in all categories are boys.

The number of young people experiencing such interventions is considerable. However, it must be emphasised that attention has to be paid to the precise age categories employed. Figures for young people under the age of seventeen are noticeably different from those for the under-eighteens. In addition, most statistics refer to the offender's age on sentence which means that, especially in the case of youth custody, the average age of residents will be higher. Furthermore, it should be noted that 'young prisoners' are defined as those under 21.

As we saw in Part 1, in the year ending June 30th 1985, 2,000 young people under the age of seventeen were sentenced to a period in youth custody and 4,000 to a period in a detention centre. This is, of course, only a small proportion of all sentenced juvenile offenders. In that year about four per cent of those who were convicted went to youth custody and about eight per cent to detention centres. In addition, in 1985 some

1,500 juveniles were remanded to remand centres or to prison, although only half of those found guilty subsequently receive a custodial sentence.

The figures in Part 1 also indicated that the number of young people committed to youth custody (Borstals) and to detention centres has risen steadily since 1970. More recently the number sent to youth custody centres has stabilised whereas the number sentenced to detention centres is beginning to fall. When the seventeen-year-olds are included in the figures for youth custody a much more pronounced increase in this disposal is revealed. The effect of the new requirements introduced in the Criminal Justice Act, 1982 seems to have been an increase in the use of youth custody rather than a reduction, as had been intended, largely because, by shortening the average duration of custody, more young men are being dealt with in this way. However, as the length of stay, particularly in detention centres, can be short, the number of young people in prison department establishments at any one time is considerably less than the number of annual entrants.

The average daily population in all prison department establishments in the age group 14–20 rose from some 8,000 in 1973 to 12,800 in 1985 (England and Wales). Although the distribution between different kinds of establishments has varied, the trend in the total number of young adults in all prison department centres steadily rises. However, additional information about those under 17 at the end of August each year shows a reduction from 336 to 178 between 1981 and 1984 in those held in prisons or remand centres although, of course, because their stay is usually short many more will have experienced these disposals in any one year.[64]

All detention centres are secure but some youth custody centres (about a third, but declining) are open in that they have no perimeter fence and allow unescorted mobility on campus. However, younger juvenile offenders are more likely to be sent to closed youth custody centres because of their offences and previous histories and 70 per cent of those sentenced spend their time in maximum security. Thus, it should be noted that not only does the department provide a substantial amount of residential care for young people aged between 14 and 16 but that much of this is secure. The regimes are explicitly controlling and, in the case of some detention centres, deliberately punitive. Only one detention centre and two youth custody centres are known to offer an overt treatment and therapeutic regime in spite of the generally high levels of psychological disturbance among young offenders. In addition, juveniles on remand may have to live alongside adult criminals.

It is important to stress the deteriorating residential experiences of offenders in their mid- and late-teens. Prior to the implementation of the 1969 Children and Young Persons Act, most of these young people would have been placed in approved schools. The approved school system provided for some 7,000 boys and 1,000 girls at any one time and a third of these young people were over the age of 15 on admission. As the length of stay was relatively long (usually eighteen months for older juveniles), many offenders remained in these establishments until the age of 18, or 19 if the court order was made after their sixteenth birthday. As a result, the approved schools 'contained' a high level of delinquency over these years. Approved schools ceased to exist as such in 1974. Most were redesignated community homes with education. Since then many of them have been closed and most of the provision for senior boys and girls has gone. As a result it has become less common for children over school age to be accommodated in a community home with education on the premises. The PSSRU survey found that only 27 per cent of all the children in CHEs fell into that age band. They were just as numerous in 'ordinary' children's homes.[65]

Nowadays, many of the older juvenile offenders who are deemed to require residential intervention are earlier routed to a detention centre or to youth custody. As we saw in Part 1, whereas the number and proportion of young offenders committed to care on a care order rose steadily for a while after the 1969 legislation they have now fallen significantly.

The only change for the better in all this is that periods in detention centres and many youth custody sentences are shorter than the old approved school training. As most of the young people return home on leaving, the duration of absence from family and community has been reduced.

The intake into youth custody centres warrants careful scrutiny. As the prison department reports indicate, many disoriented and disruptive as well as delinquent young people end up in these establishments.[66] For instance, it might be noted that between the beginning of 1984 and the end of March, 1985 'there were 110 instances of non-fatal self-injury with apparent suicidal intent in youth custody centres.'[67] As these centres are required to admit all who are sent by the courts the proportion of young people passing through the reception centres who display symptoms of serious emotional and behavioural disturbance is high and, even though the Home Office has some special provision, such as in the new Feltham youth custody centre, most experience a traditional youth custody approach. Youth custody centres come to shelter a wide variety of the failures (or rejects) of the welfare system, child care, special schools and mental health. The use of unruliness certificates for children in care who are deemed too disruptive to be remanded to or kept in care is one example. Of the 1,700 certificates issued in 1984 for boys of 15 or 16, 1,500 resulted in their being sent initially to remand centres or prison and most thereafter went on to youth custody if sentenced.[68]

It seems that the increasing number of young people in youth custody and detention centres combined (although it has been noted that the balance between the two disposals has changed) raises considerable problems for understanding residential services for young people. First, many young people may enter the prison system because local authorities and other welfare agencies are reluctant to accept responsibility for older children or have no suitable provision—as the use of unruly certificates (amongst other things) indicates. Disposals to the prison service cost local authorities nothing whereas many specialist treatment establishments and secure child care units are expensive. Yet, despite a few attempts at treatment and therapy, it must be concluded that prison department institutions usually impose a spartan and regimented experience. In style, they have not been designed to meet the needs of emotionally disturbed adolescents, many of whom are physically and mentally immature.

The trade training elements that research suggests are one of the activities most positively regarded by the inmates are in decline.[69] The variation in sentences now possible under the 1982 Criminal Justice Act means that the trade training found in the old Borstal system has virtually collapsed. The Borstal approach relied on a fixed and longer period, but most sentences now are relatively short. This means that the alleged trade training benefits are virtually non-existent; and they have never been a feature of the detention centre system. The rationale for trade training, of course, was partly based upon the expectation that there would be appropriate work for youngsters to do upon discharge. It might be argued, therefore, that these changes in the youth custody system accurately reflect the mass unemployment which adolescents now face.

As the more disturbed and criminal young people will have already been in other types of residential care, most juvenile entrants are allocated to closed institutions. A number of these are located in old prisons, such as Rochester and Portland, and while modifications to the buildings have been made, it does mean that adolescents in their mid-teens spend much of their time in prison surroundings, considerable periods locked-up in cells, and in the case of those on remand they may be in the company of adult criminals. It is also the case that despite the efforts of prison department staff to make the experience beneficial, there is little indication that their efforts achieve a great deal in terms of preventing further offending. The rates for long-term recidivism among this group are high and some 80 per cent are likely to re-offend and some 50 per cent to re-enter custody within two years of release. The younger the offender, the higher is the rate of recidivism.[70]

Offenders in their mid-teens require more consideration than they receive. While the old senior approved schools did not offer difficult young people a great deal, their regimes contained them passably well and at least spared them a premature prison experience. Directing or returning persistent 14 and 15-year-old offenders to the child care system is likely to provide an interlude of protection even though it may only achieve limited results with regard to long-term offending. Yet such deflection towards 'welfare' options also calls for a re-appraisal of the role of residential care for deprived and difficult boys and girls in their mid-teens. A more flexible approach is indicated, possibly imitating the Community Service projects and alternatives to custody that are available in some parts of the country.[71] Unfortunately, there appear to be few positive ideas on what to do with these young people and one has to conclude that their plight has worsened in the last few years. In 1975, in a report on approved schools, Millham and his colleagues wrote of the establishments for senior boys that 'in the senior schools, any observer can see the debris of countless, ineffective institutional placements floating out with a tide of rejected, defeated older boys towards Portland Borstal'. If anything, the tide is running even more swiftly today. With the exception of one or two courageous experiments, there is no evidence that, generally, local authority social services departments are concerning themselves with the deeper issues raised by these older adolescents. It is, in fact, singularly depressing to find how far recent research, such as the recent survey by the Carnegie Working Party, has corroborated the research findings of several years ago.[72]

Disquiet about the strength and direction of this tide is emphasised in Tutt's recent (as yet unpublished) survey of youngsters under 17 in penal establishments in 1984. He points out, for instance, that

> children who were in remand centres or adult prisons, and particularly those who were remanded in custody and not yet convicted or sentenced, were the least likely to receive special consideration because of their age.

More generally, his results drew attention to the irony that

> the current British response to children in prison is not to protect them nor to make their experience of custody less harsh than for adults. Instead, the British policy is to ensure that child prisoners have it even 'tougher' than adults.[73]

The fact that a recent Home Office study found that harsher regimes in detention centres made no difference to rates of reconviction (yet they continue) suggests that these tougher regimes fulfil symbolic rather than substantive purposes.[74]

The relationship between the prison system and child care is, therefore, a matter of considerable concern. Had the spirit and intention of the 1969 Children and Young Persons Act been realised then social services departments would almost certainly be having to accommodate many more delinquent (and often disturbed) young people than at present. At the moment 45 per cent of all the young offenders who have been committed to care on a full care order live in child care residential homes and another eight per cent are in hospitals, youth treatment centres or prison department establishments. Another 35 per cent are allowed to live with their parents or relatives.

Only five per cent are in foster homes. Thus, it is clear that were social services departments to receive into care more adolescents who are at present sent to the penal system many of them (if present patterns are any guide) would have to be placed in residential homes. The increasing use of custodial disposals to the prison system for young offenders is one of the factors, together with the greater use of cautioning and 'community alternatives', that has enabled local authorities to reduce their provision of residential care places.

* * *

Each of these four examples illustrates how residential establishments serve purposes which are functional for other parts of the wider welfare, education and penal systems. However, it is important to stress that such functions should not be used to justify an establishment's existence or to indicate that it is being successful. Many functions can be fulfilled by other means; so some of those outlined for o and a centres could equally well be served by community and fostering alternatives. But, in an imperfect world, residential care often survives by virtue of these important wider functions rather than because of its success in meeting primary goals associated with the needs of individual children. Nonetheless, it should not be concluded that all wider functions are to be deplored, for in some instances these may enable *another* system, or a part of a system, to operate in ways which encourage it to meet *its* primary goals more successfully in the interest of children's well-being.

2 Individual Children

Having examined several examples of the functions of residential care for the wider welfare system we turn to consider some of the purposes it may serve for individual children. These are often referred to as its primary goals. Five such goals furnish useful examples: care; rehabilitation; preservation; education; and the preparation for independence.

i Residential Caring
The term 'residential care' has a wide currency but the goal, albeit temporary or short-term, of providing a child with the experience of

caring people and a caring environment tends to be taken for granted or, indeed, overlooked. If an organisation is acting *in loco parentis* then this is its foremost priority, ideally establishing a firm base from which other goals may be successfully pursued. Yet, in analyses of the goals for residential living, 'caring' fails to figure prominently. One reason is undoubtedly the pervasive assumption that really good care for children is only to be found in family settings; another is the long-standing association between institutions and instrumental goals (reform, industrial training, discipline or education); a third reason might be found in the fact that residential life rarely allows the development of the kind of close, intimate, partisan and reliable relationship between an adult or adults and a child upon which the sense of being cared for and loved depends. There are too many children; too many staff move too frequently and, in any case, the children themselves have competing loyalties. Some of this is true also for some foster homes and for the children's own homes as well; but care in a residential setting has to face problems peculiar to itself. At the same time, as Beedell emphasises, 'the essential character of residential work for children is that it takes over a more or less substantial part of responsibility for "parenting" '.[75]

He goes on to suggest that parenting covers three main functions: holding (care, comfort and control); nurturing (the development of social, physical and intellectual skills), and the encouragement and maintenance of personal integrity (the whole person). Unfortunately, the available research does not lend itself to an exploration of this sensitive framework but, at least, it does suggest that the first requirement of good 'care' is to meet a child's physical needs, with all the emotional connotations that includes. As he says,

> Like good hospitality it does not basically alter one's life situation but it does renew hope. Simple food and drink, warmth, bodily comfort and opportunity for peace are essentials . . . the symbolic scrap of sticking plaster and kiss on a scratch for a small child or hot drink and cossetting for an adolescent are quite as important as aseptic medical care. The roots of our dependence on sound physical care begin at birth and we are never free of them.[76]

How does residential care measure up to these basic ingredients of care? There is a mixture of evidence which can be divided broadly into information about physical standards and emotional warmth.

The provision of high material standards in children's homes will rarely, if ever, compensate for the emotional hurt which many separated children suffer. Some would argue that rather modest standards are desirable in that they resemble more closely the home circumstances from which children come and to which most of them will return. However, neither public, voluntary nor private homes aim to replicate the child's own home and, in some cases, they would be guilty of negligence if they did. A sensible balance has to be struck in which both the opportunities and special circumstances of group living have to be taken into account. What is the present position?

Two inspectorate reports provide some answers. During 1981 and 1982 the London region of the DHSS social work service conducted its sample survey of 83 establishments in Greater London.[77] Just over half the homes had been purpose-built while most of the remainder were large Victorian houses or other kinds of family dwellings. No clear picture of prevailing standards emerged. There was considerable variation in homeliness, comfort, decoration, furnishing, food, cleanliness and the state of repair. Reports recorded conditions which ranged from the outstanding to the bleak and depressing. These differences were reflected in the inspectors' general summary which concluded that:

> Many of the homes were beautifully kept and imaginatively decorated, with both staff and children clearly concerned to maintain good standards and to provide a warm and homely environment. But a worrying number of homes showed signs of serious neglect. . . These conditions occurred most often in homes for adolescents. The standards in some of these homes reflected a lack of good management by staff and an absence of home-making example for the young people living in them.[78]

The national inspection of homes which the DHSS inspectorate undertook in 1985 sounded a rather more critical note.[79] The general level of comfort, they said, 'was disturbingly low'. They commented that homes were often cold (especially the bedrooms) and poorly lit (again especially in the bedrooms). Many children had to share storage space. They reported adversely on the general state of maintenance: 'all too often', they said, 'premises were uncared-for and in urgent need of repair'. There was, however, little evidence of vandalism. There was an absence of colour and although musical instruments and electronic equipment were often provided books were not prominent. Food was generally wholesome and adequate though rather monotonous, partly because of the practices of central supplying and bulk buying.

In his study of 'ordinary' children's homes Berridge adopted a three-fold classification: homes based on the 'family group' approach, hostels, and multi-purpose homes. This trichotomy is useful for many purposes, amongst which is that of showing how material conditions vary between each class of home. The family group homes (looking after from six to ten children) resembled ordinary family houses. 'Furnishings are comfortable, children's bedrooms are individually decorated and there are cats and dogs and other pets'. Nevertheless, 'household defects such as broken windows or faulty locks are sometimes left unrepaired for several months because of bureaucratic delays'. Although the family group home may be homely it 'still retains distinctive features: aluminium teapots, washing-up rotas and stacked chairs'.[80] However, since these homes are also the homes of the heads and their husbands (usually employed elsewhere) they share most of the material conditions, and this tends to ensure that at least an adequate standard is maintained. This was particularly noticeable, Berridge reported, in the private sector, where homes were usually staffed solely by the proprietors with occasional or part-time help. 'By contrast with the local authority homes proprietors are frequently from middle class backgrounds: a pattern often reflected in the physical environment and ethos of the home'.[81]

Berridge found that the quality of the physical environment in 'hostel-style' homes varied considerably.[82] Even so, they were generally better equipped than family group homes and had more facilities for leisure pursuits. Furthermore, they offered more opportunities for privacy: they were less crowded and most of them provided single bedrooms. The larger multi-purpose homes, often accommodating 20 to 25 children, were usually purpose-built and exhibited 'some of the least appealing features of modern architecture'.[83] Berridge characterised their internal decor as 'consisting of bright contrasting colours, modern fittings, identical living areas and plastic crockery' all of which 'can recreate something of the warmth and intimacy of an airport lounge'. Nevertheless, these multi-purpose homes were usually well-equipped, comfortable and spacious. He offered two other interesting observations. First, that because the atmosphere is more impersonal than in other homes they are 'often successful in encouraging local people to use their facilities' (echoes of the community resource centre idea). This, however, was not always welcomed by the residents, however temporary their stay. The second thoughtful observation was that because local authorities were conscious of the possible need to use such buildings for other purposes later on (the infirm elderly or the physically disabled) they had been designed accordingly: light switches, rails and special toilets positioned or installed to cater for the needs of a quite different class of resident.

A good many of these points were also made by Colton in his recent study of the differences in care practice in children's homes and foster homes.[84] He devised a physical environment inventory and, as might be expected, foster homes compared favourably with children's homes. Nonetheless, the smallest home and the largest foster home showed only modest differences. Children's homes tended to score badly on measures of the ratio of facilities to children; facilities such as baths or showers, television sets or radios, occasional tables to sit at or 'dayrooms'. The fact that all but one of the homes in his study were immediately identifiable, even from a distance, contributed to the sense of stigma which the children frequently felt. For instance, two council houses might be obviously converted into one; notices erected which told of a building's purpose, and there were purpose-built homes whose architecture at once betrayed who lived there. Design often resembled school or office development, favouring large windows; and Colton, too, noted the kind of open-plan arrangements which would permit the buildings to be converted easily and cheaply to other uses.

There are few other enquiries which provide detailed information about the material standards that now prevail in residential homes for children, although there is a good deal from the past, especially concerning the old approved schools. However, there are several studies of the daily life in homes which convey an impression of the atmosphere and regime. Juliet Berry's research in 1972–3 was based upon reports compiled by students on placement in 44 different residential settings.[85] Her general thesis was that good quality care is characterised by the purposeful and sensitive use which is made of the inevitable daily activities and interactions between staff and children. The way in which twelve typical daily activities were accomplished served as the basis for dividing the establishments into those which provided 'good enough' care; those where it was 'more positive' and those where it was 'more negative'. Twenty units were assessed as 'good enough'; six as 'more positive' and 17 as 'more negative'. The size of this last group was disturbing since, as Berry points out, 'the quality of care received may be experienced not only as less than life-enhancing but as actively harmful'.[86] She summarises the essence of her findings in this way: 'the central, indisputable fact is that a sizeable proportion of children have a comparatively poor experience of daily care in residential life, and this appears to be linked with their caregivers receiving similarly poor experience of ongoing support'.[87] The provision of that support is, she argues, an imporant means of improving the quality of child care.

The deliberate use of social interactions in residential homes emphasises social contact as a means of enabling children to learn from the way staff behave towards them and others. Even so, a child's development also depends upon the sense of individuality; upon time for quiet reflection; escape from the demands which living with other people impose as well as the enjoyment of intimate relationships. By its very nature, therefore, residential care needs to offer opportunities for privacy, and this must be regarded as an equally important aspect of a caring environment.

Yet privacy is not always readily available in residential homes, even though children in care tell us that they value it highly. With the rising age of children in homes it has probably become more important, although the need for younger children to be able to enjoy privacy should not be underestimated. Although little attention has been paid to privacy as a dimension of care there is some evidence about its availability in children's homes.

The PSSRU survey of residential homes for children recorded the number of places which were available as single rooms—something which was virtually unknown in the 1940s and 50s. In local authority 'ordinary' children's homes the proportion was 21 per cent, but in their hostel accommodation it rose to 61 per cent.[88] Overall, a quarter of all children in local authority residential accommodation were sleeping in single rooms. The proportion was roughly the same in the voluntary and private sector homes. At the other end of the scale almost 14 per cent of all bedrooms contained four or more beds, but that meant that a much greater proportion of children were accommodated in larger dormitories.[89] These were most common (36 per cent) in CHEs.

This theme is echoed in the recent DHSS inspectors' report and in the earlier investigation undertaken by the London region of the Social Work Service. The London study, conducted during 1981 and 1982, reported that 'in a considerable number of homes...there was no privacy' and that children had 'little opportunity to be by themselves or to withdraw from the hurly-burly of everyday life'. Furthermore they found that it was 'rare for the child's need for some privacy to extend to the provision of lockable cupboards or for children to hold the keys to their own bedroom doors'.[90] Staff found it difficult to find a place to talk privately with a child. However, it was pointed out that privacy was not only a matter of adequate space but of the regime as well. For example, it was noted that although one of the London observation and assessment centres contained plenty of space, there was little privacy 'because of the regime and the way in which the children are managed...children are not encouraged or indeed allowed to have private corners'. The fear that privacy might lead to the loss of control seems to be at the root of such restrictions—despite the fact that we know that much misbehaviour is a group phenomenon.

The inspectorate's national study, undertaken three years later in 1985, found much the same. Many young people, they reported, shared chests and wardrobes; bunk beds were used more often than they had expected; and poor heating limited the amount of usable space. Indeed, they commented that many homes 'seemed cramped and too small for the boisterous young people who lived in them'.[91] Despite its dominant influence on the lack of privacy, limited space was not the only issue to be noted. For instance, the inspectors reported that whereas nearly all children had access to a telephone it was rarely possible to use it privately. Similarly, there was unlikely to be much opportunity for parents or others who visited the children to find a private space in which to talk.

In their study of absconding, Clarke and Martin found that one of the variables that was significantly associated with running away was the amount of overcrowding.[92] Even when children go home legitimately, as they do at weekends in large numbers, they may be unable to find much privacy there either. Several studies indicate that children in care come from disproportionately large families as well as from poor housing conditions.[93] If one of the functions of care (and therefore of residential care) is to provide experiences which compensate for the impoverishment of a child's family life, then creating the opportunity for some privacy may be an important objective. Certainly, it appears to affect children's views of the quality of life which they enjoy in residential homes as the *Who Cares?* group of children so cogently made clear.[94]

Similar views were expressed by the children in Dorothy Whitaker's study of their residential experience. The issue of privacy was important for many of them.

> Few liked sharing bedrooms, usually because of the personal habits of one or more of the others in the room. Being allowed access to bedrooms during the day was greatly appreciated and there were complaints about homes where access was restricted. In such homes, children who needed to get away from others for a time resorted to the toilets or a park.

The author adds that 'Homes tended not to have a private area for receiving guests. This was awkward when parents and others visited: other children, for example, made demands on the parents, or confidentiality could not be maintained'.[95] Such problems are not unique to children's homes as Lambert's study of boarding-school life, as portrayed through the writings of the boys and girls, confirms. He concluded that 'many problems spring from continuously having to live a public life, for even in the most generously provisioned school, most teaching, sleeping, eating and leisure are spent in the company of other people'.[96]

It might be thought that the decline in occupancy rates in some homes will ease the problem of too little space for privacy but, as the PSSRU study points out, although these rates in all three sectors presently run at about 75 per cent many of the unfilled places are reserved for those who are temporarily absent. This was most common in local authority homes, where some 10 per cent of places were being kept for such children at the survey date. The major reason was that children were away in boarding or special schools and returned in the holidays (about five per cent of the 'resident' children fell into this category). Other reasons for temporary absence included being tried out 'home on trial'; visiting parents; having absconded; being in custody or being in hospital.[97] The space made available by children being away was, therefore, not entirely free and available for reoccupation. Indeed, the space and possessions of children who are temporarily absent may be better protected than those of the children who are present.

Given the undoubted importance of some privacy for successful group living, it is surprising that relatively little attention has been paid to the matter in children's homes. By comparison it has become a much more lively issue in the field of the elderly who live in homes. Many of the suggestions and proposals being made in that quarter might usefully be transferred to child care. There is, perhaps, the unspoken belief that children are more fitted to group living than their elders and that they have less need for privacy. It seems unlikely that either assumption is correct although it is interesting to consider why and how such beliefs might have arisen. The nature of the school system may well have helped to engender such views.

Privacy is but one of the elements which go to produce a caring environment in residential units. What is important to stress is that in regarding 'care' as a primary goal it may also become the means to other future objectives for the well-being of children.

ii Residential Care and Rehabilitation

One of the main arguments adduced in favour of residential care as a means of achieving the return of children to their own homes is that, unlike foster care, it does not discourage parental contact. This we know from numerous studies is a crucial factor in increasing the likelihood of a child's return.[98] Its importance was captured in the conclusion reached by Millham and his colleagues that:

> even after controlling for other variables, we find that a weakening of parental links is strongly associated with declining chances for a child returning home. Naturally parental links are not a sufficient condition ...[but they are] a necessary condition.[99]

The same study, like others before, also found a relationship between the reduction in parental contact and a child's unsettled behaviour as well as the breakdown of placements. For example, three-fifths of the children whose links with their mothers over two years had declined had experienced a crisis breakdown at some time. However, it should be noted that where there had been little contact throughout these rates were much lower.[100]

There is also considerable evidence from several of the studies included in the recent DHSS review of child care research to show that family links were seldom accorded much consideration by social workers. Circumstantial factors played the most important part in deter-mining whether or not contact was maintained.[101] If a child's place-ment in residential care creates such conditions better than foster care then it may facilitate the achievement of a principal goal of child care; that is, the rehabilitation of child and family. The most compelling evidence for this proposition is provided by Aldgate's 1977 study of 244 Scottish families with children in care.[102] The children had been admitted on a voluntary basis; the study therefore excluded neglect or abuse cases as well as offenders. The results showed that there was significantly greater contact between parents and children in residential care than between parents and children in foster care.

The interviews that Aldgate conducted with the parents suggested very strongly that foster homes presented more difficulties for them than children's homes. This applied to the mothers much more than to the fathers—especially fathers who had been left on their own with children. Unlike mothers they were often pleased to see foster mothers as mother substitutes. This difference was also found by Colton in a more recent study.[103]

When asked about their views the parents in the Aldgate study expressed a marked preference for residential homes rather than foster homes. For instance, only five per cent of those whose children were in homes said that they would have preferred a foster home whereas 48 per cent of those with children in foster homes felt that residential care would have been better. They gave a variety of reasons for preferring residential care, amongst which were: that residential care staff were more likely to encourage and welcome their visits; that homes were more flexible about the times and durations of visits; that they could keep in contact with their children by telephone (only 40 per cent of the foster parents had telephones); that there was more chance to be alone with their children and that, since it was more likely that their children would be kept together in a home than in foster homes, it was easier to arrange the visits (especially for those who had no car). This was not simply a matter of geography for, as Aldgate points out, 'reaching one destination was bad enough but having to brave several different homes, new faces and different expectations was too much for some parents to cope with'. Furthermore, 'seeing children in one place had helped parents accustom themselves more quickly to the strangeness of the new environment and set up meaningful patterns of contact which were within their capabilities'. Given the stressful circumstances faced by parents with a child in care encouragement is important, but whereas 80 per cent of the residential staff who were interviewed believed that parents should be encouraged to visit and maintain contact only half of the foster parents shared that opinion.[104]

Thus, as Aldgate suggests, residential care may help to promote (or sustain) a child's sense of family identity as well as enhancing the competence of parents 'by not placing them in direct competition with another family'.[105]

Similar evidence of parental preference for residential care had been provided earlier in the Rowe and Lambert study *Children Who Wait*.[106] The Sheffield study by Fisher, Marsh and Phillips, however, suggests that these conclusions should be approached with a degree of caution. They found 'that one of the dominant disappointments among many parents was...that residential care *contaminated*' (their emphasis).[107]

The apparent laxity of the regimes, the freedom the child enjoyed to come and go, to stay out or to smoke were all criticised. 'The perception of laxity in exercising control over young people applied to all types of residential care, from remand homes to the smallest family group home.'[108] The solution, however, was often perceived as moving the child to another (more disciplined) residential unit—not to a foster home. It is noteworthy that the children themselves did not generally object to strictness—only when it was seen to be inconsistent or unfair.

Unfortunately, we do not have similar evidence about parental attitudes to the question of control in foster homes. However, we do have some further evidence about the differences in the amount of parental contact with children in homes and foster homes. Berridge and Cleaver's study of foster homes divided them into long-stay, inter-mediate and short-stay. The rate of 'no parental contact at all' was about 40 per cent in each category; but there was more frequent contact amongst the shorter placements. Whilst 38 per cent of the children in short-stay placements had at least monthly contact, this fell to 18 per cent for the intermediate group and to 7 per cent for the long-stay foster homes.[109] Relating the levels of contact to the outcomes of the place-ments they found the most significant relationship in the intermediate group—less contact being associated with more breakdowns and more contact with more success.[110] For the other two categories the relationship was by no means so clear.

These results bear some similarity to the Dartington study of children's links with their parents. However, in that, no marked differ-ence existed between the amount of parental contact as between children in residential care and those in foster care; but there were other differences. Children in residential placements who had little contact with parents were 'the most ill-at-ease' confirming, as the authors remind us, Lasson's findings on children in long-stay homes[111] as well as those of Hall and Stacey and Oswin on children in hospitals.[112] In these situations increased contact with home reduced the amount of stress for children and problem behaviour.

The picture of foster homes derived from the Dartington work was more complicated. After six months in care, for example, children with-out contact with their mothers tended either to be well settled or to show various signs of strain and distress. The researchers suggest that 'children in foster homes are more upset by changes in existing arrange-ments, either when long-absent family figures reappear or, more often, when there is a reduction in contact with home. Relations between the child's foster family and the natural parents are also likely to deteriorate'.[113]

Obviously, it is necessary to distinguish between different circum-stances and different children in drawing comparisons between residential care and foster care in terms of their contribution to the maintenance of family links. For instance, it may be that it is those children for whom parental contact is expected to be weak who are placed in foster homes. Likewise, as the Dartington research indicates, there are many ways in which contact can be interpreted: it is not only a matter of parental visiting. There is much home visiting by children. Amongst those who had continued to have contact with parents after two years in care, most contact (70 per cent) took the form of home visits or weekend 'leave', irrespective of whether the children were in residential homes or foster care.[114] This reflects the finding in Juliet Berry's study of the daily experience of residential life. She showed that the pattern of parental visiting (in 1972–3 in 44 residential settings) was fairly infrequent; but, she argued, one reason for this was that many of the children were going home regularly for weekends 'sometimes every week, sometimes monthly or perhaps three week-ends a term', not to mention the longer holidays.[115] This was not just the case in the boarding special schools but in community homes too—especially for the adolescents.

We know that although parents are rarely legally debarred from access to their children in care various restrictions are consciously imposed by local authorities whilst others are allowed to develop. Jean Packman found that restrictions were imposed in the case of seven per cent of the cases in her sample where the child had been admitted to care on a voluntary basis and that this applied to 21 per cent of those who were committed to care;[116] but, as she points out, the inadvertent barriers were no less powerful. This reflected the results in the Dartington study.[117]

It is not clear, however, how far the existence of explicit restrictions upon parental contact are made necessary by the need to sustain a foster home which may otherwise collapse under the pressure of erratic, abusive or frequent parental visiting. Recent work by Colton suggests that this might be so.[118] If that is the case it would seem likely that difficult or demanding parents could be better dealt with by residential care staff without resort to the limitation of contact and all that that entails. Where there is a need for a clear and deliberate curtailment of parental access this may also be more easily achieved in the setting of a residential home.

The weight of the available evidence therefore suggests four main features of residential care and rehabilitation:

(1) The maintenance of parental contact is shown to be a major factor in all routes to restoration;

(2) There is some (but mixed) evidence to show that residential care encourages this vital continuity of contact, although short-term foster care may do as well;

(3) Children certainly appear to return home more often (either

unconditionally or 'home on trial') from residential homes than they do from foster homes, and

(4) Whether or not the child returns home parental contact seems to ease the turmoil of separation for the child and to reduce the likelihood of troubled behaviour. This is particularly so in residential care. In foster care what appears to be more disturbing for the child is a change in the pattern of contact.

On the face of it it seems that residential care could play a special part in the rehabilitation of children, especially for those who, *faute de mieux* have to be in care for moderately long periods. If that is to happen, however, two things need to be done. First, it should be established for which groups of children it can do this better than foster care and, secondly, it has to be conceived as an explicit function and not as a coincidental result of the circumstances. Some simple but deliberate decisions, such as keeping children close to their home areas, may produce good results.

iii Residential Care and Preservation

We have already embarked upon the exploration of this theme in connection with the maintenance of parental contacts; but there are other dimensions as well. One of the central dilemmas that is faced in planning for children who are separated from their parents is how best to balance the claims of the past, the present and the future. Permanency planning looks firmly towards settling and stabilising the future. Yet for many children in care, in boarding special schools or in penal establishments the future is, to a significant extent, a reintegration in, or with, the past. The futures of children in care are 'in trust' as the Jasmine Beckford inquiry argued but, in a complicated fashion, so too are their pasts.[119] For the professionals and even for foster parents acquaintance with a child is an episode (note the use of the term 'care episodes' in the statistics); but for the child it is a continuation of a career, however disrupted and chequered that might be.

One of the functions which residential care may fulfil better than foster care for some children is the preservation of important parts of their personal histories. Parents are crucial elements of those histories even though, in practical terms, they may be unable or unfit to assume the responsibility for their child's care and upbringing. The other significant people in the personal histories of separated children are their brothers and sisters and for some they will be their present and immediate future family to all intents and purposes.

One of the strengths of residential care has been held to be its ability to keep brothers and sisters together. There is also a widespread conviction that it is important for children who are separated from their parents to retain contact with their siblings, especially when they are also in care. Those who lose contact often try very hard to regain it. If, therefore, despite any other shortcomings, residential care is able to secure this where other forms of care fail, then it may be an achievement upon which to build.

In Berridge's study 92 of the 234 children in the homes lived there with brothers and sisters. However, many others had siblings in homes elsewhere.[120] The crucial question, then, is whether this number can be regarded as a 'good' achievement in light of the total number of brothers and sisters who are in care together. We also need to know how it compares with other kinds of care—in particular the principal alternative, foster care.

The Dartington 'links' study found that after two years in care 51 per cent of those children who had brothers and sisters also in care were in placements together with some of them. At the six months stage this had only been 42 per cent. They suggest, therefore, that it may be that the longer children are in care the more likely they are to be reunited with their siblings. It was also found that the larger sibling groups were more likely to be placed in residential care than the smaller ones.[121]

The DHSS inspectorates' report on residential homes discovered that of the 1459 children in the homes that they visited two-thirds had no other siblings in care. Of the remainder who did 37 per cent were with them in the same home and 63 per cent were separated.[122] The regional variation ranged from 63 per cent being together with some brothers or sisters in the Northern region (the region with the highest proportion of groups of siblings in care) to 12 per cent in neighbouring Yorkshire and Humberside. Most of the other regions, however, clustered around the national average (it should be borne in mind that CHEs, O and A centres and secure accommodation were not included in this exercise: it is hardly likely that they would have demonstrated a higher rate of siblings being kept together). So, along with Berridge's evidence, this enquiry suggests that in most areas between 30 and 40 per cent of children living in homes, and who also have siblings in care, are placed together with at least some of them.

Foster care studies have also provided information of a partially comparable kind. In my study the following pattern at placement emerged: of the children in the sample 69 per cent had brothers and sisters in care; of these children 43 per cent remained separated at the foster placement in question; 17 per cent were separated in the process; 34 per cent were kept together with all or some siblings and six per cent were reunited with all or some of their brothers and sisters.[123] However, the success of the placement seemed unaffected by whether or not siblings were together. In Trasler's study 27 per cent of the children in foster homes were placed there with some brothers or sisters and he did find that these were more likely to succeed than those where they were not.[124] It should be noted that his proportion was based upon all child-ren placed, whether or not they had siblings; had the calculation been made for only those children with brothers and sisters in care then it would certainly have been higher. In George's study 42 per cent of the children were in the same foster home as all or some of their siblings.[125] Jane Rowe's more recent research on long-term foster care found that 57 per cent of the children had at least one brother or sister also in care and that of these 51 per cent were together with at least one of them in the same foster home.[126] In Triseliotis' small-scale study of children who had grown up in foster care 48 per cent had lived together with all or some of their siblings and almost all these children fell into his 'mutually satisfying relationships' designation; that is, into that group of placements considered to be the most satisfactory by both the children and their foster parents.[127] The Berridge and Cleaver study of foster care discovered that 58 per cent of the children had siblings who were also in care and that of these, 53 per cent lived in the same foster home as some or all of their brothers and sisters.[128]

Thus, from the admittedly patchy information which has become available over the years the rate of fostering with some siblings amongst those who have them in care as well seems to fall somewhere between 35 per cent and 50 per cent. There is, therefore, no conclusive evidence that residential care (even excluding CHEs and O and A centres) shelters any greater proportion of groups of brothers and sisters than foster care. However, the ages and the sizes of the respective groups may well be different and the whole analysis is certainly complicated by the existence of step and half sibling relationships which have never been untangled in the analyses. Many of the studies amalgamated the children who were together with all their siblings with those who were with some of them. The Berridge and Cleaver study, however, has differentiated between the two categories. Thirty per cent of those who had siblings in care as well were with only some of them whilst 23 per cent were with all of such brothers and sisters.[129] But we still do not know the size of these sibling groups, although it is likely, as the Dartington study suggests, that children's homes shelter the larger groups of siblings and foster homes the smaller.

What is particularly noteworthy, however, is the fact that about half of all those children in care who have brothers and sisters in care too, appear to be separated from them at any one time. When one bears in mind that about 17 per cent of all children in care are 'home on trial', and that this usually means reunification with siblings (who are likely to be in care and 'home on trial' at the same time), then the proportion of separations amongst those *living away from home* and in care will certainly rise beyond the 50 per cent level. If, in addition those children who are separated from *some* siblings are taken into account, the overall separation figure could well be nearer 75 per cent than 50 per cent.

Earlier child care practices have been severely criticised for the way in which they placed brothers and sisters apart and a few of those involved have recorded the pain and anguish of these separations in their auto-biographies.[130] It is therefore disturbing to find that siblings in care are still very likely to be parted.

The practical problems of keeping brothers and sisters together in care are, of course, considerable. There is, for example, the need to have a sufficient number of vacancies available in any one form of care to accommodate them all. Where high occupancy rates prevail this has always been difficult. Berridge makes the valuable point that the function of children's homes in caring for groups of siblings entering care is quite different from that of bringing together brothers and sisters who have been in care for some time.[131] In light of the evidence from the Dartington study it may be that the latter role is better performed than the former by residential care. Either way, if more sibling groups are to be kept together then residential care may have to play a much more deliberate part than it does at present. In their hey-day family group homes were often portrayed as serving just such a purpose, though how far they ever did so remains unclear. Likewise, the cottage system of an earlier era had similar claims made on its behalf.

Apart from the practical difficulties other factors in the history of residential care and in the history of child development theory may have militated against a strong tradition of keeping siblings together in residential care. For instance, there has been a long-standing practice, only recently reversed, of separating children into groups by reference to their age and gender; and such classification inevitably led to the fragmentation of family groups—even, in the past, within the same large home. On a quite different front psycho-analytic theory influenced the emerging ideas about child development; but, amongst other things, it emphasised the importance and intensity of sibling rivalry for parental affection, a rivalry which was generally regarded as antagonistic and negative. The positive strength of sibling relationships, especially in the absence of parents, was rarely if ever noted.

The whole question of sibling relationships warrants closer and more imaginative investigation, especially given what we know about the importance to children of having brothers and sisters with them in adversity (perhaps especially those who are older). They provide a link with the past as well as with the future after care; they offer the opportunity to form defensive alliances against the adult world and all its uncertainties as well as the chance to share unhappinesses or fears. Sibling relationships are often intimate and loyal, even though they can also be disruptive and antagonistic. This is how the matter was described by a thirteen-year-old girl in Berridge and Cleaver's study:

> Me and me two brothers, they're both younger than me, got put into care five years ago when me Mum died. Me Dad didn't give a damn, he never

has. To start with we got put in a children's home but after a while they said we were going to be fostered and it meant me going to one family and the two of them going somewhere else. I cried for days and I haven't seen them for two years. Me social worker said they've got to have a fresh start. I've got nobody now. We used to fight and that but we'd been through a lot together and we understood each other. I'll find them when I'm eighteen, nobody will be able to stop me then.[132]

Similarly, in Dorothy Whitaker's recent detailed study of the views of children in a number of community homes she found that those who were placed with their siblings almost always valued it. 'They acknowledged quarrelling and other difficulties but, at the same time, saw their siblings as a source of support and protection' (often against the bullying and aggression of other children—which was one of the things they found frightening about residential care).[133]

When a child is unable to be rehabilitated with his or her family, either temporarily or permanently, there is no reason why they should also be separated from other relatives, especially their brothers and sisters, but also grandparents or aunts and uncles. Indeed, for those whose links with their parents are fractured, for whatever reason, the maintenance of contact with other relatives becomes increasingly important. If residential care is able to help preserve these relationships better than other forms of care then this may be regarded as a significant goal.

iv Residential Care and Education

One of the reasons why children in care secure such a poor foothold in the labour market is their lack of educational achievement. This is not surprising given their poverty-stricken backgrounds, the number of different schools many of them have had to attend and the frequent history of non-attendance. A significant minority have also experienced special education of one kind or another.

Given this plethora of educational disadvantage it might be thought that residential care could play a special role in compensating for these losses, especially where education is provided on the premises or where children have been specifically committed to care to ensure their attendance. Department of Education inspectors undertook a survey of 21 CHEs in England and Wales in 1978 and concluded that almost all the children were under-achievers. They were also able to say that the 'education provided...is frequently at fairly low overall standard, despite the commitment of many teachers'.[134] Whether residential education is to be favoured or not, its existence (together with small classes) ought to provide an opportunity for imaginative and intensive compensation. Yet this is not simply a school problem, whether in the boarding or the day sectors. We know that children's success in education depends as much upon the stimulation and encouragement they receive at home. That ought to be a priority in any home; yet, as Sonia Jackson's report to the SSRC pointed out, this happens rather infrequently.[135] It depends upon staff according it priority; upon space and time being available; upon the availability of personal attention (for example, in helping with homework) and upon the provision of supporting resources (not least appropriate books). Sadly, the DHSS inspectors reported that staff generally had little or no knowledge about the ability of the children in their homes except for those admitted from O and A centres and accompanied by various test results.[136] Furthermore, staff often considered 'that once a satisfactory pattern of attendance had been established their responsibilities in relation to education were at an end', although the inspectors acknowledge that it was indeed often 'a considerable achievement to persuade some children to attend school'.

Berridge made a special examination of the educational experiences of the children in the twenty homes he studied. He advanced three reasons for their poor performance. First, they came from deprived backgrounds. Secondly, the educational climate within the homes was often not conducive to progress. Although there were notable exceptions 'the relatively unstimulating environment of some children's homes does little to ameliorate...poor educational performance'.[137] Thirdly, many of the children suffered many changes of school that were often precipitated by their moves whilst in care. Almost a third of the children in his sample of homes had experienced five or more moves since coming into care, commonly entailing a move to a new school. As Berridge points out, 'for children who lack social skills and who find it difficult to function in large social groups, these frequent interruptions must hinder educational progress'.[138] They also make it difficult to sustain continuity in the collaboration between social services departments and children's schools. Nevertheless, Berridge found that in most of the homes a good relationship had been established with the local schools. Three-quarters of the heads of homes considered that they had good contact with year tutors as well as with other teachers responsible for pastoral care. In the same number of homes a teacher regularly attended reviews or case conferences and in the remainder written reports were usually submitted. These relationships appeared to be least firmly established in the smaller family group homes.

Both educational progress and emotional security depend upon a reasonable degree of stability. Moving children from one placement to another and at the same time obliging them to change schools is a multiple burden on them. Indeed, mobile middle-class parents often arrange boarding education for their children in order to avoid constant upheaval and service families receive allowances for this purpose.[139] Yet the main focus of boarding schools is upon education; that is their rationale and the yardstick (perhaps wrongly) against which they are judged. In many other countries the care of separated children is firmly located within the educational system and, especially in eastern Europe, education is regarded as the vehicle for achieving social compensation. For all its faults that was a view widely shared within the poor law system of child care, albeit linked with the idea of breaking the chain of generational pauperism. How far today's system of child care could achieve a measure of compensation through education remains unclear, as does the part which residential provision might play.

At the moment there is a sorry record. It was plain from the National Child Development Study that children in care (or who have been in care) exhibit significantly poorer educational performance and achievement than other children.[140] Given that a considerable number of children enter care because of truanting and that repeated absence from school is often associated with other reasons for separation it might be expected, as Stein and Carey point out, that the carers would put a high value on education, and great improvements would follow. The truth was, they went on,

> that whether they were in care for shorter or longer periods the level of attainment was extremely low...there was little interest in school...the exception to this was the attitude towards the remedial unit attached to one assessment centre: the young people enjoyed the small groups, and even individual attention; they liked the informality and personal closeness of the teachers and thought more interest was taken in them.[141]

The comparative evidence of the success of different forms of care in enhancing educational achievement is sparse. Triseliotis' study provides some information, albeit from a small sample. In comparing the educational attainments of the group who had been adopted with those brought up in children's homes he found little difference, although the adoptees did slightly better. The residential group did much better than other studies of children in care would lead us to suppose—20 per cent had obtained some kind of higher qualification by the time they were interviewed in their mid-20s (City and Guilds, ONC, HNC, HND or degree).[142] However, when he compared these results with those in his separate study of people who grew up in foster homes Triseliotis found a lower proportion staying on at school or obtaining qualifications.[143] He suggests that this might be a reflection of the different socio-economic backgrounds of foster parents compared with those of residential care staff and adopters. One thing to note about the residential group, however, was that they had spent relatively long periods in the same homes—they had spent, on average, eleven years in residential care and, on average, had four moves since their reception into care. This suggests a greater measure of stability than that experienced by many others in similar circumstances.

Further evidence that stability and individualised attention pay educational dividends comes from work on secure units within the child care system. Millham and his colleagues draw comparisons with boarding school regimes. 'All the boys spend much of their daytime hours in the classroom and', they add, 'benefiting from regular attendance, sufficient sleep and physical care, the children make rapid advances in educational skills. Remedial teaching is a strong feature of the provision. Some boys may increase their attainments, particularly in reading, by several years whilst they are in the units. Naturally those children who stay the longest make the greatest educational gains'.[144] Cawson makes the same point and argues that we should seek to replicate these advantages in open conditions while allowing some move towards 'independence in daily domestic living'.[145]

Yet the drawbacks of small intensive care and educational units should not be overlooked. Whilst education provision was generous in terms of the staff-pupil ratios in the secure units Millham studied, the breadth of stimulation was 'inevitably restricted'. The lack of access to laboratories was noted and 'in some of the units expressive subjects such as music, the plastic arts and drama are hardly developed'.[146] Sports and team games were also poorly served by these arrangements. Furthermore, the educational routine was liable to drive out the care and the pastoral and counselling elements. Clearly there is a balance to be struck that might be more achievable were there not a professional divide between care and teaching staff.

Nancy Hazel's evidence from the Kent special fostering project reaches a rather different conclusion about the role of foster parents and school achievement. However, as part of the project schools were told about the scheme and asked for regular reports on the youngsters' progress. It was anticipated that the foster parents would play an active role in promoting their education. The results were encouraging. From poor starting positions the reports mostly noted favourable progress: Hazel suggests that this showed that 'the foster parents' interest and hard work clearly paid off'.[147]

What suggests itself from these limited studies is that

(1) the repeated moving around that is associated with care is detrimental to the child's education;

(2) despite non-attendance and other school problems being important contributors to the reasons why a child is admitted to care, education does not receive much priority, in particular children's homes may do little to provide a stimulating atmosphere or individual attention on educational matters;

(3) where *special* attention is provided and careful arrangements made with schools the results may be encouraging in both residential and foster care—although it may be more practical to modify regimes and attitudes in residential homes than in a multitude of foster homes;

(4) given the problems of achieving a measure of stability for children in care and their problems in coping with school there may be a case for a closer integration of the functions of boarding education and children's homes. The tension between care and education has always been a difficulty but for children in care in particular, care will not be fully realised without more attention to education, and education will hardly be successful without a clearly child-oriented and caring approach. This is surely what happens in the best special schools, especially those for the mentally handicapped. As the NCB report on *Caring for Separated Children* concluded: 'some of the best care can assume an educational form; and some of the best education and efficient learning can be attained in what is narrowly regarded as a ''care'' setting'.[148]

The role of residential care in education is as important an aspect of 'preparation' as the maintenance of parental contacts and assisting children towards their eventual independence. Each provides an example of preparation which, from some of the available evidence, residential care may be geared to undertake. At the moment it is not regarded as a central function and where it is done it may not be pursued systematically or with the necessary vigour. There are, however, other functions which residential care does or could fulfil for individual children: one of them is preparation for independence.

v Residential Care and Preparation for Independence

One of the longstanding indictments of residential care is that it fails to prepare older children for independence. Group living may drive out the day-to-day experiences upon which children depend for their progress to self-confident adulthood. 'With a predominantly adolescent population', the DHSS inspectorate explained, 'it is generally recognised that preparation for independence is a crucial part of the residential child care task'.[149] This is especially important in the case of those who will not be able to rejoin their own families.

The national inspection survey found that in about a quarter of the general homes some accommodation was available for older adolescents which offered an opportunity for independent living. Its provision often required considerable ingenuity where there were only communal kitchens or where bulk buying systems operated. In many other homes older children

> had no opportunity to buy or cook food, to do their own laundry or to buy their clothes...more importantly, they were never alone. Some staff argued that the pattern of life in many working class homes did not allow for any privacy, or for experimenting with cooking, but this argument had little validity for young people who were going to face life without the support of a family.[150]

Most authorities offer some older children in their care special accommodation which is usually referred to as independence units or hostels, although it does not necessarily follow that these facilities prepare their residents adequately for living on their own. Indeed, neither the older children in hostels nor those in lodgings or in flats of their own (whilst still in care) may have received much preparation for such ventures. More care seems to be taken in these matters for the placement of mentally handicapped adolescents from homes or hospitals into semi-independent living units located in the community.

The considerable variety of transitional living arrangements for adolescents as they approach the time when they have to leave care is exemplified in the Stein and Carey study which looked at the recent past and the future of a group of youngsters who left care in 1982 when they were between 16 and 18 years of age: most left on becoming 18, none stayed on beyond that age.[151] About a third were in foster homes or in some other kinds of family, usually with relatives. These young people mostly did not anticipate any immediate move, with the exception of those in special fostering schemes where it was clear that, at 18, they were expected to make way for other younger adolescents.[152] Likewise, in residential accommodation directly provided by the social services department there was the necessity to move out at 18 when their eligibility for care ceased. In accommodation provided by other agencies with no such upper age limit the arrangement seemed to be more flexible. Hence, one of the disadvantages of local authority residential care is that it has to end when the youngster reaches the age of 18 or, occasionally, 19. Although foster parents cease to be paid when a child is no longer in care, placements tend to continue, albeit with longer and longer periods away. In any case, some children are placed with relatives who will have been designated foster parents in order to be able to receive the allowances. Hence, the need for planned transition for children who are in residential care would seem to be especially presssing.

It is surprising, therefore, to find a decline in hostel accommodation for older chidlren in care. The number living in hostels (local authority or voluntary but excluding those for the mentally handicapped) fell from 2,000 in 1976 to 900 in 1984 or, as proportions of all children over school age in care, from 10 per cent to a little over three per cent.[153] On the other hand, the number in 'lodgings' rose in the same period from 1,500 to just over 2,000, from eight per cent to 10 per cent of those in care who were over school leaving age.

This national pattern was reflected in a recent study of residential homes in Leicestershire where although 72 per cent of the children in care were over 14 only eight per cent were in semi-independent accommodation. Many were in all-age homes and then left at 16 for lodgings or their own accommodation.[154] Lupton reported similar results in

Hampshire for the same period.[155]

Another worrying trend is the reduction in the use of section 72 of the Child Care Act, 1980 which allows authorities to retain children in care until they are 19 (instead of 18) if they are considered unready or unprepared to live independently. Of course, this could be an indication of better earlier preparation but, whatever the reason, in 1976 a total of 700 children left care in England and Wales at 19, whereas by 1984 the figure had fallen to 300.[156]

Thus, there are two aspects of local authority residential care which need to be emphasised in considering its role in the preparation of children for independence. The first is that, by comparison with other forms of care (fostering or 'home on trial' in particular) there is a foreseeable and unavoidable termination at 18: something has to happen. Secondly, and in addition to this, it may be that residential care, and particularly certain kinds of residential care, can be deliberately and skilfully used in the preparation process. There are some good examples but the need is still considerable as a recent report by Pat Cawson on regional residential provision in London makes plain.[157] One of her main recommendations was that 'for boys and girls needing new placements close to their sixteenth birthday a completely new approach is needed'. Amongst these might be small residential units with further education (CHFEs)—and further education would be interpreted to include the inculcation of community survival skills. One of the problems at present, she pointed out, is the reluctance of some independence units to accept children who are regarded as immature or who are considered to be problematic in other ways.

It is vitally important that, wherever possible, children leaving care should have a job to go to. If residential care, in whatever form, is to play a special role in the preparation of older children for independence then it must be expected to enhance their chances of getting work. The record, however, is not impressive, although there is little comparable evidence of the success of other forms of care in this direction. However, in his retrospective study of children brought up in residential homes and those from similar backgrounds who had been adopted, Triseliotis found much better employment records amongst the latter group. His interviews took place in 1980–1 with people in their mid-20s so that their experience may not be typical today. Overall about 70 per cent of the adopted were mostly in regular employment compared with 50 per cent of the residential group,[158] and at the time of the interview the proportion of them out of work was six times greater than the adoptees. The residential group also experienced longer periods of unemployment. However, Triseliotis reported that 'the amount of unemployment experienced by those who grew up in residential establishments was unrelated to the amount of preparation and help they said they had received before or after leaving the institution'. That must raise questions about the appropriateness of the help. Triseliotis was also able to compare the work experiences of these two groups with that of a group of former foster children whom he had interviewed in an earlier study. The foster children's record settled about mid-way between the others.[159]

One of the handicaps residential staff and social workers face in assisting children into work may arise from their lack of knowledge of the local employment networks, a knowledge which both adopters and foster parents would be more likely to possess. In Nancy Hazel's study of the Kent special fostering scheme for adolescents, for example, she reported that the 'foster-parents knew the district well, could liaise with employment services and were rather successful in helping adolescents to find jobs'.[160] However, as more of them become unemployed themselves that advantage may be lessened, whilst an increasing localisation of social services may strengthen the position of the professionals.

The 1980 national survey conducted by the DHSS inspectorate was concerned with those young people between 16 and 18 who were still in care. Their experience was much more bleak. Forty per cent of them were unemployed; a further 30 per cent were in work experience schemes and 12 per cent were still in the education system. Only 17 per cent had a job.[161] The smaller group (45) in the Stein and Carey study told an even sorrier story (though only 13 per cent left from residential care). After leaving, the young people in the project 'inhabited a world of benefits, work schemes, casual labour and other practices (legal or otherwise) on the margin of employment. A "proper" job, full-time and permanent, was a rarity few could hope to obtain'.[162] The largest number to have a job at any of the five successive interviews was five (out of 45, or 11 per cent) and all were poorly paid. The changes over time were in the direction of more unemployment or temporary work. This small study of young people leaving care from various kinds of accommodation suggests that the low rate of employment amongst the residential homes' leavers is no different from what might be expected amongst those who had been in lodgings, foster care or 'home on trial'. The rate of unemployment amongst children who have been in care may be universally high, and high compared with this age group amongst the general population.

In the spring of 1985, for example (by which time general unemployment had increased substantially), 19 per cent of the 16–19 year-olds in the Labour Force Survey described themselves as unemployed[163] and a year later about six per cent of the under 18s were officially returned as claiming benefits as unemployed.[164] Whatever the exact state of youth unemployment throughout the country it is plainly significantly higher amongst children who are in care or who have been in care, and those in or from residential homes are no exception. Although prospects have worsened dramatically in the last decade or so this picture is in rather sharp contrast to the success of the old approved schools in finding work for youngsters when they left.

However, the relationship between juvenile employment and residential care may be more complicated than it appears to be. For instance, the DHSS inspectors' survey found that 'in some homes in areas of high unemployment every young person had a job. By contrast there were homes, or hostels, in more affluent parts of the country where no one was employed'.[165] Even so, the report concluded that in general 'the number of young people who were unemployed, and for whom no action appeared to be taken, was disturbing'. It is noteworthy that in homes looking after numerous school leavers who were unemployed there was the problem of just how the routines should or could be organised during the day when school children were absent and when, conventionally, homes were expected to be empty of children. These new problems (compared with those of the 1950s or the 1960s) may well exacerbate the problems of control.

If residential care is to provide an improved springboard for employment for more children in care then the task must surely be embraced more vigorously and deliberately than hitherto. It must certainly not be an additional handicap. The preparation of adolescents for independence extends beyond the examples which have been discussed. The National Children's Bureau paper on *Leaving Residential Care* suggests that it should be regarded as falling into three stages: preparation whilst in a home, intermediate help in the transitional stage, and then support once young people are in the community on their own.[166] The use of residential resources to provide continuity into the second and third of these stages could well be an important development. Done successfully, such work will be a remarkable achievement given the deprivations and disadvantages suffered by many of the children as well as their immaturity. But, like so much else, that will require a radical overhaul of the organisation and priorities for residential care and, possibly, new legislation.

                              *   *   *

This section has considered some of the functions that residential care may fulfil for individual children. There are others, of course, which could be added; but these—care, rehabilitation, preservation, education and preparation—seem to offer specific and realistic possibilities. What is clear from a wide spectrum of research is that the identification and adoption of tangible goals for individual children is of the utmost importance, albeit that they will include the short-term as well as the long-term. However, three taxing questions remain:

(1) How are the tensions between the functions which residential care serves for the wider welfare system to be reconciled with those which it fulfils on behalf of the children who are being looked after?

(2) How are the child-orientated goals that should inform the canons of general policy to be balanced against those which are unique to a particular child?

(3) How far is residential care 'successful' measured in the light of either of these requirements and, furthermore, how do different regimes, or the major alternatives to residential care, perform in comparison with each other?

Part 3   Treatment and Outcomes

Much residential child care aims to change children's behaviour. A few homes and schools make this the rationale for their existence. Many others tend to refer to any interventions that endeavour to modify behaviour as 'treatment', even though they may be punitive and oppresssive. Some establishments misleadingly describe themselves as therapeutic in order to gain status. The majority of homes, however, would probably not consider that they were engaged in systematic and carefully designed treatment. Despite that, we know that behaviour is modified in various ways as the result of everyday social interactions which lay no claim to treatment. Good daily care and nurture help children to develop, to learn, to gain self-confidence and to mature emotionally.

Generally speaking research tells us two things about the effect of residential care on behaviour: first that different regimes lead to different patterns of behaviour during a child's stay in a home and, secondly, that these experiences have little discernible effect on behaviour outside of that context. However, whereas there is compelling evidence for the first of these conclusions that for the second is less reliable. Studies of the subsequent outcomes of different kinds of residential care regimes are limited, heavily concentrated in the field of delinquency and difficult to undertake. Furthermore, there is virtually no research that compares the outcomes of particular forms of residential care with possible alternatives like foster care.

Important evidence about the impact of different residential regimes on child behaviour was gathered together by Tizard, Sinclair and Clarke in 1975.[167] Two examples from that collection will serve to show how much regimes can vary (even in supposedly similar establishments) and how those variations influence behaviour.

In a study of institutions caring for similar types of retarded children Tizard found that there were marked differences in the pattern of their upbringing.[168] It was possible to characterise units as either 'institutionally-orientated' or 'child-orientated'. In the child-orientated settings staff interacted with the children more frequently and more warmly and there was less division of labour. The attitudes and behaviour of the heads of the units were considered to be the principal influences upon the style of regime. The more they were 'involved in the everyday care and supervision of children, the more they talked to them, the more likely were junior staff to behave warmly towards their charges'. The differences in the behaviour of the different heads were attributable to two main factors: the amount of autonomy that they enjoyed and their training. Those accorded most autonomy and with child care rather than nursing training ran the most child-centred units. The effect on the children of the two different types of care was also noted. For similar children, 'those in child orientated units were significantly more advanced in speech and feeding than those in institutionally-orientated units'.

Another of the reported results came from a study of probation hostels for young people conducted by Sinclair. Again, there were large differences between the regimes, and these differences were related to the attitudes and approaches of the wardens—particularly towards matters of control and regulation. Measuring 'failure' in terms of absconding or the commission of further offences, wide variations were found between the hostels—from 14 per cent to 78 per cent. These could not be accounted for by differences between the boys. Failure rates, it was concluded, were characteristic of wardens. Wardens who were strict, agreed with their wives on how the hostel should be run, and were apparently warm towards the residents had lower failure rates than others.

Juliet Berry published her study of the daily experiences of residential living at the same time that the Tizard collection of studies appeared. She also drew sharp contrasts between the regimes in various residential settings for children.[172] The ways in which routine activities (like getting up, eating and going to bed) were managed enabled her to devise a means of dividing the 44 establishments in the study into three groups according to the quality of care being provided. As we have noted, there were comparatively few in the 'more positive' category and she concluded that poor daily care was linked to the staff themselves receiving poor support.

Other studies, mainly of residential provision for delinquents, have shown equally wide variations in regimes and that such differences are associated with different patterns of behaviour within the establishments. Absconding and violence have been two of the issues explored from these perspectives.

The large-scale study of boys in approved schools conducted by Millham and his colleagues in the early 1970s showed that there was considerable variation in the amount of running away between one place and another, and that this was related to a cluster of school characteristics, but particularly to the level (rather than the style) of control: less control, more absconding. Yet the picture was not as simple as this implies. For instance, 'in unsatisfactory schools boys run away and quickly get transferred. In other schools, there is less likelihood of ever running...and in the three "exceptional" schools, absconders are numerous but are generally readmitted, so that they share in the generally high success rate of the schools'.[173] Clarke and Martin arrived at somewhat similar conclusions but added that the opportunity to run was in itself important.[174]

The complicated issue of control threads its way through much of the literature and research on residential child care. Violent behaviour is taken to be one manifestation of the problem although it is less common than is imagined.[175] Again, the work of Millham and his colleagues at the Dartington Social Research Unit provides a useful example. As they observe, there are considerable difficulties in the definition and recording of violent events. There is staff violence to children; child to staff violence as well as the violence that one child vents on another. Substantial differences in the amount of violence as between schools were recorded in the study of approved schools and in subsequent studies of four community homes over time. The amount of violence appeared to be increasing, but the Dartington team suggest that the evidence indicates that it does so 'when the stability of the inmates' world is threatened', in particular by 'successful attempts to bring about closer relationships between boys and staff through small group living'.[176] Therefore, different patterns and rates of change in homes partly account for different amounts of violent behaviour; but it is also a function of the skill with which staff prevent the escalation. The research on violence in homes confirms the importance of the social situations, rather then the uncontrolled drives of the children and young people, in accounting for variations in behaviour.

Much of the research on the impact of different regimes has been conducted in the former approved schools and prison department establishments. That is particularly true of the study of the relationship between different residential regimes and outcomes as measured by reoffending. In this area the overwhelming weight of evidence is that different regimes make little or no difference to rates of recidivism. For instance, Clarke and Cornish compared the subsequent records of boys in different units at the former Kingswood classifying school. One group was offered treatment within a 'therapeutic community' whilst the others received the usual training experience of approved school boys at the time. The conclusion, however, was that although the regimes differed considerably their ineffectiveness in reducing future delinquent behaviour was 'virtually identical' with about a 70 per cent failure rate.[177]

A more recent Home Office study has examined the effects of the tougher regimes which have been introduced in a number of detention centres. The conclusion was clear: that the new projects 'had no discernible effect on the rate at which trainees were reconvicted'. Furthermore, the harsher regimes seemed to have almost no effect upon the behaviour of boys whilst they were within the detention centres.[178]

There are several reasons why different residential regimes have so little long-term effect, at least upon those behaviours which have been the subject of research. Clarke and Martin have argued that since institutions are able to condition the behaviour of their residents it is only to be expected that, once away from these influences, other equally strong pressures will succeed them. The residential contribution is overridden by problems of background, family, community and poverty. As Cornish and Clarke explain:

> The failure to consolidate gains made during institutional intervention is as much a feature of 'training' as of 'treatment' programmes. In token economies, for example, where therapy is directed primarily towards bringing about changes in behaviour, the problems of generalising behaviour gains to the post-institutional environment, or of resisting their extinction there, has yet to be given adequate consideration.

For example, they go on,

> Where programmes stress the importance of manipulating the inmate's environment through the systematic application of operant and classical conditioning procedures, it is the institutional environment's very capacity to exert far-reaching control over rewards and punishments for the purpose of promoting pro-social behaviour which distinguishes it from the post-institutional situation.[179]

The thrust of these arguments is borne out by research from a different setting. Bartak and Rutter studied the effects of different approaches to autistic children in their special educational treatment.[180] The results indicated that high staff-child ratios and a large amount of specific teaching in a well-controlled classroom produced the greatest educational benefit. However, if these achievements were to be sustained when the child returned home then considerable attention had to be paid to collaboration and close co-operation between school and home.

In a nutshell, therefore, the various studies suggest

(1) that different regimes have a differential effect on children's behaviour;

(2) that the style of regime which has the 'best' results is child-orientated rather than institutionally-orientated;

(3) that the role of heads is important in establishing a particular kind of regime, and

(4) that although success in modifying children's behaviour in sought for directions can be achieved in residential settings, it is singularly difficult to sustain this once they leave unless considerable preparatory work has been undertaken.

However, three notes of caution should be sounded. The first is that it may be dangerous to place residential establishments on a single continuum from good to bad according to their degree of child-centredness because the dimensions in which they need to be perceived are so numerous. For instance, in the Dartington study of young people in maximum security it was found that their commitment to the units was often considerable and, in their study of approved schools the same team warn that 'if the equilibrium is lost between different kinds of aims, and expressive goals are stressed to the detriment of instrumental aims and organisational needs, child commitment can diminish sharply'.[181] Likewise, in examining the regimes of eight approved schools Anne Dunlop found that those which boys regarded most favourably were the ones that offered effective trade training and emphasised responsible behaviour.[182]

A second note of caution must be that virtually no studies have compared the performance of residential homes (or different residential homes) with the principal alternatives. Colton's research compared the amount of child-orientated contact in residential homes and foster homes and found the latter to offer more.[183] Nevertheless, he also discovered that residential staff held child-orientated views but were constrained by the settings in which they worked from putting them into practice fully, particularly in homes run with a bureaucratic style. There is also Triseliotis' research which has already been mentioned. He interviewed groups of adults who had been brought up for long periods in either residential care or foster homes or had been adopted. On various measures of well-being his broad conclusion was that residential care was the least satisfactory and adoption the most satisfactory.[184] Nonetheless, there were exceptions and in this and other retrospective accounts provided by adults and young people who had been in care it is the sense of receiving understanding, sympathetic, comforting and individual attention which stands out as the hallmark of the experiences which they cherish. The lack of these things characterised the bleak and unhappy periods of their lives.[185] Good and bad experiences are recorded in all types of care although group living, by its very nature, presents more obstacles to achieving reasonably stable individual attention.

The third and final note of caution must be about the time perspective that is employed in evaluating the outcomes of residential care. Dorothy Whitaker argues from the evidence of her study, that long-term goals may drive out the short-term; simply helping a child to cope with day-to-day life within the home or helping a child to make sense of his or her current and past life are worthy enterprises.[186] Likewise, she warns that it is unlikely to be helpful to think in grand terms of eventual 'success' or 'failure'. Her work suggested that it is more profitable to assess the mixed *pattern* of gains and losses. It ought to be possible, she argues, to increase the benefits and reduce the costs through skilful and sensitive care on an individual basis.

The lack of conclusive evidence about the effect of different residential regimes on children's longer-term futures ought not to detract from the fact that we do know from research studies and from children's own accounts, that the quality of their daily life in a residential home is affected by how it is run, by the warmth of relationships, by whether they are with brothers or sisters, by their contact with parents and by the methods employed to secure the control that is necessary. None of this should be overlooked or its importance minimised. Furthermore, in striving to obtain the best quality of care for children in residential homes we may find, almost incidentally, that some of the goals of the more ambitious treatment programmes come to be realised.

Part 4   Summary and Conclusion

The quality and nature of the evidence

Although there is a growing body of empirical research on residential child care it is deficient in four main respects:

(1) Apart from Moss's enquiry, the PSSRU survey and the report of the DHSS Inspectorate there are no large-scale and national studies upon which to draw. Even these concentrate upon England and Wales: Scotland and Northern Ireland are not included although the different legislation and administrative organisation might provide valuable lessons.

(2) Few studies look across the full range of residential child care and hence important interconnections are liable to be overlooked.

(3) Hardly any enquiries adopt a systematically comparative approach in which residential care is studied and assessed in conjunction with the major alternatives.

(4) There is virtually no evidence about outcomes, except in the field of juvenile delinquency where these have been measured narrowly against rates of reconviction.

However, this rather gloomy picture may be counterbalanced by three further observations.

(5) Partly as a result of the DHSS and ESRC research initiatives in child care (sadly discontinued) we do have a number of good small-scale studies. They provide useful and up-to-date illustrations as well as elaborating important themes. They have not approached residential care from a negative or unsympathetic position but have aimed to set it in a wider framework. In terms of the quality of care some of the results are quite encouraging.

(6) There is also a number of studies which have elicited the opinions of children and parents as well as members of staff and field social workers. These suggest that not all views about residential care coincide.

(7) The substantial evidence about the ill-effects of residential child care referred mainly to pre-school aged children. It is now less relevant with the virtual disappearance of residential nurseries and a growing preponderance of adolescents.

If we are to move towards an integrated approach to child care planning then it is vital that the research evidence and basic information is of a kind that enables us to do so. A start has been made with the PSSRU costing exercises and with some of the local authority research initiatives; but there is still an urgent need for across-the-board research (or closely integrated separate pieces of research) if the role and nature of residential child care is to be objectively determined and appropriately modified as time passes.

The diverse functions
Even the most cursory review of research and information about residential child care reveals its many functions—at different levels, at different times, for different children and with different consequences. It is not simply the system which exhibits this diversity but individual establishments as well. Although homes have been designated for special purposes or to take particular groups this may actually be misleading if, as a result, other functions are obscured. It is crucial, therefore, for this mixture of purposes to be appreciated and decisions taken about which should be served or, at least, in what order of priority.

Three points in particular are worthy of reiteration:
(1) There is an inevitable tension between the functions fulfilled for 'the system' and those for individual children. However, it would

be an over-simplification to regard these as necessarily in conflict. Much depends upon what *kinds* of purposes residential child care serves for other parts of the wider system. They may be such that although they do not enhance a particular child's well-being they do enable the welfare of *other* classes of children to be more efficiently and humanely met.

(2) Although it is imperative for each establishment to appreciate the range of functions that it does or could fulfil, these should not be clarified at the expense of individualisation. As Dorothy Whitaker has been at pains to stress, the pursuit of what is generally considered to be good for children (or good for children in care) has to be tested repeatedly against the question 'what is good for *this* child?' Some children may suffer in what is undoubtedly a beneficial regime for the majority. The challenge of individualisation is faced on two fronts: first in the daily routine and group living and, secondly, in deciding what best needs to be done to ensure a child's longer-term well-being. The latter may prove to be less difficult than the former. Indeed, there is evidence that reviews and case conferences are more regularly and fully undertaken on children in residential care than for those in other placements, although implementing agreed courses of action is another matter.[187] In day-to-day care, however, there appear to be two large obstacles. One is that there are rarely enough people to offer undivided and individual attention to each child and the other is that routines and styles develop which preclude that possibility.

(3) In taking the analysis of goals and functions further it may be useful to concentrate upon certain groups of children. The evidence suggests four in particular: adolescents; groups of brothers and sisters; those variously described as 'maladjusted'; and youngsters in penal establishments.

Regimes are important

The evidence from a number of different fields clearly shows that different residential regimes achieve different results with similar children. Furthermore, it is apparent that children appreciate and feel more settled in some rather than in others. All of which points to the fact that generalisations about the nature of residential child care ignore a considerable amount of variation. The evidence about the effect of different regimes on the subsequent behaviour of children elsewhere is, though, inconclusive.

Nevertheless, when the effectiveness of residential care is measured by the use of independent indicators of various kinds, nine factors seem to stand out:

(1) Establishments do 'best' when the children feel that they are cared for, listened to and responded to in a quiet, sympathetic and consistent fashion. Such environments are usually characterised as 'child-orientated' rather than 'institution-orientated'—but that may be too simple a distinction.

(2) The atmosphere and quality of relationships in a residential establishment owe much to the style of the leadership. That style appears to be influenced by training.

(3) A necessary but not sufficient condition for any beneficial effects achieved by residential care to have an enduring influence is a reasonable agreement between all concerned about the goals and about how to achieve them. In particular, attention has to be paid to the situation in which a child or young person will find themselves after they leave residential care. Neither planning nor daily care can be effective in the long run unless they take into account the external social and economic forces.

(4) Children are best settled and have the greatest chance of returning home where contact with their parents is actively maintained and encouraged. Children are likely to be distressed by being separated from brothers and sisters—they gain much support from their presence.

(5) The opportunity for privacy should be regarded as an essential part of good residential care.

(6) Children continue to feel stigmatised because they live in a 'Home'. Steps can be taken to minimise that hurt, not least by avoiding distinctive buildings and separate services.

Other factors are more relevant to adolescents in particular:

(7) Establishments do well where young people see themselves as acquiring some instrumental skills during their stay.

(8) It is important to start to equip young people with the social skills for independent living as early as possible. Regimes which make children over-dependent and allow them to become isolated from the community do not help in this.

(9) Clear, consistent and firm control is important for effective residential care. Children and young people acknowledge this but react negatively against what they perceive as trivial rules, unpredictable decisions, public castigation and unjust treatment.

A final note
It was pointed out in Part 1 that there has been a notable reduction in the number of children in residential care over the last twenty or thirty

years. Undoubtedly, too many children were inappropriately placed in establishments and many were damaged in the process. There were many rationalisations and assumptions. They have been superseded by others which now, in their turn, need to be identified and tested.

The reduced size of the residential sector in child care provides a unique opportunity to decide how it should develop and for what reasons. In particular, a growing number of commentators plead for a purposeful use of residential care for children to replace the residual functions which its long history has imposed upon it.

Notes and References

1. Moss, P. (1975), 'Residential care of children: a general view', in Tizard J., Sinclair, I. A. C. and Clarke, R. V. G., (eds), *Varieties of Residential Experience*, Routledge and Kegan Paul, p. 17.

2. Department of Health and Social Security (1984), *Children in the Care of Local Authorities in England*, feedback statistics, DHSS.

3. Department of Health and Social Security (1986a), *Children in the Care of Local Authorities in England and Wales, 1984*, DHSS.

4. Knapp, M. and Smith, J. (1984), *The PSSRU National Survey of Children's Homes*, Report no. 2, Discussion paper 322, University of Kent, Personal Social Services Research Unit, table 21, p. 27.

5. Department of Health and Social Security (1986b), *Inspection of Community Homes, 1985*, DHSS Social Services Inspectorate, table 1.1, p. 62.

6. Berridge, D. (1985), *Children's Homes*, Blackwell, p. 33.

7. As note 3.

8. Department of Health and Social Security, annual statistics, *Children in the Care of Local Authorities in England and Wales*, various years, DHSS.

9. *Ibid.*

10. Knapp, M. and Smith, J. (1984) *op. cit.*, p. 27.

11. *Ibid.*

12. As note 8.

13. Department of the Environment, District Audit (1981), *The Provision of Child Care: A Study of Eight Local Authorities in England and Wales—Final Report*, HMSO, p. 30.

14. Home Office, *Approved School and Remand Home Statistics*, various years and Department of Health and Social Security, *Children in Care* annual statistics.

15. Knapp, M. and Smith, J. (1984) *op. cit.*, table 2, p. 8.

16. Department of Health and Social Security (1982), *Social Services for Children in England and Wales, 1979–81*, DHSS, p. 28.

17. Berridge, D. (undated), *Private Children's Homes*, (unpublished), p. 5.

18. As note 15.

19. These and other statistics assembled by F. Loughran, unpublished, University of Bristol.

20. Home Office, *Criminal Statistics*, England and Wales, various dates, HMSO.

21. Home Office, *Prison Statistics*, England and Wales, various dates, HMSO.

22. See, for example, Aldgate, J. (1987), 'Residential care—a revaluation of a threatened resource', *Child Care Quarterly*, Spring, or, Ainsworth, F. (1985), 'Residential programmes for children and youth: an exercise in re-framing', *British Journal of Social Work*, 15, 2, Apr., pp. 145–154.

23. See, for example, Millham, S., Bullock, R. and Cherrett, P. (1975), 'A conceptual scheme for the comparative analysis of residential institutions', in Tizard, J., Sinclair, I. A. C. and Clarke, R. V. G. (eds), *Varieties of Residential Experience*, Routledge and Kegan Paul.

24. Berridge, D. (1985), *Children's Homes*, Blackwell, p. 41.

25. Berridge, D. and Cleaver, H. (1987), *Foster Home Breakdown*, Blackwell, pp. 60 and 111.

26. Ongoing research R. A. Parker and E. Farmer, Department of Social Administration, University of Bristol.

27. Millham, S., Bullock, R., Hosie, K. and Haak, M. (1986), *Lost in Care: The Problem of Maintaining Links Between Children in Care and Their Families*, Gower, pp. 149 and 192.

28. *Fostering and Adoption Disruptions: A Preliminary Study* (1982), discussion paper no. 2, Research team, Social Work Headquarters, Strathclyde Regional Council, Glasgow.

29. Newman, N. and MacIntosh, H., (1975), *A Roof Over their Heads? Regional Provisions for Children in South East Scotland*, University of Edinburgh: Department of Social Administration, p. 10.

30. Social Services Research and Intelligence Unit, Portsmouth Polytechnic and Hampshire County Council (1976), *First Year at Fairfield Lodge*, p. 16.

31. South West Children's Regional Planning Committee, South West Social Services Research Group (1976), *Observation and Assessment: A Study of Children's Progress through Centres in the South West, 1976–7*, p. 21.

32. Parker, R. A. (1985), 'Planning into practice', *Adoption and Fostering*, 9, 4, pp. 25–28.

33. See, for example, Parker, R. A. (1966), *Decision in Child Care*, Allen and Unwin.

34. Berridge, D. and Cleaver, H. (1987), *op. cit.*, p. 56.

35. Research and Training Section, Social Services Department, Exeter, (undated), *Fostering in South Devon: A Study of Terminations in 1980–81*.

36. Department of the Environment, District Audit (1981), *op. cit.*

37. Redfern, M. (1983), 'Successes and failures in family placement', *Adoption and Fostering*, Autumn.

38. Avon Social Services (Domiciliary) Sub-Committee, (1982), *Foster Home Breakdowns, 1981–2*, Report.

39. Berridge, D. and Cleaver, H. (1987), *op. cit.*, p. 111.

40. *Ibid.*, p. 57.

41. See Warwickshire's evidence to the Social Services Committee, Session 1982–3, Children in Care, Minutes of Evidence, 6 Dec. 1982, HC 26-iii; for example, pp. 94 and 102. Figures from DHSS feedback statistics, England, 1984.

42. Fuller, R. (1983), CHE *Withdrawals in Sandwell: A Case Study in Policy Change*, University of Keele, p. 227.

43. Department of the Environment, District Audit (1981), *op. cit.*, pp. 15–16.

44. Berridge, D. (1985), *op. cit.*

45. Parker, R. (1966), *op. cit.*, pp. 48–9.

46. Berridge, D. and Cleaver, H. (1987), *op. cit.*

47. Department of Health and Social Security (1986b), *op. cit.*

48. SW Children's Regional Planning Committee (1976), *op. cit.*, p. 37.

49. Social Services Research and Intelligence Unit (1976), *op. cit.*, p. 74.

50. Millham, S., *et al.* (1986), *op. cit.*

51. Fisher, M., *et al.* (1986), *In and Out of Care*, Batsford/British Agencies for Adoption and Fostering.

52. For a discussion of residential assessment issues see, Hoghughi, M. (1980), *Assessing Problem Children*, Burnett Books, and, more generally, Fuller, R. (1986), *Issues in the Assessment of Children in Care*, National Children's Bureau.

53. SW Children's Regional Planning Committee (1976), *op. cit.*

54. Social Services Research and Intelligence Unit (1976), *op. cit.*

55. Wessex Children's Regional Planning Committee (1976), *A Study of Placement Recommendations*.

56. Department of Health and Social Security, annual statistics, *Children in the Care of Local Authorities in England and Wales*, and fuller information for England only for 1984.

57. Department of the Environment, District Audit (1981), *op. cit.*, p. 31.

58. Department of Health and Social Security (1984), *op. cit.*

59. Knapp, M. and Smith, J. (1984), *op. cit.* pp. 21–23.

60. See, for example, Feldman, B. (1983), 'Contract IT in a residential setting', *Orchard Lodge Studies of Deviancy*, 3, 2, Spring, p. 47.

61. Knapp, M. and Smith, J. (1984), *op. cit.*, p. 24.

62. Department of Health and Social Security (1986b), *op. cit.*, pp. 23 and 34.

63. Department of Health and Social Security, Social Work Service, London Region, (1982), *Residential Care for Children in London*, p. 100.

64. *Hansard* (HC), 20.11.84, cols. 113–114.

65. Knapp, M. and Smith, J. (1984), *op. cit.*, table 21, p. 27.

66. See, annual reports on *The Work of the Prison Department*, HMSO.

67. *Hansard* (HC), 29.1.86, col. 524.

68. *Hansard* (HC), 16.1.85, cols. 149–50.

69. See, Dunlop, A. B., (1974), *The Approved School Experience*, HMSO.

70. See, annual *Prison Statistics*.

71. For examples, see Thorpe, D., *et al.* (1980), *Out of Care*, Allen and Unwin.

72. *Report of the Carnegie Working Party on Young People in Custody in the United Kingdom and Eire*, (1986).

73. Tutt, N. (1986), *A Survey of Young People Under 17 in Prison Establishments in 1984*, (unpublished).

74. Thornton, D., *et al.* (1984), *Tougher Regimes in Detention Centres: Report of an Evaluation by the Young Offender Psychology Unit*, Home Office.

75. Beedell, C. J. (1970), *Residential Life with Children*, Routledge and Kegan Paul.

76. *Ibid.*, p. 27.

77. Department of Health and Social Security (1982), *op. cit.*

78. As footnote 63, p. 28.

79. Department of Health and Social Security (1986b), *op. cit.*, sect. 6.

80. Berridge, D. (1985), *op. cit.*, p. 72.

81. *Ibid.*, p. 80.

82. *Ibid.*, pp. 74–5.

83. *Ibid.*, p. 77.

84. Colton, M. (1986), *Dimensions of Substitute Care*, D. Phil., Oxford.

85. Berry, J. (1975), *Daily Experience in Residential Life: A Study of Children and their Caregivers*, Routledge and Kegan Paul.

86. *Ibid.*, p. 150.

87. *Ibid.*, p. 157.

88. Knapp, M. and Smith, J. (1984), *op. cit.*, table 9, p. 16.

89. *Ibid.*, table 8, p. 14.

90. Department of Health and Social Security (1982), *op. cit.*, p. 84.

91. Department of Health and Social Security (1986b), *op. cit.*, p. 28.

92. Clarke, R. V. G. and Martin, D. N. (1975), 'A study of absconding and its implications for the residential treatment of delinquents', in Tizard, J. *et al.* (eds), *Varieties of Residential Experience*, Routledge and Kegan Paul, pp. 259–261.

93. Summarised for example, in Holman, R. (1980), *Inequality in Child Care*, Child Poverty Action Group.

94. Page, R. and Clarke, G. A. (eds) (1977), *Who Cares? Young People in Care Speak Out*, National Children's Bureau, pp. 26–7.

95. Whitaker, D. S., Cook, J. M., Dunne, C. and Rockliffe, S. (1985), *The Experience of Residential Care from the Perspective of Children, Parents and Caregivers*, Report to the Economic and Social Research Council, University of York, (unpublished).

96. Lambert, R. (1968), *The Hothouse Society*, Weidenfeld and Nicholson, p. 280.

97. Knapp, M. and Smith, J. (1984), *op. cit.*, table 5, p. 12.

98. The evidence is reviewed in ch. 7 of Millham, S., *et al.*, (1986), *op. cit.*.

99. See also Department of Health and Social Security (1985), *Social Work Decisions in Child Care: Recent Research Findings and their Implications*, HMSO, p. 11.

100. *Ibid.*, p. 191.

101. *Ibid.*

102. Aldgate, J. (1977), *The Identification of Factors Influencing Children's Length of Stay in Care*, Ph.D., University of Edinburgh, also summarised in J. Triseliotis (ed), (1980), *New Developments in Foster Care and Adoption*, Routledge and Kegan Paul, pp. 22–40.

103. Colton, M. (1986), *op. cit.*

104. Aldgate, J. (1987), *op. cit.*, pp. 6 and 14 (MS).

105. *Ibid.*, p. 17.

106. Rowe, J., and Lambert, L. (1973), *Children Who Wait*, Association of British Adoption Agencies.

107. Fisher, M., *et al.* (1986), *op. cit.*, p. 84.

108. *Ibid.*, p. 90.

109. Berridge, D. and Cleaver, H. (1987), *op. cit.*, calculated from various sections.

110. *Ibid.*, p. 125.

111. Lasson, I. (1981), *Where's My Mum?* Pepar Publications.

112. Hall, D. and Stacey, M. (eds), (1979), *Beyond Separation*, Routledge and Kegan Paul, and Oswin, M. (1978), *Children Living in Long-Stay Hospitals*, Spastics International Medical Publications.

113. Millham, S., *et al.* (1986), *op. cit.*, p. 161.

114. *Ibid.*, p. 195.

115. Berry, J. (1975), *op. cit.*

116. Packman, J. (1986), *Who Needs Care? Social Work Decisions about Children*, Blackwell, p. 163.

117. Millham, S., *et al.* (1986), *op. cit.*

118. Colton, M. (1986), *op. cit.*

119. London Borough of Brent (1985), *A Child in Trust*, The Report of the Panel of Inquiry into the Circumstances Surrounding the Death of Jasmine Beckford.

120. Berridge, D. (1985), *op. cit.*, p. 93.

121. Millham, S., *et al.* (1986), *op. cit.*, p. 188.

122. Department of Health and Social Security (1986b), *op. cit.*, table 1.2, p. 63.

123. Parker, R. (1966), *op. cit.*, p. 61.

124. Trasler, G. (1976), *In Place of Parents*, Routledge and Kegan Paul, p. 220.

125. George, V. (1970), *Foster Care: Theory and Practice*, Routledge and Kegan Paul, pp. 86–7.

126. Rowe, J., *et al.* (1984), *Long-term Foster Care*, Batsford/British Agencies for Adoption and Fostering, pp. 95–6.

127. Triseliotis, J. (1980), 'Growing up in foster care and after', in Triseliotis, J. (ed) (1980), *op. cit.*, pp. 132 and 134.

128. Berridge, D. and Cleaver, H. (1987), *op. cit.*, pp. 81–82.

129. *Ibid.*

130. For instance, O'Neill, T. (1981), *A Place Called Hope*, Blackwell.

131. Berridge, D. (1985), *op. cit.*, p. 93.

132. Berridge, D. and Cleaver, H. (1987), *op. cit.*, pp. 72–3.

133. Whitaker, D. *et al.* (1985), *op. cit.*, p. 14.

134. Department of Education and Science (1980), *Community Homes with Education*, HMI series, no. 10, HMSO, p. 21.

135. Jackson, S. (1983), *The Education of Children in Care*, Report to the Social Science Research Council.

136. Department of Education and Science (1980), *op. cit.*

137. Berridge, D. (1985), *op. cit.*, p. 115.

138. *Ibid.*, p. 116.

139. See, for example, Towey, J. V. (1986), *Data Sheet*, Service Children's Education Authority. The total number of Boarding School Allowances being paid to servicemen in 1985 (59 per cent to officers) was 21,500.

140. Essen, J., Lambert, L. and Head, J. (1976), 'School attainment of children who have been in care', *Child Care, Health and Development*, 2, 6, pp. 339–351.

141. Stein, M. and Carey, K. (1986), *Leaving Care*, Blackwell, p. 45.

142. Triseliotis, J. and Russell, J. (1984), *Hard to Place*, Heinemann, p. 77.

143. *Ibid.*, p. 76.

144. Millham, S., *et al.* (1978), *Locking Up Children*, Saxon House, p. 117.

145. Cawson, P. (1986), *Long-Term Residential Care for Adolescents: An Analysis of Gaps in London Regional Provision*, London Boroughs Children's Regional Planning Committee, p. 34.

146. Millham, S., *et al.* (1978), *op. cit.*, p. 117.

147. Hazel, N. (1981), *A Bridge to Independence*, Blackwell, p. 109.

148. Parker, R. A. (ed), (1980), *Caring for Separated Children*, Macmillan, p. 142.

149. Department of Health and Social Security (1986b), *op. cit.*, p. 56.

150. *Ibid.*

151. Stein, M. and Carey, K. (1986), *op. cit.*, p. 52.

152. *Ibid.*, p. 54.

153. Department of Health and Social Security, annual statistics, *op. cit.*

154. Goble, J. and Lymbery, M. (1983), *Surviving the System*, Leicester Family Housing Association and CHAR.

155. Lupton, C. (1985), *Moving Out: Older Teenagers Leaving Residential Care*, Portsmouth Polytechnic Social Services Research and Intelligence Unit. Both this and the previous reference are more fully reviewed (together with other studies) in Cawson, P. (1986), 'Older teenagers in residential care', *Concern*, 60, Autumn, p. 11.

156. Department of Health and Social Security, annual statistics, *op. cit.*

157. Cawson, P. (1986), *op. cit.*, p. 30.

158. Triseliotis, J. and Russell, J. (1984), *op. cit.*, p. 112.

159. Triseliotis, J. (1980), *Growing Up in Foster Care and After*, Report to the Social Science Research Council.

160. Hazel, N. (1981), *op. cit.*, p. 117.

161. Department of Health and Social Security (1986b), *op. cit.*, p. 74.

162. Stein, M. and Carey, K. (1986), *op. cit.*, pp. 93–4.

163. Department of Employment (1980), *Gazette*, May, p. 140.

164. Department of Employment (1986), *Gazette*, August.

165. Department of Health and Social Security (1986b), *op. cit.*, p. 46.

166. Robinson, A. (1985), *Leaving Residential Care*, National Children's Bureau.

167. Tizard, J., *et al.* (1975), *op. cit.*

168. Tizard, J. (1975), 'The quality of residential care for retarded children', in Tizard, J., *et al.*, *op. cit.*

169. *Ibid.*, p. 60.

170. *Ibid.*, p. 64.

171. Sinclair, I. (1975), 'The influence of wardens and matrons on probation hostels', in Tizard, J., *et al.*, *op. cit.*

172. Berry, J. (1975), *op. cit.*, esp. p. 157.

173. Millham, S., *et al.* (1977), 'Absconding—part I', *The Community Homes Schools Gazette*, Oct., p. 287.

174. Clarke, R. V. G. and Martin, D. N. (1975), 'A study of absconding and its implications for the residential treatment of offenders', in Tizard, J., *et al.*, *op. cit.*

175. See Millham, S., Bullock, R., Hosie, K. and Haak, M. (1981), *Issues of Control in Residential Child Care*, HMSO.

176. Millham, S., Bullock, R. and Hosie, K. (1976), 'On violence in community homes', in Tutt, N. (ed), *Violence*, HMSO, pp. 126–165.

177. Cornish, D. B. and Clarke, R. V. G. (1975), *Residential Treatment and its Effects upon Delinquency*, Home Office Research Studies, HMSO.

178. Thornton, D., *et al.* (1984), *op. cit.*, p. 243.

179. Cornish, D. B. and Clarke, R. V. G. (1975), *op. cit.*, p. 38.

180. Bartak, L. and Rutter, M. (1975), 'The measurement of staff-child interaction in three units for autistic children', in Tizard, J., *et al.*, *op. cit.*, p. 196.

181. Millham, S., *et al.* (1975), *After Grace—Teeth*, Human Context Books, p. 85.

182. Dunlop, A. B. (1974), *op. cit.*

183. Colton, M. (1986), *op. cit.*

184. Triseliotis, J. and Russell, J. (1984), *op. cit.*

185. See, for example, Kahan, B. (1979), *Growing Up in Care*, Blackwell, and Loveday, S., (1985), *Reflections on Care*, The Children's Society.

186. Whitaker, D., *et al.* (1985), *op. cit.*

187. See Sinclair, R. (1984), *Decision Making in Statutory Reviews on Children in Care*, Gower.

Residential Care for Children and Adults with Mental Handicap

Dorothy Atkinson

Department of Health and Social Welfare
The Open University

CONTENTS

Residential Care for Children and
Adults with Mental Handicap

1 What is Residential Care?

'Residential care', in relation to people with mental handicap, has a short history. It may have a restricted future.

Until the 1960s, people with mental handicap mostly lived either at home with their families or in long-stay institutions. 'Residential care' in hostels evolved as an alternative to long term, or even life-long, 'care' in mental handicap hospitals. The hostels were, and are, part of the policy of 'community care'. Community care, in residential terms, meant the development of residential units on a smaller scale than the long-stay hospitals and located 'in the community'. Tyne[1] has argued that community care has suffered by being thus ''negatively defined'', a situation which led to ''mini-institutional'' services being developed in its name.

Residential care evolved from institutional care. Now the notion of residential care itself is challenged by the widespread adoption of the principle of 'normalisation'. Instead of residential care for people with mental handicap, a *residential service* is proposed. (See, for example, Towell[2,3] and Shearer[4]). A residential service aims to cater for the personal, social *and* accommodation needs of individual people.

Although new hostels are still being planned and built,[5,6] it could be that the present generation of purpose-built hostels is the last. There is a growing feeling that a buildings-based service is inflexible. The Independent Development Council,[7] for example, hold this view. Buildings quickly become dated as ideas about 'care' change. They are not easily dismantled, however, and although there may be fewer new hostels built in the future, it is likely that existing ones will be incorporated into any new residential service that emerges, with some changes made in their focus, philosophy and practices.

This paper looks at the whole spectrum of residential provision for people with mental handicap. This includes hostels, staffed and unstaffed group homes, ordinary housing and 'core-and-cluster' schemes.

[127]

2 Historical Background

The 1913 Mental Deficiency Act established a network of institutions, or 'colonies', for 'mental defectives' who were said to need 'institutional care'. This Act also required local authorities to provide training, occupation and supervision for those 'mental defectives' in their areas who continued to live with their families. The idea that many 'mentally defective' people could, with support, live outside large hospitals ('hospitals' since the 1948 National Health Service Act) was enshrined in the 1959 Mental Health Act. This Act encouraged local authorities to provide day services for people living with their families and residential care for those unable to do so who did not need hospital 'treatment'. Residential care took the form of accommodation provided in residential homes and hostels.

In practice the large hospitals continued to be the main providers of accommodation outside the family home. Local authorities developed some training facilities in the community and appointed Mental Welfare Officers to make routine visits to the family homes. A few residential homes, or hostels, appeared here and there. There was, however, no wholesale move from hospital care to community care.

In the 1960s, the long-stay hospitals became major news items. Two hospitals, Ely and Farleigh, attracted media attention following reports of staff misconduct. Pauline Morris' book, *Put Away*,[8] published in 1969, provided evidence of the poor conditions prevailing in the long-stay hospitals. It was against this background that the 1971 White Paper, *Better Services for the Mentally Handicapped*,[9] was published. A major aim of this document was to speed up 'the shift in emphasis from care in hospital to care in the community'.

The desirability of 'care in the community' has been stressed in subsequent policy statements. The 1980 Review of Services,[10] the 1981 *Care in Action*[11] guidelines and the 1981 Consultative Document, *Care in the Community*,[12] continued to press for an accelerated, and major, shift of emphasis from hospital to community care. The latter document begins with these words: 'Most people who need long-term care can and should be looked after in the community. This is what most of them want for themselves and what those responsible for their care believe to be best'. Two documents on *Care in the Community*,[13,14] issued in 1983, made adjustments in joint finance arrangements, eased the transfer of funds from health to local authorities and set aside £16 million for the development of innovative schemes to move people and residents into 'community care'.

The move from hospitals to 'community care' is finally on its way. It is a complicated move however. Residential care outside hospital is not the prerogative of local authorities. Health authority hostels, 'community units'[15] and 'locally based hospital units'[16] have grown-up alongside, and sometimes instead of, local authority homes and hostels. The House of Commons Social Services Committee Report, on *Community Care* (1985)[17] explains this involvement: 'The fundamental reason for the NHS becoming increasingly involved in community-based residential provision for mentally handicapped people is that they have the funds and local authorities do not'. Whilst acknowledging the current NHS involvement in providing residential care in the community, the Social Services Committee Report assumes that in the long-term this will be the responsibility of local authorities.

This picture of residential provision is incomplete. There is now a groundswell of opinion that seeks to replace traditional large and small 'institutions' and 'units' with ordinary housing. The idea that people with mental handicap could live in domestic housing, in local neighbourhoods, grew both from a practical and a philosophical base. On the practical front, local projects were using ordinary houses for their group homes and early reports were encouraging. (See, for example, Jones *et al*,[18] Gardham *et al*[19] Tyne,[20] Chant[21] and Race and Race[22]). At the same time, the principle of 'normalisation' (see Wolfensberger[23]), was becoming influential in people's thinking and practice.

Two recent reports have recommended ordinary housing as the accommodation of first choice for people with mental handicap. The Jay Committee Report (1979)[24] stressed that 'ordinary houses' were to be part of its model of care. The Social Services Committee Report (1985) commended the ordinary house as 'the living arrangement most likely to provide high quality care'.

3 The Consumers of Residential Care

Who are the consumers of residential care? They include people already living in some form of residential establishment, and others who may wish to, or need to, at some future date. Some live in hospitals, others in local authority homes and hostels, and a smaller number live in voluntary and private homes.

Most of them live at home with their families. What is their future? The increase in day centre places and, latterly, the growth of short term care provisions has enabled many people with mental handicap to stay in the family home not only into adulthood but also into middle age and beyond. An often-voiced anxiety of parents, especially ageing parents, is 'What will happen after I'm gone?'[25] The fear is placement, or misplacement, of their son or daughter, during a crisis, in a residential situation which is unfamiliar and unwelcoming. Surveys in Devon,[26] Somerset[27] and Lambeth[28] confirmed that many adults now living with ageing, ill or frail parents were 'at risk' of sudden admission to residential care at a time of family crisis.

(i)   **PRESENT CONSUMERS**

- HOSPITALS AND NHS UNITS

   In 1985, 36,300 people were living in mental handicap hospitals and units in England.[29] This figure includes 2,079 people living in small NHS units in the community.

- LOCAL AUTHORITY HOMES AND HOSTELS

   In 1984, 14,346 people were living in local authority homes and hostels.[30]

- VOLUNTARY AND PRIVATE HOMES

   In 1984, 4,200 people were living in voluntary and private homes.

(ii) **FUTURE CONSUMERS**

   There are four trends which may help shape the level of future demand for residential care:

- the rundown, and closure, of hospitals and the relocation of people in alternative residential care;

- the growth of short-term care in residential units of all kinds;

- the development of the 'right to leave home' for adults with mental handicap.

- the admission into residential settings of adults following the illness or death of an elderly parent.

- HOSPITAL RESIDENTS

   There has already been a reduction in the number of people living in hospitals, from 56,000 in 1969 to 36,000 in 1985. Current hospital residents are all at least potential consumers of alternative residential care.

- SHORT-TERM CARE

   Most children, and many adults, live with their families. How many of these will become consumers of residential care in the future? There has been an increase in the demand for *short-term care* in recent years and this may continue to be a growth area in the residential field. This may reduce, or delay, *long-term* admissions to residential care.

   In the case of hospitals, this trend is already noticeable. Alongside the reduction in the number of residents, and the reduction of people admitted for long-term care, is a large increase in short-term admissions. In 1984, 35,000 people were admitted to hospitals and units; of these, 33,600 were re-admissions or people admitted on a short-term basis.[31]

   Local authorities are also providing a variety of short term care schemes both in hostels and with families. Again this trend may slow down requests for *long-term* care.

- LEAVING HOME

  The Jay Report (1979) states: 'Any mentally handicapped adult who wishes to leave his or her parental home should have the opportunity to do so'. The All-Wales Strategy[32] likewise looks to a time when those people with mental handicap who wish to leave home are given the support to do so. The Independent Development Council[33] echoes this point. How many people will seek this option remains to be seen. It is, however a possible source of future demand for residential accommodation.

- CRISIS ADMISSIONS

  The growth of day services and short term care have enabled many people with mental handicap to stay in the family home. Residential alternatives to home, especially the long-stay hospitals, have often been unacceptable to parents; to such an extent that many have opted to 'live for the present'.[34] There is now an accumulation of adults, some middle-aged, with ageing and elderly parents, whose futures are still unplanned and uncertain, and who are at risk of being admitted to a residential setting during a major family and personal crisis.[35]

4 Patterns of Residential Care

The following categories of residential provision will be reviewed in this paper:

- residential accommodation for children
- hostels
- group homes
- ordinary housing
- residential accommodation for people with 'special needs'
- private and voluntary homes.

This is an artificial distinction and there is considerable overlap between categories. For example, the early history of residential accommodation for children was very much to do with the development of hostels. The recent history of projects for people with profound handicaps and challenging behaviour involves the use of ordinary housing. And 'group homes' are usually 'ordinary houses' too!

i Residential Accommodation for Children

The 1948 Children Act established 'a new pattern of care for most children'.[36] However, it excluded children with mental handicap who were unable to live with their families. These children were seen as needing 'treatment' in long-stay institutions. In 1969, 7,400 children were living in mental handicap hospitals. The 1971 White Paper envisaged that by 1990 this number would be reduced to 6,400. In fact, the fall in numbers has been dramatic and in 1984 only 1,117 children (Hansard, October 1985) lived in mental handicap hospitals and units in England and Wales. Some of the fall in numbers is attributed to the natural ageing process and the reclassification of 'children' to 'adults' at the age of 16. The growth of alternative residential provision for children has, however, also played a significant part, and now has an established history.

An early initiative in providing alternative care for children in hospital was the 'Brooklands experiment' in the 1950s. Sixteen children with severe mental handicap, living in Fountain Hospital, were placed by Jack Tizard in an ordinary house. The regime was based on the Home Office's 1955 guidance for residential nurseries, which stressed education and care. The children's personal and social skills improved in their first year and, over two years, Tizard[37] found they developed favourably compared with similar children who remained in hospital.

A further impetus was provided by the work of King, Raynes and Tizard[38] who distinguished 'resident-oriented' care practices from the 'institution-oriented' practices found in hospitals. Institution-oriented practices included block treatment, rigidity of routine, social distance and depersonalisation. In the 1960s and 1970s, the Wessex Regional Hospital Board (now Health Authority) began to develop small units situated in residential communities. These 'locally based hospital units' were, according to Felce *et al*,[39] designed to avoid the negative characteristics itemised by King *et al*. They were, at the time, considered small with 20–25 beds. They allowed staff a degree of autonomy in their work, and were located within easy reach of community facilities. The units themselves were 'designed to imitate ordinary housing' with rooms of domestic size and scale.

Comparisons were made with the quality of care provided in hospitals, along a series of dimensions: client progress,[40] level of client engagement in activity,[41] contact with family,[42] social interaction with staff and staff performance.[43] The results, according to Felce, Kushlick and Smith,[44] were unequivocal; 'superior outcomes were achieved (in the small units) at no greater revenue cost'.

In Sheffield, in the 1970s, specially designed purpose-built hostels were planned and developed as part of the Sheffield Development Project. They were to be provided by both health and local authorities although, in practice, the health authority moved much more quickly towards its target number of places. The model was the 24-place hostel, with children accommodated in 'family groups' of eight children. In her evaluation of these units Dalgleish[45] noted problems with hostel and group size, as well as with design and physical features. The director of the Evaluation Research Group in Sheffield, Alistair Heron, suggests that this 'marked preoccupation with buildings' led to the provision of 'purpose-built miniature institutions'.[46] The lack of any underlying philosophy meant that the children lived in hostels, and *not* in the community.

The provision of residential accommodation for children, in the 1970s, proceeded along two routes; 'special' provision continued to be made, especially for children living in hospitals, but at the same time local authorities and voluntary agencies began to include children with mental handicap into their mainstream child care provisions. Two well-known examples of 'special' homes, catering mostly for children coming out of hospitals, are the Barnardo's Skelmersdale project (described by Kendall[47]) and the Northumberland Health Authority houses in Ashington (reported by Thomas[48]). The Skelmersdale project began in 1976 when Barnardo's rented two houses and began providing accommodation for six children. In 1981, five children moved from Northgate Hospital to live in a rented council house in Ashington.

In the mid 1970s an adoption agency called Parents for Children began finding adoptive parents for children with special needs. Other adoption agencies, including Barnardo's, have also found homes for children with mental handicap. (An account of this work is given by Macaskill[49]). Successful fostering of handicapped children is now well established, and Shearer[50] cites some pioneering work carried out in Camden, Barnardo's North West division, Leeds and Coventry. Ordinary children's homes are used too; Camden and Barnardo's (North West) pioneered this approach to making mainstream child care facilities available to children with handicaps, and many local authority social service departments have followed suit.

These developments reflected the thinking of the 1970s. The Court Report (1976)[51] commented: 'severely mentally handicapped children have more in common with other children because of their childhood than they do with severely mentally handicapped adults because of their common disability'. This view was echoed by the National Development Group in 1977[52]: 'these children are children first and mentally handicapped second'. Oswin's book, *Children Living in Long Stay Hospitals*[53] published in 1978, advocated the adoption of a child care policy for children currently living lives of deprivation and neglect on hospital wards. The Jay Report (1979) described mental handicap hospitals as 'quite unacceptable' places for children, and recommended that substitute family homes should, wherever possible, be found for children unable to live with their families.

The parallel development of 'special' and 'integrated' residential services for children have been mirrored in the provision of short term care facilities. The effects of placing children, especially very young ones, in hospitals and large hostels have been researched and reported by Oswin. The 'strange environment and multiplicity of carers'[54] are factors additional to the inherent emotional effect of separation from family. By way of contrast, family support schemes were operating in 50 local authorities in 1983. These schemes are 'child orientated' rather than providing a 'separation service'.[55] Consequently they are more likely to be local, flexible and based on close relationships between the child and support family, and between parents and substitute parents.

ii Hostels

The typical purpose-built hostels, homes and community units have, according to the Social Services Committee Report (1985), several disadvantages: 'They cannot be said to be a "natural" domestic setting, nor to merge unobtrusively into the surrounding community. Their high visibility may exacerbate local resistance.' Their 'institutional feel' made them 'a pale reflection of hospital wards, transplanted almost intact to the community'.

Hostels are the main providers of 'residential care' for people with mental handicap. They fulfil the functions, spelled out in the Bonnington Report,[56] of providing living space for people at crisis point, offering time-limited programmes of training-for-independence and providing an alternative long-term home life. As hostels most closely resemble the accepted concept of residential care, a detailed account of them, along a series of key dimensions, is provided below. These dimensions are:

- Size and scale
- Physical appearance
- Internal arrangement
- Care practices
- Aims and objectives
- Client progress
- Community acceptance
- Opportunities for integration.
- SIZE AND SCALE
  The 1971 White Paper preferred the term 'home' to 'hostel' as it better conveyed the homeliness, domesticity and family size of the residence it envisaged. Such a home would cater for up to 25 adults, and would provide permanent places for them. Single rooms were

recommended so that adults could enjoy privacy, and homes should have access to local facilities. The 24- or 25-bed hostel, described in the White Paper, became the preferred model in the buildings-approach to residential care.

The Sheffield Development Project explicitly set out to put these proposals into practice on a large scale, with a variety of new purpose-built accommodation. The overall size of the hostels meant that the resident groups were also large. In her detailed study Dalgleish[57] also found there were difficulties in enabling a group identity to form, as units were linked and dining facilities shared.

- PHYSICAL APPEARANCE

One consequence of a building which is larger, newer and otherwise different from neighbouring homes is that it is conspicuous.

Neighbours draw conclusions about the people who live there, whose 'special needs' have led to the creation of a 'special' building. Dalgleish[58] reports how a purpose-built hostel with unusual features drew unfavourable comments from neighbours: 'I thought, it's a funny house having windows like that . . . until I found out what it was and then I thought, well, probably they have to have kind of windows like that . . .'

Brandon and Ridley[59] describe Hornby House: 'Both in style and size it looks very different from the rest of the neighbourhood with a bronze plaque on its outside wall marking the opening ceremony by a local dignitary, and the extensive parking space in front of the building.' Tyne[60] describes Primrose Lodge: 'The hostel is a large, new building at the edge of a housing-estate some 10–20 years old . . . A large notice says only "Primrose Lodge (Blankshire Social Services)". A large, formal garden separates the hostel from the pavement. The front door has a sign "Visitors please ring the bell", and inside it "Office" is clearly seen.'

- INTERNAL ARRANGEMENT

The 1971 White Paper envisaged the hostel as 'home' to its residents; a permanent home. Yet the typical hostel incorporated many of the familiar features of hospital life, both physically with its corridors, 'day-room' (lounge) and out-of-bounds kitchen, and organisationally with its employment of separate domestic and catering staff, and its engagement of residential staff to work shifts and 'long days'. (See, for example, Dalgleish[61] and Gunzburg[62]).

Many features were, however, deliberately different from hospitals. The latter had been criticised for being over-crowded, with people having no personal space or privacy. The new hostels provided single rooms in a light, bright, modern environment. Providing individual space, it was assumed, would lead to people expressing their individuality. This, as Gunzburg points out,[63] may not be enough. Private space is not the same as 'a personalised space which has been moulded, furnished and adorned to spell laughter and fun'. If no thought is given 'to loneliness, to anxiousness and lack of human closeness' then that prized single room all too easily becomes 'an isolating cell'.

- CARE PRACTICES
  The physical features of a hostel can help determine care practices. Dalgleish,[64] in her Sheffield study, commented: 'The impression gained is that perhaps the single most important factor in creating a domestic environment is the relationship of the kitchen to the unit'. A central large kitchen, with heavy-duty equipment, is not for use by residents. Indeed, special catering staff are employed to cook for residents and residential staff. This leads to lack of opportunities for learning and experiencing everyday domestic activities: 'the smell of burnt toast; the crackling noise of fying; the feel of sharp edges, pointed gadgets, smooth tiles, rough rendering . . '[65] More importantly, it rules out a major area of everyday living which residents and staff could experience *together*. The spin-offs of close daily 'doing' and 'teaching' sessions are several, according to Tyne;[66] improvements in skills, confidence, engagement and interaction.

  The size and scale of the typical hostel mean that a daily routine is necessary for residential workers, domestic and catering staff, and residents. A routine requires careful timetabling of events and the movement of groups at predetermined intervals. King *et al*[67] posed some key questions about 'resident-oriented' practices. Is the hostel regime flexible? Does it promote individuality? How close are staff and residents? Some accounts of hostel living suggest that even with 'warm and caring' staff (Brandon and Ridley[68]) daily life may easily become routinized (Coulter[69]).

- AIMS AND OBJECTIVES
  What are hostels for? Are they to provide a homely domestic environment for people to live in? Are they training units, acting as stepping stones to greater independence? Are they there to provide short term care for large numbers of people?

  Hostels have evolved over the years. The 1971 White Paper saw them as 'homes' for people. Many started out that way. In time their residents, with 'mild' or 'moderate' handicaps, were able to move on as the establishments developed an additional training function. The through-put of residents has enabled another function to emerge: the use of spare beds for short term care.

  A hostel may be involved in all three functions; providing a long-term home for some residents, running a training regime for a few people and offering short breaks to others. The lack of clarity about objectives, and uncertainty about functions, can lead to staff depression, according to Anderson.[70] The belief, on the part of staff, that the hostel is the resident's home can obscure or jeopardise the added, or imposed, training function (Mittler and Serpell[71]).

- CLIENT PROGRESS

  Some evaluative studies of hostels have suggested a 'good client outcome'. People's skills improve. For example, in a study of hostel care Locker *et al*[72] found that residents improved significantly in the following areas: self help, communication, socialisation and occupation.

  Other 'client outcomes' are dealt with elsewhere in this paper; in the sections on children, ordinary housing and people with special needs. Otherwise, as Mittler and Serpell[73] observe, 'remarkably few hard data exist to evaluate the work of hostels and their impact on residents'.

- COMMUNITY ACCEPTANCE

  Locker *et al* carried out two surveys of neighbourhood opinion: (i) two months before a hostel opened[74] and (ii) two years later.[75] In the two year period between studies the number of people with no objections to the hostel rose from 60 per cent to 90 per cent. Was this a sign of community acceptance? Or indifference? There was little contact between local people and the hostel residents, and few neighbours had ever visited.

  A similar acceptance-without-involvement was described by Tyne[76]: 'Broadgate is known and accepted in the neighbourhood, although there is minimum integration with local community life.' Similarly, Brandon and Ridley's interviews[77] with neighbours of Hornby House indicated that people regarded the hostel residents as 'no trouble' but had little actual contact with them.

- OPPORTUNITIES FOR INTEGRATION

  Siting a building 'in the community' does not itself promote integration, a point made by Dalgleish *et al*[78]: 'In the development of new residential provision in Sheffield the assumption seems to have been that smaller, more physically homelike units would in *themselves* promote a life in the community'. This was not the case; other considerations were necessary before *involvement* in community life became possible. There may be more *access* to community facilities for hostels appropriately sited, but this does not in itself mean that residents become integrated in their neighbourhood, a point made by Raynes.[79] She comments: 'Part of living in the community implies other ways of ending segregation, apart from using locally-available amenities.'

  It is the degree to which hostels are able to promote the integration of their residents into the community that has evoked criticism. Mittler and Serpell[80] observed that 'many hostels are too institutionalised in their regimes and by definition are unnecessarily segregated from the mainstream of community activities and provision'. Tyne[81] comments from his study of hostels: 'Contacts with "the community" tended to be formal and organised in many ways. The residents were invited *out*—to clubs, concerts and entertainments; and "the community" came *in*—to the annual garden-fete, or as "volunteers" on a regular basis, or as occasional groups for a show or a party.' Parker and Alcoe[82] point to the difficulties of hostel residents becoming integrated: 'The number of residents is, in any case, too large for them to be absorbed by, and integrated into, the neighbourhood.'

iii Group Homes

Are group homes part of 'residential care'? In the sense that group homes provide accommodation and need some staffing input then they are part of a broad spectrum of residential care. Some group homes are 'satellites' to their parent hostels, with residents looking to residential staff for continuing help and support. Satellite group homes are thus part of residential care in its widest sense.

In their traditional form, group homes provided early examples of small-scale domestic living for groups of fairly able people who needed only domiciliary support. Guidance about acquiring property, training clients, making links with the local neighbourhood and giving appropriate help and support to residents is provided by Gathercole.[83] Advice about obtaining property and managing group homes is given by Heginbotham.[84,85]

There are now several published studies of group homes in operation, and the lives and lifestyles of people who live in them. The Cherries Group Home was designed and established in the early 1970s, providing accommodation for 12 adults. The difficulty of getting 12 people to live together 'in harmony' was a major problem; Race and Race[86] describe the formation of subgroups and the occurrence of leadership clashes. Group homes have reduced in size over the years, with four people now widely regarded as the maximum number. The tensions and conflict of small group living have been charted by Tyne,[87] Atkinson[88] and Malin[89]. Factors promoting 'group harmony'[90] and the 'right mix of personalities'[91] are important, but remain elusive.

A small group of people living in an ordinary domestic house would seem better placed than hostel residents to become integrated into local neighbourhoods. This has not always been borne out in practice. Malin,[92] for example, found that group home residents in Sheffield looked for support from official networks rather than informal sources. A similar point is made by the present author in relation to group homes in Somerset[93]: 'A designated group home, situated in an ordinary street may, at best, draw minimal neighbourly kindness but, at worst, may draw negative reactions, from the teasing of children to actual hostility or fear. Otherwise a casual indifference may prevail, as the group is perceived as being in receipt of special support and not in need of neighbourhood kindness.' This aspect of group life remains a major challenge for the support staff involved and it may be that the more 'interventionist' approach, described by Atkinson and Ward,[94] is needed to promote social contacts.

A *staffed* group home is described by Gathercole[95] as: 'an ordinary, domestic scale house in which not more than five or six people who are mentally handicapped live together, cared for by a number of paid staff.' People who can benefit from small-scale domestic living with resident staff include those with severe, profound and multiple handicaps. Three published evaluative studies of staffed group homes, by Evans *et al*,[96] Thomas[97] and Firth,[98] show that group home living can be beneficial in terms of client progress, engagement and opportunities for integration. The people in the three studies came from hospitals. Their new environments, in practice, led to increased levels of interaction between staff and clients; a wider range of activities both at home and outside; increased family contact; contact with local people; and increased choices and new skills.

A special sort of group home is the co-residence, a house shared by students and people with mental handicap. The earliest reported project was the co-residence set up by the Cardiff University Social Service Group in 1974 (described by James[99]) though other similar schemes have since been established elsewhere, for example in Derbyshire (an account of this is given by Malin[100]). The combination of a supportive environment and contact with, and help from, co-tenants has meant little input from staff other than a visiting social worker.

iv **Ordinary Housing**
Staffed and unstaffed group homes, and co-residences, are examples of the use of ordinary housing. They have tended to appear in a piecemeal fashion, in response to local needs and opportunities. These small scale projects are now widespread and they have done much to convince planners and service providers that living in ordinary domestic housing can be beneficial to clients. Ordinary houses avoid the more obvious pitfalls outlined in the discussion above about hostels. They are, by definition, domestic and homelike, and are part of ordinary streets and neighbourhoods. They have a positive function too; they provide access to the community, with opportunities for contact with local people.

Current interest in ordinary housing comes from a theoretical, or philosophical, basis as well as from reports of practical examples. The 'principle of normalisation' has gained widespread support since its earliest conceptualisation in the late 1960s. It combines a *set of values* about the rights of people with mental handicap to enjoy a valued lifestyle, with a *design of services* which promote opportunities for developing reciprocal relationships with others and becoming integrated into wider society. Wolfensberger, one of the earliest and best known proponents of normalisation, has recently suggested[101]: 'The most explicit and highest goal of normalisation must be the creation, support and defence of valued social roles for people who are at risk of social devaluation.'

Normalisation is very much about providing opportunities for people to lead socially valued lives and thereby become valued themselves. Living in an ordinary house is a first step in this process. Many recent, and influential, documents stress this requirement. For example, the Jay Report (1979) and the Social Services Committee Report (1985) advocate the use of ordinary houses. The government's response[102] to the Social Services Committee Report made this point: 'The importance for mentally handicapped people of ordinary housing in the wider community is fully recognised.'

The King's Fund Project Paper, *An Ordinary Life*,[103] appeared in 1980. It drew on the experience of the Eastern Nebraska Community Office of Retardation (ENCOR) in establishing guidelines for a comprehensive locally-based residential service. This took the form of a 'core-and-cluster' system: a 'core' unit supporting a dispersed network of 'cluster' homes. These ideas have been written into detailed local plans, for example the Guy's Health District plan,[104] which envisaged a range of ordinary houses supported by flexibly deployed staff, providing a 'client-centred' residential service. There are other examples too; the Wells Road service in Bristol,[105, 106] Preston 'Integrate', Cardiff's Nimrod Scheme[107] and Barnardo's Skelmersdale project[108] (in its later development).

Many practitioners, planners and researchers have attended Normalisation Workshops, Ordinary Living Workshops,[109] PASS[110] (Program Analysis of Service Systems) or PASSING[111] (Program Analysis of Service Systems Implementations of Normalisation Goals) Workshops. The extent of the interest and involvement in the principle of normalisation, and its practical application, has led Russell[112] to suggest that services in most parts of the country have been influenced to some extent.

Core-and-cluster schemes, and other variations of dispersed ordinary housing projects, have implications for the training, deployment and support of the residential staff involved. As experience is gained in the field, so guidance is beginning to appear in the literature about some of the key staffing issues. For example, Mansell and Porterfield, Ward, Tyne, Mathieson *et al* and Porterfield have produced advice on the following areas of interest:

- selection and organisation of staff[113]
- initial training[114]
- home-making skills[115]
- defining tasks[116]
- staff support[117]
- in-service training[118]
- positive monitoring[119]
- training of service designers[120]

'Open learning' materials can provide cost-effective training to large numbers of staff. The Open University course, *Mental Handicap: Patterns for Living*,[121] is a comprehensive set of learning materials designed to meet the training and support needs of unqualified staff, volunteers and others, especially people already working in community settings and those preparing to do so.

v **Residential Accommodation for Adults with 'Special Needs'**
The split service between health and local authorities has its origins in the 1971 White Paper's assumption that hospitals should continue to provide specialist skills, assessment, treatment and hospital care. The 1978 National Development Group Report (*Helping Mentally Handicapped People in Hospital*)[122] supported this notion, expressing the view that some people with additional severe disabilities and impairments, and those with multiple handicaps, would continue to need specialist hospital services and treatment. The Jay Report (1979) moved away from this view, however, suggesting that people with special needs did *not* need specialist hospital services and treatment. The Committee did concede, though, that its model of care 'would encompass the possibility of some small specialised residential accommodation' for the small number of people with special needs.

The 1984 DHSS Study Team Report (*Helping Mentally Handicapped People with Special Problems*)[123] comments: 'Experiments in providing a more normal domestic environment for mentally handicapped people have shown that it is possible to look after even former long-stay severely mentally handicapped clients in ordinary houses which can be rented or bought and adapted to meet the needs of those with restricted mobility.' The Team concedes, however, that people with severely restricted mobility or who otherwise have a high degree of dependency may need a small purpose-built residential unit.

Do people with special needs require hospital treatment? Or 'special care' in units run by health authorities? The Development Team[124] recommended the 'community unit' as a local residential and treatment resource for people with special needs. The unit would provide a residential service, offering long-, medium- and short-term placements, as well as providing a local base for personnel and resources. Some areas, for example the West Midlands Regional Health Authority,[125] have made extensive plans for setting up community units in local areas.

Some health authorities have sought other ways to meet the needs of people with severe, profound and multiple handicaps, and those with difficult behaviour. In Wessex, some early experimental schemes involved adults with severe handicaps living in health authority hostels, or 'locally based hospital units'. Early success in terms of the progress made by residents and the improved quality of their care (reported by Felce *et al*[126]), has led to the use of ordinary houses for people with special needs. This was not the only departure from tradition. Domestic and catering staff were no longer appointed, and 'all staff are care staff' (Felce *et al*[127]).

A study by Thomas *et al*,[128] of adults with severe and profound handicaps living in two small homes (five in each) in the community, showed increased levels of client engagement in activity and staff inter-action, when compared with residents in larger units and institutions. Felce *et al*[129] found that 'the materially enriched environments' of the ordinary houses, when compared with institutional settings, also had a beneficial effect on residents, with people having opportunities for example, to join in household and domestic activities. De Kock *et al*[130] reported other beneficial effects; clients in the ordinary houses used community amenities more than their peers elsewhere, and experienced greater family contact. People in the shops, bars and cafes visited most frequently by clients were also interviewed. Felce[131] reports that there seemed to be acceptance both of the frequency of visits *and* people's appearance and behaviour. Most respondents (97.4 per cent) felt the individuals concerned benefited from community involvement.

A study, by Evans *et al*,[132] of a group of five people showing 'problem behaviour' in a staffed house in Cardiff, has also produced encouraging results. The authors commented: 'The findings of this preliminary study add to the growing body of literature which shows that severely mentally handicapped people with problem behaviours can be accommodated in small community settings.' There are, how-ever, implications for the training and support of staff in managing these problem behaviours.

In a comparative study of residential provision for people with severe or profound handicaps, Rawlings[133, 134] found that the small residential homes had features not found in the hospital wards. The small homes had better staff ratios, more staff autonomy, resident-orientated care practices, occupational and leisure pursuits, and more client engagement in simple constructive activities.

The Guy's Health District Plan[135] aimed to cater for all people regardless of handicap. This meant confronting the issue of what to do with people who showed difficult or disruptive behaviour. The solution was to provide 'massive levels of staff' to meet these demands. Any individual's behaviour which proved quite intolerable would live, not with other clients, but with full-time staff. The Social Services Committee Report (1985) echoed this view: 'with sufficient resources available to provide, for example, one-to-one staffing where that is necessary, it has been amply demonstrated that severely handicapped people can be properly cared for in some ordinary domestic surroundings'.

vi **Private and Voluntary Homes**
The Social Services Committee Report (1985) views the sheltered village type communities (for example, Association of Residential Communities for the Retarded (ARC) and Rudolph Steiner settlements) as selective and segregationist, but notes that they hold some appeal for parents. The Independent Development Council[136] notes that *voluntary homes* may be high quality, flexible and innovative but are not necessarily so, and in *private homes*, the level and quality of services is based on the profit motive rather than on considerations of need.

The MENCAP Homes Foundation is based on ordinary houses and the home-making skills of staff. (See reports by Capewell[137] and Murray[138]). The aim of the Foundation is 'to provide permanent homes with appropriate care, in small local units, preferably in ordinary housing, within easy reach of public transport, shops and other community facilities'.[139] L'Arche is also involved in developing small local housing projects for people with mental handicap. The L'Arche message is that the most important part of care is 'to have a relationship with handicapped people and allow them to reciprocate, and housing that allows that to happen should be encouraged' (CEH Seminar Report[140]).

5 A Residential Service

Towell[141] has stated: 'The aim of a residential service is to provide a home and home-life for people who cannot find these independently'. What are the elements of a residential service? They include:

 i Consumer views

 ii Individual programme plans (IPPs)

 iii Friendship

 iv Staff

v Opportunities for integration

vi Daytime and leisure opportunities

vii Quality assurance

i Consumer Views

People's 'rights' to make choices about where and how they live, and how they spend their time, are widely acknowledged (for example in the 1971 United Nations Declaration of Rights[142]; the Jay Report, 1979; the King's Fund Project Paper, *An Ordinary Life*; the Guy's Health District Report; and the Campaign for People with Mental Handicaps' Report, *Hope for the Future*.) But how are people to find their voice in expressing these choices? This remains, according to Carle[143] and others, a special challenge for staff. Meanwhile some consumers have spoken out about their experiences in hospitals, hostels and 'in the community', sometimes with a critical voice (quoted by Wertheimer[144]).

ii Individual Programme Plans (IPPs)

IPPs ensure individuality. The involvement of the consumer, family and staff in making, and carrying out, plans helps make services become client-centred. (For more details about IPPs see Blunden[145]). The concept of Individual Programme Planning has been refined and developed by Brechin and Swain into the Shared Action Plan.[146]

iii Friendship

A residential service is not just about accommodation, it is about relationships. Shearer[147] notes how important it is for people 'to make links of friendship' within and beyond their homes. A study of people living in Somerset (reported by Atkinson and Ward[148]) found: 'the quality of their lives was, to a great extent, determined by the range, and type, of their social relationships'. Of special importance was the friend or companion; someone to go out and about with.

iv Staff

Tyne[149] and Towell[150] suggest that 'home-making' staff are needed at the frontline of services. Local people bring special advantages, according to Thomas[151] and Firth[152], in helping residents slot in to their own existing family and neighbourhood networks.

v Opportunities for Integration

Local staff can provide opportunities for making contact with local people. Otherwise the 'interventionist' approach used in the Wells Road service (reported by Atkinson and Ward[153]) can help extend people's social contacts.

vi Daytime and leisure opportunities

The Independent Development Council pamphlet, *Next Steps*, suggests that accommodation is only one element in a 'package' of services for people with mental handicap. Individuals also need access to day-time and leisure opportunities. Some of these may be provided by existing day services, but more innovative schemes using colleges, work placements and other community provisions may involve residential staff in planning, initial introductions and ongoing support. (See reports by MENCAP[154] and the IDC[155] and an account by Shearer[156].)

vii Quality assurance

How are high quality services established and maintained? Towell[157] suggests that positive monitoring of staff can help, and that external monitoring (for example, using the PASS evaluation) is beneficial. Mittler[158] suggests the IPP can also be a tool for a continuous review of services. The Independent Development Council[159] suggests that staff, consumers, families and others form local Quality Action Groups to monitor and review the quality of services.

6 A Residential Service for the Future

In many areas, both health and local authorities are involved in providing residential accommodation in the community. This is seen by some bodies as a transitional arrangement, which has come about for reasons of history, tradition, organisation and financial structures. The parallel provision may continue in the short to medium term but then it is envisaged that local authorities will take on overall responsibility for providing residential accommodation for people with mental handicap. This view is expressed by the Social Services Committee Report (1985) and the Independent Development Council in *Next Steps*.

In a few areas, attempts have been made to set up *comprehensive* local services. Two examples are the NIMROD project in Cardiff, set up in 1981, and the Wells Road service, established in 1983. Both projects are being systematically evaluated. The NIMROD project (see Mathieson and Blunden,[160] Mathieson[161] and Evans *et al*[162]) serves all people with mental handicap and their families within a total population of 60,000. Key features of the project include individual programme plans for all clients, the use of ordinary houses, positive monitoring of staff and the adoption of quality control procedures (described further by Blunden[163]). It is run jointly by the health and local authorities, with some additional funding from the Welsh Office. It is assumed that the local authority will take over the services at the end of the seven year evaluation of the project.

The Wells Road service aims to provide a comprehensive residential service for individuals and families in an area of Bristol with a total population of 35,000. It was set up as a 'core-and-cluster' scheme which aimed, in time, to provide a wide range of residential options including group homes, family placements, independent bedsits or flats, supported lodgings, staffed houses and co-residences. The service is being systematically evaluated as it develops. (See reports by Ward[164, 165, 166]). Key features include the IPP, use of ordinary houses and positive monitoring of staff. This residential service was set up by the health authority, but it is anticipated that it will be transferred to the local authority.

The All-Wales Strategy (Welsh Office, 1983) provides guidelines for new patterns of comprehensive community-based services. The strategy is based on identifying individual needs and meeting these needs with services rather than buildings. It aims to provide a 'people-centred' service. The main responsibility for developing the new services lies with local authorities.

Both the *parallel provisions* model and the *comprehensive local service* model look set to become the responsibility of local authorities in due course. This development has implications for the organisation of local services, and the training and deployment of staff. There are some known, and a few *unknown*, factors to be considered when thinking about the future provision of residential accommodation:

(*i*) **Known Factors**
- Residential accommodation will be needed for the *full range* of clients including those currently living in hospitals and health authority units.

- Residential accommodation, or supported housing, will be needed for people with mental handicap now living in their family homes.

- The move towards ordinary housing raises questions about new and innovative uses of existing hostels.

- Care is needed to identify and meet the *training and support* needs of staff working in dispersed small units.

- The inclusion in residential services of clients with profound or multiple handicaps, or challenging behaviour, has implications for the training and deployment of staff.

- The provision of *short term care* for people of all abilities, including those with special needs, also has implications for residential staff.

(*ii*) **Unknown Factors**
- What accommodation is to be provided for the thousand or so children still living in hospital? Will they be offered places in

'special' local authority homes or will they be absorbed in mainstream children's accommodation?

- Some provisions for children (with substitute families) and adults (in family placements—see Gathercole[167] and Penrose[168]) are residential solutions not requiring residential staff. How many people might be involved?

- How fast will the voluntary sector and, in particular, the private sector grow in this field?

- How many people already in the community are 'lost' from records or 'forgotten' by statutory services but who will, one day, need a residential service?

There may be little future for *'residential care'*, in its traditional sense, for people with mental handicap but there is considerable scope for an expanding and innovative *'residential service'*.

Notes and References

1. Tyne, A. (1982), 'Community care and mentally handicapped people', in Walker, A. (ed), *Community Care: The Family, the State and Social Policy*, Basil Blackwell.

2. Towell, D. (1984), *Developing Community Based Residential Services for People with Mental Handicap*, King's Fund Centre.

3. Towell, D. (1985), 'Residential needs and services' in Craft, M., Bicknell, J. and Hollins, S. (eds), *Mental Handicap: A Multi-Disciplinary Approach*, Balliere Tindall.

4. Shearer, A. (1986), *Building Community with People with Mental Handicaps, their Families and Friends*, Campaign for People with Mental Handicaps and King Edward's Hospital Fund for London.

5. Campaign for People with Mental Handicaps (1984), *Hope for the Future?* CMH.

6. House of Commons (1985), *Second Report from the Social Services Committee, Session 1984–85. Community Care with Special Reference to Adult Mentally Ill and Mentally Handicapped People*, Vol. 1, HMSO.

7. Independent Development Council for People with Mental Handicap (1982), *Elements of a Comprehensive Local Service for People with Mental Handicap*, Independent Development Council.

8. Morris, P. (1969), *Put Away: A Sociological Study of Institutions for the Mentally Retarded*, Routledge and Kegan Paul.

9. Department of Health and Social Security (1971), *Better Services for the Mentally Handicapped*, Cmnd. 4683, HMSO.

10. Department of Health and Social Security (1980), *Mental Handicap: Progress, Problems and Priorities. A Review of Mental Handicap Services in England since the 1971 White Paper*, HMSO.

11. Department of Health and Social Security (1981), *Care in Action. A Handbook of Policies and Priorities for the Health and Personal Social Services in England*, HMSO.

12. Department of Health and Social Security (1981), *Care in the Community. A Consultative Document on Moving Resources for Care in England*, HMSO.

13. Department of Health and Social Security (1983), *Care in the Community and Joint Finance*, Circular HC (83) 6, HMSO.

14. Department of Health and Social Security (1985), *Care in the Community: Follow-up*, Annexe HC (83) 6, HMSO.

15. Development Team for the Mentally Handicapped, *First Report, 1976– 1977; Second Report, 1978–1979*, HMSO.

16. Felce, D., Kushlick, A. and Smith, J. (1980), 'An overview of the research on alternative residential facilities for the severely mentally handicapped in Wessex', *Advances in Behaviour Research and Therapy*, 3, pp. 1–4.

17. House of Commons (1985), *op. cit.* (Referred to subsequently as the Social Services Committee Report, 1985, in the text).

18. Jones, K., Brown, J., Cunningham, W. J., Roberts, J. and Williams, P. (1975), *Opening the Door: A Study of New Policies for the Mentally Handicapped*, Routledge and Kegan Paul.

19. Gardham, J. H., Wardell, K. D. and McKeown, K. (1977), 'Community care for the mentally handicapped. Minimum support homes in Humberside', *Social Work Services*, 14, pp. 31–34.

20. Tyne, A. (1978), *Looking at Life in a Hospital, Hostel, Home, or Unit*, Campaign for People with Mental Handicaps.

21. Chant, J. (1978), 'Group housing for the mentally retarded' in Wynne Jones, A. (ed), *What About the Retarded Adult?* Taunton: SW MENCAP.

22. Race, D. G. and Race, D. M. (1979), *The Cherries Group Home: A Beginning*, HMSO.

23. Wolfensberger, W. (1972), *The Principle of Normalisation in Human Services*, Toronto: National Institute on Mental Retardation.

24. The Jay Report (1979), *Report of the Committee of Enquiry into Mental Handicap Nursing and Care*, Cmnd. 7468, HMSO.

25. Sanctuary, G. (1984), *After I'm Gone: What Will Happen to My Handicapped Child?*, Souvenir Press.

26. Devon County Council (1975), *Caring for the Mentally Handicapped: A Discussion Document*, Devon County Council: Social Services Department.

27. Somerset County Council (1976), *Survey of Mental Handicap, Stage I: Adults Living at Home*, Somerset County Council: Social Services Department.

28. Lambeth Council (1979), *Mentally Handicapped People Living at Home*, Research Section Report No 102, Lambeth Council: Directorate of Social Services.

29. Department of Health and Social Security (1986), *Mental Handicap Hospitals and Units in England*, Statistical Bulletin, 7/86, DHSS.

30. Department of Health and Social Security (1985), *Homes and Hostels for the Mentally Ill and Mentally Handicapped*. Personal Social Services Local Authority Statistics, DHSS.

31. Department of Health and Social Security (1985), *Mental Handicap Hospitals and Units in England*, Statistical Bulletin, 7/85, DHSS.

32. Welsh Office (1982), *The Development of Community Care for Mentally Handicapped People. Report of the All-Wales Working Party on Services for Mentally Handicapped People*, Welsh Office.

33. Independent Development Council (1984), *Next Steps*, IDC.

34. Wertheimer, A. (1981), *Living for the Present: Older Parents with a Mentally Handicapped Person Living at Home*, Campaign for People with Mental Handicaps.

35. Richardson, A. and Ritchie, J. (1986), *Making the Break. Parents' Views about Adults with a Mental Handicap Leaving the Parental Home*, King Edward's Hospital Fund.

36. Shearer, A. (1980), *Handicapped Children in Residential Care. A Study of Policy Failure*, Bedford Square Press.

37. Tizard, J. (1960), 'Residential care of mentally handicapped children', *British Medical Journal*, pp. 1041–6.

38. King, R. D., Raynes, N. and Tizard, J. (1971), *Patterns of Residential Care*, Routledge and Kegan Paul.

39. Felce, D., Kushlick, A. and Smith, J. (1983), 'Planning and evaluation of community based residences for severely and profoundly mentally handicapped people in the United Kingdom', *Advances in Mental Retardation and Developmental Disabilities*, 1, pp. 237–271.

40. Smith, J., Glossop, C. and Kushlick, A. (1980), 'Evaluation of alternative residential facilities for the severely mentally handicapped in Wessex: Client Progress', *Advances in Behaviour Research and Therapy*, 3, pp. 5–11.

41. Felce, D., Kushlick, A. and Mansell, J. (1980), 'Evaluation of alternative residential facilities for the severely mentally handicapped in Wessex: Client Engagement', *Advances in Behaviour Research and Therapy*, 3, pp. 13–18.

42. Felce, D., Lunt, B. and Kushlick, A. (1980), 'Evaluation of alternative residential facilities for the severely mentally handicapped in Wessex: Family Contact', *Advances in Behaviour Research and Therapy*, 3, pp. 19–23.

43. Felce, D., Mansell, J. and Kushlick, A. (1980), 'Evaluation of alternative residential facilities for the severely mentally handicapped in Wessex: Staff Performance', *Advances in Behaviour Research and Therapy*, 3, pp. 25–30.

44. Felce, D., Kushlick, A. and Smith, J. (1983), *op. cit.*

45. Dalgleish, M. (1979), *Children's Residential Accommodation: Policies and User Reaction*, Sheffield Development Project, Mental Health Buildings Evaluation, DHSS.

46. Heron, A. (1982), *Better Services for the Mentally Handicapped? Lessons from the Sheffield Evaluation Studies*, King's Fund Centre.

47. Kendall, A. (1983), 'England: services to mentally handicapped children and their families' in Jones, G. and Tutt, N. (eds), *A Way of Life for the Handicapped. New Developments in Residential and Community Care*, Residential Care Association.

48. Thomas, D. (1985), 'Putting normalisation into practice' in Karas, E. (ed), *Current Issues in Clinical Psychology, No. 2*, New York: Plenum Press.

49. Macaskill, C. (1985), *Against the Odds. Adopting mentally handicapped children*, British Agencies for Adoption and Fostering.

50. Shearer, A. (1981), *Bringing Mentally Handicapped Children out of Hospital*, King's Fund Centre.

51. The Court Report (1976), *Fit for the Future. The Report of the Committee on Child Health Services*, Cmnd. 6684, HMSO.

52. National Development Group (1977), *Mentally Handicapped Children: A Plan for Action*, Pamphlet 2, HMSO.

53. Oswin, M. (1978), *Children Living in Long Stay Hospitals*, William Heinemann Medical Books.

54. Oswin, M. (1981), *Issues and Principles in the Development of Short-term Residential Care for Mentally Handicapped Children*, King's Fund Centre.

55. Oswin, M. (1984), *They Keep Going Away*, King's Fund Centre.

56. The Bonnington Report (1984), *Residential Services: The Next Ten Years. Trends and Developments in Residential Services*, Social Care Association.

57. Dalgleish, M. (1979), *op. cit.*

58. Dalgleish, M. (1983), 'Environmental constraints on residential services for mentally handicapped people: some findings from the Sheffield Development Project', *Mental Handicap*, 11, pp. 102–105.

59. Brandon, D. and Ridley, J. (1983), *Beginning to Listen. A study of the views of residents living in a hostel for mentally handicapped people*, MIND.

60. Tyne, A. (1978), *op. cit.*

61. Dalgleish, M. (1979), *op. cit.*

62. Gunzburg, A. L. (1982), 'The essential environment', in Wynne Jones, A. (ed), *Residential Care for Mentally Handicapped People*, Taunton: SW MENCAP.

63. *Ibid.*

64. Dalgleish, M. (1979), *op. cit.*

65. Gunzburg, A. L. (1982), *op. cit.*

66. Tyne, A. (1978), *op. cit.*

67. King *et al* (1971), *op. cit.*

68. Brandon, D. and Ridley, J. (1983), *op. cit.*

69. Coulter, R. (1977), *No Longer a Child*, Campaign for People with Mental Handicaps.

70. Anderson, D. (1981), *Social Work with Mentally Handicapped People*, Heinemann Educational Books.

71. Mittler, P. and Serpell, R. (1985), 'Services: an international perspective', in Clarke, A. M., Clarke, A. D. B. and Berg, J. M., *Mental Deficiency: The Changing Outlook (4th Edition)*, Methuen.

72. Locker, D., Rao, B. and Weddell, J. M. (1984), 'Evaluating community care for the mentally handicapped adult: a comparison of hostel, home and hospital care', *Journal of Mental Deficiency Research*, 28, pp. 189–198.

73. Mittler, P. and Serpell, R. (1985), *op. cit.*

74. Locker, D., Rao, B. and Weddell, J. M. (1979), 'Public acceptance of community care for the mentally handicapped', *Apex*, 7, 2, pp. 44–46.

75. Locker, D., Rao, B. and Weddell, J. M. (1981), 'Changing attitudes towards the mentally handicapped: the impact of community care', *Apex*, 9, 3, pp. 92–93, 95, 103.

76. Tyne, A. (1978), *op. cit.*

77. Brandon, D. and Ridley, J. (1983), *op. cit.*

78. Dalgleish, M., Barnes, S. and Matthews, R. (1983), 'External contacts of residents in hospitals and hostels for mentally handicapped adults', *Community Medicine*, 5, 3, pp. 227–234.

79. Raynes, N. (1986), 'Getting out and about in the community', *Community Care*, 9 Oct.

80. Mittler, P. and Serpell, R. (1985), *op. cit.*

81. Tyne, A. (1977), *Residential Provision for Adults Who Are Mentally Handicapped*, Campaign for People with Mental Handicaps.

82. Parker, C. and Alcoe, J. (1984), 'Finding the right way out', *Social Work Today*, 16 April.

83. Gathercole, C. E. (1981), *Group Homes—Staffed and Unstaffed*, Kidderminster: British Institute for Mental Handicap.

84. Heginbotham, C. (1980), 'Housing choice for mentally handicapped people', *Design for Special Needs*, 23, Sep–Dec, pp. 11–15.

85. Heginbotham, C. (1981), *Housing Projects for Mentally Handicapped People*, Centre on Environment for the Handicapped.

86. Race, D. G. and Race, D. M. (1979), *op. cit.*

87. Tyne, A. (1978), *op. cit.*

88. Atkinson, D. (1982), 'Distress signals in the community', *Community Care*, 22 July.

89. Malin, N. (1983), *Group Homes for the Mentally Handicapped*, HMSO.

90. *Ibid.*

91. Race, D. G. and Race, D. M. (1979), *op. cit.*

92. Malin, N. (1983), *op. cit.*

93. Atkinson, D. (1983), 'The community—participation and social contacts', in Russell, O. and Ward, L., (eds) *Houses or Homes? Evaluating Ordinary housing schemes for people with mental handicap*, Centre on Environment for the Handicapped.

94. Atkinson, D. and Ward, L. (1986), *A Part of the Community: Social integration and neighbourhood networks*, Campaign for People with Mental Handicaps.

95. Gathercole, C. E. (1981), *op. cit.*

96. Evans, G., Todd, S., Blunden, R., Porterfield, J. and Ager, A. (1985), *A New Style of Life. The Impact of Moving into an Ordinary House on the Lives of People with a Mental Handicap*, Cardiff: Mental Handicap in Wales—Applied Research Unit.

97. Thomas, D. (1985), *op. cit.*

98. Firth, H. (1986), *A Move to Community: Social Contacts and Behaviour*, Northumberland Health Authority.

99. James, H. (1979), 'A better way of life?', *Social Work Today*, 10, 45.

100. Malin, N. (1982), 'Living together', *Community Care*, 11 Feb.

101. Wolfensberger, W. (1983), 'Social role valorisation: a proposed new term for the principle of normalisation', *Mental Retardation*, Dec., pp. 234–9.

102. House of Commons (1985), *Government Response to the Second Report from the Social Services Committee (Session 1984–85) on Community Care with Special Reference to Adult Mentally Ill and Mentally Handicapped People*, HMSO.

103. King's Fund Centre (1980), *An Ordinary Life. Comprehensive locally-based residential services for mentally handicapped people*, King's Fund Centre.

104. Guy's Health District (1981), *Development Group for Services for Mentally Handicapped People: Report to the District Management Team*, London: Guy's Health District.

105. Bristol and Weston Health Authority (1983), *Operational Policy for the Wells Road Project*, Bristol and Weston Health Authority.

106. Ward, L. (1983), 'An ordinary life', *Community Care*, 10 Nov.

107. Mathieson, S. and Blunden, R. (1980), 'NIMROD is piloting a course,' *Health and Social Service Journal*, 25 Jan., pp. 122–124.

108. Kendall, A. (1983), *op. cit.*

109. Dyer, L. (1984), 'Working to build a sense of value', *Social Work Today*, 6 Aug.

110. Dickens, P. (1984), 'Evaluating services for people who are mentally handicapped using program analysis of service systems (PASS)' *Mental Handicap* 12 Sept., pp. 102–3.

111. Renshaw, J. (1986), 'Passing understanding', *Community Care*, 17 July.

112. Russell, O. (1985), 'The organisation of services towards greater co-operation: patterns of support and care', in Craft, M., Bicknell, J. and Hollins, S. (eds), *Mental Handicap: A Multi-Disciplinary Approach*, Balliere-Tindall.

113. Mansell, J. and Porterfield, J. (1986), *Staffing and Staff Training for a Residential Service*, Campaign for People with Mental Handicaps.

114. Ward, L. (1985), 'Developing a local service: what kind of training do staff need?', in Ward, L. and Wilkinson, J. (eds), *Training for Change. Staff Training for 'An Ordinary Life'*, King's Fund Centre.

115. Tyne, A. (1981), *Staffing and Supporting a Residential Service*, Campaign for People with Mental Handicaps.

116. Mathieson, S., Wilson, C., Jordan, P. and Rowlands, C. (1983), 'Defining tasks: from policies to job descriptions', in Shearer, A. (ed), *An Ordinary Life. Issues and strategies for training staff for community mental handicap services*, King's Fund Centre.

117. Porterfield, J. (1983), 'The staff—monitoring staff performance, training and the need for support', in Russell, O. and Ward, L. (eds), *Houses or Homes?* Centre on Environment for the Handicapped.

118. Porterfield, J. (1985), 'After initial training, then what? In-service training, positive monitoring and staff support', in Ward, L. and Wilkinson, J. (eds), *Training for Change*, King's Fund Centre.

119. *Ibid.*

120. Mansell, J. and Porterfield, J. (1986), *op. cit.*

121. The Open University (1986), *Mental Handicap: Patterns for Living*, Milton Keynes: Open University Press.

122. National Development Group (1978), *Helping Mentally Handicapped People in Hospital*, HMSO.

123. Department of Health and Social Security (1984), *Helping Mentally Handicapped People with Special Problems*, HMSO.

124. Development Team for the Mentally Handicapped (1977, 1979), *op. cit.*

125. West Midlands Regional Health Authority (1980), *Operational Brief for Community Units for the Mentally Handicapped*, Birmingham: West Midlands Regional Health Authority.

126. Felce, D., Smith, J. and Kushlick, A. (1981), 'Evaluation of the Wessex experiment', *Nursing Times*, 77, 49, pp. 213–216.

127. Felce, D., Mansell, J., de Kock, U., Toogood, S. and Jenkins, J. 'Housing for severely and profoundly mentally handicapped adults', *Hospital and Health Services Review*, 80, 4, pp. 170–174.

128. Thomas, M., Felce, D., de Kock, U., Saxby, H. and Repp, A. (1986), 'The activity of staff and of severely and profoundly mentally handicapped adults in residential settings of different sizes', *British Journal of Mental Subnormality*, 32, 2, pp. 82–92.

129. Felce, D., Thomas, M., de Kock, U. and Saxby, H. (1985), 'An ecological comparison of small community-based houses and traditional institutions—II: physical setting and the use of opportunities', *Behaviour Research and Therapy*, 23, 3, pp. 337–348.

130. de Kock, U., Felce, D., Saxby, H. and Thomas, M. (1985), *Community and Family Contact: An Evaluation of Small Community Homes for Severely and Profoundly Mentally Handicapped Adults*, University of Southampton: Psychology Department.

131. Felce, D. (in press), 'Behavioural and social climate in community group residences', in Janicki, M. P., Krauss, M. W. and Seltzer, M. M. (eds), *Community Residences for Persons with Developmental Disabilities: Here to Stay*, Baltimore: Paul H. Brookes.

132. Evans, G., Blewitt, E. and Blunden, R. (1983), *A Preliminary Study of Problem Behaviours within a Staffed House for Severely Mentally Handicapped People*. Cardiff: Mental Handicap in Wales—Applied Research Unit.

133. Rawlings, S. A. (1985), 'Lifestyles of severely retarded non-communicating adults in hospitals and small residential homes', *British Journal of Social Work*, 15, pp. 281–293.

134. Rawlings, S. A. (1985), 'Behaviour and skills of severely retarded adults in hospitals and small residential homes', *British Journal of Psychiatry*, 146, pp. 358–366.

135. Guys Health District (1981), *op. cit.*

136. Independent Development Council (1984), *op. cit.*

137. Capewell, R. (1982), 'On the philosophy and concept of the Homes Foundation', in Wynne Jones, A. (ed), *Residential Care for Mentally Handicapped People*, Taunton: SW MENCAP.

138. Murray, N. (1983), 'A permanent home', *Community Care*, 13 Oct.

139. Royal Society for Mentally Handicapped Children and Adults (1983), *The Mencap Homes Foundation*, MENCAP.

140. Centre on Environment for the Handicapped (1981), *Housing Projects for Mentally Handicapped People*, (Seminar Report) CEH.

141. Towell, D. (1984), *op. cit.*

142. United Nations (1971), *Declaration of the Rights of Mentally Retarded Persons*, United Nations.

143. North East Campaign for People with Mental Handicap and Carle, N. (1986), *Helping People To Make Choices: Opportunities and Challenges*, CMH.

144. Wertheimer, A. (1986), *Housing: A Consumer Perspective*, Campaign for People with Mental Handicaps.

145. Blunden, R. (1980), *Individual Plans for Mentally Handicapped People: A Draft Procedural Guide*, Cardiff: Mental Handicap in Wales—Applied Research Unit.

146. Brechin, A. and Swain, J. (1987), *Changing Relationships: Shared Action Planning with People with Mental Handicap*, Harper & Row.

147. Shearer, A. (1986), *op. cit.*

148. Atkinson, D. and Ward, L. (1986), 'Friends and neighbours. Relationships and opportunities in the community for people with a mental handicap', in Malin, N. (ed), *Reassessing Community Care*, Croom Helm.

149. Tyne, A. (1981), *op. cit.*

150. Towell, D. (1985), *op. cit.*

151. Thomas, D. (1985), *op. cit.*

152. Firth, H. (1986), *op. cit.*

153. Atkinson, D. and Ward, L. (1986), *A Part of the Community (op. cit.)*.

154. MENCAP (1986), *Day Services Today and Tomorrow*, MENCAP.

155. Independent Development Council (1985), *Living Like Other People: Next Steps in Day Services for People with Mental Handicap*, IDC.

156. Shearer, A. (1986), *op. cit.*

157. Towell, D. (1984), *op. cit.*

158. Mittler, P. (1984), 'Evaluation of services and staff training', in Dobbing, J., Clarke, A. D. B., Corbett, J. A., Hogg, J. and Robinson, R. O. (eds), *Scientific Studies in Mental Retardation*, The Royal Society of Medicine and the Macmillan Press.

159. Independent Development Council (1986), *Pursuing Quality. How Good are your Local Services for People with Mental Handicap?* IDC.

160. Mathieson, S. and Blunden, R. (1980), *op. cit.*

161. Mathieson, S. (1982), *op. cit.*

162. Evans, G., Todd, S. and Blunden, R. (1984), *Working in a Comprehensive Community Based Service for Mentally Handicapped People*, Cardiff; Mental Handicap in Wales—Applied Research Unit.

163. Blunden, R. (1984), 'Behaviour analysis and the design and evaluation of services for mentally handicapped people', in Breuning, S. E., Matson, J. L. and Barrett, R. P. (eds), *Advances in Mental Retardation and Developmental Disabilities, Vol. 2*, Greenwich, Connecticut: JAI Press.

164. Ward, L. (1984), *Planning for People. Developing a local service for people with mental handicap*, King's Fund Centre.

165. Ward, L. (1985), 'Training staff for an "ordinary life": experiences in a community service in South Bristol', *British Journal of Mental Subnormality*, 32, 2, pp. 94–102.

166. Ward, L. (1986), 'Changing services for changing needs', *Community Care*, 22 May.

167. Gathercole, C. E. (1981), *Family Placements*, Kidderminster: British Institute for Mental Handicap.

168. Penrose, M. E. (1980), *Family Homes for the Handicapped. Final Report*, North Yorkshire Social Services Department.

Residential Care for Mentally Ill Adults

Jane Gibbons

National Institute for Social Work

CONTENTS

Residential Care for Mentally Ill Adults

Plan Of the Review

This review of the needs of mentally ill adults for residential care will treat the literature selectively, focussing on only the main issues, and on the evidence from England. There is general consensus that Department of Health and Social Security (DHSS) 'community care' policies, involving a shift from mental hospitals to locally based services, raise the most important issues to be confronted. The people most affected by these policies are those with persistent, relapsing mental disorders and their carers. This review will be principally concerned with them but will consider more briefly the problems posed by people who have abused alcohol and drugs, and by 'difficult' personalities who are a cause of nuisance and complaint to those around them. In this field, even more than others, the role of Local Authority Social Services Departments (LASSD) cannot be considered in isolation from that of the National Health Services (NHS) and the voluntary and private sectors.

The review will start in the early 1970s—the period when 'Seebohm' reorganisation of local authority services took place,[1] and when the DHSS published Hospital Services for the Mentally Ill.[2] I shall attempt to review the evolution of policy on residential care of the mentally ill and research evidence on its implementation in England up to 1985. References to literature published elsewhere, or outside this period, will be highly selective. In this review I shall interpret 'residential care' broadly, to mean, not just care in a residential institution, but care in a variety of sheltered settings in the community. The discussion will be confined to adults over 18 and under 65, falling into three main parts, the first dealing with policy developments in the period, the second with their effects and the third with research studies of residential care. The review will be concerned principally with the needs of adults suffering from mental disorders that persist over a long period, often fluctuating in severity, and that cause serious impairments and handicap. Schizophrenia is the prime example of such disorders. In its acute phases, the sufferer is likely to have unusual and frightening experiences, such as thoughts that are not his own intruding into his mind, or voices perpetually commenting on his behaviour. Such experiences

[159]

are often accompanied or followed by chronic symptoms, such as a loss of drive and energy, social withdrawal and a general slowing down, which produce permanent 'social disablement'. Schizophrenia is a fairly common disorder: in a population of 100,000, 10 to 15 new cases would be expected each year, and some 200 to 400 cases would be receiving psychiatric treatment during the year.[3]

Part 1   Policy: The Mental Hospital

1   The Rise of the Asylum

Up to the second half of the eighteenth century, mentally disturbed people were not categorized separately from other indigent people, and were very seldom cared for in segregated institutions, apart from the rest of society. By the mid-nineteenth century, however, the insane found themselves incarcerated in a specialised, bureaucratically organised, state-supported asylum system which isolated them both physically and symbolically from the larger society.[4]

This is not the place to discuss the conflicting explanations that have been offered for such a major change in social policy. But, in seeking to dismantle this asylum system, we need to bear in mind its history and the reasons given by those who originally constructed it. Otherwise we may find that something very like the discarded asylum is recreated as a solution for the social problems for which it was originally set up. The reformers who succeeded in 1845 with the passing of the Lunatics Act and the County Asylums Act in establishing a network of publicly supported institutions, regularly inspected, within whose walls all lunatics were to be treated by specialised doctors, had struggled from the early years of the century to rescue the mad from appalling conditions in private madhouses and workhouses. They, with members of the medical profession, believed that not only was it more humane to care for the insane in specially designed institutions, but that early treatment would produce cures. The alternative to confinement in the institution was believed to be neglect and ill-treatment outside it.

However, the consequence of the policy of institutional care was the accumulation of ever-larger numbers of chronic cases in institutions of increasing size, with ever-fewer therapeutic pretensions. By 1890 there were sixty-six county and borough asylums in England and Wales with an average 802 inmates, and 86,067 officially certificated cases of insanity in England and Wales, more than four times as many as forty-five years earlier. By 1930 there were nearly 120,000 patients in public asylums, and by 1954, at the peak in numbers, there were over 148,000. Scull has argued that this rise in numbers reflected declining tolerance of 'the awkward and unwanted, the useless and potentially troublesome... The importance of the asylum lies in the fact that it makes available a culturally legitimate alternative, for both the community as a whole and the separate families which make it up, to keeping the intolerable individual in the family'.[5] If this is so, the effect of abolishing the asylums, without having invented new ways of carrying out their function, is likely to be socially unacceptable.

2 Declining Provision in Hospital

During the period under review the decline in the numbers of resident in-patients, which started in the mid 1950s, has steadily continued. In 1970 there were 107,977 resident inpatients in England—a rate of 233 per 100,000 of the general population. By 1982 this had fallen to some 71,000—a rate of 151. This represents a decrease of approaching a third in the amount of hospital provision over the period. Over half the resident in-patients were over 65. Two-thirds of all patients were in older mental hospitals with more than 500 beds.[6]

First admissions between 1970 and 1981 fell from 63,480 to 56,621; while readmissions rose from 109,451 to 132,893. However these admissions figures conceal important variations for different diagnostic groups, illustrated in Table 1. The fall in first admissions did not apply to personality disorder and alcohol problems, while the rate of first admissions for psychotic disorders fell markedly from 44 to 29 per 100,000. The rise in readmissions did not occur for patients with schizophrenia and was largely accounted for by elderly patients suffering from dementia and patients with alcohol problems. Patients suffering from psychotic disorders, especially schizophrenia, largely make up the group with long-lasting illnesses, with frequent relapses, often leading to permanent handicap. This group is affected by the drop in hospital beds in two ways. Declining numbers of beds mean that those already in hospital (the so-called 'old' long-stay) are more likely to be discharged back into the community. Equally important, people becoming ill for the first time, or relapsing after a period outside hospital, are less likely to be admitted or readmitted.

Table 1 **Admissions to Psychiatric Hospital by Diagnostic Group England, 1970–1981**

Diagnostic Group	First Admissions Rate per 100,000		Readmissions Rate per 100,000	
	1970	1981	1970	1981
Schizophrenia	16	9	59	53
Other psychoses	28	20	52	58
Dementias	13	13	9	21
Neuroses	24	15	27	27
Alcohol problems	5	8	10	24
Drug problems	1	1	2	3
Personality disorder	12	10	23	23
All diagnoses	137	112	237	284

Source: DHSS (1984), *In-patient Statistics from the Mental Health Enquiry for England 1981* (HMSO).

3   The Evolution of DHSS Policy

Sir Keith Joseph, speaking in 1972, clearly explained what was to be the main thrust of DHSS policy for the mentally ill.

> We are trying to shift, deliberately, from a service based on the large, relatively isolated mental illness hospital to a service based equally on the psychiatric unit in the district general hospital and the community services... It is no good whatsoever trying to improve the hospital-based services for mental illness unless at the same time equal—no, probably more—emphasis is put on improving and expanding the community services... Of course, no mental hospital will be closed until the necessary alternatives for care of the chronically mentally ill are available in the area.[7]

This policy was more fully described in 1975.[8] The DGH psychiatric unit was to develop at the centre of a network of local psychiatric services. It would provide facilities for day, as well as in-patient care, and would be the base from which 'specialist therapeutic teams provided advice and consultation outside the hospital'. The scale of provision suggested was 0.5 beds and 0.65 day hospital places (0.35 of them for in-patients) per 1,000 population, with additional provision for the elderly severely mentally infirm and for the 'old' and 'new' long-stay whose needs will be considered in more detail later in this review.

A 'substantial expansion' of social services provision was recognised as 'an essential element' in the new strategy. It was stressed that needs should be individually assessed and services geared to meeting individual requirements. Social services would need to provide various forms of residential accommodation to cater for different degrees of dependency and length of stay. These were, firstly, hostels for short-term care and rehabilitation, serving as half-way houses on discharge from hospital or temporary refuges at times of stress, and providing a relatively intensive programme of rehabilitation. It was tentatively suggested that between eight and twelve places of this sort would be needed per 200,000 population. Staffed homes for up to twenty-five residents would be needed for people discharged after long spells in hospital who had lost their roots in the community. Various forms of unstaffed, but supported, accommodation would also be necessary, such as bed-sitters and group homes. Altogether, local authorities were expected to provide between thirty and forty-eight places in various kinds of long-stay accommodation per 200,000 population.

Comparatively little attention was given to two issues which have subsequently emerged as of crucial importance in the provision of adequate locally based services: arrangements for joint health and local authority planning; and the role of mental hospitals in the transitional period.

The policy has been developed further in a series of DHSS publications. *Priorities for Personal Health and Social Services*[9] re-emphasized the strategy and gave guidance on capital expenditure, which was taken further in *The Way Ahead*.[10] In 1977, co-operation between health and social services authorities was encouraged by the establishment of Joint Finance, set aside for projects collaboratively planned.

The DHSS internal community care study[11] showed that the balance of care was not changing—severely dependent people were remaining in institutions in spite of growth in community facilities. Subsequently, the DHSS has targeted its policies to this end.

Centrally there is now a very clearly defined ministerial initiative on the problem of moving long-stay cases out of hospital care whilst at the same time renewed efforts are being made to encourage co-ordination of services and of service-providing agencies at the district level through collaboration and in particular through joint planning.[12]

In 1981 *Care in Action*,[13] addressed to district health authorities and local authority social services departments, described three urgent tasks, two of which are relevant to the present review: the creation of locally based psychiatric services; and making arrangements over the next ten years for the closure of mental hospitals not well placed to fit into a district service. Thirty of 100 large mental hospitals were so considered. In this document the voluntary and private sectors have chapters to themselves: not so the local authority departments. The lack of detailed guidance was deliberate.

Statutory responsibility for the personal social services rests with elected local government. The Government indicates broad national policies, issues guidance where necessary and has a general concern for standards. There are only a small number of direct controls and these are being reduced as a matter of general government policy... (p 19).

In the same year, *Care in the Community*[14] outlined possible ways in which long-term patients and resources might be transferred from NHS to alternative local services. The paper estimated that there were some 5,000 seriously mentally ill people in hospital who might be capable of leading more independent lives. (The DHSS now regard this as a low estimate, given the detail now available in Regional Health Authorities' Strategic Plans for the ten years to 1994). An unknown proportion would need local authority residential care; others would need day care only. Seven possible arrangements whereby patients could be transferred from the care of NHS to that of local authorities were considered.

1 An extension of joint finance arrangements to encourage local authorities to take on longer-term projects by postponing the time when they would have to assume the full revenue costs.

2 The payment of a lump sum, or a guaranteed annual sum, by the NHS for each person discharged to a local authority.

3 The transfer of whole buildings, with associated funds, from NHS to local authorities.

4 The pooling of funds by NHS and local authorities for a particular client group, with subsequent joint planning and administration.

5 Central transfer of NHS funds to local government.

6 Creation of a central or regional earmarked NHS fund to be drawn upon by local authorities in respect of specific developments.

7 Concentrating responsibility for meeting all the needs of a client group on either the NHS or the local authority.

Local authorities were encouraged to experiment, within existing statutory provisions. Revised financing arrangements were published in 1983.[15] Tapering for joint finance schemes intended to move people out of hospital was extended to thirteen years and lump sum or continuing payments from health to local authorities were permitted. A series of demonstration projects for the transfer of long-stay patients, directly funded centrally from Joint Finance, was set up. However, the judgement of the Social Services Select Committee on this initiative was that:

No more than Joint Finance do the Care in the Community pilot projects or the new arrangements introduced in 1983 offer a persuasive and lasting solution to the problems of transferring resources together with people.[16]

The policies in these various documents were summarised by the DHSS in 1983.[17] This Note prepared for NHS Regions restated:

The main long-term aim... for mental health services, including services concerned with abuse of alcohol and drugs, is the creation of a comprehensive range of psychiatric services provided... within a district. Such a service is only possible if... it takes full account of the contribution social, educational, housing, employment and all other voluntary and statutory services can make.

The shape of the future hospital services is clearly described. Much less clear is the shape that community services are expected to take. General statements on the 'essential' role of the local authority in joint planning and in providing a 'complement to NHS services' are not expanded into detailed guidelines or numerical norms.

The priority tasks in each region will be to build up new patterns of comprehensive service in districts which do not have a suitable psychiatric hospital while carrying out the closure of hospitals which are not being fitted into the new pattern. However, the DHSS emphasised that:

The closure of hospitals is a consequence, not a cause of the reduction of in-patient care. Patients who would be better off outside hospital should have a planned discharge to suitable care even if no closure is foreseen; patients who are better off in in-patient care should receive such care, by a transfer if necessary, even if a closure is planned.

In summary, over the period under review the DHSS has consistently expressed its determination to move to a new pattern of locally based, comprehensive psychiatric services. However, the tone of the various policy documents has changed, to reflect a new attitude to public expenditure. The later documents are based on the assumption that the changes must finance themselves, through savings, and that no new monies will be made available. The strong lead which the DHSS was giving at the beginning of our review period, in issuing guidelines on the extent and nature of provision needed to replace the old pattern of services, was no longer evident in the 1980s. The DHSS is no longer attempting to establish national standards against which services can be judged. Progress towards the new pattern has been as slow as predicted in the foreword to the 1975 White Paper, as can be seen from the reiteration of the same messages over ten or more years.

Social Services: Policy Developments

4 Legislation

The Mental Health Act of 1959 followed on the Report of a Royal Commission on the Law Relating to Mental Illness and Mental Deficiency that had begun work five years earlier. The Act's importance in establishing a legal framework for mental health services not based on a specially designated and segregated hospital need not be expounded here. So far as the local authorities were concerned, the Act set out the powers that they had to provide residential and day services, as well as social work support, but it did not make such provision obligatory, nor did the Government of the day provide any funds earmarked for the development or expansion of community services. The forebodings of many were expressed by Titmuss:

> To scatter the mentally ill in the community before we have made adequate provision for them is not a solution; in the long run not even for HM Treasury. Considered only in financial terms, any savings from fewer hospital in-patients might well be offset several times by more expenditure on the police forces, on prisons and probation officers; more unemployment masquerading as sickness benefit; more expenditure on drugs....[18]

Other legislation is relevant in considering the powers and duties of local authorities. The 1948 National Assistance Act placed a duty on them to provide residential accommodation, and empowered them to make other arrangements to promote the welfare of certain groups, including mentally ill people. (These provisions were updated in Local Authority Circular 13/74). Under the Health Services and Public Health Act of 1968 local authorities were empowered to provide accommodation and other services for the care and aftercare of people suffering from 'illness' in a section subsequently consolidated in the National Health Service Act of 1977. Section 21(1) and Schedule 8 of this give social services departments powers to make arrangements for prevention, care and aftercare of people suffering, or likely to suffer, from 'illness'. Local Authority Circular 19/74 does actually *direct* authorities to provide specified services for mentally ill people, albeit in an appendix.

The legislative position relating to local authorities was altered in two ways by the 1983 Mental Health Act. Section 114 laid on them the duty of appointing a sufficient number of approved social workers with appropriate competence in dealing with persons suffering from mental disorder. Section 117 reinforced the duty of health and social services authorities to provide, in co-operation with voluntary bodies, aftercare services for patients discharged after compulsory detention in hospitals. Authorities now had a clear duty to provide aftercare for as long as needed in the case of three groups of detained patients: those held under Section 3; Section 37 (under a hospital order); and those transferred to hospital under Sections 47 and 48. Although this is only a very small minority of patients, and the extent of the services to be provided is not made clear, the section could lead to a higher priority being given to this area of social services' responsibilities.

5   Seebohm Reorganisation

The reform of local authority based social services at the beginning of our period had major effects on mental health services. Before 1971, social services to the mentally ill had been provided by a comparatively small group of psychiatric social workers employed by health authorities, and a larger group of local authority based mental welfare officers under the control of medical officers. The establishment of unified local authority social services departments, staffed by 'generic' social workers, was a radical change, involving the complete disappearance of the profession of psychiatric social work—a dissolution actually encouraged by that profession's leaders—and a deepening of the already existing split between hospital and community based services for the mentally ill. As Martin has pointed out, the consequences in terms of quantitative provision by social services for the mentally ill are difficult to assess, but, in the absence of research evidence and statistics,

> there developed among psychiatrists and many of their colleagues an almost universal impression that the mentally ill received scant attention from the reorganised social services; and that this was due to... the emergence of entirely different and unanticipated priorities.[19, p 38]

6   Residential Services Provided by LASSDs: Numbers

Figures produced by the Association of Metropolitan Authorities for the Social Services Select Committee give some picture of the scale of local authority and voluntary bodies' expenditure on residential care between 1975 and 1982 (Tables 2 and 3). By the end of the seven year period the number of places in total had increased from approximately 4,000 to over 6,000. The association described this as 'slow progress', in contrast to the picture for mental handicap. The rate of growth in local authority day care for the mentally ill was slower still.

Table 2 Expenditure by Social Services Departments on Residential Care for Different Client Groups

	Gross Current Expenditure £s million, average 1981–2 prices	
	1975/6	1981/82
Mentally ill	11.4	16.7
Elderly	463.5	506.8
Children	302.5	304.6
Younger physically handicapped	28.5	40.1
Adult mentally handicapped	34.1	62.4
Mentally handicapped children	12.4	24.6

Source: Minutes of Evidence to House of Commons Social Services
         Committee Session 1984–5. Evidence by Association of
         Metropolitan Authorities.

Table 3 Places in Homes and Hostels for the Mentally Ill Provided by Social Services and in Registered Voluntary and Private Homes

	1975	1982
Social services	2,545	4,063
Voluntary and private	1,366	2,157
Total	3,911	6,220

Source: *ibid*.

The Association described a number of obstacles to further major expansion of local authority provision in the future. These were the overall reduction envisaged in local authority expenditure, and the competition for diminishing resources from the growing numbers of people over the age of 75. Thus 'it is not politically possible to guarantee priority for the mentally ill'.[20]

Local authorities have been particularly concerned by the absence of new, bridging finance to cover the costs of closure of mental hospitals. Savings cannot be realised until institutions are closed, but in the meantime costs arise from the maintenance of the institutions as well as from the development of new community resources.

7 Collaboration: LASSDs and Health Authorities

Other difficulties in the way of joint planning and co-operation between health and social services authorities are the lack of coterminous boundaries and the different planning cycles of the two organisations, as well as more general differences.[21] A joint working group was set up in 1984 bringing together representatives of DHSS, and the health and local authorities:

> To review the working of the present arrangements of joint planning between health and local authorities including the arrangements for transferring resources; to consider what steps could be taken to improve joint planning and the more efficient and more effective use of all available resources in the delivery of services.

The history of the organisations' attempts to respond to previous central exhortations to collaborate has been recently reviewed. In its latest draft circular the Government proposes joint planning groups for the priority clients, including one for drug and alcohol abuse, which will cover total resource provision for these areas. Regional Health Authority chairs are supposed to establish formal contact with chairs of local authority social services committees to initiate collaboration at the earliest planning stage, with subsequent joint staff groups and information bases. It has been suggested that the implications are far-reaching, and may lead to some degree of *de facto* unification.[22]

The Audit Commission, reporting at the end of 1986, concluded that progress in implementing community care policies had been very slow and uneven.[23] Hospital beds for the mentally ill had closed faster than community services had been built up so that a loss of 25,000 beds over the last decade was matched by only 9,000 extra day places. The social security system was funding uncontrolled expansion of private residential care. Progress in developing community care was blocked by inadequate funding mechanisms; lack of bridging finance; the fragmentation of responsibility between different agencies, managed in different ways; and by inadequate staffing and training arrangements. The Commission proposed a choice between two methods of organising services for the mentally ill in the future:

- the NHS would have responsibility for all services for the mentally ill, buying in local authority and other services as necessary.

- a new system of joint NHS and LASSD management (with a single manager and a single budget) would be created.

The Commission called for an urgent review at ministerial level, warning that the one option not tenable was to do nothing. The government immediately set up a review. Its results were not known at the time of going to press.

Part 2 Effects Attributed to the Policies

There has been much adverse publicity about the consequences of running down the mental hospitals without building up alternative local provision. As I have shown above, there has certainly been an absolute loss of residential provision for the mentally ill during our review period: the slow increase in residential places provided by local authorities and the voluntary and private sectors is far from compensating for the loss of about a third of places in hospitals.

I shall review the evidence on unmet needs for residential care as it relates to the various charges that have been made.

1 Hospital Closure

In the period, few of the old mental hospitals have closed—one, Powick, in Worcester, as the result of a centrally funded demonstration project dating from 1970. A number of publications have described this operation, from which the major lesson appears to be the long time-span necessary for closure.[24] A survey by MIND in 1983 found that none of the fourteen regional health authorities had actually closed a large mental hospital or had immediate plans to do so.[25] There are about 160 psychiatric units in general hospitals, about half of which are small—additions to, rather than replacements for, the mental hospitals.[26] The next ten years, however, will see a quickening of the pace, due to more pressure from the centre, and might see the closure of at least thirty large psychiatric hospitals. The numbers of long-stay beds in the remaining specialised mental hospitals are expected to continue to decline. Thus, not only will some regions be caring in the community for patients with chronic mental illnesses who have been discharged after long periods in hospitals which have closed; but all regions will be maintaining in the community patients who would formerly have been admitted to hospital for long periods.

What the effects of hospital closure will be on the remaining long-stay patients in these hospitals is not yet clear. The Kings Fund has published optimistic accounts of progress in some areas[27] and large-scale evaluative research is planned at Friern Hospital in the NE Thames Region. Newspaper accounts illustrate what can happen in some circumstances:

> Saxondale long-stay psychiatric hospital at Radcliffe-on-Trent is due to close by 1988. Nottingham Health Authority says the hospital is too big and uneconomic and that the patients can be placed in better accommodation elsewhere... Most of the 400 patients still there are due to be transferred to other hospitals over the next twelve months with only about fifty now

on rehabilitation wards expected to move into the community... The health authority hopes to sell the site of the hospital, a former county asylum which opened in 1902 standing in eighty-eight acres of countryside... At the last survey 35 per cent of the patients were over 70, and forty-seven patients had been there for more than forty years. In November 1984, a member of Nottingham community health council found dozens of Saxondale patients wandering about the corridors carrying their belongings in black dustbin bags. She had stumbled into 'sorting day', when the patients were being shaken out of their previous wards, breaking old friendships, and herded into 'places of origin' groups prior to transfer. 'Too much of the planning is simply moving people from one institution to another as a matter of convenience' says....the secretary of the community health council.[28]

There is very little published research on the wishes of long-stay patients themselves. One study carried out in Goodmayes Hospital found that only about a third of long-stay patients interviewed actually wanted to remain in hospital; and only 10 per cent said the reason why they stayed in hospital was because they liked it there. Most feared they would be unable to cope outside, and were generally ignorant of community services and social security benefits that would be available to them.[29]

2 Deaths

It is sometimes alleged that the policy of early discharge from hospital leads to more patients dying prematurely.

MIND claimed that the effects of hospital closures and inadequate community care on the safety and mental health of discharged patients were leading to an increase in suicides... Trent Regional Authority announced last week that it would hold an independent inquiry into (15) suicides at St John's Hospital in the past nineteen months, after relatives had complained that the hospital may have released patients too early. COHSE, the health service union, has threatened to take industrial action at the hospital, due to close in 1991, in protest against the alleged early discharges.[30]

There is evidence from surveys of high death and suicide rates among patients suffering from schizophrenia. A survey of all such patients under 65 in a Southern city who were out of the mental hospital but in contact with psychiatric services in the course of a year, found that eleven of 360 patients were dead by the end of a follow-up year. Six had committed suicide, producing a suicide rate approximately seventy times that of the city's general population.[31] A study in London found similarly raised suicide rates among schizophrenic first-admissions,[32] but long-term users of psychiatric community services did not have raised suicide rates.[33] Over half the patients with chronic schizophrenia admitted to hospital may have made a previous attempt at suicide.[34] However, there is no clear evidence to link high death rates with 'community care' policies. This is an area where more research is needed.

3   Rise in Prison Population

The British Medical Association, in its evidence to the House of Commons Social Services Committee, wrote

> There is a danger that the prison service will become the sump for the social services in caring for the mentally ill.[35]

The Committee concluded that there was evidence to substantiate this fear.

> If there are no alternatives in the community, mentally disabled people will increasingly end up in the care of the prison service.

In a survey of prisoners on remand in Brixton prison on charges involving violence, people suffering from schizophrenia were over-represented by 22.5 times. This, if true elsewhere, would be a great change from earlier surveys showing that the ratio of schizophrenic patients committing violent crimes corresponded to the proportion of them in the population as a whole.[36] It has been urged that the increase in the prison population of some 14 per cent a year is due to the corresponding decrease in the number of mental hospital beds,[37] but this causal association has been shown to be statistically in error.[38] There in fact appears to be no evidence that discharged long-stay patients will go to prison, and some evidence to the contrary, which we will discuss shortly. It is more likely that, if schizophrenic people are really becoming over-represented in prisons, this is due to changing admission policies and reluctance to admit aggressively difficult patients to psychiatric hospitals.[39]

4   Homelessness

It is difficult to evaluate claims from several sources that the reduction in mental hospital beds has caused an increase in the numbers of homeless and destitute. It is certain that in this country the picture is different from that found in some large American cities, where shelters have had to be set up to cope with chronic patients discharged from state hospitals with nowhere to go. However, voluntary bodies providing shelter in Britain who gave evidence to the Social Services Committee agreed on the high, and rising, proportion of their clients who were mentally ill.

The Church Army, which has deliberately specialised in this area of work, told the Committee that of the 1,000 people in their hostels, 268 had recently been discharged from mental illness hospitals. The National Cyrenians suggested that between a quarter and a third of their residents were mentally ill. A high proportion of men using DHSS Reception Centres are mentally disabled,[40] and the Committee reported fears that the programme to replace the units may compound the problem of homelessness. St Mungo's estimated that up to 8,000 bed spaces for homeless destitute people may disappear in London over the next five years.[41]

5 Difficulties of Relatives

Several surveys have documented the problems of parents and spouses who are caring for relatives with chronic mental illnesses.[42, 43] Between 80 and 90 per cent of supporters of schizophrenic patients reported some adverse effects on themselves during a previous year. Distress was greatest among 'new' supporters, whose relatives had become ill for the first time, but also among all supporters when their relatives relapsed with acute symptoms. Supporters found their relatives' decreased social performance easier to tolerate. Supporters appeared to become more resigned or detached over time, as they learned their roles by trial and error. They received little help from health or social services in learning how to cope with odd or difficult behaviour, and they generally found it very hard to get professional help promptly when the patient relapsed. The majority of supporters felt dissatisfied with helping services. However, very few indeed expressed any wish for residential care for the patient. Of a representative sample of some 150 supporters in one city, only 5 per cent wished their relative to be in a long-stay hospital; and only 4 per cent expressed any wish for a place in a hostel or group home. 83 per cent preferred the patient to continue to live at home.[31] However, approximately one quarter of patients lived with supporters over 65, and many of these had an unmet need for some form of sheltered housing, or would develop such a need.

The National Schizophrenia Fellowship, in its evidence to the Social Services Committee, pointed to the shortfall in residential provision.

> As things are, most (discharged patients) are returned to their 'families', if any. The rest are on park benches, in prisons, doss houses or seedy and rapacious lodgings... Sufferers from schizophrenia are mostly cared for by their families, with little or no support from anyone and no idea of how to cope till they painfully learn by trial and error... Specialised residential care outside hospital is available for very few; and is almost always selective. It is practically non-existent outside sizeable centres of population, leaving large areas with no provision and little likelihood of any.[44]

6 Evidence from Follow-up Studies

There has been a surprising absence of large-scale research to assess the quality of the lives of patients living in the community who would formerly have remained in hospital. The important study of patients discharged in the 1950s has never been replicated.[45] A study of long-stay in-patients who were discharged in Nottingham showed that most achieved 'revolving door status'.[46] A recent survey of long-stay patients discharged into the York Health District showed that few returned to their homes. Most had been carefully resettled. None were in prisons and only one (of 34) lacked a settled home. Some had made repeated moves in the months after leaving hospital, but only two were back in hospital. Patients who moved to their own homes were mostly living fairly satisfying lives and receiving adequate support. Those in local authority hostels were also satisfied with their accommodation, though the few in homes had less autonomy. Seven, of 34, were in private homes. Although their conditions appeared satisfactory, the researchers were concerned to find that neither health nor social services were willing to offer domiciliary support to the private homes. As increasing numbers are moved out to the private sector, this is a policy issue that will have to be resolved. Five people had been resettled in two group flats, with continued support, an arrangement that had worked well. The five in lodgings had helpful landladies, providing good care and were better off than they had been in hospital.

This small survey gives no support to the pessimistic literature reviewed above. The researchers concluded that resettlement had been undertaken with much care and forethought and was generally success-ful. There was, however, evidence of lack of co-ordination between health and social services and with primary health care services. Establishment of a case management system was recommended to keep track of patients in their own homes and support and recruit volunteers. However, this survey included only patients selected as suitable for discharge—presumably those most easy to resettle.[47]

7 The Social Services Committee's Conclusions

On the basis of its wide-ranging review of the problem, the Committee gave its wholehearted support to the policy of caring for mentally ill people in local communities. However, it stated that:

> The pace of removal of hospital facilities for mental illness has far outrun the provision of services in the community to replace them. The Minister must ensure that mental illness... hospital provision is not reduced with-out demonstrably adequate alternative services being provided beforehand both for those discharged from hospital and for those who would otherwise

seek admission. We recommend that nobody should be discharged from hospital without a practical individual care plan jointly devised by all concerned, communicated to all those responsible for its implementation, and with a mechanism for monitoring its implementation or its modification in the light of changing conditions; and that the resources for this be made available.[48]

In its response, the Government did not commit itself on these points.[49] A private members' bill which would have enacted the Committee's proposals on carrying out a detailed assessment of a disabled person's needs before discharge from hospital has been passed, but in a severely weakened form.[50]

Part 3   Residential Care: Research Evidence

1 Needs of Different Groups

Professor Wing[51] has analysed the concept of need, in this context, to include:

(i)   The causes of social disablement, ie intrinsic impairment; social disadvantage; and personal demoralisation

(i)   Specific, effective and acceptable forms of care

(iii)   Efficient service delivery systems

The range of care needed may be illustrated in the form of 'ladders', with levels corresponding to different dependencies.

Table 4

Dependency	Occupation	Residence	Recreation
Low	Can occupy self	Maintains own home	Own and shared activities
	Sheltered work	Supervised lodging	Accompanied to public amenities
Moderate	Industrial therapy	Group home	Reserved hours
	Occupational therapy	Staffed hostel	Restaurant/club
	Special unit	Special hostel	Private grounds
		Sheltered community	
High		Secure unit	

This approach to the problem envisages a 'stairway', with individuals of greatest dependency on the lowest rungs but able to move up or down, as their needs vary. It is based on a body of research on the characteristics of people who stay in the large, old institutions (reception centres as well as hospitals) for long periods, in spite of all efforts to 'rehabilitate' them.[52] The intractibility of their social disablement has been attributed to factors which are common to the group, although formal diagnostic labels may vary. These are the risk of harm often posed to themselves or others; unpredictability and frequent relapse into acutely disturbed states; inability to motivate themselves or care for their own physical needs; lack of insight into their own problems; and low public acceptability. These disabling factors operate most negatively in socially impoverished environments, such as have been documented in the old mental hospitals and also in newer community settings.[53] They are most effectively combated in good quality 'neutrally stimulating' environments.[54]

There is general agreement in the literature that some form of 'asylum' will continue to be needed, not only for people with severe disabilities who are already in the old mental hospitals—'old' long-stay—but for similar people who continue to accumulate despite active treatment and rehabilitation—so-called 'new' long-stay.[55-60] These are the highly dependent people on the lowest rungs of Professor Wing's three ladders. Disagreements exist about the numbers of such people and the nature of the 'asylum' they need. Some have concluded that comparatively large numbers of dependent patients needing long-term care in segregated, sheltered communities will continue to accumulate. Wing,[61] for example, using the projections of a DHSS statistician, quotes an estimated rate per 100,000 population of fifty-three people continuing to need a modern version of the sort of care that used to be provided in the best mental hospitals. (This is an average, since districts' needs for places would in fact vary widely). Those who take a different view of the sort of provision that is needed also tend to take a more optimistic view of numbers. One psychiatrist working in an inner city area has claimed that although his district had large numbers of chronically mentally ill, not a single one under 65 was in need of long-stay hospital accommodation.[62] The local authority and voluntary sector in this health district would be faced with different demands from those in a health district which retained the major responsibility for the chronically ill. In fact, the rate of accumulation of such patients does vary widely in different parts of the country.[63] In general, areas with declining populations near the centre of large conurbations are likely to have higher rates.

2   Forms of Asylum

There is agreement that, whatever its precise form, the modern asylum must provide security, protection and shelter for people who cannot provide these things for themselves. There is, however, an important disagreement about how these functions should be fulfilled.

Some, including many psychiatrists and relatives' pressure groups, believe that what is needed is essentially a modified version of the old segregated institutions. Only in this way could one of the most essential functions of the mental hospital of former times, that it would never refuse to accept a patient in need, no matter how difficult, be preserved.[51] However, the new asylums would differ in important ways from the old ones. 'Campus communities', or 'haven communities' are envisaged, occupying part of an accessible mental hospital estate. Most of the site would be sold off, but enough land would be retained to set up a number of houses, on a 'core and cluster' principle, to cater for the needs of the most dependent group. Plans to develop such a 'haven' are in hand on the site occupied by Friern Hospital.

> One house (or hostel) with twelve residents, will serve as the heart and resource centre of the Community. It will provide for relapsing 'revolving door' patients and younger persistently disturbed people. The three other core houses will each have six residents. One house will cater for the long-term severely disabled with physical problems. . .another house will provide treatment and containment for those who tend, if unsupervised, to wander without regard for common danger. The third house will provide for frail elderly people with functional psychiatric disorders. . .The remaining twenty residents will live in a range of housing and flatlets with a lower degree of supervision. They will provide a gently graduated range of facilities. . .Each resident will have a personal bed-sitting room. . .Residents will participate in running their own houses, including cooking, cleaning and repairs. . .Linked to the Haven but scattered among the local housing estates would be peripheral group homes and supervised apartments. . .There will be plenty of space where people can wander and be private and where oddities of gesture or demeanour will not incur arrest or public ridicule. Ideally, some amenities would be created that were shared with the locality.

A different approach to the problem starts from the assumption that services for the mentally ill should enable them to lead as normal a life as possible, and that people should not be in hospital unless they need services which are only available there. The goal is to make available:

> Patterns and conditions of everyday life which are as close as possible to the norms and patterns of the mainstream of society.[64]

In a service of this sort, a handicapped or deviant person:

> lives in a culturally normative community setting in ordinary community housing, can move and communicate in ways typical for his age and is able

to utilise, in typical ways, typical community resources: developmental, social, recreational, and religious facilities; hospitals and clinics; post office; stores and restaurants; job placements. . .[65]

Thus services for the mentally ill, in this pattern, are not based on segregated residential communities, but on domiciliary support services geared to maintaining even severely handicapped people in ordinary housing. Midway between these two approaches would come a pattern of services providing specialised residential care, but in small, dispersed units in local communities rather than in 'haven communities'.

These new approaches to the creation of asylum have not yet been tested in practice. The supporters of the 'haven' ideal argue that insisting that handicapped and deviant people live in ordinary communities may mean exposing them, by administrative fiat, to a very poor quality of life without regard to their needs; and that people severely disturbed or disabled by mental illness may well, in some districts, need protection from the local cultural norm. Opponents point to the evidence from official enquiries of the difficulties of maintaining civil liberties as well as good quality care in settings where all aspects of a resident's life are under the control of one authority;[66] and lay stress on the opportunities, as well as the dangers, offered by ordinary life.

3   Surveys of Residential Provision

Surveys during the period of our review provide information about the amount and nature of housing provision for the mentally ill.[67] The most informative is the national survey undertaken for the Department of the Environment.[68] This revealed a total of 662 housing schemes in operation in England and Wales in 1981, probably representing 80 per cent of all provision. Some 3,300 mentally ill people were living in these schemes, which were far from evenly distributed across the country. Housing was provided by local authority housing departments in 61 per cent of cases; by housing associations in 31 per cent; and by voluntary bodies in 8 per cent. Involvement by housing associations was likely to grow, as statutory services became more knowledgeable about their use. Only 4 per cent of the provision was in staffed hostels, while 84 per cent was in unstaffed group homes. Core and cluster units were just starting to develop. In the majority of schemes, some form of continuing support was provided for residents, most commonly by community nurses and social workers, though voluntary groups alone were supporting a quarter of the schemes. The vast majority of the schemes were in ordinary or converted housing, in fairly central locations with easy access to town centre facilities, and often in areas with mixed residential and other uses. The acquisition of properties for the schemes had not caused particular problems. Case studies of thirty schemes found that only about half were offering direct tenancies, although this was recommended as the best arrangement. About half the residents had rooms of their own. The majority of residents were very satisfied with their homes and the researchers rated two-thirds as working well.

> These schemes were characterised either by having groups who had clearly sorted out their roles within the household, and perhaps because of this, their relationships with each other, or because they allowed a degree of privacy and independence within the accommodation. In the remaining cases some implicit or explicit problems were raised related to the composition of the group or the personalities within it. All of these involved a high degree of communal living.[68, p5]

The selection, preparation and subsequent support of residents was found to be crucial to a scheme's success. Schemes could be supported in a variety of ways, such as by befrienders, able tenants, non-resident housekeepers or resident staff, provided that the form of support was appropriately geared to the needs and abilities of residents. This 'matching' did not always take place. Support should involve help with practical tasks such as budgeting and food preparation, as well as counselling.

The authors concluded that there was a sizeable and urgent need for more housing provision in the future. However, the balance of provision needed to be rather different. There was a need for more staffed, hostel-type provision to accommodate, permanently, more dependent people. Group homes, on the other hand, were thought to be a form of provision that may have outlived its usefulness. Their cheapness was outweighed by the problems of selection, replacement and vacancies; and their somewhat forced style of group living. Cluster schemes were thought to provide a more desirable alternative, and core and cluster units might have application for more dependent people. In all cases there was a need for schemes to have some method of allowing priority access to ordinary lets for tenants who were able to move on.

The main restriction on the provision of housing schemes for mentally ill people was not the supply or allocation of properties, but the resources available for support. This was seen to be largely the responsibility of health and social services departments, although the voluntary contribution was emphasized. Hence, there was a need for more resources and more collaborative planning with housing departments to extend the range of support for schemes.

The MIND survey[25] found that different districts were adopting very different approaches to housing needs of the mentally ill in their plans for the future. The examples included a combination of hospital-hostels for high and low-dependency patients combined with group homes; homes with a resident warden combined with housekeeper-supported hostels and flats. One district's plans have been more fully described.[69]

Preliminary research in Hackney identified a range of needs, progressing from the total dependence of the hospital ward through to the independence of the ordinary flat. The basic elements in the district's plan were ordinary council flats, in which a person could be given more or less support according to need by a multi-disciplinary community psychiatric team. Thus, it is the support system which is flexible, rather than the person who has to move from one building to another as his needs change. In addition to these flats, there were projects to cater for special needs. These included accommodation with one or more resident housekeepers and visiting community nurses and occupational therapists for the most handicapped; other hostels with less support; group homes and flatshares; and 'cluster flats'—several flats on the same estate within easy reach of each other and supported by social services staff. In this district, the hospital will be a resource for short-stay admissions, not a source of long-term care. It will be important to find out whether this pattern of residential provision can meet the needs of the most severely handicapped and difficult people. Evidence from the United States suggests that it probably can, provided that intensive day care and domiciliary support is organised for an indefinite period by a highly motivated professional team.[70]

4   Different Types of Residential Care

In this section I will briefly consider the literature on different forms of residential care. Much of it is descriptive or anecdoctal and space will not permit reproduction of these individual accounts. A useful bibliography has been compiled by Baruch.[71]

i Hospital-Hostels
In 1975 the DHSS suggested that the need for long-term residential care for mentally ill people who developed persistent disorders which did not respond to treatment might best be met though hospital-hostels.

> On present thinking such hostels are likely to be fairly large houses reasonably close to the general hospital psychiatric unit, with the patients being cared for in a domestic atmosphere but with night nursing supervision.[8]

Three experimental hostels of this type, staffed by nurses and occupational therapists with psychologists and psychiatrists, have been opened in different parts of the country and evaluative research on each has been published[72-76]. The results showed that residents who moved to the hostels from hospital wards became less withdrawn, communicated more with others, became more active and made more use of community facilities. On most, though not all, measures their quality of life improved. None wanted to return to hospital, though some would have preferred to live with their families or independently. A place in a hospital-hostel cost at least twice as much as one in a mental hospital long-stay ward, but it provided a better alternative for the small minority of mentally ill people who continued to need medical and nursing care for a long time. However, the two hostels that were in ordinary property off hospital premises were selective and could not cope with all such patients. Younger people who were over-active or a danger to themselves or others were most likely to be rejected.

At present staff in the hospital-hostels all come from the health service. Staff for this setting need adequate experience of dealing with very withdrawn and sometimes disturbed people, and of providing socially rich but not over-stimulating environments. Staff who push residents too hard and expect too much may precipitate further breakdown.

ii Staffed Hostels

The 'half-way' hostel, intended to provide a transition between hospital and ordinary living, was a favoured form of provision in the 1960s. However, experience showed that it was impossible to supply a regular flow of residents who would move on within the prescribed time limits. Apte[77] carried out a survey of a national sample of hostels for the mentally ill, to test the hypothesis that 'permissive' regimes in hostels were more successful in encouraging residents to move to independent living than were 'restrictive' regimes. More people did move on from 'permissive' hostels after shorter stays. However, 40 per cent of residents in this survey were long-stay. Apte's conclusion was a pessimistic one:

> Without a clarification of purpose, the halfway house could turn into a diffuse and aimless institution, similar to the workhouse of former years.

In the early 1970s a survey was carried out of mentally ill residents from three London boroughs living in ten different hostels in Southern England.[78] Nine were run by voluntary bodies and one by a social services department. The hostels were categorised, by the intentions of their managers, as rehabilitative (short-stay) or permanent (indefinite periods of stay). Most hostels were found to have 'permissive' environments, regardless of their category, and there was no relationship between residents' ability to move on and the permissiveness of the environment. Two-thirds of residents in the so-called rehabilitative hostels had needed to stay for more than a year. It was notable that remaining in employment was a condition of acceptance and continuing residence in these hostels, and that 80 per cent of the sample was in full-time, open employment. Even though residents mostly had long histories of hospital treatment, this finding suggested that these hostels were selecting a comparatively able group of residents, in contrast to the 'compensatory' long-stay hostels. In contrast to the previous survey, the authors found that in general the hostels seen provided a high quality environment. Staff, most of whom had hospital backgrounds, did not operate restrictive regimes. A number of items scored as restrictive in Apte's original survey were still in common use, however. These were, having to leave an address when going away for the weekend; limited choice of menu; residents having no keys to their rooms, and staff able to enter at any time; the prohibition of smoking in bedrooms; some restrictions on visitors; staff calling residents in the morning; and supervision of medication. The researchers felt that many of these practices had a positive value for mentally disabled residents and were experienced as 'caring' rather than restrictive. Some were practices that would be found in most ordinary domestic settings. However, supervision by resident staff also had negative aspects when it involved unnecessary extensions of 'parental' responsibility.

> Adult residents, to put it simply, must be allowed to be 'at risk' in ways which are unacceptable for children. They must also have a greater degree of reciprocity with staff than is practicable between children and parents. . .In many hostels the residents are called by their Christian names but they do not call the warden by his or her Christian name. . .There may be notice boards in the hall, books for residents to sign in when they go out and when they come back in. Medicines may be put out in the front hall, where anyone can see them, or people may queue up to get them at the office door. These all seem to the visitor to suggest an 'institutional' approach, although residents do not always resent them.[79]

iii Group Homes
Group Homes have been defined as:

> Ordinary residential accommodation in the community in which a small group of people, having been discharged from mental hospital, are able to live as a family unit, without resident supervision.[80]

As we have seen, the unstaffed group home where a varying number of mentally disabled people share a household, is by far the commonest form of provision. Schemes are most often set up by hospitals in partnership with housing associations or voluntary bodies, although social work support is often included. Not very much systematic evaluative research has been carried out during our review period. An evaluation of a social services supported group home over a two year period found that it was fulfilling a 'compensatory' function. Residents showed no change in the direction of greater independence, but neither did they slip back from the levels they had reached in the staffed hostel where they had lived before. Residents and supervisors had somewhat conflicting perceptions of the home's purpose, which were never resolved.[81]

Most information comes from a study of four local authority areas where a range of accommodation for the mentally ill, which included group homes, was provided.[82] The study compared hostels with group homes in these areas. The hostels expected residents to move on after relatively short stays, while the group homes placed more emphasis on maintenance and support. Those living in the group homes were more disadvantaged and more handicapped. They were older and had spent longer periods in hospital. Women were more likely to be in group homes. Group homes accepted more 'old long-stay' patients with a history of prolonged handicap and an apparently smaller chance of eventually achieving independence. Hostels on the other hand also accepted younger people with less handicapping conditions and a possibly better prognosis. The former group might be expected to be more amenable but more withdrawn; the latter more troublesome but more lively.

There were marked differences between the environments of group homes and hostels, as measured by the degree of autonomy experienced by residents. People in group homes had much greater freedom and took more decisions. They also took more responsibility for practical tasks, such as cooking and shopping. Group home residents expressed less anger and hostility. Three-quarters of group home residents wanted to stay permanently in their homes, whereas the hostel residents were much more eager to move on. Neither group wanted to return to hospital.

Although the group homes were in ordinary houses in the community there was very little contact between residents and local people, apart from volunteer visitors. The residents were not integrated into their local neighbourhoods.

The researchers considered that neither the hostels nor the group homes would be able or willing to deal with the more severely disturbed group of people who are accommodated in the new hospital-hostels. Since group homes were much cheaper than hostels, because of the very limited staff involvement, the researchers considered that a wider use of them for current hostel residents was desirable. At the same time, more staff support and more occupational opportunities would have created a richer social environment in the group homes. Domiciliary occupational therapists could have encouraged more activity in the homes, and residents should also be given more say in their management.

A more recent survey[83] of group homes in a Northern metropolitan authority identified eight, most of which dated from the mid-1970s and resulted from a partnership between a psychiatric hospital and a voluntary body. Nearly all residents were still coming directly from hospital or from other specialised settings, but more younger people were being admitted and more were in some form of employment. There was more turnover of residents.

All the homes received at least a weekly visit from staff, who were fulfilling a role more like that of an ordinary landlord than any other, although they were maintaining some rules—for example about smoking and visitors. In some of the homes a resident appeared to fulfil some of the roles expected of a warden. Contact with the surrounding community was variable, but appeared more extensive than in the earlier survey.[82] There was not much group solidarity among residents, although there was a degree of co-operation. The nearest analogy was with the model of sheltered housing. The author considered that an increasing proportion of group home residents will be younger, less institutionalised and more lively. More may come direct from the community. A changing population will call for a different model of staff support, with more stress on residents as individual tenants, rather than as a group.

iv Boarding-Out
Boarding-out, or substitute family care schemes, have until recently made little contribution to accommodation for the mentally ill in this country, though they have been used extensively in parts of Europe.[84] The boarding-out of large numbers of chronic patients to commercially-run boarding houses is a discredited form of provision. Boarding-out into supported lodgings, with specially recruited landladies who receive professional support, is very different. The Health Service and Public Health Act (1968) enabled local authorities to finance schemes. There are several published accounts of schemes[85-87] but little controlled research. Common to schemes that work well are a specialised lodgings officer who selects potential landladies, visits premises and is available for advice and support; and a contractual arrangement which binds the landlady to provide bed, breakfast and an evening meal—with full board at weekends—services and baths. There must be careful selection of lodgers, who need to be reasonably stable and competent to care for their own hygiene. Daytime occupation needs to be available. The consultant psychiatrist guarantees readmission to hospital if necessary, and social workers or community nurses provide continuing support to the lodger. Costs are met from a mixture of social security and social services payments. Olsen concluded that boarding-out offered the opportunity to return to and be supported by the community, personal family-based care, employment, increased privacy, greater self-determination, a greater dignity from the opportunity to contribute to their own and others' well-being as opposed to the passive acceptance of institutional care.

v Private Homes
The placement of discharged adult psychiatric patients in private residential and nursing homes, often run by former mental hospital staff, is almost certainly increasing, but I have been unable to trace systematic

research on this topic. The York follow-up study showed that about a fifth of discharged adults were in private homes and that standards were generally satisfactory. However, it would be easy for poor standards to become established in isolated and forgotten homes. Under the Registered Homes Act (1984) LASSDs have an obligation to register and inspect residential homes, and nursing homes are inspected by the District Health Authority under the Health and Social Services and Social Security Adjudications Act (1983). This is an important area of work, which we must hope will be monitored by future research. Standards of practice in the residential field have been recently established. These should provide a common measure that can be used in the inspection process.[88]

5 The Role of Social Security

It is clear that all forms of alternative residential provision rely heavily on social security payments to underpin them. The AMA Evidence already quoted[20] argued strongly for a comprehensive disablement allowance to replace the myriad contributory and non-contributory benefits of the present system, and pointed out the various anomalies that exist between long-term patients in hospital and in other residential settings. The Government's review of the social security system has resulted in a separation of single and urgent needs payments, important to ex-patients trying to establish themselves in independent accommodation, from the main Income Support scheme into the proposed social Fund. The Social Fund will be cash-limited and discretionary, offering mainly loans. It is expected to play an important part in furthering the Government's objectives of moving patients out of hospitals.

The fund will promote further the objectives of encouraging care in the community for the mentally and physically handicapped, the elderly and the mentally ill.[89]

The Government appears to intend that Social Fund officers should have a role in co-ordinating activities by health and social services staff in the discharge of long-stay patients. Researchers have pointed out that the Social Fund will not be able to enter into regular commitments for the financing of alternatives to hospital care.[90].

Groups with Special Needs

6 The Need for Secure Accommodation

Social services departments do not have responsibilities for the provision of secure accommodation, but they should be concerned with the issue, since a failure to provide such accommodation leads to strains elsewhere in the system as well as unnecessary detention in Special Hospitals. Gostin has reviewed the available provision and proposed that the time has come to phase out the Special Hospitals altogether. Regional Secure Units should be increased so that more localised subunits could be set up, making it easier to maintain family links. These units should develop exchange systems of patients and staff with the rest of the NHS so that waiting lists do not build up.[91]

7 Recovering Alcoholics and Drug Abusers

The needs of alcohol abusers for residential care were reviewed by the DHSS Advisory Committee.[92] People with homes and those without homes were considered to need somewhat separate provision. For the former, the Committee considered that local authorities and voluntary organisations should experiment with small, staffed hostels where people would stay for short crisis or transitional periods. Such hostels could also offer some day care. Homeless problem drinkers were considered to have special needs. Entry points to services need to be accessible and welcoming, situated near places where the homeless congregate. These entry points should be linked with more specialised residential services, of graded levels of structure. Homeless problem drinkers may graduate from hostels and rehabilitation units to unstaffed group homes and other sheltered housing. The Committee envisaged that ultimately some 100 additional specialised social worker posts would be required, as well as large increases in voluntary provision.

The value of residential care for 'recovering' drug abusers is not altogether clear. The best documented approach is the one based on the work of the Synanon communities that developed in the USA in the late 1950s. At least two communities of this type, in Portsmouth and Oxford, exist in England with support from local authorities. Synanon is the creation of former alcohol and drug abusers. The community attempts to simulate the structure of an imagined nineteenth century authoritarian family. Its values are expressed in 'concepts' which explain the nature of the addicts' problems and what must be done to effect change. The structure is hierarchical, with rules governing behaviour and strong pressure to conform. At the same time, intimacy is fostered through confrontational encounter groups, where members' defences are broken down by direct attack. The new member is the 'baby' of the family, a mere crew member with menial jobs to do and no other responsibilities. He gradually progresses through the hierarchy (though failure can lead to his being shot down to lower levels) to become a staff member or even the community's director. The risks of this type of therapeutic community are high, in the sense that members who do not drop out may become alienated from ordinary life altogether. In certain circumstances, the community may then become a religious, rather than a therapeutic one in the usual sense of that term, as happened to Synanon in the USA.[93]

8 Anti-Psychiatry

In this paper, I have not expounded the ideas of writers belonging to the anti-psychiatry movement, since they are not based on research evidence of the kind which I have tried to review. However, such ideas did give birth to a number of alternative havens which sheltered some people with psychosis. Members of these communities would not see formal evaluation as appropriate, but have published descriptions and autobiographical accounts—both positive and negative.[94-95] Most writers of this school rejected the reality of schizophrenia as 'illness' and believed that medical treatment for sufferers was harmful, since it interrupted a healing journey which eventually led naturally to recovery. The small communities established, for example, by the Philadelphia Association were intended to provide an environment where such journeys could take place, with the support of other community members. These were often professionals—sympathetic psychiatrists and others—who stayed for a time in the community as equals with those who in other settings would have been patients. A community in the USA based on somewhat similar principles was formally studied and found to be at least as successful as conventional in-patient treatment.[96]

Part 4 Conclusions

It must be admitted that there are not many controlled research studies on which to base firm conclusions. The available research cannot tell us with any certainty what forms of residential care work best for what kinds of people with mental illness. However, research in this field will probably continue to be almost entirely local and descriptive, not through any wish of the researchers, but because of the very great difficulties in persuading administrators, clinicians and patients and their families of the importance of controlled evaluation. In any case, there may be more to be gained from cumulative evidence from careful descriptive studies carried out in different areas (provided they are planned to take advantage of previous work) than from specially designed experiments whose results may not be generalisable to ordinary settings. The work in this field, over many years, of the MRC Social Psychiatry Research Unit, has provided most of the cumulative knowledge on which planning can be based, and illustrates the need for a similar effort over a long time-span in social services research.

In spite of the limitations of the research, there is a wide measure of agreement on most of the major issues, starting with the DHSS policy itself. No writers openly argue for the retention of large mental hospitals, distant from the populations they serve, as the best way of caring for people with persistent and severe disorders. There is general agreement that the principles of care in the community are the right ones. However, the majority of independent reviewers of the policy have concluded that it is being carried out in ways that are likely to result in a loss of services and care to some vulnerable groups. There is agreement that services outside hospital have not developed fast or coherently enough to compensate for the loss of hospital places, and that this is due, not just to underfunding, but also to the difficulty of co-ordinating the plans and services of the many different agencies and people involved. The effectiveness of new arrangements for interagency collaboration which are shortly to be introduced will need to be monitored in the next few years.

The evidence in support of claims that the shift to local services has already, or will in the future, result in higher death rates and rising prison numbers did not appear very strong. There is also no research evidence that relatives of sufferers from chronic psychiatric illness would prefer them to remain in hospital for long periods. Evidence from surveys of relatives still living with their mentally ill spouses or children shows that, while the majority is dissatisfied with the level of support they receive from health and social services, few would prefer patients to remain permanently in any form of residential institution. The small body of research into the preferences of patients themselves shows that the majority do not want to remain in old mental hospitals, and those who move out into smaller hospital-hostels, or into group homes, do not want to return.

It is difficult to make precise numerical estimates of the unmet need for all forms of residential care for the mentally ill from the available research. In any case, evidence from psychiatric case registers shows that need varies according to area, with cities with declining populations probably showing the greatest relative need. DHSS statistics have shown a loss of nearly 14,000 residental places in total for the mentally ill between 1975 and 1982. This was due to a loss of over 16,000 health service beds, balanced by a rise of only 2,309 places provided by local authorities, the voluntary and the private sectors.

There is wide general agreement on the need for a range of residential provision within each district to cope with differing levels of dependency. At the extreme end of the continuum is the need for a small number of places in secure accommodation within the health service. Also within the health service is the need for specialised facilities for adults who are physically as well as mentally disabled and who need prolonged nursing care and medical supervision. There is agreement that staffed accommodation will be necessary for the so-called 'new' long-stay group of adults, mainly though not exclusively with schizophrenia, who need skilled care for long periods to combat crippling withdrawal and lethargy as well as actively disturbed behaviour. In a district with a population of a quarter of a million there is likely to be a minimum of five new people in this category each year. Districts appear to be making different plans for this group. Some are developing small, decentralised hospital units run by nurses. These units may be dispersed in local neighbourhoods with access to a general hospital psychiatric unit, or they may be grouped on part of the site of a former mental hospital as part of a campus development. Other districts seem to be planning to accommodate this group of patients in hostels staffed by lay wardens or residential care workers with support from visiting nurses and doctors. As yet we do not know which pattern will prove most effective. Different kinds of sheltered, but unstaffed, housing will be needed for people moving out of hospital after many years who no longer need intensive supervision, people with chronic disorders who are ready to move on from parental homes, and mentally ill people who are in unsatisfactory refuges and lodging houses—the single homeless. As part of new arrangements for better co-ordinated planning between health, social services, housing and the voluntary sector, it will be necessary to set up a database containing information on these various needs. In addition, in some areas there will be a need for staffed short-term accommodation and unstaffed accommodation for longer-term needs of recovering alcoholics. At the lowest point on the continuum, there needs to be some arrangement whereby mentally ill people who cannot compete in the open market for ordinary housing can yet gain access to it. The chances of achieving all this without additional central funding seem small.

The move away from the mental hospital involves decentralisation, and splitting responsibilities between more different groups. This could result in haphazard development, with units springing up under different auspices with no common standards. Some districts are considering tackling this problem by the establishment of a planning commitee involving representatives of the various interests (NHS, local authority, social security, housing associations and other voluntary bodies and the private homes) under strong leadership. This committee would be concerned with planning for and funding new initiatives within an agreed overall policy, and also with the monitoring of standards.

We now consider the conclusions suggested by research into the effects of regimes of residential care on residents' behavioural problems and quality of life. Again, there is not a great deal of systematic research—less than in the field of mental handicap. The evidence suggests that smaller, self-contained units (which might be linked in a 'cluster' arrangement) are more successful than ward units in a larger institution. Although single bedrooms are probably desirable, residents do not object to sharing rooms. In a self-contained unit, the staff in charge are able to take day-to-day decisions, and such matters as food preparation, minor repairs and staff rotas are within their control. Units containing twenty residents are probably too large since there is likely to be crowding and excessive noise in shared leisure spaces. However, units of under twenty are even more expensive to run. The evidence consistently suggests that the less the regime resembles Goffman's 'total institution', the better the results from the residents' point of view. Thus, it is better if residents' daily programmes are individualised, and they are not made to do the same things at the same time; if there is reduced social distance between staff and residents, for example, if the use of first names is mutual and not confined to staff using residents' first names; if there are opportunities for daytime occupation on a different site from the living unit; and if the accommodation is not marked out from its surroundings and residents can make use of community facilities.

The whole question of daily activities, for this group of severely handicapped people, some of whom can lose all ability to act, even to keep themselves clean, is of great importance. In the better mental hospitals, occupational and industrial therapy were available and patients were usually compelled to attend. The first hospital-hostel provided activities of this kind in a day hospital on the same site as the hostel, which most residents attended. The Manchester and Southampton hospital-hostels have adopted somewhat different approaches, not offering traditional occupational therapy at all, but attempting to involve residents in more individualised domestic tasks and social outings. Residents (in Southampton) appeared to increase their activity level as compared to the hospital setting, but much of their increased daytime activity was due to short trips, on their own initiative, from the hostel into the neighbourhood to shop, visit cafes, go for walks on the common. This increase in activity, for most, appeared to take place spontaneously, and to be a consequence of moving to an accessible site with a more flexible regime that encouraged freedom and initiative. The question of whether formal daytime occupational activities need to be provided off-site in the new patterns of staffed accommodation is one that needs further empirical investigation.

Research has found that new accommodation for the mentally ill tends to be sited in or near the centre of cities. This has definite advantages: because residents are very poor, anything that reduces transport costs and makes it easier to take advantage of cheap amusements such as window-shopping and visiting junk shops is a good thing. In these areas there are fewer intolerant citizens to make complaints about odd behaviour, and there are more struggling cafes and tobacconists to welcome new customers, as well as more people looking for the sort of employment that a new hostel can bring. On the other hand, such areas can be dangerous, and they could easily be asked to absorb too many ex-patients, since they make little organised protest when hostels or group homes are planned.

There appears to be no research into what sort of qualifications are needed by staff working in residential alternatives to the mental hospital. At present, most staff running accommodation for the mentally ill, whether provided by the health service or social services, appear to have nursing backgrounds. Experience and training in using rehabilitative techniques with chronically ill patients may well be an essential prerequisite for this work. The research suggests that staff in hospital-hostels identify more problem behaviours and intervene in a more active way to help residents change behaviour than either staff in the old mental hospitals or staff in other hostels. However, there is no reason to think that people without nursing qualifications cannot acquire these skills, with appropriate training and experience. This is an area of work that needs to grow, but at present there are no joint nursing/social work structures within which new training methods could develop.

Research suggests that the crucial factor in the continuing development of unstaffed accommodation is not the supply of housing, but the funding and organisation of adequate support systems. The support system provides a number of vital functions: location of suitable property, selection and preparation of residents, and continuing support through visits to the residents in their ordinary housing. A number of people with different skills need to be involved in a properly co-ordinated system. This is an area that calls for more research, since we know little about the kinds of structures that work best nor the kinds of skills that are most needed. Although the national survey of housing for the mentally ill concluded that the future of group homes was in doubt, research evidence from more detailed studies suggested that they had considerable advantages. The quality of support is probably particularly important here, since strains in personal relationships among residents are a frequent cause of breakdown. So far there have been no evaluative studies of different methods of support.

The next twenty years hold out great promise that new structures will be created which will improve the quality of life of people who suffer the cruel blow of developing a chronic psychosis—often just as they approach adult life—and reduce the burdens on their relatives. The research findings, with all their limitations, do provide some clear directions for the development of residential care. However, without renewed investment of resources—both material and intellectual—there is a real danger that services overall could become worse, not better.

Notes and References

1 Local Authority Social Services Act, 1970, HMSO.

2 Department of Health and Social Security (1971), *Hospital Services for the Mentally Ill*, HM(71)97, HMSO.

3 Wing, J. K. (1978), *Reasoning About Madness*, Oxford University Press.

4 Scull, A. T. (1982), *Museums of Madness: The Social Organisation of Insanity in Nineteenth-century England*, p. 14, Penguin.

5 *Ibid.* p. 240.

6 Department of Health and Social Security (1985), *Facilities and Services of Mental Illness and Mental Handicap Hospitals in England 1982*, HMSO.

7 Cawley, R. and McLachlan, G. (eds), (1973), *Policy for Action: A Symposium on the Planning of a Comprehensive District Psychiatric Service*, Oxford University Press.

8 Department of Health and Social Security (1975), *Better Services for the Mentally Ill*. Cmnd 6233, HMSO.

9 Department of Health and Social Security (1976), *Priorities for Personal Health and Social Services in England: A Consultative Document*, HMSO.

10 Department of Health and Social Security (1977), *The Way Ahead*, HMSO.

11 Department of Health and Social Security (1981), *Report of a Study on Community Care*, DHSS.

12 Hunt, L. B. (1985), 'Implementation of policies for community care: the DHSS contribution', *Health Trends*, 17, pp. 4–6.

13 Department of Health and Social Security (1981), *Care in Action: A Handbook of Policies and Priorities for the Health and Personal Social Services in England*, HMSO.

14 Department of Health and Social Security (1981), *Care in the Community: A Consultative Document on Moving Resources for Care in England*, DHSS.

15 Department of Health and Social Security (1983) *Health Service Development: Care in the Community and Joint Finance.* Circular HC(83)6/LAC(83)5, DHSS.

16 House of Commons (1985), *Second Report from the Social Services Committee Session 1984–85* HMSO.

17 Department of Health and Social Security (1983), *Mental Illness: Policies for Prevention, Treatment, Rehabilitation and Care,* DHSS.

18 Titmuss, R. M. (1968), *Community Care: Fact or Fiction?* Lecture delivered at 1961 Annual Conference of the National Association for Mental Health and reprinted in Titmuss, R. M., *Commitment to Welfare,* Allen and Unwin.

19 Martin, F. M. (1984), *Between the Acts: Community Mental Health Services 1959–1983,* Nuffield Provincial Hospitals Trust.

20 House of Commons Social Services Committee (1984) on Community Care: Minutes of Evidence, 14 November, HMSO.

21 Glennerster, H., Korman, N. and Marslen-Wilson, F. (1983), *Planning for Priority Groups,* Martin Robertson.

22 Smart, C. (1986), 'A marriage of two minds', *Community Care,* 24 April, pp. 20–21.

23 Audit Commission (1986), *Making a Reality of Community Care,* HMSO.

24 See, for example, Dorwick, C., Marwick, M., Martin, S. and Smith, L. (1980), 'The Worcester experiment', *Social Work Today,* 11, 23, pp. 10–15; DHSS Works Group, Worcester Development Project Psychiatric Provision (1982), *Where Do We Go from Here?* Mental Health Buildings Evaluation Pamphlet 3.

25 MIND (1983), *Common Concern,* MIND Publications.

26 Reed, J. and Lomas, G. (eds), (1984), *Psychiatric Services in the Community,* Croom Helm.

27 Kings Fund (1983), *Creating Local Psychiatric Services,* Kings Fund Centre.

28 *Guardian,* August 13, 1986.

29 Abrahamson, D. and Brenner, D. (1982), 'Do long-stay psychiatric patients want to leave hospital?' *Health Trends,* 14, pp. 95–97.

30 *Times,* August 11, 1986.

31 Gibbons, J. S. (1983), *Care of Schizophrenic Patients in the Community 1981–1983,* Report to DHSS.

32 Wilkinson, D. G. (1982), 'The suicide rate in schizophrenia', *British Journal of Psychiatry,* 140, pp. 138–141.

33 Sturt, E. (1983), 'Mortality in a cohort of long-term users of community psychiatric services', *Psychological Medicine,* 13, pp. 441–446.

34 Roy, A., Mazonson, A. and Pickar, D. (1984), 'Attempted suicide in chronic schizophrenia', *British Journal of Psychiatry,* 144, pp. 303–306.

35 House of Commons Social Services Committee (1985), *Second Report from the Social Services Committee Session 1984–5 on Community Care*, p. 161, HMSO.

36 Taylor, P. J. and Gunn, J. (1984), 'Risk of violence among psychotic men', *British Medical Journal*, 288, pp. 1945–1949.

37 Weller, P. I. and Weller, B. (1986), 'Crime and psychopathology', *British Medical Journal*, 292, pp. 55–56.

38 Altman, D. G. (1986), 'Crime and psychopathology', letter, *British Medical Journal*, 292, p. 340.

39 Orr, J. H. (1978), 'The imprisonment of mentally disorded offenders, *British Journal of Psychiatry*, 133, pp. 194–199.

40 Tidmarsh, D. and Wood, S. (1972), 'Psychiatric aspects of destitution' in Wing, J. K. and Hailey, A. M. (eds), *Evaluating a Community Psychiatric Service*, Oxford University Press.

41 House of Commons Social Services Committee (1985), *op. cit.* p. 165.

42 Creer, C. and Wing, J. K. (1974), *Schizophrenia at Home*, National Schizophrenia Fellowship.

43 Gibbons, J. S., Horn, S. H., Powell, J. M. and Gibbons, J. L. (1984), 'Schizophrenic patients and their families', *British Journal of Psychiatry*, 144, pp. 70–77.

44 House of Commons Social Services Committee (1984), on Community Care: Minutes of Evidence, 25 May. HMSO.

45 Brown, G. W., Bone, M., Dallison, B. and Wing, J. K. (1966), *Schizophrenia and Social Care: A Comparative Follow-up of 339 Schizophrenic Patients*, Oxford University Press.

46 Howat, J. G. and Kontny, E. L. (1982), 'The outcome for discharged Nottingham long-stay in-patients', *British Journal of Psychiatry*, 141, pp. 590–594.

47 Jones, K. (1985), *After Hospital: A Study of Long-term Psychiatric Patients in York*, University of York: Department of Social Policy and Social Work.

48 House of Commons Social Services Committee (1985), *op.cit.* p. CXIII.

49 Department of Health and Social Security (1985), *Government Response to Second Report of Social Services Select Committee*, HMSO.

50 Disabled Persons' (Services, Consultation and Representation) Bill (1986), HMSO.

51 Wing, J. K. and Furlong, R. (1986), 'A haven for the severely disabled within the context of a comprehensive psychiatric community service', *British Journal of Psychiatry*, 149, pp. 449–457.

52 Mann, S. and Cree, W. (1976), '"New" long-stay psychiatric patients: a national survey of fifteen mental hospitals in England and Wales 1972/3', *Psychological Medicine*, 6, pp. 603–616.

53 Schmidt, L. J., Reinhardt, A. M., Kane, R. L. and Olsen, D. D. (1977), 'The mentally ill in nursing homes', *Archives of General Psychiatry*, 34, pp. 687–691.

54 Wing, J. K. and Brown, G. W. (1970), *Institutionalism and Schizophrenia*, Cambridge University Press.

55 Bewley, T., Bland, J. M., Ilo, M., Walch, E. and Willington, G. (1975), 'Census of mental hospital patients and life expectancy of those unlikely to be discharged', *British Medical Journal*, 4, pp. 671–675.

56 Bennett, D. (1980), 'The chronic psychiatric patient today', *Journal of the Royal Society of Medicine*, 73, pp. 301–303.

57 Babiker, I. E. (1980), 'Social and clinical correlates of the "new" long-stay', *Acta Psychiatrica Scandinavica*, 61, pp. 365–375.

58 Bewley, T., Bland, M., Mechen, D. and Walch, E. (1981), '"New chronic" patients', *British Medical Journal*, 283, pp. 1161–1164.

59 Early, D. F. and Nicholas, M. (1981), 'Two decades of change: Glenside Hospital population surveys 1960–1980', *British Medical Journal*, 282, pp. 1446–1449.

60 Freeman, H. and Choudhury, M. H. P. (1984), 'Social characteristics of newly admitted mental hospital patients—a replication study', *Health Trends*, 16, pp. 55–57.

61 Wing, J. K. (1986), 'The cycle of planning and evaluation' in Williamson, G. and Freeman, H. (eds), *The Provision of Mental Health Services in Britain*, Gaskell.

62 Reed, J. (1984), 'The elements of an ideal service: The clinical view' in Reed, J. and Lomas, G. *op. cit.*

63 Gibbons, J. L., Jennings, C. and Wing, J. K. (eds) (1984), *Psychiatric Care in Eight Register Areas, 1976–1981*, Southampton Psychiatric Case Register.

64 Nirje, B. (1969), 'The normalisation principle and its human management implications' in Kugel, R. B. and Wolfensberger, W. (eds), *Changing Patterns in Residential Services for the Mentally Retarded*, Washington: President's Committee on Mental Retardation.

65 Wolfensberger, W. (1972), *The Principle of Normalisation in Human Services*, Toronto: Leonard Crainford, for the National Institute on Mental Retardation.

66 Martin, J. P. and Evans, D. (1984), *Hospitals in Trouble*, Blackwell.

67 Murray, J. (1978), *Special Housing*, Report no. 9, MIND.

68 Ritchie, J., Keegan, J. and Bosanquet, N. (1983), *Housing for Mentally Ill and Mentally Handicapped People*, HMSO.

69 Lovett, A. (1984), 'A house for all seasons' in Reed, J. and Lomas, G., *op.cit.*

70 Stein, L. I. (ed) (1979), *New Directions for Mental Health Services: Community Support Systems for the Long-term Patient, No 2*, San Francisco: Jossey Bass.

71 Baruch, G. (1984), 'Residential Care and Occupation Bibliography' in Reed, J. and Lomas, G. *op.cit.*

72 Wykes, T. (1982), 'A hostel-ward for "new" long-stay patients' in Wing, J. K. (ed), 'Long-term community care: experience in a London borough', *Psychological Medicine*, Monograph Supplement 2.

73 Garety, P. A. and Morris, I. A. (1984), 'A new unit for long-stay psychiatric patients: organisation, attitudes and quality of care', *Psychological Medicine*, 14, pp. 183–192.

74 Goldberg, D. B., Bridges, K., Cooper, W., Hyde, C., Sterling, C. and Wyatt, R. (1985), 'Douglas House: a new type of hostel ward for chronic psychotic patients', *British Journal of Psychiatry*, 147, pp. 383–388.

75 Gibbons, J. S. (1986), 'Care of "new" long-stay patients in a district general hospital psychiatric unit', *Acta Psychiatrica Scandinavica*, 73, pp. 582–588.

76 Gibbons, J. S. and Butler, J. P. (1987), 'Quality of life for "new" long-stay patients: the effects of moving to a hostel, *British Journal of Psychiatry*, 150.

77 Apte, R. Z. (1968), *Half-way House*, Occasional Papers on Social Administration, No. 27, Bell.

78 Hewett, S., Ryan, P. and Wing, J. K. (1975), 'Living without the mental hospitals', *Journal of Social Policy*, 4, pp. 391–404.

79 Hewett, S. (1979), 'Somewhere to live: a pilot study of hostel care' in Olsen, M. R. (ed), *The Care of the Mentally Disordered: an examination of some alternatives to hospital care*, BASW.

80 Capstick, N. (1973), 'Group homes: rehabilitation of the long-stay patient in the community', *Proceedings of the Royal Society of Medicine*, 66, 12, pp. 1229–1230.

81 Pritlove, J. H. (1976), 'Evaluating a group home: problems and results', *British Journal of Social Work*, 6, pp. 353–376.

82 Ryan, P. and Wing, J. K. (1979), 'Patterns of residential care: a study of hostels and group homes used by four local authorities to support mentally ill people in the commmunity', in Olsen, M. R. (ed), *op.cit.*

83 Pritlove, J. H. (1983), 'Accommodation without resident staff for ex-psychiatric patients: changing trends and needs', *British Journal of Social Work*, 13, pp. 75–92.

84 Martin, D. (1979), 'Family care for the mentally disordered in Belgium', *Health and Social Service Journal*, LXXXIX, 4671, pp. C33–C40.

85 Olsen, M. R. (1976), 'Boarding-out the long-stay psychiatric patient' in *Differential Approaches in Social Work with the Mentally Disordered*, BASW.

86 Smith, G. (1975), 'Institutional dependence is reversible', *Social Work Today*, 6, pp. 426–428.

87 Anstee, B. H. (1985), 'An alternative form of community care for the mentally ill: supported lodging scheme. . .a personal view', *Health Trends*, 17, pp. 39–40.

88 Aves Report (1984), *Home Life: A Code of Practice for Residential Care*, Centre for Policy on Ageing.

89 Department of Health and Social Security (1985), *Reform of Social Security*, *Vol. 2*, HMSO.

90 Stewart, G. and Stewart, J. (1986), *Boundary Changes: Social Work and Social Security*, Child Poverty Action Group/British Association of Social Workers.

91 Gostin, L. (1986), *Institutions Observed: Towards A New Concept of Secure Provision in Mental Health*, King Edward's Hospital Fund for London.

92 Advisory Committee on Alcholism (1978), *The Pattern and Range of Services for Problem Drinkers*, DHSS.

93 Kennard, D. (1983), *An Introduction to Therapeutic Communities*, Routledge & Kegan Paul.

94 Berke, J. (1979), *I Haven't Had to Go Mad Here*, Penguin.

95 Reed, D. (1976), *Anna*. Secker and Warburg.

96 Mosher, L. R. (1975), 'Soteria: evaluation of a home-based treatment for schizophrenia', *American Journal of Orthopsychiatry*, 45, pp. 455–467.

Residential Care for Younger Physically Disabled Adults

Diana Leat

University of Warwick

CONTENTS

Residential Care for Younger Physically Disabled Adults

1 Introduction

Research into residential care for the adult physically disabled is remarkably sparse. There is research in the general area of disability and there is research into residential care for other groups; two significant studies of the organisation of residential care for the adult physically disabled provide the basis for much of this review.[1, 2] Both of these studies are relatively small scale but they are significant not only as oases in a research desert but also in their quality and insight. Other studies, smaller in scale or concerned with narrower groups or particular settings are also referred to. At a different level is the recently published study for the Royal College of Physicians by Harrison; this study provides relatively up-to-date information on the scale and nature of provision nationally.[3]

It may be worth speculating briefly here on this lack of research. The numbers of adult physically disabled in general are, of course, relatively small, and of these only a tiny proportion* are in residential care. In numerical terms therefore, the adult physically disabled are not a major problem for policy-makers. Research into residential care for the adult physically disabled may also be regarded as relatively unimportant insofar as there are few wider social and economic benefits attached to the provision of such care. For these reasons research into residential care for the adult physically disabled may be sparse because it has not attracted adequate funding. Another reason for the relative lack of research may be the complexity of the variables involved and the methodological difficulties in communicating with some groups. More encouragingly there is a small amount of recently commissioned research in progress. Although not specifically concerned with residential care the OPCS studies of the needs of the disabled and their carers will produce valuable data of relevance to the future of residential

---

* The exact proportion is not known but it is estimated to be less than 5 per cent.

care. OPCS are also undertaking a separate study of private residential homes for the disabled of all ages. The York University Social Policy Research Unit are undertaking a study of the 'teenage transition' of disabled people.

Despite the lack of research into residential care for the adult physically disabled there is, of course, a considerable amount of research into residential care in general and at another level, into the organisation and effects of total institutions. While it is clearly important to be aware of this wider body of research, in assessing its relevance to residential care for the adult physically disabled it is equally important to be aware of the differences between the provision of residential care for this group and for other groups.

Residential care institutions for the adult physically disabled display some of the defining characteristics of total institutions in general. 'A place of residence where a large number of like situated individuals are cut off from the wider society for an appreciable period of time', and where the three normally separate activities of sleeping, playing and working are carried out in the same place.[4] However, unlike some total institutions they are not concerned with curing, nor are they concerned with control or reform of their residents. Because they are not in the business of any activity which will end in the 'release' of residents, residential care institutions for the adult physically disabled are unlike many other total institutions in that residents are the 'permanents' and staff the 'transients'. Nevertheless, because staff in such institutions are structurally more powerful and physically stronger, or at least less dependent, they may despite their transience exert considerable influence over not only the organisation but also the general culture of a home.

Miller and Gwynne have described residential institutions for the adult physically disabled as institutions which import the socially dead and export the physically dead. One problem arising from this 'permanence' of residents is that it becomes difficult to maintain the separation of the young disabled from the elderly. Despite the efforts (noted below) to cater specifically for the young disabled, the fact remains that without further disruption and rejection residents become progressively older.

The lack of a clear goal in homes for the adult physically disabled creates further problems. If homes are not about cure or control or reform but about care and development what are the rights and duties of residents? Do residents have the right, for example, to refuse medication, to put themselves at risk in dangerous situations or, more mundanely, to get drunk occasionally or often?

The complexities and contradictions within provision of residential care for the adult physically disabled are compounded by the current emphasis upon the care institution as the resident's home.

Before looking in more detail at the reality of residential care for the adult physically disabled it may be useful to make two further general points. First, the label 'adult physically disabled' is used here to refer to those physically disabled who are neither children nor elderly but, beyond that, the label conceals a wide diversity. Apart from the very wide age range there are also differences in duration of disability, type of disability, degree of disability and whether the condition is stable or deteriorating. It is arguable that these differences and the associated differences in needs and expectations are more significant than the somewhat artificial distinction between those aged under and over 65 on which current policy and provision is based.

Second, as noted above, residential care for the adult physically disabled is currently provided for a tiny proportion of a relatively small total population. The research reported below, and in particular the future demand for residential care, must be viewed in the light of changes in the expectations, characteristics and circumstances of the disabled and their potential carers, as well as wider social changes. As Topliss has remarked: 'Residential care provision needs to be organised to meet the demand that really exists, not a demand that may have existed once'.[5] The problem is that of predicting just what demand will exist.

The congenitally handicapped and others disabled in youth usually only enter residential care when their parents become unable to cope at home; because in recent years women have completed their families at a younger age it is likely that in future these groups will be cared for at home until late middle age. Other disabling conditions begin in adult life and many do not become severely incapacitating for some time. Thus, the future demand for residential care for the young physically disabled may well be less than current supply. However, the demand for care from severely incapacitated late middle-aged or 'young elderly' adults may well exceed supply. Having secured separate provision for the young adult disabled this provision may become increasingly irrelevant.

Whether or not the younger parents of the future will go on caring for their handicapped offspring for longer seems likely to depend on a number of factors.

The current emphasis upon the value of informal or 'community' care, including the emphasis upon the responsibility of families to care, may well create a climate in which family caring will be pursued. The current political emphasis upon the value of community care may also increase further the availability of appropriate accommodation for the disabled and their families although, clearly, resource constraints are likely to militate against this.

The growing recognition of the strains imposed upon carers and their needs for financial and other support may also serve to maintain informal care. However, against the effects of greater support on carers' capacity to go on caring must be set changes in the expectations and role of women, and the fact that families are not only completed earlier, they are also smaller and may consist of only one parent. Will women continue to be willing, or if willing will they be able, to devote their lives to caring—especially if they are without the support of a spouse or other female relatives? And, despite the rhetoric, will adequate income and support services actually be available to carers?

Other changes which must be taken into account in estimating future demand for residential care relate not to carers but to the disabled themselves. The expectations and expressed demands of the disabled have changed considerably in the last decade (see, for example, Davis[6]). Some of these expectations and demands are likely to decrease the demand for residential care and increase that for more viable 'community care'. As I shall suggest below, the growth in owner occupation must also be considered as a factor influencing demand for residential care.

The results of the national OPCS survey of the disabled and their carers currently in progress should be available in 1988. Although this survey will provide valuable data relating to the future demand for residential care these data will require interpretation in the light of the factors discussed above.

2   From the Poor Law to the Present Day

It is only relatively recently that the need for residential care for the young adult physically disabled as a separate group has been formally recognised in statutory policy. The current structure and content of provision still clearly reflects the 19th century origins of residential care for the adult physically disabled. For this group there have been fewer 'breaks with tradition' than has been the case in provision for some other groups.

During much of the 19th century the adult physically disabled were provided for under arrangements designed to help the poor in general rather than as a separate category with special needs. Under the Poor Law acts, disabled people with no alternative source of care or appropriate accommodation were housed in Public Assistance Institutions along with a variety of other groups in need. Towards the end of the 19th century voluntary organisations began to develop more specific provision.

In 1948 there were two important events in the history of residential care for the physically disabled. First the National Assistance Act replaced the existing Poor Law and made provision for the National Assistance Board, together with local authorities, to make further provision for the welfare of the disabled, sick, aged and other persons. The Act also made provision for the statutory regulation of homes for disabled and aged persons and charities for disabled persons.

Under the 1948 National Assistance Act it became the duty of every local authority to provide 'residential accommodation for persons who by reason of age, infirmity, or any other circumstance are in need of care and attention which is not otherwise available to them' and 'temporary accommodation for persons who are in urgent need thereof, being need arising in circumstances which could not reasonably have been foreseen or in such other circumstances as the authority may...determine'. Furthermore, the local authority '...shall have regard...in particular to the need for providing accommodation of different descriptions suited to different descriptions of such persons...'. The 1948 Act is significant in the history of residential care for the physically disabled not only because it remains the basis of provision today but also because it implies a recognition of the need for different types of provision for different groups.

The second significant event in 1948 was the foundation of the Cheshire Homes. The Cheshire Foundation is not only today the largest single voluntary provider of residential care for the physically disabled but has also been highly influential in developing the notion of 'family homes' specifically geared to the special capacities and limitations of the physically disabled.

Thus by the end of the 1940s there was limited recognition in legislation of the duty of local authorities to provide for the physically disabled as a group separate from the poor, and in the voluntary sector the creation of an organisation which was to become influential in translating recognition of the special needs of the disabled into practice.

In reality, however, the duties of the local authorities to provide residential care 'with regard to' the different needs of different groups did not immediately imply much change as far as the physically disabled were concerned. The bulk of what separate provision there was continued to be made by the voluntary sector; this was partly because the elderly were the largest group in need and in many areas the numbers of physically disabled did not justify expenditure on separate homes. A number of local authorities did, however, begin to provide separate homes in the 1950s and 1960s as they became aware of an increase in the numbers of disabled people resulting from the war, the polio epidemic of the 1950s and medical practices which have changed the pattern of disability and increased the life expectancy of disabled people.

Recognition of the special needs of the young disabled was not formally expressed in legislation until the Chronically Sick and Disabled Act of 1970. Under that Act the Secretary of State was required to make an Annual Report to Parliament on the number of younger people in homes, provided by local authorities under the National Assistance Act, which also housed people aged over 65. In 1972 it was estimated that there were 8,000 younger people in homes also housing the elderly (over 65) but more than half of these younger people were aged 60–65. Up to date data are difficult to piece together but Harrison[3] suggests that today less than half the younger adult physically disabled in residential care are in places specially catering for them. However, the hospital data suggest that 70 per cent of those 'misplaced' are over 55 and only 10 per cent under 45. Comparable data for local authority, voluntary and private homes are not available.

In 1986 only 54 of the 115 local authorities in England and Wales have set up homes catering specifically for younger physically disabled people.[3] Of course, other authorities may rely on voluntary and private homes for such provision.

Thus from 1970 onwards the need for residential provision specifically for the younger physically disabled was formally recognised, but health and local authorities varied in the speed with which they translated this formal recognition into practice.

As at the beginning of this century, today the voluntary sector continues to be a key provider of residential care for the physically disabled. In 1986 it is estimated that there are in England and Wales 72 Younger Disabled Units, 58 local authority homes and at least 198 voluntary and private homes.[3]

Many local authorities have, for various reasons, preferred to support voluntary homes rather than make their own direct provision and most, if not all, voluntary homes are directly or indirectly financially supported by the statutory sector. However, it is worth noting here that neither local authorities nor health authorities make any direct contribution within fees paid to voluntary homes to the capital cost of the homes. Thus the voluntary sector remains not only a major provider of care but also a major financer of residential provision for this group.

Alongside local authority and voluntary sector residential provision for the physically disabled there is, of course, provision by the Health Service.

The disabled have, of course, always been cared for in hospitals in so far as they could be categorised as chronically sick. However, in 1957 central government interest in the special needs and problems of the disabled in hospital was shown in a memorandum to Regional Hospital Boards, drawing attention to the difficulty of caring for the younger chronic sick patient at home. Following a small survey of chronic sick patients in 1965, a comprehensive national enquiry was conducted into hospital provision for the younger chronic sick, to discover the extent to which they were being cared for in geriatric wards. This in turn led to a memorandum in 1968 emphasising the need for units specially designed and equipped for care of the chronic sick. The memorandum provided fairly detailed guidance on the appropriate size, facilities and organisation of such units.

In 1970 the Chronically Sick and Disabled Persons Act reinforced the responsibility placed on Regional Hospital Boards to make special provision for the younger chronic sick. In the same year Regional Hospital Boards were asked for a progress report on accommodation provided exclusively for the younger chronic sick; later that year (1970) an extra £3 million was allocated over the following 4 years for special units for the younger chronic sick. Perhaps unsurprisingly this appears to have had a dramatic effect. Whereas in February 1970 it had been estimated that there were 26 units in use and a further 7 expected to open in the following year, by May 1971 28 units were in use and a further 21 planned to start that year (18 of those financed from the extra £3 million). In 1986 it is estimated that there are 72 such special units in use in England and Wales.[3] Although in the last few years the numbers of Young Disabled Units may have remained fairly static it appears that their turnover has increased due to a greater emphasis on short stay care.

Throughout the 1970s there was increasing questioning of both the proper functions and organisation of residential care and the desirability of provision of residential care rather than the creation of greater opportunities for independent living.

In the last ten years the major changes in statutory regulations have had their greatest impact on the voluntary and private sectors. The Nursing Homes Act 1975, the Residential Homes Act 1980, and the Registered Homes Act 1984 (attempting in part to remedy the 'deficiencies' of the former acts) have, it is suggested, led to a rapid growth in private and voluntary homes for the elderly and disabled. It seems likely, however, that this growth is closely related to changes in the regulations regarding use of social security payments in order to fund places in residential care. Not only does this use of DHSS payments provide private and voluntary homes with a much wider population from which to draw (ie those who can pay or be paid for), it also enables local authorities to support placements not from their own restricted budgets but from the, in effect, unrestricted social security budget.

The present financial and administrative structure of provision of residential care for the younger physically disabled is outlined on the next page.

Harrison provides data on the cumulative effect of changes since 1970 on the number of younger disabled people in residential care in England and Wales. He concludes: 'Despite the greater emphasis on community care during that time, the total number of occupied places has significantly increased, and the principal cause can only have been the change in social security entitlement'[3] (see also Department of Health and Social Security).[7] A working party within DHSS is currently

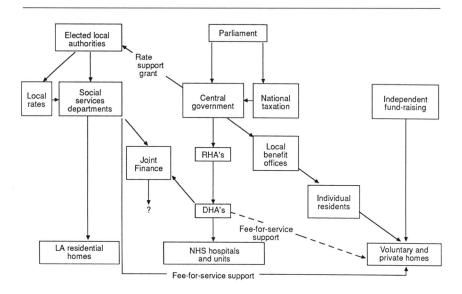

(Harrison, 1986)[3]

discussing the apportionment of funds for the provision of care between central and local government and it seems unlikely that current funding arrangements will continue unchanged.

The 1986 Disabled Persons (Services, Consultation and Represen-tation) Act which has been enacted but not yet implemented is not directly concerned with residential care though some clauses may have implications for the provision and organisation of such care. For example, the 1986 Act gives the appointed representatives of disabled persons right of access to residential homes; it requires local authorities to make an assessment of the needs of children leaving special education. The 1986 Act also brings into legislation the term 'carer' and, more significantly, the notion that the ability of the carer to continue caring should be taken into account in decisions regarding provision of care.

Three key points emerge from this very brief historical review. First, the relative lack of change in the basic structure of residential provision for the physically disabled. The State has never 'taken over' residential provision for this group and the basic three pronged parallel structure of local authority, voluntary sector and health service provision remains. It is still unclear to what extent the private sector must now be included as a fourth 'partner' in provision for the younger physically disabled.

Second, the review demonstrates the relative recency of the recog-nition of the younger disabled as a group requiring separate or different provision. When discussing residential care for the younger physically disabled it is perhaps important to remember that as a specialist form of provision this is still in its infancy relative to provision for some other groups.

Third, and perhaps more contentiously, the review may be interpreted as suggesting the limited change which guidance and/or legislation alone may affect and the much quicker change produced by allocation of additional resources or by changes in funding regulations.

3 Who Enters Residential Care and Why?

In 1986 it is estimated that 'overall provision of designated residential care is at the level of 16 per 100,000 total population in England and Wales'. But less than half of the younger physically disabled residents are in places catering specifically for them; and more than 10 per cent of residents in homes and units for the younger disabled are aged over 65.[3]

Who enters residential care and why? In what ways do residents vary in their social circumstances and levels of physical dependence? Do different types of home cater for people with different needs? How and by whom, is the entry into residential care managed?

i Age and Sex

The available data suggest that a rather higher proportion of women than men enter residential care. It is unlikely that the greater demand for residential accommodation for women is a reflection of distribution of disability and much more likely that it reflects differences in availability of alternative forms of care. I shall return to this point below.

Although the younger physically disabled in residential care may cover an age span of 50 years, in the study by Canter *et al*, the age band containing the highest proportion of residents was 50–59 years. This is similar to the survey carried out by Harris[8] which reported an average age of 50.8 years for disabled people under retirement age.

There appear to be significant differences in age of residents between different types of organisation. Younger residents (under the age of 30) are more likely to be in local authority homes whereas those over 50 are more likely to be in voluntary homes and health authority units.[2] In part these differences in age may be related to the admission policies of different homes.

Miller and Gwynne report that half of the residents in the homes they studied were aged 35–50. Given that the main requirement for residential care comes from the upper age groups Miller and Gwynne conclude '...there is a discrepancy in residential accommodation between the patterns of demand and supply. The under 35s find it relatively easy to get into the specialised institutions—in the two voluntary homes, a third and a half of the inmates respectively, were in this age group—whereas the over 50's appear to obtain much less than their fair share of places even in the special RHB Units'.[1]

As Topliss points out the discrepancy between demand and supply in terms of age may be seen as one effect of the emphasis placed in the Chronically Sick and Disabled Persons Act 1970 on the separation of younger and older residents. This emphasis on separation made '...natural ageing of residents seem undesirable, and reinforced the tendency of units established to care for younger disabled adults to impose quite a low upper age limit for admission in order to delay the time when any resident should reach the age of sixty-five'. Although middle-aged people were increasingly accepted to 'fill the gaps' Topliss suggests that preference continued to be given to the young person with a static disability. 'The severely handicapped person over 55, who has struggled against progressive disability to maintain an independent home life as long as possible, is still often dismayed to find that no residential unit has room for him when he finally asks for care'.[9]

ii Marital Status

In the homes studied by Canter *et al* 24 per cent of male residents and almost 20 per cent of female residents were married. In Miller and Gwynne's study nearly three-quarters of the residents had never been married; of those who had married slightly less than half were divorced or legally separated.

Compared with Harris's figures for married disabled people in the community (62 per cent married) the proportion of married residents of homes is low.[8]

Given that for some (though not for all) entry into residential care is a result of lack of available community care the higher proportion of single people (and the relatively high proportion of separated/divorced in Miller and Gwynne's study) in residential care might be expected. However, Canter *et al* cast some doubt on the simple explanation that people enter residential care because there is no-one to look after them at home. I shall return to this point below.

iii Disabilities and Dependence

Four major conditions appear to dominate in residential care: multiple sclerosis, cerebral palsy, stroke and rheumatoid arthritis.[2] Whereas in terms of sex and marital status residents do not appear to be characteristic of the disabled population in general these major conditions are the same as those reported for the young disabled in the general population.[10]

However, the proportions with these conditions are different between residential homes and the disabled in general. Compared with the disabled population in general, Canter *et al* found a smaller proportion of residents with stroke and cardio-respiratory diseases but a larger proportion with multiple sclerosis and disorders of infancy and youth. As they point out, the higher representation of certain conditions within residential care may reflect the ability of families and health and social services to cope with these conditions. Multiple sclerosis is a deteriorating condition and is likely to make heavy physical and psychological demands upon carers. Disorders of infancy and youth are not deteriorating conditions in the same way but this group may impose other demands or have other needs which cannot easily be met by carers in the community, eg to make friends, to be more independent, etc.

The incidence of certain conditions may also vary between different types of organisation. In the study by Canter *et al*, over half the residents in health authority units had multiple sclerosis compared with around one third in voluntary homes and only 12 per cent in local authority homes. In local authority homes around 40 per cent had cerebral palsy compared with a quarter in voluntary homes and only 3 per cent in health authority units. Similar findings are reported by Harrison.[3]

How do these differences in conditions between homes relate to the levels of dependence for which homes must cater? Clearly, both cerebral palsy and multiple sclerosis may appear in an extreme or a mild form and the condition alone does not indicate level of dependence. Canter *et al* report that in their sample health authority units had the most dependent residents which, given the available medical and nursing facilities, is as might be expected. It might also be expected that voluntary homes, having no statutory requirement to provide accommodation to those in need, cater for the less dependent while local authority homes cater for the more dependent. However, Canter *et al* suggest that in reality, voluntary homes display a wide range of dependency levels. They conclude: 'While voluntary homes may in theory have the opportunity to pick and choose, it appears that level of dependency is not an over-riding criterion. Local authority homes had a surprisingly wide range of dependency although tending towards less dependent residents when compared to health authority units'.

iv Education and Training
181 of the 214 residents studied by Canter *et al* had no school leaving qualification; 141 residents had been in paid employment. In terms of previous paid employment there were some differences between types of home with health authority units having the highest and local authority homes the lowest proportion of residents with paid work experience.

v Reasons for Entering Residential Care
There is now a growing amount of research evidence to demonstrate the strain on those caring at home for dependent groups such as the elderly

and mentally handicapped children. It is therefore perhaps unsurprising to find that the most common reason given by the adult physically disabled for entering residential care is 'the physical strain on carers', closely followed by 'My disability got worse'. Only 12 of the 213 respondents in the study by Canter *et al* gave 'Nobody to look after me' as a reason for entering residential care. It would seem from this study that the majority of the adult physically disabled in residential care are there not because of a lack of informal care but rather because despite the best efforts of informal carers the strain eventually becomes too great.

It is important, however, to note that although the majority of residents may enter residential care for negative reasons there are also some young residents who enter residential care for positive reasons—to make friends and to be more independent.

The tension between these two basic factors underlying entry into residential care is obvious. On the one hand are those who enter because they are becoming increasingly dependent (and unable to be cared for at home) and, on the other hand, there are those who enter in order to become more independent.

vi Admissions

As I have pointed out above the residents of homes are not exactly representative of the disabled population in general. Furthermore, it appears that the residents of any one home or type of home are not representative of the general population within residential care. In part these latter differences may reflect the different admissions policies of homes.

Admission policies of residential homes for the adult physically disabled are a complex issue and rather different in some respects from that of admission policies in other types of residential institution. Three problems arise in considering the issue of admission policies in residential care for the younger physically disabled. The first problem is that (with the exception of respite care) as few people leave homes (other than at death), new admissions are infrequent. As noted elsewhere this basic fact means that homes which have an explicit policy of admitting only the younger adult disabled capable of development over time find themselves with an increasingly elderly and more disabled population. In other words, because residents rarely 'voluntarily' leave, admission policies logically require consideration of 'exit policies'. Harrison reports an average length of stay of 30 years in The Spastics' Society Units, 10 years in the Cheshire and local authority homes and only 6 months in the YDUs which, like some local authority homes, have become involved in providing short stay programmes.

The second problem relates to the criteria for admission. Should admission be based on some sort of queueing system or on individual need? If admission is to be based on need are different types of need, and their short and long term implications, recognised and distinguished? To what extent is provision for short-term respite care compatible with provision for long-term permanent care? Is provision for the very dependent compatible with provision for the less dependent?

Third, given that residential institutions for this group generally subscribe to the philosophy of providing a *home* for residents what role should residents themselves play in selecting new members of their home?

As noted above different types of home do indeed have different types of residents in terms of age and disability. But to what extent these differences are a result of different admission policies is not entirely clear. Both Miller and Gwynne and Canter *et al* suggest that differences in admissions policy play a part in the different composition of homes. Harrison reports significant differences between types of home in admission criteria, especially in relation to age, behavioural difficulties and need for nursing. He also reports differences in decision-making processes regarding admissions.[3]

Underlying the lack of clear policies on admissions are the problems noted above which in turn may be related to a lack of clarity in the aims of homes (on which criteria for admission to different homes might be based). This lack of clarity in aims and thus in admission criteria is nicely illustrated by Battye (himself a voluntary home resident):

> What kind of people are they (homes) for? Should admission be confined to the merely handicapped who simply want somewhere suitable to live and who can actively participate in running their home or should they also include the genuinely sick and dying? Should they be places to live in or die in? Also the problems of short-term rescue operations were hopelessly confused with the quite different problems of providing long-term accommodation.[11]

If aims and therefore admission criteria are often confused it appears that admission procedures are equally ill-thought out.

vii Admission Procedures

Just as the reasons why people enter residential care may affect their subsequent adjustment there is now a body of evidence which suggests that the way in which a major life change is managed may have an important effect on the long term outcome for the individual.

Given the considerable differences in age, family circumstances/ relationships, type and duration of disability, previous life-style and reasons for entry of residents it seems likely that new residents may need and have available to them very different types and levels of physical and emotional support. Having been admitted they are also likely to need and demand different types and levels of support from the home.

Canter *et al* graphically illustrate the differences, in terms of available and required support, between new residents with two case histories:

1. This is a young man of 21 who is now living in a local authority home. He has been disabled from birth. He received all his schooling in a special residential school, left at 16, and has never had a job. After being at home for 18 months he asked his social worker to find some way for him to leave home because he felt lonely and cut off.

2. This is a woman of 56 who is now living in a health authority unit. She had a sudden stroke and was immediately hospitalised three months ago. Prior to the stroke she had a secretarial job, lived with her husband and two grown up children and was friendly with her neighbours. She wanted to go home from hospital but was transferred to a younger disabled unit because her husband and children were all at work and couldn't look after her.[2]

There is little detailed research evidence on the admission process and in particular how the very different needs of residents are met.

Canter *et al* report that 'In the majority of cases the residents felt that social workers and doctors were mainly responsible for the admission arrangements' and they go on to suggest: '...for most residents control over the event was out of their hands, although some did get a chance to look round their home before they came to live there'. More disturbingly: 'The fact that so few residents had an opportunity to look around cannot be explained by emergency admissions'.

Canter et al were unable to examine systematically whether those very few residents who had information, involvement and control over their admission were better able to cope with admission than those who did not. They do note, however, that the few people in their sample who had visited the home prior to admission were less likely to feel negative about admission than those who had made no prior visit.

It appears then that the, for many, traumatic process of admission to residential care has been given little thought by those responsible for admission arrangements. Once admitted, the 'philosophy of the happy home' and the refusal to face up to the 'real purpose' of homes as a staging post between social and physical death may further serve to discourage homes from recognising and dealing with the negative feelings of new residents.[1]

Canter *et al* suggest that the admission process might be improved if residents were given

Before admission...information about possible homes, some choice of home and involvement in any decisions which are taken, and opportunities to visit the home and meet people there before admission. After admission...information about routines and what is expected of a new resident, someone with time to help with adjustment to this new way of life, being able to bring personal possessions, and an opportunity to take on a new role in the home.[2]

4 The Organisation of Residential Care

Above I have briefly alluded to some of the characteristics which residential care institutions for the adult physically disabled share with other total institutions and some ways in which they differ from other total institutions. I also mentioned the philosophy of the 'home' to which many such institutions subscribe. Furthermore, I have noted above that the aims or purposes of residential care for the physically disabled are varied and often confused.

The combination of the varied and often unclear purposes of residential care for this group, the philosophy of the 'home' with all its uncertain and amorphous implications, the variety in both 'parent' institution and the characteristics and needs of residents is likely to produce variety and tension within the culture and organisation of residential institutions.

For example, the fact that the purpose of residential care for this group is neither cure nor control but 'care' or 'development' lends itself to adoption of the notion of such institutions as a home for residents. But what does providing a home imply? Is home a place where one has rights, where one can be oneself or a place where one must give up individual rights in favour of collective comfort? The home philosophy may be used as a justification for allowing residents to stay out as late as they wish or as a justification for a single inflexible meal-time.

Is the provision of a home compatible with the bureaucracy, the rules, procedures and standards necessary within, say, a health authority? For example, do residents have the right to choose who shall be invited to live in their home or should the decisions be based on the criteria of need and equity which underlie the provision of (other) statutory services?

The lack of clarity in the purposes of residential care for the physically disabled is not solved by adoption of provision of a home as the purpose. The notion of providing a home contains its own complexity and confusion and these are compounded when account is taken of the fact that these are homes which are run by and within structures with their own organisational requirements.

In view of the above it is perhaps unsurprising that there appears to be considerable variety in the culture and organisation of residential institutions for the physically disabled.

Miller and Gwynne attempt to impose some order on this variety by suggesting two models of residential care. These two models differ in the way in which they define the primary task of the institution and from this different task definition flow differences in organisation and approach.

In the first model—the warehousing model—the primary task is that of prolonging physical life. The resident is a patient defined in terms of physical malfunctioning and therefore in need of medical and nursing care. If the role of staff is to provide care, to do things to and for the 'patient' the role of the resident is to be a patient, to be dependent.

> To the extent that effective performance of the warehousing task requires the inmate to remain dependent and depersonalised, any attempts by the inmate to assert himself, or to display individual needs other than those arising from his specific disability, are in the warehousing model constraints on task performance. They are therefore to be discouraged. The 'good' inmate is one who accepts the staff's diagnosis of his needs and the treatment they prescribe and administer.

In the second—the horticultural—model, the needs of residents for physical care are the constraints on the essential purpose of the organisation. In this model the resident is conceived of as a deprived individual with unsatisfied drives and unfulfilled capacities. The primary task is to develop these capacities by providing the conditions for greater independence. The role of the staff is not to treat disability, not to minister to dependents but rather to encourage independence.

Miller and Gwynne suggest that:

> The warehousing model represents the conventional approach to residential care and is still found in relatively pure form, especially in some medically based institutions...The horticultural model on the other hand, is less likely to be found in a pure form—it is an aspiration rather than a reality—in some institutions the two models coexist somewhat uncomfortably together.[1]

Decision-making

The identification of decision-makers is central to an understanding of the culture and organisation of the residential institution. Who makes the decisions is important in relation to the philosophy of 'the home'— for the able-bodied person his/her home provides the greatest opportunity for making his/her own decisions. The role of residents in decision-making may also be related to the warehousing and horticultural models outlined above. Dependence implies that decisions are taken by others on behalf of the dependant; independence implies the right and the capacity to take decisions. Finally, participation in decision-making may be seen as important in relation to the more fundamental effects of institutionalisation. Denial of the right to make decisions may be seen as one of the ways in which total institutions strip residents of their own identities.

What evidence is there on the involvement of different groups in decision-making in homes? Are there differences between types of home and what factors relate to or explain these differences?

Canter *et al* report that although parent organisation staff often had considerable management responsibility for the home or unit, they were perceived by residents and staff as less influential in decision-making than senior staff within the home. Residents were generally seen as being relatively uninvolved in decision-making.

There were, however, some differences between types of home in resident involvement in decision-making. Residents in health authority units tended to be less involved in decisions than residents in voluntary homes and they in turn were less involved than residents in local authority homes.

The lower involvement of residents in voluntary homes may be explained in terms of the number of factors which have to be taken into account in decision-making and the limited resources of such homes. The relative autonomy of local authority homes coupled with relative flexibility of resources may provide more 'space' for resident involvement in decision-making.[2]

Other factors which may be relevant in the degree of resident and basic staff involvement in decision-making include the age of the home. Canter *et al* hypothesised that an older home would be more likely to have a core of long standing residents and staff whose views would be valued. But they found exactly the reverse—perhaps incorporating modern ideas at the outset, newer homes were more participative than older ones.

Is there any evidence to suggest that a high level of resident participation in decision-making is 'better' than a lower level?

Interestingly, the available data suggest a slight negative relationship between feelings of participation and satisfaction; this may, however, be a function of the degree of institutionalisation of residents. Institutionalisation implies both a lack of involvement in decision-making and an acceptance of things as they are.[2]

In all homes which promote individual independence for residents this must, of course, be combined with the constraints of group living. The study by Miller and Gwynne vividly illustrates the tensions, conflicts and scapegoating which may arise when residents are encouraged to participate in decision-making.[1]

The limited available research evidence suggests that residential homes and units for the adult physically disabled may generally offer relatively few opportunities for resident participation in decision-making. But this may have rather less to do with autocratic staff and rather more to do with basic approaches to care and with the structure and constraints of parent bodies.

Canter *et al* suggest that homes display two main types of organisation which may be related to decision-making, to approaches to the organisation of care and to characteristics of the residents.

One covers what can be thought of as the Local Authority model. Here, decision-making is integrated. Decisions are taken by staff in the home, in some cases in consultation with parent organisation staff. Where consultation occurs it is with only one or two staff of the parent organisation.

A care staff hierarchy is adopted with care assistants doing different jobs to the senior staff in the home. There is some overlap of jobs but both groups have a number of distinctly separate jobs. The residents here tend to be younger and less dependent and quite local. The staff are older. The home itself is purpose built and of a 'hall of residence' type.

The other model is the Health Authority model. Decision-making is dispersed, decisions are taken by staff within the parent organisation occasionally with some consultation with staff in the home or unit. Each decision is taken by a different person or group of people. A nursing staff hierarchy is adopted. Here senior staff do essentially the same work as basic grade staff plus some additional tasks. Residents tend to be older and more dependent and staff are younger. Homes can be either purpose built or adapted and are sited at a hospital. Residents here are very local and have lots of visitors.[2]

The voluntary homes display characteristics of both patterns. Canter *et al* conclude that the parent organisation of the home fundamentally affects the organisation of the home.

Harrison drawing similar distinctions and conclusions points to 'inappropriateness of the medical model as a long term way of living', the 'inadequate goals' of YDUs and the 'divided and often ill-informed' management support in such units.[3].

5   Who Provides Care?

I have discussed above who enters residential care for the physically disabled in order to *receive* care. In this section I shall look at the data on who enters residential care in order to *provide* care.

Despite the fact that in this type of residential care residents are the permanents and staff the transients there is some evidence to suggest that it is staff who have a powerful influence on the culture and organisation of the home. For example, Miller and Gwynne suggest that: 'it is felt that tiresome routine is almost inescapable when trained nurses determine the staff: they expand a concept of efficiency that runs counter to the value of what is meant by a home'[1]. Similarly, Shearer comparing a hospital based unit with a voluntary home notes that the two homes employ staff with different types of training and background. In the hospital unit with a high proportion of hospital trained staff, residents spend most of the morning in bed or watching television. In the voluntary home, employing staff with a variety of training and experience, residents appear constantly active and busy. Shearer concludes that the former 'looks after people, because that is what nurses are trained to do' whereas the latter 'helps people as far as possible to run their own show'.[12]

Another reason for looking at the characteristics of staff employed in residential institutions is that it may help to explain the practical problem of staff shortage and high staff turnover. The DHSS 1970 Census of Residential Accommodation shows that one third of all staff employed in April 1970 had been recruited in the last 12 months. Similarly, Miller and Gwynne suggest a 30 per cent staff turnover rate in the homes they studied. Such a turnover rate is likely to create not only administrative and management problems but also a lack of enduring, secure relationships within the home; for residents who already have ample experience of rejection this lack of security in relationships with staff is likely further to compound existing problems.

Staff Characteristics, Experience and Satisfaction
Somewhat disturbingly, Miller and Gwynne report that:

> We had repeated evidence that staff vacancies in residential institutions attract candidates who, while not having a visible physical handicap are, in some measure, socially handicapped themselves. For instance, the proportion of divorced or separated staff members in these institutions almost certainly exceeds the proportion in the population at large.[1]

In the larger and more recent study by Canter *et al* 92 per cent of staff were women and almost three-quarters had been or were still, married. Almost two-thirds of staff had children and one-third had young children (under 16). As Canter *et al* comment:

> With such a group of staff with family commitments, there may be attractions in working in a residential home which are not necessarily to do with the work itself; such as shift hours which fit in with the children's schooling, availability of part-time work and ease of travelling.[2]

Given these characteristics of staff one might also suggest that the relatively high level of staff turnover may have less to do with the job *per se* and more to do with changes in individual, domestic or other circumstances.

Looking at reasons given for taking a job in a residential home Canter et al suggest that the most frequently mentioned reasons were concerned with a desire to care for or to nurse people. For some respondents the job was a means of gaining experience in order to go on to other things. Staff with children mentioned the convenience of shift work or location close to home more often than those without children. The level of pay was not generally mentioned as a reason for taking the job and indeed several respondents demonstrated their awareness of the low pay level and said they had taken the job *despite* this.

What experience or training do staff bring to the job? As noted above there have been suggestions that where a high proportion of hospital trained staff are employed in a home this will produce a particular approach to the work, to the resident and to the organisation and ethos of the home. Is there any evidence to suggest that hospital trained staff predominate in homes in general? What experience and training, if any, do other staff have?

Canter *et al* found substantial differences in previous experience (relevant to the job) of staff between different types of home. Whereas 40 per cent of staff in voluntary homes had no previous relevant experience, 24 per cent of staff in health authority units and only 16 per cent of staff in local authority units had no such experience.

Over half the sample had no qualifications at all but again there were differences between types of home. Predictably, the health authority units had the largest proportion of staff with nursing qualifications; voluntary homes had the smallest number of staff with qualifications of some sort. As Canter *et al* point out, at the time of their study the recently established training courses on residential care had not yet had any effect on staff in post. It would be interesting to discover whether the health services are still the major source of staff and training in homes today. Harrison's more recent national survey suggests 'wide individual variations, especially in the employment of trained, un-trained, full-time and part-time staff'[3].

Given the relatively high proportions of staff with no relevant previous experience or qualifications it is perhaps surprising that Canter *et al* report that on starting work 31 per cent of staff were given no form of induction or training; of those who were given some form of induction just over half worked with another member of staff for their first day.

Staff working in health authority units were rather more likely to be given some formal induction though the percentage is still low. Somewhat surprisingly, however, three-quarters of staff included in the study felt that their initial induction and training were adequate and reported that they had settled into the job within a few weeks.

How satisfied are staff in residential care institutions for the physically disabled and what, if any, are the sources of dissatisfaction?

Canter *et al* distinguish between four different need levels which staff were asked to rate on both importance and satisfaction.

The first level of need—social needs (belonging to a group, making friends, etc)—was rated highly on importance and satisfaction by staff in all 3 types of home. The second level of need—social esteem needs—was rated by staff as even more important than the first level but a smaller proportion rated it as satisfactory in their present job: '. . . staff knew they were doing a worthwhile and valuable job, however, a little more recognition for their efforts would have been welcomed'.

The third need level—autonomy, the opportunity for independence and decision-making—was also rated as important but again there was a gap between importance and satisfaction. Given the data presented above on decision-making within homes the fact that only half of all staff felt this need to be satisfied in their current job is perhaps unsurprising.

The fourth level—need for self-actualisation—includes opportunities for self-development, learning and promotion. Although considered by most staff as less important than the other three levels of need there was again a discrepancy between importance and satisfaction. Those who were interested in further training were often unaware of any appropriate training other than nursing and of other types of home.

What about satisfaction with pay? Canter *et al* suggest that the importance of and satisfaction with pay changes over time and is related to family circumstances and commitments and to feelings of fairness and equity in relation to other jobs. Furthermore, 'There was no great difference in satisfaction with pay between the different homes although there were substantial differences in rates of pay'.[2] The role and meaning of payment in a range of 'caring' jobs both within and outside of residential care is clearly a subject on which more research is needed.

6 Staff and Resident Activities and Relationships

In theory it would be reasonable to suppose that staff and resident activities and relationships are more or less directly related to the goals of residential care and to the needs of residents. As noted above, however, there is a certain lack of clarity in the main purpose of residential care for the adult physically disabled as well as differences between residents in their degree of physical dependence and independence. I have also noted above Miller and Gwynne's two models of residential care for this group—the warehousing and horticultural models. These models imply not only a difference in approaches to the purpose of residential care and to the resident but also a corresponding difference in staff and resident roles and activities. Miller and Gwynne point out that these two models are ideal types in the sense that they represent 'the extremes' which may not be found in a pure form in reality.

To what extent do staff activities differ in reality and are these differences related to different ideologies of residential care or to other factors such as staff training or degree of physical dependence of residents? More fundamentally, to what extent are staff activities related to resident needs and to what extent to organisational and staff needs?

i Staff Activities and Relationships

There are, of course, certain basic 'constraints' on staff-resident relationships with which all residential care institutions for the physically
disabled must contend. First, in most institutions a relatively small
number of staff must relate to a larger number of residents. Second, all
residents are to some degree physically dependent and therefore require
a greater or lesser amount of physical care from staff. These two
'constraints' when put together imply some degree of conflict: to what
extent are staff and resident needs complementary and to what extent
in conflict?

Miller and Gwynne highlight the way in which measures designed
to share an actual or perceived scarce resource (ie staff) among residents
within an institution may also defend staff—to the ultimate detriment of
relationships between them (ie staff and residents). For example, duty
rosters which ensure that staff are rotated between inmates are designed
to 'share' equally the least and most skilful staff and the least and most
difficult residents. However, they suggest that

> By denying that some inmates may prefer less skilled attention from staff
> they like to more efficient attention from those they dislike, the convention
> of fairness preserves the interpersonal distance between staff member and
> inmate as individuals. Avoidance of favouritism can thus inhibit develop-
> ment of a potentially supportive relationship between them.[1]

More fundamental than avoidance of favouritism, Miller and
Gwynne suggest that in every institution there are implicit or explicit
rules which prohibit close personal relationships between staff and
residents. Although, as they point out, the logic of this rule is clearly
that staff exist to serve the collectivity: '...the stringency of the
sanctions against the development of such relations suggests that there
are strongly irrational elements at work. In other words, the fantasies
about the consequences of such relationships are scarcely related to
reality'.[1]

It is, of course, arguable that the way in which the structure of
institutions actually creates barriers in relationships between staff and
residents is indeed, on balance, for the benefit of residents and is of little
significance given that residents have intimate, individual relationships
with others. However, as I shall point out below, there is some evidence
to suggest that in many institutions residents have limited opportunities
for the development of close personal relationships with others inside
or outside the institution.

Given the fact that residents are by definition physically dependent
to some degree, the provision of basic physical care is clearly one of the
major tasks of staff. How is staff time organised to provide physical care
and how much time is left over for other activities?

Canter *et al* report that most of the care and nursing staff's day was spent giving basic physical care to residents. In the evening, and more especially the morning, staff felt under particular pressure in providing physical care.

Although most residential homes operate a shift system, how this system is organised may vary. Canter et al report that in some homes the shift system was organised in relation to local needs, in others it was imposed by the organisational needs of the parent body. For example, the health authority units operated the three shift system of the hospital of which they were a part. Some of the staff had complained that this system was inappropriate for the needs of long-stay heavily dependent residents whose needs were greatest in the morning and evening. Staff in one unit had agreed to work out a different schedule better related to residents' needs but this had been vetoed by management.[2]

The shift system may be not only inappropriate to residents' needs but may also cause friction between staff; shift hours may cut across the busy morning and evening periods and give ample opportunity for accusations of one shift leaving all the work for the next shift.

Interestingly, Canter et al found that whereas one particular shift system and a 40 hour week over 5 days were common in the health authority units, in the voluntary homes staff worked a variety of hours and shift systems, and '...appeared willing to work the longest and least convenient shifts among the organisations studied'. It is worth considering whether flexible organisations/management encourage flexibility among staff.

Basic nursing and care staff may also be expected in some homes to spend time cleaning and cooking. Although most homes are likely to employ domestic and housekeeping staff their numbers may be reduced in the evenings and at weekends.

Senior staff in the study by Canter *et al* did not work the shift system worked by basic grade staff but nevertheless were often available in the evenings and at weekends, especially if they lived on the premises. Like the other grades, senior staff were prepared to give their 'own' time to help with residents' outings and social events but 'These activities were not usually seen as normal ''work'' which could be carried out during paid working hours'.[2]

Are these activities viewed in this way because they are not defined as part of the primary purposes of the organisation or simply because there is no time for them within working hours?

Miller and Gwynne explain the proportion of time spent on providing physical care largely in terms of the prevailing task ideology of the institution. Thus, they state, 'Staff in warehousing institutions characteristically over-emphasised the amount of physical care required'. Because, they suggest, a high proportion of qualified nursing staff tends to be correlated with adoption of a warehousing model, but not necessarily with a high degree of physical incapacity, the conclusion is presumably that the time spent on physical care is related to training and ideology rather than to residents' needs. However, Miller and Gwynne also emphasise the way in which residents are affected by and collude with the definitions of staff. In a warehousing institution the emphasis on dependence and physical care forces residents into almost total dependency. In a horticultural institution, they suggest, catering for dependence and independence '...seems characteristically to be split between staff and inmates, a formal staff organisation being responsible for care and, in conflict with it, an informal inmate organisation for activities'.[1]

Miller and Gwynne's relatively straightforward explanation of time spent on physical care and on other activities is illuminating and challenging but it may also be over simplified.

Although the quantity of physical care necessary may indeed be overestimated in some institutions it is nevertheless true that residents have different degrees of physical dependence and that some types of home have more dependent residents than others. In addition, as Canter *et al* suggest, the time spent by senior staff on administration and other organisational maintenance activities is also likely to vary between types of home. In the homes they studied senior staff in local authority and voluntary homes spent considerable time on administration (and, especially in voluntary homes, other organisational matters), whereas in health authority units much of the administrative work was carried out by central departments within the parent body.

Senior staff are therefore likely to spend rather different proportions of their time in direct contact with patients. As Canter *et al* point out, it is worth noting that these differences cannot be entirely put down to the original nursing training of senior staff in all homes—organisational characteristics also play a part.

The significance, or lack of it, of training in influencing staff activities is further underlined in consideration of the activities of basic nursing and care staff. Few basic nursing and care staff had nursing qualifications and yet in all homes studied by Canter *et al* much of their time was taken up with providing basic physical care.

Neither senior staff nor basic grade staff spent much time on encouraging independence, therapy, outings or social relationships. Canter *et al* conclude: 'Discussion is needed in some of the homes, particularly by senior staff who influence activities, to resolve the feeling that social and leisure activities with residents are a luxury which should be indulged in the staffs' own time, or after all possible physical care has been completed'.[2]

It would appear that the potential conflict within the aims of residential care—provision of physical care and provision of opportunities for development—is further underlined by limited resources. Harrison suggests that few YDUs have senior staff who are not 'almost wholly preoccupied elsewhere' and, at worst, are constantly being 'raided' to provide nurses to help in other wards.

> Many nurses find it very hard to explain their units' commitments and ideals, such as they are, to colleagues and seniors in the main hospital. When YDUs are attached to a geriatric department...the YDUs can only achieve the standards expected of them by claiming a degree of privilege which the main department can resent.[3]

But it remains unclear whether, if more time/resources were available, staff would still regard social and leisure activities with residents as a luxury.

Would the time taken by the provision of physical care simply expand to fill the extra capacity? With existing levels of resources *could* the time spent on physical care be reduced? How, if at all, would a reduction in levels of physical care relate to the difficult decisions which all residential institutions must make about 'proper' levels of care and protection? This last question clearly takes us back to the question of the proper role and purpose of residential care for the adult physically disabled. It is perhaps not surprising that when society in general is so unclear about what is expected or required from residential care institutions for this group, residential care staff focus their time and energy on the most tangible and immediate task at hand.

ii Space and Moving Around

'Severely disabled people are space guzzlers of necessity'.[2] The space required by disabled people includes physical space for manoeuvering and storing wheelchairs and other special equipment, as well as space for social activities and private space to be alone or to entertain friends.

The availability of both private space (single rooms) and space for social activities (common rooms, etc) may vary between different types of home. The health authority units studied by Canter *et al* had the least number of single rooms and the least number of common rooms whereas local authority homes had most single rooms *and* most common rooms. Amount of private and social space appeared to be negatively related to degree of disability and therefore, in a sense, negatively related to need. In other words, health authority units with the least amount of private and social space also had the most severely disabled residents who rarely went out and had most visitors coming in; local authority units with the most individual and common space had the least severely disabled residents, many of whom regularly attended workshops and day centres. Lack of space, they suggest, may not only impoverish the quality of life and relationships of residents but may also lead to tension between staff and residents. However, flexibility is needed in planning accommodation because, although single rooms were generally preferred, some residents enjoyed the benefits of sharing a room.[2]

One explanation for the differences in individual and common space between types of homes may lie in their different approaches to care. 'The lack of space in the health authority units perhaps reflects the health care focus of these units and the model of patient care which emphasised the "ward" features'[2]. Health authority units have space but it is likely to be organised along 'medical' lines (eg sluice, sister's office, etc). The local authority homes in the study by Canter *et al* had been purpose built for residential care and designed in terms of a social model of care which attached significance to gardens, television rooms and patios.

Miller and Gwynne focus not so much on space *per se* but rather on the ability of residents to move around the available space. They too emphasise the importance of the prevailing model of care in influencing residents' ability to make use of or move around available space: 'Indeed, we postulate that staff attitudes toward the use of electrically operated wheelchairs are perhaps the best single indicator of the prevailing value system'. In institutions adopting the horticultural model residents were encouraged to use any equipment which maintained or extended their independence. In the institutions where the warehousing model prevailed various reasons were given for not using various forms of equipment and aids but, Miller and Gwynne suggest, such rejection may reflect '...an inability to tolerate a measure of independence in those they look after'.

It is worth pointing out here that although some types of residential care may discourage moving about and may provide too little personal and common space this lack of mobility and space is probably also true for many of the disabled people who live outside such institutions. The 'outside world' is not generous in its provision of ramps and lifts and space in buildings and on pavements for wheelchairs. Similarly, the average disabled person living on a low income is unlikely to have the space in his/her accommodation for all the aids and adaptions he/she ideally may need.

iii Providing Work

In addition to meeting needs for physical care and for individual and social activities it may be expected that homes should also provide for the work needs of their residents. Work in our society is, of course, not only a source of income but also conveys certain other social benefits such as individual identity and feelings of self-worth, opportunities for social contact, exercise of skills and self-development. Although our ideas about the value and functions of work and leisure are changing it is nevertheless true that considerable significance is still attached to work and being able to work. Although work is unlikely to be a source of financial independence for the majority of residents in homes for the physically disabled it may nevertheless be important in other ways.

Miller and Gwynne identify two basic approaches to work in residential care institutions. These two approaches—the occupational therapy approach and the work approach—correspond to their 'warehousing' and 'horticultural' approaches to care noted above. Within the occupational therapy approach work provides diversional activities in which the resident adopts an essentially passive role, exchanging dependence on a nurse for dependence on a therapist. The resident has little or no control over the nature of the work and its organisation, nor over what is done with any profit gained. 'The crucial point is not whether the task is basket-weaving or light assembly work for a factory, but to what extent it gives inmates a role that is differentiated from that of psycho-physical dependence'.[1] The 'work approach' is distinguished by the characteristics of inmate participation and involvement. Residents are involved in, or take full responsibility for, the acquisition and organisation of the work and what is done with the proceeds. Miller and Gwynne conclude that:

> . . . while inmates' work can seldom be judged by the same criteria or confer the same status as work in the outside world, it should, as far as possible, simulate the meaning of 'real' work in terms of affording them the experience of a second role, through which to relate to the institution and to the environment, and of the choices and conflicts that go with it.[1]

Canter *et al* report that three main issues arose in relation to the provision of work: whether to adopt a 'work' approach with emphasis on contracts and production, how much and on what basis to pay residents and the availability of transport to and from workshops. The main factor affecting these three issues was the severity of the residents' disability. The data from this study suggest that there are no simple solutions to the provision and the role and organisation of work within residential care institutions for the physically disabled. Some workshops, having adopted one approach, were having to adapt arrangements to the needs of an increasingly incapacitated clientele. Workshops attached to homes were able to involve those who could not travel any distance but, it was suggested, this arrangement failed to provide residents with a change of environment and social contacts. Bringing in local disabled people from outside the home was sometimes limited by transport difficulties and, it was suggested, could lead to a division between those required to attend (the residents) and those for whom attendance was voluntary.[2]

Although the place and organisation of work within residential homes for the physically disabled is likely to remain an important issue for some years to come it is worth considering its future significance. What significance will the disabled resident of tomorrow attach to work given that he/she may never have had a job? What effects will widespread unemployment have in the long term on our attitudes to the meaning of work for the able-bodied and the disabled?

iv Moving In and Out

In the sections above I have presented the research evidence concerned with what goes on inside residential care institutions for the adult physically disabled: the characteristics of those who enter residential care as residents and as staff as well as some data on the structure and culture of homes. In this section I shall consider the extent to which homes may be regarded as total institutions in the sense of being closed to the outside world.

Before looking at the data on movement in and out of homes it is important to point out that for this particular group difficulties in getting out are not peculiar to living in residential care. The physically disabled living 'in the community' may nevertheless find it difficult to go out for a variety of reasons ranging from perceived stigma to the inadequacies of public transport.[13] It is possible that for some people residential care does not make these difficulties any greater, it merely does little to reduce or overcome them.

Canter *et al* found that 28 per cent of all residents studied had not been out at all in the previous week. Nineteen per cent had had more than five outings in the previous week. Attending a day centre or going to work both counted as outings. But, as they point out, there are no comparable statistics for non-disabled people, nor for disabled people living in the community. In general visits were a less frequent occurrence than outings: 26 per cent had no visitors at all and only 5 per cent had had 6 or more visits in that week.

Although there are variations between the homes within the categories, it appears that residents in local authority homes go out more than they receive visits and the same is true for voluntary homes, although the difference between outings and visits is smaller. In health authority units the pattern is reversed with visits on average outnumbering outings.

Canter *et al* report that the majority of residents were satisfied with the level of social contact they had but rather more satisfied with the level of visits than the level of outings. Over three-quarters of the sample received visits from relatives and almost two-thirds had visits from friends. Surprisingly, only 17 per cent reported receiving visits from a social worker. Residents perceived visits as being controlled by other people whereas they felt they had rather greater control over outings, especially to shops, clubs, etc.

One interpretation of these positive findings is that, 'It is likely that residents were evaluating their social contacts in the context of the home or unit and their condition rather than in relation to some criteria relating to the life of people who are not disabled'.[2]

What factors influence the amount of social contact residents have?

Miller and Gwynne have suggested that where it was easier to go out it was also generally easier for visitors to come in; Battye makes the same suggestion.[1, 11] According to Miller and Gwynne movements out, and in, varied according to the approach to residential care adopted. Under a warehousing regime the boundaries are strictly regulated by staff, and residents go out less often and when they do go out are more likely to do so in batches and to activities specifically for the disabled.

Interestingly, Miller and Gwynne suggest that excursions out of the institution may be related to the encouragement of incoming visitors—in particular, volunteers. Where volunteers are discouraged the additional work falls on staff and excursions are then less frequent.

Drawing on previous research related to social contact in other settings, Canter *et al* consider a number of factors which might affect levels of social contact among residents in homes for the physically disabled. These include age (of resident), proximity of last accommodation, proximity of family, time since onset of disability, accessibility of facilities, degree of dependence, age of home, and time in the home. They conclude that:

> A study of outings alone showed that the most important factor was mobility, followed by accessibility of the home followed by age. The oldest and the least mobile residents in homes with not very good access were least likely to go out.

It is the everyday shopping trips or visits to the pub rather than the special outings which are excluded when homes are inaccessible.

However,

> It proved much more difficult to identify what factors affected people's visits. The only two things which showed any influence at all were proximity of last accommodation and onset of disability.[2]

If visits are indeed increased in relation to proximity of the home to last accommodation then the policy implications would seem to be that residents should be encouraged to enter homes nearer where they used to live rather than near relatives. Here, however, Canter *et al* identify a further factor of relevance. Health authority units have smaller catchment areas, local authority homes rather wider areas and voluntary homes the widest catchment areas. Furthermore, whereas there tends to be transfer of residents between local authorities little transfer occurs between health authorities. Whether or not the likelihood of transfers given the current financial situation of local and health authorities has decreased since the study by Canter *et al* is debatable.

The data presented above suggest that, for various reasons, residents' relationships with staff and with others outside the institution are constrained in different degrees and ways.

According to Miller and Gwynne relationships with staff and with 'the outside world' are not only significant in themselves but also in their effects on interaction between residents. Where there is greater quantity and quality of residents' interaction with 'the outside world' there may also be greater quality and quantity of interaction *within* the institution. Miller and Gwynne suggest that where there is tight control of the boundary there is also a rigid, hierarchical distinction between staff and 'patient'. Where there is greater involvement in and out of the institution there is more likely to be a more egalitarian relationship between staff and residents in which friendships and leisure time spent together become possible. Furthermore, 'We found that greater openness in transactions across the boundary was associated with a higher quantity and quality of interaction. There were more interpersonal bonds and more friendship groups'. It is suggested that staff control over the boundaries of the institution and of the individual, by reduction of choice, diminishes the individual's personal identity and thereby reduces his/her ability to make and maintain relationships.

Apart from the value of operating an open-door policy which they suggest generates more visits and maintains relationships with friends and kin, Miller and Gwynne also highlight the importance of enabling the resident to take the role of host to visitors. In taking the role of host the resident is able to exercise not only choice (in who visits and when and with what level of hospitality) but also experiences the role of giver rather than taker (dependant). Miller and Gwynne emphasise that 'Benign permissiveness is not enough' in encouraging a resident to overcome his/her dependent role as recipient of care '...a powerful countervailing social system is needed to allow and encourage him to take up less passive roles'.[1]

Paradoxically, it is arguable that although some residential institutions may encourage dependence they may also be in a better position than possessive, protective or hard-pressed families and well-meaning friends to provide the structure for opportunities for greater independence.

7 The Financial Costs of Residential Care

Although there are very few data on the costs of residential provision for the young adult physically disabled it seems reasonable to suppose that they will vary between types of home and between homes in different locations. Harrison attempted to compare costs between types of home in his national survey but found that many respondents could not provide costs and that data from different types of homes were not comparable. Data from voluntary homes are likely to represent charges rather than costs, omitting any subsidy from independent funds. The ceiling rates for Social Security payments also appear to influence the data presented on costs.[3]

It is, of course, important to distinguish in considering costs between capital and revenue costs and between costs *per se* and costs to the state. These distinctions are particularly significant given the proportion of homes run by voluntary bodies to many of which the state directly contributes little or nothing in terms of capital costs.

Data on the costs of residential care are of little value in policy terms unless there are data on the costs of similar alternative forms of provision with which they may be compared. A detailed and complex review of the relative costs of residential and home care for the disabled was prepared some years ago by the Economist Intelligence Unit.[14] Although the figures in this report are now out of date it is worth noting the main conclusions of this very detailed analysis.

Having distinguished between single and shared home accommodation and between intensive and moderate packages of domiciliary services the report concludes that:

> Firstly, it is clearly normally cheaper to care for people at home than in institutions. Secondly, the difference, whilst varying between cases, is of the order of £10 a week, which is significant but certainly less than the figures sometimes quoted. Quite apart from the preferences of patients, the standard of home care assumed is higher than hospitals in that single bedrooms are assumed which is not the case for the hospital.

The report explains the difference in cost in terms of the lower capital cost of an *extra* bedroom and full quota of special fittings in a family house compared with the capital cost of a place in a new institution. Much more contentiously the report goes on:

> 'Secondly, the family can cope with constant attendance at less cost than an institution, even allowing for incidental expenses and some earnings losses. Finally, organising the logistics of constant attendance, which effectively cost a hospital £5 a week, costs the family nothing directly. Indirectly, it may be the main cause of the severe stress families caring for the disabled often suffer, but no simple financial cost can be attached to that burden'.[14]

The importance of distinguishing between tangible financial costs and other costs and between costs to the state and to others is clearly apparent here. It is also important in assessing the significance of this conclusion to note that the cost of providing continuity in home care has been assessed at the level of statutory attendance allowance. Clearly this measure of the real cost of constant attendance at home depends upon certain assumptions about the adequacy of attendance allowance, the availability of a carer at home and the opportunity costs of such a carer being available.

Having concluded that home care is generally cheaper than residential care, the report further suggests that if relative costs are compared over time, 'savings' are evident. Most crippling diseases entail some element of progressive deterioration but if the rate of deterioration is slowed down and hospitalisation delayed this is

> ...distinctly advantageous from an economic point of view:
> (a) because an expense postponed, on a present value basis, costs society less:
>
> (b) because any disabled person who avoids hospitalisation or institutionalisation for a time, is at risk of death from some other cause...and may therefore never become institutionalised.

An approximate estimate of the savings from a year's postponement of institutionalisation is put at 15–20 per cent of the cost of a year's institutional care.[14]

The report makes two further important points. First, it is not sufficient to show that home care is cheaper if in fact the necessary domiciliary services do not exist to provide standards of care similar to those in institutions. 'Discharging institutional patients would, and sometimes does, lead to even lower costs—at the price of neglect and low standards'.

Second, given competition for limited domiciliary services the use of such services to maintain severely disabled people at home may not be regarded as the most efficient use of resources, ie even though care at home is cheaper than residential care. In other words, when domiciliary services are in short supply it may be more efficient to allocate those services to those who need *least* care in order to remain at home and thus prevent or postpone the institutionalisation of the maximum number of people.

In view of the present shortage of domiciliary services in most local authorities and the increasing numbers of elderly people it seems likely that analysis of the relative costs of home care versus residential care for the younger physically disabled will carry little weight in decisions about effective resource allocation.

8 Conclusion

At various points in this brief review I have drawn attention to the *relative* advantages or disadvantages, strengths or weaknesses of residential care for the younger physically disabled. The very small amount of research evidence on the organisation and 'effects' of residential care for this group is, in many respects, critical and depressing. Without wishing in any way to suggest that the criticism is misplaced it is obviously important to put residential care into a comparative perspective, to view the data on residential care in the light of data on alternative forms of care. Residential care may not be ideal but how does it compare with the alternatives? Without writing a similar review on the alternatives to residential care it is obviously impossible properly to provide this wider perspective within which to place residential care but it may be worth noting briefly a number of points.

There is, however, another reason for looking at the data on residential care against the background of the available alternatives. The characteristics of those in care and their reasons for entering care highlight both the importance of informal care and the strains such caring involves. For many entry into residential care is a last resort and the demand for residential care is, in an important sense, a reflection of the real availability of satisfactory alternatives to residential care. It is arguable that we cannot begin to consider the future of residential care without *first* considering the current and future alternatives to residential care. Before briefly reviewing some of these alternatives it is worth noting that one of the difficulties in assessing their significance for the future of residential care is that many are currently presented as local 'experiments'. Whether or not the many local experiments when added together currently constitute, or have the potential to constitute, part of a systematic, national package of provision is debatable.

For the vast majority of adult physically disabled people the current alternative to residential care is care in their own homes. Furthermore, it seems reasonable to suppose that a proportion of those currently in residential care institutions could be cared for at home were the 'right' packages of domiciliary and day care support services available. Current government policy emphasises the value of informal care but unfortunately this theoretical commitment has not been accompanied by positive measures designed to increase the quantity and distribution of services to support informal care. At present care in the community is not a viable alternative for some because of the lack of support services and benefits—or is an alternative but only at considerable cost to the carers and the disabled.

Although informal care is currently the dominant means of provision for the majority of the adult physically disabled there are, as noted above, reasons to doubt whether it will be available on the same scale in future.

There is, of course, no legislation at present which requires local authorities to provide care services to support carers of the disabled. However, some local authorities do directly or indirectly, via aid to voluntary organisations, provide limited forms of regular and respite support.

The home help service is of limited relevance to most disabled people and their families partly because it is, in practice, primarily confined to the elderly and partly because it is not in any case organised to give the type of help needed by most families with a disabled member. Of much greater potential relevance are the various forms of domiciliary care attendant schemes now being developed throughout the country. Crossroads Care Attendant Schemes, the voluntary sector pioneers, are growing rapidly in number but there are still areas in which there is no scheme of any sort. In areas where a scheme does exist demand is likely to exceed supply.

An alternative to residential care, or some would argue an alternative form of residential care, which has grown considerably in recent years is 'fostering' or 'family placement'. Although initially used for children and then extended to the elderly, many local authorities are now using family placement schemes for a wide range of client groups including the physically disabled. The placement of those in need of care with carers in their (the carers') own homes in return for a relatively small payment has the advantages of being relatively inexpensive and providing individual, local, family care.

I have discussed elsewhere the reported advantages and some of the disadvantages and difficulties presented by this approach to the provision of care[15]. Certainly, this approach would seem to overcome some of the difficulties and disadvantages of institutional care for the physically disabled. It would appear that there is considerable scope for development of such schemes. Scheme organisers report that carers are able to cope with far more dependent groups than originally envisaged. However, one of the difficulties reported by schemes is that of finding sufficient carers with appropriate accommodation (particularly in some areas) for the frail elderly, eg ground floor bedroom, toilet and bathroom. These difficulties are likely to be even greater in relation to the provision of appropriate accommodation for the physically disabled. Another disadvantage of this approach is, of course, that although individual, local, family care may be what some require, others, perhaps especially the young physically disabled, are looking for the benefits of group living.

There has been very little research into family placement schemes in general and more is certainly needed[15, 16, 17]. It is obviously important that further research focusses upon the potential of schemes to meet the needs of particular client groups and, in this context, that such research recognises the existence of different needs within the range of 'adult physically disabled'. In considering different needs it is clearly necessary to distinguish between age groups as well as between the need for respite care (to enable a young person to remain at home) and for long-term care. In considering provision of long-term care by means of a family placement scheme it is essential to distinguish between those with deteriorating and 'stable' conditions and, in particular, to consider the implications of deteriorating conditions for both the disabled person and the carer.

I have mentioned above the difficulties faced by some respite and long-term care schemes of finding carers with appropriate accommodation. This is, of course, only one aspect of the much wider problem of suitable accommodation for the adult physically disabled. Again it seems reasonable to suppose that with more appropriate accommodation not only might family placement schemes be extended but more disabled people might be able to live independently or remain with their own families for longer and/or to do so more comfortably.

The Chronically Sick and Disabled Persons Act of 1970 expressly charged local authorities with making special housing provision for this group (to be subsidised by central government) and there has been some increase in the supply of purpose-built accommodation for the disabled since the Act. However, it is very unlikely that present supply meets more than a fraction of the need.[5]

Local authority housing provision does not, of course, benefit the disabled who are owner-occupiers. Owner-occupation has risen dramatically in recent years in the general population. Because the future population of disabled is likely to be composed largely, as it is now, of people who become disabled in middle age the proportion of disabled owner-occupiers is likely to increase. This growing group may be helped by local authorities to make adaptations to their own properties. However, many of the most desirable adaptations are expensive and local authorities may consider it a more efficient use of resources to spend money on building hostels or residential homes or local authority owned purpose-built accommodation, ie continuing accommodation for disabled people which will not be lost to the authority after the sale of the privately owned adapted accommodation.

The Economist Intelligence Unit report recommended the creation of a Finance House for the disabled which would lend money for house improvements and other purposes. However, it is unclear what impact this would have if, as the report suggests, it operated within the normal commercial framework.[14]

Various other proposals have been made for increasing the supply of appropriate accommodation for the disabled.[5] Proposals need to take into account the current needs of the disabled person, those of his/her relatives for continuing accommodation, as well as the need to retain scarce accommodation for the use of other disabled people. Topliss suggests:

> The existence of a pool of accommodation run by the housing authority on behalf of the families of disabled people to whom they allocate special accommodation would not only preserve the ownership of a home to which the surviving relatives could ultimately return but would also, in the interim period, give the housing department useful temporary accommodation for others on their list.[5]

In the last ten years there have been a number of interesting developments in the provision of accommodation adapted to the needs of the disabled. The development of housing schemes by the Cheshire Foundation, by the Multiple Sclerosis Society and by Habinteg (an offshoot of the Spastics Society), among others, are interesting not only as experiments in appropriate accommodation but also as examples of statutory-voluntary collaboration in provision for the disabled. There are, however, difficulties in such collaboration as well as the design and subsequent allocation, organisation and operation of accommodation; such developments cannot be seen as a 'simple' alternative to residential care. (See for example, Dartington, Miller and Gwynne.[18])

Perhaps the most basic message to emerge from this review of research into residential care for the adult physically disabled is that many of the disadvantages and difficulties in providing such care stem from a failure to recognise the inadequacy of the label itself. There is no one group 'the adult physically disabled' but rather a variety of groups distinguished by age, type of condition, degree of dependence, family circumstance and so on. In the laudable attempt to distinguish the (young) adult physically disabled from the elderly it seems that we have failed to pursue the further distinctions which are necessary. The failure to distinguish within the category of adult physically disabled has meant that the *different* needs of 'the disabled' have been inadequately identified. Without adequate analysis of the (different) needs of the adult physically disabled it is perhaps unsurprising that the (different) purposes of residential care are confused. Lack of clarity in the purpose of residential care for the adult physically disabled has been a key theme running through this review. Without clear analysis of for *whom* residential care is provided confusion over purposes, tasks, and roles of staff and residents is likely to remain.

In addition to recognising that 'the adult physically disabled' does not exist as an entity but is rather composed of a number of groups with different and sometimes conflicting needs, discussion of residential care for these groups must also adopt a dynamic approach. Disablement implies progressive deterioration for *some*, and natural ageing for all. The distinction between the young adult physically disabled and the elderly may be a 'once and for all' distinction in policy, but in reality it is one which must be constantly, and often painfully, reapplied.

Any discussion of the future of residential care for the adult physically disabled must take into account not only the changing context of informal care but also the different and changing needs, resources and expectations of the very different groups concealed behind the label 'adult physically disabled.'

It may not be only needs which are changing but the expectations of the future generation of younger disabled adults may also be very different. For example, the growth in technological aids for disabled children in schools are likely to create new needs and expectations of provision after school. It is against this background that the future relevance and appropriate purposes, forms and standards of different types of residential care may be assessed.

Increasing experimentation with alternative forms of accommodation and care coupled with the demographic factors outlined above may produce a very different population of customers of residential care. In future the greatest demand for residential care may come not from the young adult physically disabled but from the older, more severely disabled requiring some level of nursing care. This will clearly present a number of resource problems but it may, in effect, serve to clarify and narrow the purposes of residential care for this group, thus 'solving' one of the key problems identified in this review.

Finally, it is worth noting the list of recommendations drawn from a number of sources and presented by Harrison. This list provides specific suggestions for local and national action but, more fundamentally, considers residential care as part of a wider programme designed to extend and improve the living options of the younger physically disabled.

(1) Establish some kind of local disability register.
(2) Establish 'physical handicap teams' for planning and the provision of services.
(3) Improve facilities for individual assessment.
(4) Improve and coordinate conventional rehabilitation.
(5) Cooperate with and encourage the relevant authorities in respect of housing.
(6) Improve and widen the availability of personal equipment.
(7) Establish and extend care attendance schemes.
(8) Ensure that there are the best possible opportunities for occupation, social contact and employment.
(9) Ensure that there is adequate provision for the relief of carers.
(10) Take steps to spread information and understanding about disability, both to those individuals who require it and to the public at large.

In an important document produced in 1985, the Prince of Wales' Advisory Group on Disability added to that list several more items which may be summarised as follows:

(11) Involve disabled people and their carers on advisory and consultative committees.
(12) Develop more flexible and creative responses for funding, and consider the establishment of a shared budget between Health and Social Services.

(13) Before planning any new residential facilities, consider the use of available funds for a radical improvement in domiciliary services.

(14) Encourage the establishment of local disablement associations and centres for independent living.

(15) Acknowledge that some physically disabled people have behavioural problems and are not receiving adequate help or rehabilitation.

(16) Be specially aware of the needs of young people, particularly those with multiple handicaps, as they move from paediatrics and education to adult services.

(17) Give special attention to an adequate and reliable service for incontinence.

(18) Give special attention to the adequacy of transport.

(19) Review the use of existing YDUs to see if they can be more generally used for other functions than permanent residence.

(20) Be aware of training needs for all staff concerned with services for disabled people.[3]

Notes and References

1. Miller, E. J. and Gwynne, G. V. (1972), *A Life Apart*, Tavistock Publications.

2. Canter, H., Barnitt, R. and Buckland, S. (1981), *This is Their Home: A Study of Residential Homes for Adults with Physical Disablement*, unpublished report, DHSS.

3. Harrison, F. J. (1986), *The Young Disabled Adult, The Use of Residential Homes and Hospital Units for the Age Group 16–64: A Report of the Royal College of Physicians*, Royal College of Physicians.

4. Goffman, E. (1961), *Asylums*, Penguin.

5. Topliss, E. (1975), *Provision for the Disabled*, Basil Blackwell.

6. Davis, K. (1984), 'Consumer participation in service design, delivery and control' in *Seminar Report: Centres for Independent Living*, Centre on Environment for the Handicapped.

7. Department of Health and Social Security (1984), *Residential Accommodation for the Elderly and for Younger Physically Handicapped People*, RA/84/2, DHSS.

8. Harris, A., Cox, E. and Smith, R. (1971), *Handicapped and Impaired in Great Britain, Part 1*, HMSO.

9. Topliss, E. (1982), *Social Responses to Handicap*, Longman.

10. Wood, P. N. H. (1978), 'Size of the problem and causes of chronic sickness in the young', paper given at Symposium: The Young Chronic Sick, *Journal of the Royal Society of Medicine*, 71, pp. 437–442.

11. Battye, L. (1975), 'Caring for the disabled', *Social Service Quarterly*, 48, 4, pp. 298–300.

12. Shearer, A. (1975), *No Place Like Home: Hostels and Homes for Mentally Handicapped Adults*, Discussion Paper 5, Campaign for Mentally Handicapped People.

13. Sainsbury, S. (1970), *Registered as Disabled*, Bell.

14. Economist Intelligence Unit (1973), *Care with Dignity: an Analysis of Costs and Care for the Disabled*, Action Research for the Crippled Child Monograph, National Fund for Research into Crippling Diseases.

15. Leat, D. and Gay, P. (1987), *Paying for Care*, Policy Studies Institute.

16. Thornton, P. and Moore, J. (1980), *The Placement of Elderly People in Private Households: an Analysis of Current Provision*, University of Leeds.

17. Leat, D. (1983), *A Home from Home?*, Age Concern Research Unit.

18. Dartington, T., Miller, E. J. and Gwynne, G.V. (1981), *A Life Together: the Distribution of Attitudes Around the Disabled*, Tavistock Publications.

Residential Care for Elderly People

Ian Sinclair

National Institute for Social Work

CONTENTS

Residential Care for Elderly People

Part 1   The Background to Policy

The post war home was not a hospital and yet it was not a home. It lay uncertainly somewhere between and in a thousand details there was no clear answer to the problem of how it should be managed (Townsend, 1962).[1]

Public authorities also need to work together in both planning and service organisation to ensure the most effective collaboration possible and reduce overlapping or duplication of activity (DHSS, 1981).[2]

The general view of both researchers and practitioners is that joint planning has, at best, achieved very limited results and, at worst has been a total waste of time (Wistow, 1986).[3]

1   Introduction

A residential care home has been defined as 'any establishment which provides or is intended to provide, whether for reward or not, residential accommodation with both board and personal care for four or more persons in need of personal care by reasons of old age, disablement, past or present dependence on alcohol or drugs or past or present mental disorder'.[4] This paper examines what is known from research about this form of provision for the elderly.

2   Aims

Until recently, explicit policy in the field of residential care for the elderly has focussed on local authority homes, attempting to define their objectives in relation to hospitals on the one hand and community care on the other. At the same time, efforts have been made to ensure that the homes provide enough places for those who want and need them, and have adequate standards of care. More recently, policy debates have focussed on the growth of private residential care for the elderly.

[243]

In tracing these developments it is convenient to begin with the National Assistance Act of 1948. In the rhetoric of that time old people's homes were to be 'hotels' in which the relationship between staff and residents was analogous to that between guests and hotel keepers. Admission was thus to be a matter of the old person's choice rather than necessity. As Mr Bevan put it in 1947:

> There is no reason why the public character of these places should not be very much in the background, because the whole idea is that the welfare authority should provide them and charge an economic rent for them, so that any old people who would wish to go may go there in exactly the same way as many well-to-do people have been accustomed to go into residential hotels.[5]

This hotel concept sat oddly with the public assistance institutions which provided much residential care for the elderly and was resisted by hospital doctors facing, as they saw it, the problem of old people 'blocking' hospital beds for social rather than medical reasons.[6] The doctors felt that such patients should be in old people's homes, and that some way should be found of giving the doctors the necessary control over admission to the homes. Moreover, old age pensions did not allow most old people to pay an 'economic rent', thus implicitly requiring 'need' as well as 'choice' to be considered in an admission.

In 1962 a new twist to the arguments over homes was given by Townsend, who questioned whether they should exist at all.[1] In his survey of old people's homes he found that many of them left much to be desired in terms of their physical fabric and the way they were run. He argued that most of their residents had not wished to enter the homes and that most were not so disabled that they could not be maintained in the community with the support of domiciliary services. The few old people who were too ill or frail to be cared for in this way should be cared for in hospital. The need for old people's homes would thus be reduced or disappear.

Townsend's critique did not fully prevail. In particular the number of places in homes has increased since his survey. Nevertheless, partly in response to his findings, there have been a number of official circulars designed to improve the design and fabric of homes—making them less institutional and more domestic without incurring undue costs. At the same time there have been repeated official endorsements of community care. In this context the homes are seen as:

> Primarily a means of providing a greater degree of support for those elderly people no longer able to cope with the practicalities of living in their own homes even with the help of the domiciliary services.[7]

The debate over the role of old people's homes as hotels or places for the very dependent has in a sense been revived by the growth of private residential care for the elderly. On the one hand, it can be argued that the private sector can expand the quantity of residential provision and increase choice for elderly people—rationales in keeping with the 1948 view of old people's homes as hotels. By contrast, one of the central criticisms of private provision reflects the 1977 view of homes as essentially places of last resort.

Thus it is argued that public funds are being used to finance in private homes old people 'who do not need to be there',[8] and that social security funds should not be more easily available for residential than community care.

3 Need for Residential Care

The concept of 'need' for residential care has not been precisely defined in statute or agreed in practice. Whatever the definition of such needs, however, recent demographic and social trends are likely to have increased them. Basically, the number of frail elderly people is growing and the number of family members available to look after them falling. At least five major trends are involved:

- The growth in the elderly population—particularly the very elderly (those aged 85 or more).

- The consequent growth in the number of people who are very disabled or suffer from dementia.

- The increase in the numbers of elderly people living alone (a group, as shown later, particularly likely to apply for residential care).

- The falling pool of potential care givers (particularly women aged 40 to 49) relative to the numbers of elderly people (a marked trend since 1901, but recently reversing).

- The increasing proportion of women in this age group who work (in 1961, 44 per cent of women aged 45–54 were according to official figures in work, a proportion which rose to 68 per cent in 1981).

More detailed evidence is given in Table 1.

The effects of these trends on 'need for residential care' is likely to be increased in certain areas by migration. According to the Census, slightly over one third of heads of households in England and Wales were not in the same house as they were five years previously. Migration is much higher in some areas than others with the consequence that elderly people form a higher than average proportion of the population of inner cities, from whence younger people have often moved out, and of retirement areas.

Evidence of the effects of these trends can be seen in social surveys. For example, according to Hunt[9], in Yorkshire and Humberside, relatives and friends visit four out of ten elderly people more than once a week, and only one in twenty elderly people are never visited by a relative. In Greater London, however, only a quarter of the elderly people receive a visit from a relative more than once a week and one in six never receive one at all.[9] In a study of elderly social services clients living alone in an inner London borough, only one third were found to have relatives living in the same borough.[10]

Additional pressures on residential accommodation are likely to come from the increasing number of single, widowed and divorced people aged over 65. The numbers of such people rose by a quarter of a million between 1971 and 1981, mainly because of the increased number of elderly widows. However, patterns of marriage and divorce are also changing and may affect demand for residential care. For example, daughters may be less willing to look after their step-mothers than their own mothers.

Table 1 The Need for Care 1971–2001, Great Britain

	1971	1981	1991	2001	1971–2001 % change
Total population (thousands) aged:					
65–69	2,647	2,667	2,718	2,398	−9.4
70–74	1,957	2,265	2,233	2,176	+11.2
75–79	1,301	1,601	1,793	1,825	+40.3
80–84	773	900	1,208	1,210	+56.6
85+	462	552	843	1,047	+126.5
Estimated number (thousands) of persons aged 65+ who are:					
Living alone*	2,285	2,660	2,973	2,943	+28.8
Unable to get in/out bed unaided*	122	146	176	185	+51.9
Suffering dementia†	450	529	653	684	+51.9

Adapted from Henwood and Wicks.[11] For method of adaptation and sources of data see Annexe 1.
* In community.
† In total population.

4 Demand for Residential Care

The shortage of residential places and the inability of many elderly people to pay for private residential care means that the latent demand for residential care has to be measured hypothetically, by asking elderly people what they would like to do. To complicate matters further, demand for residential care comes from at least three sources—the elderly people themselves; their relatives; and professionals (such as hospital consultants or sheltered housing wardens).

For their part, the vast majority of elderly people do not wish to enter a home if this can be avoided. In a recent community survey of elderly people aged over 75 in South Glamorgan, 98 per cent of the respondents agreed that 'retired people should be maintained in their own homes for as long as possible'.[12] The achievement of this aim was seen to entail some sacrifice on the part of the family which most respondents, particularly men, felt was their due. Nevertheless, it was not felt that the sacrifice should be too extreme. The majority did not agree that daughters should be prepared to give up work to look after dependent parents.

This constellation of attitudes is similar to that found by West and his colleagues in a community survey in Scotland.[13, 14] They presented a large community sample in three contrasting areas of Scotland with a series of vignettes of people suffering from varying disabling conditions and asked them which of a number of care options they would choose. The least preferred options, for all but one of the vignettes, involved family and informal care only on the one hand or residential care on the other. It was striking that two-thirds of the sample felt that residential care was the best solution in the vignettes involving the elderly mentally ill. For the other groups, however, most people wanted local care which was shared between family and services.

In keeping with this evidence, sheltered housing is considered by many in the community to be a good solution to the problems of the frail—enabling them to maintain their independence while having some-one on hand if need arises.[15, 16] In another study, West and his colleagues[15] asked 104 rheumatic and arthritic patients whether, if their condition deteriorated to the point where they could not manage in their own homes, they would prefer to move in with a relative, move into a sheltered home or move into a residential home. Three-quarters said they would prefer sheltered housing, the remainder splitting their preferences equally between relatives and residential care.

The major disadvantages of residential care are described by older people in the community as being loss of independence and privacy, and to a lesser extent, the need to mix with elderly or uncongenial company.[12, 17] Most people, however, also see some advantages, mainly the provision of comfort and physical care, but also the reduction of loneliness. In the light of these advantages, 5 per cent of a community sample of elderly people aged 75 or over in Hammersmith and Fulham were 'interested' in the idea of entering a home even though most of this 5 per cent were quite fit.[17] Moreover, a further 17 per cent felt that they might 'have to' enter a home. Similarly, 16 per cent of the Glamorgan sample said that they would be 'prepared to consider' residential care if they were 'unable to prepare and cook a hot meal' and as many as 52 per cent that would do so if they were 'unable to control their bowels or bladder'.[11]

Nevertheless only a minority (about a fifth in each case) said that they would be pleased or very pleased to enter a local authority residential home, private rest home, or nursing home.

Relatives also become increasingly willing to consider residential care for an old person as the latter's disability or confusion increases. Levin and her colleagues found that roughly one in five of a sample of relatives looking after 'confused' elderly people in touch with services said they would have definitely or probably accepted residential care for them.[18] Allen studied two samples of short stay residents in local authority homes and found that nearly four in ten of their relatives would have liked permanent care for them.[19]

Evidence that the latent demand for residential care is turned into requests for care if places are available, comes from the wide variations in residential provision. Devon provides an instructive example. In 1984 this county's private homes provided about one seventh of the private residential places in England. Nevertheless they were far from being a national resource. Hardly any advertised nationally, 91 per cent of their residents came from within Devon and 81 per cent from within the boundaries of their own social services division.[20] Although there was some evidence of vacant beds in areas of Devon with a very high level of private provision, bed vacancies were far from being a major problem. Demand for residential care may be particularly high in the areas to which private homes have been attracted. Nevertheless, there have traditionally been wide variations in the number of local authority beds in old people's homes provided by authorities with apparently similar levels of need, and the more generous providers do not seem to have had trouble in filling their homes.

Further circumstantial evidence of unmet demand comes from comparison of British figures for the proportion of those over 65 who are in nursing homes or old people's homes with figures from other industrialised countries. The latest figures I have been able to get for the United States, Denmark, West Germany and Holland suggest that England and Wales are comparatively low providers of residential care. The numbers in homes or nursing homes for the elderly per 1,000 over 65 in these countries ran from 43 (in West Germany) to 112.5 (Netherlands). The comparable figure for residential homes and nursing homes in England and Wales in 1984 was 28.5.

5 Trends in Provision

Over the past fifty years, the numbers of elderly individuals in institutions has been rising, not only absolutely but also in terms of age-specific rates. This rise has been particularly marked among women, who are now more likely than men to be in institutions on the night of the Census. The differences in the trends for men and women may reflect improvements in the relative prosperity of old men as against that of old women (men, for example, benefit more from occupational pension schemes).[21] More impressive evidence for the influence of income maintenance on demand for residential care is the drop between 1901 and 1921 in the age/sex specific rates of old people in poor law institutions—a drop which Moroney has argued reflects the introduction of the Old Age Pension in 1908.[22]

Many elderly people in institutions are in hospital rather than in residential care, but, contrary to some of the arguments raised in 1948, the elderly rich are not flocking in large numbers to hotels or boarding houses, nor for that matter are the elderly poor often found in common lodgings and hostels. In the 1981 census the elderly usually resident in residential institutions were found predominantly in three places; psychiatric wards and nursing homes for the psychiatrically ill (*circa* 46,000); other hospitals and nursing home provision (*circa* 47,000); and homes for the elderly and disabled (*circa* 174,000).

Since the Second World War, the lion's share of providing this accommodation in homes for the elderly and disabled has been borne by local authorities. In absolute terms the growth of their contribution in this field has been impressive. In 1952 English and Welsh authorities supported 42.9 thousand elderly people in residential accommodation. By 1982 this figure had approximately trebled, to 124.3 thousand (including a small proportion of short stay residents).[23] In recent years, however, the number of places in local authority homes has been levelling off and decreasing relative to the rise in the number of people over 75. Local authorities have also been decreasing the degree to which they support individuals in private or voluntary establishments, feeling perhaps that such people can be supported by the social security system (see Table 2).

The reduction of local authority funding for residents in the voluntary sector has led to demands for other forms of financial support.[24] This other funding has taken the form of board and lodging allowances for residents from the supplementary benefits system. A 1980 discretionary power allowing theoretically unlimited amounts of benefit to be paid to elderly people in residential and nursing homes when it was unreasonable to expect them to move has been increasingly used. Attempts to control expenditure of this kind, by imposing local limits on the amount payable, appeared to result in a levelling-up of charges in homes. According to an Office of Health Economics survey, about 40 per cent of residents in private homes now receive support from the supplementary benefit system.[24]

Demographic change and supplementary benefit funds have fuelled a dramatic increase in the number of residents in private and voluntary homes in England and Wales (from circa 43,000 in 1974 to circa 82,000 in 1984). The great bulk of this increase was accounted for by the private sector which has nearly trebled over this period (from 19,300 occupied places to 55,000), while the voluntary sector has increased only slightly (from 23,300 occupied places to 26,900).[25] This growth is apparently continuing. In July 1984, for example, Devon County Council had 454 private homes, whereas by May 1986 these had increased by a third to 605.[20] In 1984/5 the DHSS estimated 42,000 elderly claimants for board and lodging allowances, whereas an Audit Commission survey estimates a rise to 85,000 by the end of 1986.[25]

Table 2 Rate of LA Supported Residents Per Thousand in Age Specific Population by Sector, England

	1975 1	1980 2	1984 3
Number of LA supported residents per thousand in age specific group who are:			
Aged 65–74 years in			
LA homes	4.29	6.17	4.06
Voluntary homes	0.57	0.81	0.46
Private homes	0.06	0.18	0.07
Aged 75–84 years in			
LA homes	21.4	18.46	17.90
Voluntary homes	3.06	2.06	1.31
Private homes	0.34	0.58	0.21
Aged 85+ in			
LA homes	81.85	75.20	75.27
Voluntary homes	11.25	9.75	6.94
Private homes	1.16	2.60	1.45

Notes and Sources:
Based on DHSS, PSS, LA, statistics RA/84/1–2.[26]
1. Estimated home population, mid year (revised), OPCS (1977) Table 3.[27]
   Excludes short-stay residents in LA homes.
2. Estimated home population, mid year, OPCS (1981) Table 3.[28]
3. Estimated home population, mid year, OPCS (1986) Table 1.2.[29]

These changes have been accompanied and perhaps encouraged by a fall in the number of geriatric beds and elderly patients in mental illness hospitals and units relative to the numbers of elderly people, by increasing turnover in these institutions, and almost certainly by a reduction in the numbers of long-stay patients relative to the increasing number of very old people.[30]

Table 3 Balance of Care for Elderly People, England and Wales

	1974		1979		1984	
	Nos	Nos per 1,000 75+	Nos	Nos per 1,000 75+	Nos	Nos per 1,000 75+
Occupied hospital beds (geriatrics)	54,600	22.1	54,500	19.6	54,100	17.1
LA homes (occupied places)	98,600	40.0	109,100	39.3	109,200	34.5
Nursing home (long-stay occupied beds)	11,900	4.8	13,800	5.0	24,100	7.6
Voluntary homes (occupied places)	23,300	9.5	25,600	9.2	26,900	8.5
Private homes (occupied places)	19,300	7.8	26,800	9.7	55,000	17.4
Day patient (attendance/day)	4,100	1.7	5,000	1.8	7,000	2.2
LA day centre (places)	13,800	5.6	29,100	10.5	34,400	10.9
Home help staff (wte's)	45,200	18.3	49,600	17.9	56,700	17.9
Meals (000's per year)	35,200	14.3	43,300	15.6	45,000	14.2

Source: Audit Commission.[25]

Despite the policy of community care, these changes have not been accompanied by a growth in domiciliary services relative to the numbers aged over 75. Local authority day care has indeed increased both absolutely and relative to the rising numbers of elderly. Other services, however, have at best increased in line with demographic changes or even fallen behind[25] (see Table 3).

In assessing these developments it should be remembered that at least 60 per cent of those in private homes pay for themselves. The growth in publicly funded care for the elderly has therefore been less than the growth of residential care overall. It can even be argued that the rate of publicly funded residential provision for those over 75 has fallen.[31] What has happened is that a higher proportion of the costs of residential care now falls on central Government and private individuals.

6 Variations in Provision

These trends have proceeded at different rates in different parts of the country and there are wide variations between authorities in provision and in the relative contributions of different sectors. In 1984, for example, nine authorities had no private homes, while there were nearly eleven and a half thousand beds in private homes in Devon and East Sussex alone. Whereas Kensington and Chelsea had 109.8 beds per 1,000 over 75 in voluntary homes and 169.3 beds in local authority homes, the comparable figures for Westminster were 0 and 91.5. Thameside had a combined private, voluntary and local authority bed rate per thousand over 75 of 41.7 whereas the comparable figure for Wandsworth was 118.8.[32]

In general, public provision of residential care for the elderly tends to be high in the poorer areas (those with high unemployment and low proportions of people in social classes 1 and 2), while private provision tends to be high in rich ones. Private provision is also likely to be high in areas with high proportions of old people over 75 and its growth has been highest in the retirement areas of the South and South West. It has also been influenced by the availability and cost of suitable housing, being discouraged, for example, by the high cost of housing in the capital.[24]

Within local authorities the distribution of private provision is also varied. In Norfolk, for example, the number of places in private homes in 1984 varied from 33 per thousand aged 65 or over in one area, to 5.9 in another. The highest concentration was around former seaside resorts. Commenting on this, Weaver and his colleagues[33] suggest the establishment of a private residential home is 'at least in part a pragmatic response to the availability of suitable reasonably priced accommodation.' Wide variation in the provision of private residential care within an authority has also been documented in Devon.[34]

Attempts to explain the variations in public residential provision between authorities suggest that these only partly reflect differences in 'need' and the provision of substitute services. Thus Davies and his colleagues[35] showed that the extent of provision of different services in Welfare Departments did reflect variations in need between authorities, and in certain respects variations in other services (voluntary old people's homes seemed to be used as substitutes for local authority homes in that a high provision of one tended to be accompanied by a lower than average provision of the other). The extent of service provision, however, was also related to who had been chief officer and to the political colour of the ruling party.

Following this work, Gorbach and Sinclair used 1976 data on services for the elderly to confirm that high provision of services, including residential services, tended to go with high 'need'.[36] Their evidence suggested that services which were less generously provided relative to need tended to be rationed (for example, by increasing throughput, or providing a lower intensity service or concentrating on the very elderly). Rationing in one service was sometimes associated with rationing in another (for example, a high turnover in geriatric hospitals was associated with measures of rationing in the home help service). However, the provision of residential care was not, if allowance was made for need, correlated with provision of home help, and tended to be high if the level of geriatric hospital provision was high. It appeared therefore that although services operated to some extent as a system with the level of one service influencing rationing behaviour in another, they were not at that time planned as a system.

More recent evidence suggests that the position has not changed. According to Bebbington and Tong[23]:

> Professionals widely regard geriatric hospital provision and residential care as at least partly substitutable. Yet, areas of high geriatric provision typically have greater than average provision of local authority residential places, even after allowing for apparent differences in area needs.
>
> What about co-ordination between residential and domiciliary services?... If there was co-ordinated planning between the sectors, then the community care policy of recent years should be expected to result in a transfer of resources from one to another. In this case there would be a correlation between changes in residential services and changes in the main domiciliary services. However, across the English local authorities between 1979 and 1983 there was no correlation at all between the increase in the scale of the home help service and the decrease of permanent local authority places.

7 Joint Planning

The variation in provision in different areas raises the question of planning. A coherent policy of community care seems to require that domiciliary services are substituted for residential ones. As the number of long-stay hospital patients and residents in old people's homes are reduced, so the number of day care places, home helps and district nurses must be increased. All this requires joint planning between different departments, authorities and services. Such effective joint planning appears difficult to achieve.

According to the Audit Commission[25] the difficulties start at central Government level. Thus the growth of private homes has been encouraged by payments from the supplementary benefits system, while another part of DHSS has been pursuing a policy of community care. There are potential clashes between policies on rate-capping and policies designed to shift resources away from London hospitals and more generally to redistribute care from hospitals to social services departments. Private care has grown much faster in the South than in the North and the public money channelled into it has thus not followed the priorities of Government regional policy.

These difficulties are compounded at local level where community care for the elderly requires co-operation between the authorities concerned with health, housing and social services. Joint planning at this level is very hard to achieve successfully even without the need to take into account the private sector, the voluntary sector and the supplementary benefits system.[3, 25, 37]

Authorities which have to plan together may lack co-terminous boundaries, be controlled by different political parties, have different planning and budgetary systems (hospitals may be planned on a ten year cycle, social services typically have a shorter time horizon), and take similar decisions at different levels.

The professionals involved in joint planning often have different priorities, attitudes and interests (very dependent people can block hospital beds, overload sheltered housing wardens or part III and no authority may therefore want to cater for them), and may not have the power to commit their departments.

Finally there is the sheer intellectual difficulty of joint planning, the time it requires, and the lack of analytical resources for it.

In keeping with these difficulties, the impression of local joint planning is that it is a matter of negotiation and horse trading, and incremental rather than strategic. Where successful, it results in specific joint activities rather than in grand overall shifts between residential and community provision.[3, 25, 37] Government efforts to improve this position through joint finance have had, according to the Audit Commission, only limited success since funds from joint finance are small relative to the total budget of social services departments and many local authorities are reluctant to use them for new initiatives whose total costs may later fall on themselves.

In the case of community care these problems are increased by the problem of achieving change at a time of economic stringency. The shift of resources from one service to another is inevitably met with resistance. Moreover initially there are higher costs as domiciliary care must be increased before residential care can be reduced by an equivalent amount. These problems suggest that the apparent failure to achieve a major shift between the resources devoted to residential and those devoted to domiciliary care was perhaps to be expected.

8   Levels of Disability in Different Sectors

Discussions of joint planning often assume that different kinds of residential and community care can affect the demand for each other (for example, that the adverse effects of reducing the numbers of long-stay elderly patients in hospital beds can be countered by increasing the number of places in local authority homes). Analogous assumptions underlie arguments about the role of homes in reducing bed blockages in hospitals. Such arguments presuppose an overlap in the kinds of individuals served in different sectors and researchers have explored how far this overlap exists. In practice there are difficulties in comparing the capacities of old people in the community and in different forms of institution. Different studies have tackled these problems in different ways but their results provide a consistent picture.

First it is clear that even at the highest levels of incapacity there are probably three to four times as many people in the community as in residential care (see Table 4).[23] Second, on average the residents of local authority and private homes are more dependent than those in voluntary homes.[38, 39]

Table 4 Distribution of an Index of Incapacity of Elderly Persons in Residential Care and in the Community in the Early 1980s

Index of incapacity	Elderly in residential care			Elderly in the community		
	LA supported	Not LA supported	Total	Living alone	Not living alone	Total
0	13,500	11,600	25,100	1,774,000	3,719,000	5,493,000
1–2	57,300	16,300	73,600	427,000	519,000	946,000
3–4	16,700	5,400	22,100	110,000	176,000	286,000
5–6	12,500	3,800	16,300	19,000	81,000	100,000
7–10	16,900	6,900	23,800	9,000	78,000	87,000
Total	117,000	44,000	161,000	2,339,000	4,572,000	6,911,000
Base	(10,520)	(3,179)	(13,699)	(1,357)	(2,650)	(4,007)

Notes:
1. Numbers in the Table are grossed up to national estimates for England, based on proportions in the 1980 General Household Survey (OPCS, 1982)[119] and the PSSRU Survey of residential care. A few of these estimates are based on quite small numbers and therefore have large standard deviations.
2. The index is constructed by scoring 1 for each of a list of five standard tasks (for example, feeding self) which causes difficulty and 2 for those which require assistance. A score of 0 is low and 10 is high incapacity. Elderly means persons aged 65+.

Source: Bebbington and Tong, Table 12.[23]

The evidence that private homes take old people who are as dependent as those in local authority ones is surprising. Benefit for individuals in these homes depends on the type of establishment in which they are rather than on an assessment of 'need' (for example, an elderly person in a home registered for the physically handicapped can attract more benefit than one in a home registered as being for the elderly). It is therefore in the interests of the proprietors of elderly person's homes either to register their home under a number of categories or to restrict their intake to elderly persons with low levels of disability.

The Association of Directors of Social Services[8] has argued that private homes are indeed taking less disabled people than their local authority counterparts. Unfortunately, however, they base their case on a sample which does not distinguish between voluntary and private homes. As voluntary homes are known to take less disabled residents on average the case remains unproven. Other research[20, 33, 38, 40] suggests that local authority residents may be on average slightly more disabled than those in private homes, but that the differences are not large and mainly arise from a slightly higher proportion of confused residents in the local authority sector. It is also clear that some private homes (about 16 per cent in Norfolk) specialise in old people who are ambulant[33, 41] and there is some evidence that private homes in London take old people of lower disability[38, 42].

Exaggerated too, perhaps, are claims that old people admitted to local authority homes are far more disabled than was the case heretofore. Over the 1970s the proportion of 'minimally dependent' people admitted to old people's homes decreased, with a corresponding increase in the proportion of moderately dependent and confused residents.[23, 43] Comparison of two national surveys of residents done in 1970 and 1981 respectively show that the proportion of 'severely dependent' residents only increased from 17 per cent to 24 per cent.[23]

Despite these changes many residents are not severely disabled and do not have much difficulty in looking after their own personal care. About half have been assessed as having low need for nursing care[39, 44] and about one in six as 'minimally dependent' which means in effect that they can carry out almost all self care tasks.[23] Most residents are probably, in Neill and her colleagues' phrase, 'partially dependent', which means that in the community they have problems with particular tasks at particular times and do not require continuous care.[45]

Although many old people in homes are not severely incapacitated, local authority homes nevertheless contain some old people who are as severely disabled as anyone in hospital.[39, 46, 47] Moreover, despite having proportionally fewer severely disabled old people in permanent care than hospitals, they probably have in total nearly as many as hospital wards.[46, 47] Conversely there is a small but from the point of view of the hospitals important group in hospital wards whose nursing needs are low,[39] who are not severely physically or mentally disabled,[48] and who are considered by the staff 'misplaced'.

Part 2   Reasons for Application and Admission

I suppose it's best as long as the home's nice. I'm getting too much for her. I'd really like to go to sleep and not wake up. I've had a good life. I'm not bothered about going. (Client, old lady in hospital).

I've got to the state I feel I'll have to leave home if she comes back. (Caregiving daughter).

Mrs A has somewhat reluctantly come to terms with the fact that due to family circumstances she needs to go into a home. Her main fear is that she may not be able to talk to other residents as they will either be incapable or asleep. (Social worker, on application form). Neill *et al.*[45]

1   Introduction

Most residents are not so disabled that they require the kind of constant, 24 hour care that can only be given in a relative's home or a residential setting. Are they drawn from the minority of old people who would like to enter a residential home, or do they apply in some sense against their will? This part of the paper considers the factors which, almost always in combination, lead to applications for care, and the degree of choice which the applicants have in their decision to apply. Almost all the evidence is drawn from the statutory sector, although many of the reasons appear to apply to the private and voluntary sectors as well.

2   Age and Sex

The likelihood that an old person will apply for residential care rises sharply with increasing age, and in consequence the age distribution in old people's homes is very different from that found among old people in the community.[49] As a rough guide, in a typical study of local authority homes, out of any hundred residents, roughly twenty might be aged less than 75, forty between 75 and 84 and forty, 85 or over. In all such studies the average age of the sample is high (82 to 83 years among residents, one or two years younger among applicants) and the average age has been rising since the DHSS survey of 1970. In private homes the residents are, if anything, on average even older.[40]

Partly as a result of this age distribution, women, who tend to outlive men, outnumber them in local authority old people's homes by roughly seven to three[50] and in private homes by maybe eight to two.[40] In recent years the rate of women residents per thousand population has been greater than that of male residents even when comparisons have been made between similar age groups. One explanation for this is that age for age old men are less disabled than old women.[9] More importantly, old men are more likely to be married than old women of similar age. Widowed or single men are more likely to apply for residential care than widowed or single women of a similar age, and married men are more likely to apply than married women of similar age.[45]

In keeping with these findings, there is some evidence that bereavement is a more important factor in the admission of old men than it is in the case of old women.[45] Typically, women are bereaved earlier in life than men, at a time, perhaps, when they find it easier to adapt to living on their own. Studies by Neill and her colleagues support Hughes and Wilkin's[49] suggestion that some men apply for residential care because they lack domestic skills.

3 Physical and Mental Dependency

Corollaries of the longevity of applicants and undoubtedly major factors in their admission to care are their physical and mental infirmities. Neill and her colleagues,[45] for example, found that 83 per cent of the sample of applicants in one authority could be rated according to their application forms as being 'at risk' or in need of physical care due to physical or mental incapacity. Mitchell and Earwicker[51] found a 'need for surveillance' among nine in ten of a small sample of 'accepted' applicants. Wade and her colleagues[39] found that in nine out of ten of a sample of 240 local authority residents there appeared to be physical reasons (illness, physical deterioration, mental deterioration and falls) involved in the admission.

A number of studies suggest that the difficulties of maintaining a dependent old person in a community are greater if dependency stems from dementia rather than from physical incapacity.[18, 52, 53] As already pointed out, most of those admitted to local authority residential care are, at the most, partially rather than severely dependent, facing difficulties in carrying out particular tasks at particular times of the day. Such people may well be kept out of residential care through the provision of services or diverted into sheltered housing, while diversion of the severely demented may not be possible. Determined community care policies may therefore result in an increasing poportion of confused people in local authority care.

4 Informal Support

Physical or mental incapacity is not of itself sufficient to precipitate demands for residential care. Additional reasons lie in the absence of unpaid carers or stresses upon them. One study found that daily visits from neighbours reduced the likelihood of admission among elderly social services' clients who were otherwise at high risk of entering a home.[52] Being married, having children and possibly siblings reduces the risk of entry into residential care.[1, 49, 54] A graphic illustration of the importance of carers was provided by Table 4 in Part 1 of this review. In constructing this table, Bebbington and Tong estimated that for every eight severely incapacitated elderly people living alone in the community there are twenty-one in residential care and seventy living with others.

Although lack of relatives or other informal carers makes an application for residential care more likely, most applicants nevertheless have some informal support. Studies of applications for local authority care suggest that in around two-thirds of cases problems associated with informal carers provide one of the reasons for application.[45, 51, 55] Commonly these reasons have to do with the exhaustion of carers or their difficulty in combining looking after an applicant with their other responsibilities. Caring relatives are also more likely to favour residential care as a solution for the elderly confused if they do not feel close to the old person, if the old person is living on their own or has only recently moved in with them and if the old person exhibits difficult behaviour.[18] The strains on relatives may be particularly hard to bear when the old person suffers from dementia.[56, 57, 58, 59] The attitudes of carers towards residential care are very important in predicting an old person's admission to an institution.[18]

Given the strains on many caring relatives, it is not surprising that they may encourage applications for care, either directly or by sowing doubt in an elderly person's mind about their ability to cope.[45] In a minority of cases, relatives may take more forceful action—for example, by refusing to have an elderly person home from hospital. Those who have studied admissions to private homes and nursing homes believe that relatives play an equally key role in these arrangements, being, for example, involved in initiating about half the admissions to private homes.[33, 40, 60] It should not be thought that relatives are pushing old people into homes on flimsy pretexts. They are aware that their wishes and those of the old person can conflict. In Allen's study, 39 per cent of relatives of a sample of short-stay residents wanted permanent care for them, but only 18 per cent thought the old person wanted it.[19] Carers rarely reject applicants and the great majority of residents in both private and local authority care receive quite frequent visits after they have been admitted.[33, 45, 50]

5   Poverty and Class

If old people enter residential care in part because of the pressure upon them from others, their ability to resist these pressures is likely to depend in part on the resources available to them. As mentioned in Part 1, there is some evidence that, historically, the number of elderly people in residential care has reflected the level of pensions available to elderly people. More direct evidence on the role of resources in preventing admissions has come from studies of applicants and residents, and from a follow up study of old people in the community.

Townsend[1] considered that poverty was a reason for admission to local authority care, basing his argument partly on the apparent 'poverty' or 'near poverty' of the majority of new residents. One reason for the 'poverty' of many applicants for local authority care may be that well off old people tend to apply for other types of residential care. Certainly, old people in social classes 1 and 2 are more likely than others to use nursing or private old people's homes rather than local authority ones.[1, 39, 41] However, there is some evidence that when compared with others, those who can pay for care enter nursing homes at a more advanced age[39] or when more frail.[1]

Higher incomes and higher social class are associated with avoidance of admission to institutional care among the elderly in the community[61] suggesting that comparative affluence may postpone or prevent application for residential care. Conversely, low income may be a contributory reason for applying for residential care in a small minority of cases.[45, 62]

6   Housing

The influence of old people's wealth on the likelihood of their applying for residential care may be mediated in part through its influence on housing. The relevant factors are whether an old person has a home, and if so whether they own it and whether it is convenient for them. Townsend[1] considered that loss of a home was a reason for admission to residential care but that a poor standard of housing was not. Later research has confirmed the importance of homelessness in applications and suggested that standards of housing may also be important, as too may tenure and ownership.

Neill and her colleagues found that applicants for local authority homes from the community were less likely than other pensioners to own their own homes,[45] a finding that also holds for those admitted.[52] In Neill's study, lack of tenure also seemed to make a decision to apply for residential care more difficult to reverse. Applicants who did not rent or own their homes were less likely than others to be in the community six months after application. Contrary to Townsend's opinion, case studies and the opinion of social workers, applicants and their carers suggest that poor housing interacts with physical disability and can become a contributory cause of application. For example, lack of an easily accessible toilet is more of a problem for the less ambulant.[45, 51] Bradshaw and his colleagues studying residents in private homes reported that 'housing was a dominant factor associated with unnecessary admissions to care'.

7 Services

Lack of resources may be compensated by services. Townsend[1] considered that lack of adequate domiciliary services was a contributory factor in admission to old people's homes. Only one fifth of his sample had had a home help—a far lower proportion than found more recently, where the proportion for both private residents supported by supplementary benefit and local authority residents seems around 50 per cent.[40, 45, 63, 64] Nevertheless, there is still evidence that lack of appropriate services may result in 'unnecessary admission'. Conversely, in some cases services may benignly or less benignly contribute to the reasons for admission.

In the first place, surveys of samples in the community suggest that the level of services received by very vulnerable individuals is often low even when these individuals are in touch with services.[18, 65] Moreover, a surprisingly high proportion of applicants are still not in receipt of services (in Neill's sample of applicants, four in ten—excluding those from residential institutions—were not receiving home help, district nursing or meals on wheels. The proportion receiving none of these services was particularly high among those living with younger relatives, but even among those living alone it was three in ten).

A second problem is that admission procedures can be somewhat haphazard. Decisions to admit have to take into account the potentially conflicting needs of applicants and their carers, and also the organisational needs of hospitals to clear their beds, of housing departments to avoid overloading their wardens and of old people's homes to maintain manageable levels of disability among their residents. The panel and quota systems involved in the processing of applications seem designed to handle potential organisational conflict perhaps as much as the applicants' needs.[45] Different people may take the interacting decisions over whether applicants are eligible for care, how quickly they can be given a bed and which home should receive them.[45] As a result, the admission of an applicant can depend, for example, on the number of vacancies for men at the time or the pressures under which a home is operating.[51]

Decisions to admit are often made at a point of crisis. In Avon, half the admissions from the community to non-specialist local authority homes were found to be emergencies bypassing the approved admission procedures.[63] In a sample of admissions to Surrey County Council homes, a fifth of those admitted had been known to the social services for less than a month.[64] Assessments too can be defective, in the sense that treatable illnesses may be missed,[66, 67] and social and functional assessments as judged by research social workers inadequate.[45] None of the applicants considered by Neill had received a comprehensive and integrated social, medical and functional assessment. Conversely, measures designed to promote more rigorous assessment can apparently reduce waiting lists.[68, 69]

Evidence that additional services or better assessment might have prevented admission in some cases is inconclusive but persuasive. Some researchers have asked applicants' social workers or social work interviewers to assess whether, given appropriate services and/or sheltered housing, some applicants or old people on waiting lists could be kept out of residential care. The proportions said to be capable of maintaining themselves in the community fluctuate wildly, depending on when the assessment is done (assessments made before admissions typically give higher proportions) and no doubt on other factors such as the optimism of the assessor and the assumptions made about the availability of services.

An example of 'pessimistic' assessments is provided by Bradshaw and his colleagues[40] whose study of private residents supported by supplementary benefit suggested that only 7 per cent of these (hardly any of them admitted from hospital) did not 'need' admission at the point of referral, but that a further 10 per cent could have been kept in the community if more intensive services had been available. The social work assessors who made these judgements differed considerably in their assessments. At one extreme, one thought that only 5 per cent could have been maintained in the community given additional resources, whereas the comparable percentage for another assessor was 61 per cent. Nevertheless, a number of studies which have used this method eg[45, 63, 65] suggest that, at a conservative estimate, a third of the residents could reasonably be kept out.

Experimental or comparative studies also suggest that additional services could in some circumstances have prevented an admission. The Kent Community Care Project[70, 71, 72, 73] suggests that the provision of flexible, appropriate packages of care can greatly reduce the likelihood of old people on the margins of residential care being admitted to a local authority home. Levin et al's[18] findings suggest that home helps may reduce institutional admissions among the confused elderly when the supporter is a man. Latto[74] also noted that an experimental home help service was maintaining in the community old people who would have been given high priority for admission to an old people's home if they had applied.

Services can precipitate as well as prevent admissions. Thus, doctors may use their authority to urge old people to apply,[75] and there are mentions in the literature of social workers 'persuading' reluctant applicants.[76] Above all there is evidence that hospitalisation may precipitate applications. Some old people have become long-stay hospital patients and are decanted to old people's homes as part of a policy of 'community care'. More commonly, the need to clear hospital beds, the reluctance of relatives to resume the burdens of caring or their anxieties about an old person's safety combine with the old person's own frailty and loss of confidence to produce the belief that residential care is the only option for a particular hospital patient.[45] In one study, old people applying for local authority homes from hospital were much more likely than community applicants to be in an institution on a permanent basis six months later.[45] In a small sample (thirty) of hospital applicants, six in ten of the applicants and seven in ten of their carers said that being in hospital had influenced the decision to apply.[45]

Relief admissions may also precipitate long-term admissions. A few elderly people enter homes for short-stays but remain there as long-term residents.[55] Levin *et al*'s[18] study of confused old people suggested that even after allowing for relevant background factors those receiving regular relief admissions were more likely to enter institutions on a long-term basis, although in some cases short-term admission may have been planned as part of a process of assessment for long-term care.

8   Attitudes and Choices

The 'contextual' pressures surrounding application (for example, lack of a home, hospitalisation, lack of an 'intensive' package of services) reduce the degree to which old people may exercise choice over whether or not to enter a home. In one study a key feature of the situation of two thirds of the applicants was that at the moment of application they were being looked after in an institution or in somebody else's home. In many of these cases, there was considerable pressure on them to go somewhere else.[45] In Bradshaw and his colleagues' study[40] only a third of the private residents they assessed had been living in their own homes in the community and were not in hospital at the point of admission.

In these circumstances, it is hard to assess how far applicants chose to go in to care, and how far any regrets about this are more properly seen as regrets about the circumstances that made it necessary. Some applicants are confused, and some do not wish to face painful truths—for example that their relatives cannot look after them—and some may want to put the responsibility for the decision on to others. Nevertheless, as far as the local authority sector is concerned, there is consistent evidence that the majority of those entering homes would not do so if they could avoid it.

Thus:

1. The idea of residential care often begins with someone else and referrals for residential care are not usually made by the applicant.[1, 8, 55, 75]

2. Applicants have often not been given, or have not taken in, the information they need to make an informed choice (for example, on what they can take with them).[45, 55, 77] Most have not visited the home.[78]

3. The majority of applicants appear to be resigned or ambivalent about the idea of going in or to reject the idea entirely.[45, 64, 77, 79] Only a minority appear to make a positive choice.[78]

The findings reported above relate to local authority care. One of the justifications put forward for the growth of private homes is that this has provided old people with more choice over the type of care they receive. One study did indeed find that residents in private homes were more likely to say they had been adequately consulted about the decision to apply than those in local authority care, although the numbers in the sample were very small.[39] Moreover, people in social classes 1 and 2 are more likely to want to go into a private home than local authority ones.[17] In this sense the growth of the private sector must enhance choice for the better off.

The private sector can only increase choice in the areas of the country which are well supplied with private homes which have vacancies. Even there, however, it seems that there are limitations in the extent to which applicants are able to exercise choice. Weaver and his colleagues[44] asked a sample of residents in private homes in Norfolk what feature they would look for in an 'ideal old people's home'. They found that '61 per cent of residents failed to report having made a positive choice based upon even the most arbitrary of criteria. . . . Only 26 per cent said they had had a choice of home'. They also noted that 'one third (32 per cent) could only report that—''the place was found for me'' or . . . ''I didn't want to come''.' In Bradshaw and his colleagues' study[40] only about a third of the residents claiming benefit in private homes had played a part in initiating their admissions.

In their discussion of the limitations on choice in the private sector, Weaver and his colleagues comment that four in ten of the residents interviewed were prepared to give a preference as between the private and public sector, almost always preferring private homes. Moreover, homes which had on the researchers' measures more 'liberal' regimes had a higher proportion of residents who had chosen to enter them. Nevertheless the researchers conclude that 'the proportion of residents exercising choice is so small that consumer choice serves no regulatory function'. They also note that residents supported on public funds and those who had been admitted as a result of a sudden illness or accident were less likely than others to have exercised a choice over which home to enter.

Like others, Weaver and his colleagues found that 'residents most able to come to terms with admission were those who had exercised some degree of control or choice in entering residential care.' More generally, literature on the relocation of the elderly emphasises the good effects of 'controllability' (moving voluntarily) and 'predictability' (knowledge of what one is moving to).[80] So it is, perhaps, disturbing that so many elderly people enter institutions when they are reluctant to do so, know little about where they are going, and are not so severely disabled that they require more or less constant care.

Part 3   Residential Regimes

Sitting looking out of the window, looking at the sky . . . sometimes I ask myself why I live so long . . . I'm like the old woman when they asked 'what do you do when you don't sit?' she replied 'I just sit.' (Resident quoted by Evans *et al*).[79]

You've got your washing done, you've got clean beds, they look after you. If you can't wash your hair they'll wash it. They've even got a hairdresser that comes. I mean what do you want—jam on it! (Resident quoted by Evans *et al*).[79]

It's terrible. I bloody sat in that bloody chair all yesterday, watching all the other buggers going senile.' (Views of short-stay resident quoted by Allen).[18]

The best thing is the lack of responsibility. People don't understand, you see. I nursed through two world wars, the general strike, the flu epidemic, so I think I'm justified in wanting a little respite. (Resident quoted by Power *et al*).[41]

If I have to go to the W . . . Safari Park once more, I'll know all the bloody monkeys by name. (Resident quoted by DHSS).[42]

1 Introduction

Researchers concerned with old people's homes differ over whether they are struck by their variety or their sameness. Thomas[81] noted his excitement on visiting some homes and his depression in others. More objective evidence shows that homes differ in staffing ratios and facilities, in the mortality rates and health of their residents[82], and in the proportion of residents who knit[81] or score high on scales of 'happiness'[83]. Booth, by contrast, emphasises the similarities between homes:

> Sociologically, the differences between regimes must, in the light of this study, be seen as a veneer that decorates the massive uniformity of institutional life, and catches the eye for precisely that reason. Underneath lies the same crushing panoply of controls over the lives and doings of residents. Changing the wrapper does not alter the contents.[82]

This section of the review sets out to describe the homes and to consider whether the differences between them matter. The review puts most emphasis on determining what residents want. Other evaluative criteria are clearly important—questions would rightly be raised about a home in which most residents were highly satisfied but died quickly or did nothing but stare into space. Nevertheless, the residents are adult and most are lucid. Their expresssions of what they want need to be taken seriously.

The review will therefore examine:

- What the residents want.
- What they experience (analogous to 'regime' or 'social climate').
- The determinants of this experience:
  staff
  buildings
  other residents
  inspection and other methods of control.
- Evaluation of residential care as a whole.

As in the last section the bulk of evidence comes from the public sector, but the private and voluntary sectors will be considered where possible.

2 What Residents Want

From Townsend onwards researchers concerned with old people's homes have noted the difficulty of getting an accurate picture of the residents' views. Typically these old people express satisfaction with the arrangements in their particular home, either because they are reluctant to complain or because they find it difficult to envisage alternatives. Evidence on residents' views therefore rests on large surveys which yield suspiciously high proportions of satisfied consumers or on detailed interviews and observational studies which give interesting insights but rely on small numbers. A second difficulty is that the residents do not all want the same thing. For example, some want respect and to be addressed by their surname, while others want to be cherished and called 'dear'. Some want activity, others rest. As Peace and her colleagues[83] have pointed out, no one type of home is likely to suit all residents. Yet despite these difficulties, a consistent picture of residents' preferences does seem to emerge.

In the first place, residents appreciate the comfort, physical security and freedom from worry which homes can provide.[45, 75, 83] For many life before admission was a bleak struggle and it is not surprising that they like 'being looked after/attention'. Ninety-four per cent of a large sample in local authority homes agreed with the statement, 'All of your needs are taken care of'.[78]

In the second place, residents want to control certain key aspects of their own lives. The desire for independence, which is the reason most commonly given in community surveys for a reluctance to enter an old person's home, is probably not lost on admission. Tanner in his evidence to the committee commented on a small sample of residents in a voluntary home that 'the one thing they valued above all else was the freedom they felt they had'. This freedom includes the ability to be private when one chooses and to choose one's own companions. More than three-quarters of residents in local authority homes would like a room of their own[78, 83]; most would prefer a bed-sitter to which they could return during the day.[78] A clear majority of those who express a preference would like their chairs lined against the wall rather than placed in apparently sociable groups,[84] possibly so that they do not have to be sociable. Most residents also want to control their immediate environment—for example to open the window when they want and turn the radiator on or off.[78, 84] Control over less immediate concerns does not seem so highly valued. For example in Willcocks and her colleagues' sample, only a third wanted a residents' committee and only a quarter wanted to choose the wallpaper and paint in their bedrooms.[78]

Other aspects of residential life over which residents want control concern security and tenure. Power and his colleagues[41] comment that:

> Security of stay is important to residents. Those in private accommodation were sometimes worried about money and knew that they would have to move if they could not pay . . . Those in local authority homes were worried not about money but about health for they feared they would be transferred to the local long-stay hospitals if they had a long illness.

Clough[75] and Neill *et al*[45] make similar comments although on the basis of very small samples.

Finally, if only by implication, residents value company and interesting activities of their own choice. Sizeable proportions of residents in local authority homes seem to be lonely and bored, and their visitors are highly valued.[79] Weaver and his colleagues argue that the adjustment of residents in private homes is related to their outside contacts.[33] Residents seem to have few suggestions for overcoming their loneliness, which may in some cases reflect their yearning for those they have lost, and they do not always appreciate the activities that are laid on for them.[42, 79]

3   What Residents Experience: Routines, Rules and Relationships

Once in the home the resident's experience revolves around the daily routine, the rules and social relationships which provide its context, and occasional highlights in the form of visitors from outside and outings. To judge from studies of local authority homes the routine in most of these is simple. The residents are called with a cup of tea, get up (probably earlier and in more of a rush in local authority homes than in private or voluntary ones), eat, sit in a chair, eat, doze, eat and go to bed. During this period they may receive various forms of care, such as toileting or bathing, chat occasionally, and watch television. They may also undertake various sedentary pursuits, such as knitting, writing letters and reading. Some residents may help others, do chores in the home or go out to the pub or elsewhere but on all the evidence these residents are exceptional.[19, 41, 78, 79, 84, 85]

Observers have been struck by the amount of time local authority residents spend in public and by their inactivity. Researchers and inspectors have been critical of this apparent public apathy, seeing it as evidence of a low quality of life and a lack of stimulation.[42, 79, 85] By contrast private homes where residents may spend more time in their rooms[33] have been criticised for lack of public space and because residents may, for lack of lifts, be marooned in their rooms.

A number of criticisms have also been made of the standards of physical and medical care in homes. As pointed out above, the old people themselves have few criticisms in this respect. One study, however, which concentrated on specific caring routines (bathing, toileting, and dressing) provided some horrific examples of bad practice.[72] In relation to medical care, evidence has been produced of overprescribing, particularly of psychotropic drugs, and that some residents receive potentially dangerous cocktails of drugs without proper records being kept.[86, 87, 88] Other studies have suggested that few residents in either local authority or private homes receive occupational therapy, physiotherapy or specialist services for the blind or deaf.[42, 44]

A rather different strand of criticism has focussed on the lack of normal life for residents. Clearly residential life has rules and regulations not experienced by old people in their own homes. It would, for example, be exceptional to find a local authority home in which most residents can lock their own rooms, or have their own furniture, or get up when they please, or bathe when they want. Restrictions on these choices in homes appears to arise from the exigencies of residential life and the anxieties of staff (for example the wish to be fair in the allocation of preferred bath times, the risk of fire, and shortage of time to get frail residents undressed). In general the rules are more likely to apply to the frail rather than the fit residents, thus giving rise to what Booth calls 'multiple regimes' in the same homes.[82] In this respect the homes are no different from life in the community, where old people dependent on the district nursing service for bathing also cannot choose their own bath times.

The researchers' criticisms of residential life as unnatural and unstimulating are not necessarily shared by the old people themselves. Nor is lack of choice necessarily associated with dissatisfaction. In one study a measure of the degree to which residents were able to exercise choice over certain aspects of their life in a home was not found to predict satisfaction with residential life.[83] In another study, measures of regime restrictiveness were not found to be related to changes in functional ability.[82]

The wish of some residents to put their feet up presents a dilemma for staff who may be expected to encourage a different kind of independence.[75] This dilemma appears to be heightened by experiments in group living whereby small groups of residents live in a unit and are expected as far as their abilities allow to fend for themselves with the staff providing encouragement. The pioneers of this method and the first researchers directly concerned with it were openly or cautiously enthusiastic.[89, 90, 91] However, more recent research has suggested that residents in such units tend to be less satisfied with residential life and to experience no unusual gains in functional ability.[78, 92]

One of the aims of group living was to reduce loneliness. Loneliness, in the sense of a wish for friendly company, might in theory be counteracted by residents, staff, volunteers and visitors. In general residents when questioned say that they get on with other residents and make new friends. Most observers, however, have commented on the low key nature of contacts between residents, with the atmosphere in homes being described as reminiscent of that in hotel lounges. A few residents seem to make important friendships or even to have romances. Most, however, make acquaintances. Typically staff get higher praise than other residents, featuring in interviews for their kindness and willingness to oblige. Visitors are also clearly important and the majority of residents (66 per cent to 88 per cent depending on the study) get them, although the frequency of visiting may decrease with length of residence. A recent study found that volunteer visitors were also appreciated but were nevertheless not able to affect a measure of resident satisfaction with life.[41]

One reason for the low level of sociability among residents may be the turnover among them. Between 20 and 30 per cent of those present in a home at any one time are likely to be dead within a year and others will have gone permanently into hospital.[45, 82] In such a setting it may be well to avoid becoming too fond of anyone.

4   Staffing

Most research reports on old people's homes contain references to the importance of staff. For example, social workers are said to see improvements in the numbers and qualifications of staff as the key to improving local authority homes,[19] and interviewers visiting different homes agreed that 'it was the attitudes of the staff that made the greatest difference to elderly people's lives'.[83] These statements, however, are generally given as asides in the research reports, rather than as results of the main research findings. To date, there is no statistical evidence on the importance of staff comparable to that in the fields of child care and delinquency.[93, 94, 95] Similarly although something is known about the types of training which staff have, there is almost no evidence on whether trained staff are any 'better' than those who are not.

Descriptively, it is clear that the staffing patterns of local authority and private homes are very different. The officer in charge of a local authority home runs a large establishment almost always catering for more than thirty residents, and often offering other services such as day care or meals on wheels. His, or more probably her, time is taken up with management[79] and the supervisory, care assistant, and domestic staff responsible to her have relatively specialised roles. Supervisory staff administer drugs, administer paper work, and pay attention to the residents' social lives. Care staff see to the beds, and the toileting and bathing of residents. Domestic staff prepare the food, do the washing up and keep the building clean.[96]

Private homes, by contrast, to judge from two studies of these are mostly part of a cottage industry—the majority have less than twenty residents, and around a third to a half have ten or less residents.[33, 97] Many of the homes (one study suggests 70 per cent) are run by husband and wife teams living on the premises.[97] Help from other family members is quite common, and part-time working even more common than in the public sector. Supervisory staff are rare (in one study only 8 per cent of private homes had them)[33] and other staff usually combine domestic and care duties.[33] Proprietors cannot afford to restrict themselves to management, and often take part in the cooking and shopping and care.[97] In one study, they provided half the care hours in the smaller homes.[33]

In both private and local authority sectors, staff are attracted to the work for one of three main reasons, their altruism and wish to work with the elderly, the convenience of the job (for example, their ability to work part-time) and their need for a job, money etc.[33, 78] One study suggested that staff in the private sector contained higher proportions of very young and very old staff than the public sector.[33] It also pointed out that the proprietors' need to keep down costs meant that staff were often expected to work unscheduled overtime, and that their conditions of service were less satisfactory than in the public sector.

Despite these disadvantages, staff were on the whole as satisfied with their jobs as those in the public sector, although they were more likely to draw their satisfaction from the nature of their work than from its material advantages.

In both private and local authority sectors, the overwhelming majority of staff are female, and taking all grades together, the great majority are untrained.[33, 78] However, officers in charge of local authority homes are almost always trained, the most common training being in nursing (between 65 per cent and 90 per cent of staff depending on the study) although some have been trained in social work or been on a css course.[19, 44]

From Townsend onwards there has been general agreement that the head of a home exercises a crucial influence over the life of those within it eg[1, 19, 79]. Evans and his colleagues have emphasised their importance in getting a common ethic among the staff who deal directly with residents.[79] In the private sector, the existence of husband and wife teams is likely, to judge from research in a different field[93], to mean that the degree of agreement between them is crucial to the quality of care provided.

Observational studies in the local authority sector have also documented the key role of care assistants. These staff are busy,[78] their work can be dirty and exhausting,[75] and they are expected both to provide adequate care and to enable residents to do things for themselves. Unfortunately, old people do not necessarily wish to do things for themselves,[75] it can take longer to encourage them to do so than to do it oneself,[91] and in certain homes there have been too many very disabled residents for staff to provide reasonable care (see below).[79] Although staff say they would like more time to talk to residents, staff-resident contacts become overwhelmingly focussed on the practical tasks of toiletting, bathing, feeding and dressing.[19, 79] The dependence of residents on staff for the performance of these basic tasks gives the staff power if they wish to use it. They may therefore have considerable influence over the informal rules in homes.[75]

One important constraint on the quality of care in old people's homes lies in the number of staff relative to the dependency of the residents. Local authority staff in particular are likely to attribute difficulties in making improvements in the homes to staff shortages.[19, 42] Although staff ratios in the local authority sector improved between 1971 and 1981, they are to some extent related to the level of resident dependency[98] and the standard of provision among care staff actually fell over this period relative to the dependency of residents.[23] If account is taken of reductions in working hours for staff, and the increased likelihood that senior staff will live out, the improvement in hours seems less impressive.

In contrast to the situation in the public sector, two studies have suggested that staffing ratios in private homes are not related to the dependency of residents. Staffing ratios in the private sector are probably lower than in the public.[33, 41] One reason for this is that proprietors in smaller establishments are on call at night thus reducing the need for night staff.[99] The consequences of this shortage include proprietor 'burn out' and use of unscheduled overtime. The turnover of proprietors may be as high as 20 per cent a year and is probably higher in the smaller homes where proprietors are likely to be providing night cover and involved in direct care. The small size of most private homes, which is one of their potentially attractive features, is thus also a source of one of their weaknesses.[33]

Moreover, residents in both sectors can deteriorate—facing heads of homes with dilemmas over whether to discharge them, face the consequences of dual-registration as a nursing home (in the private sector) or provide a poor standard of care. A potential answer to these dilemmas might be to make additional calls on the community nursing service. However, one study suggests that district nurses give low priority to patients in local authority homes, and that most nursing tasks in these homes are carried out by staff.[44]

5   Residents

The atmosphere of a home is necessarily affected by its residents. Some old people find congenial companions with whom to make friends, others complain of poor table manners, 'doziness' or cattiness, others of room-mates who steal their things or pull their clothes off their beds in the middle of the night. Staff may enjoy life with an easy group, or be run off their feet with the demands of very dependent residents, or driven to distraction by the 'chaos' caused by the confused. Such issues have led to an enduring research concern with the proportion of dependent people a home may accommodate, and in particular with the degree to which the confused should be mixed with the lucid.

The first major research study of this issue was mounted by Meacher.[100] He studied three homes which were known to contain sizeable proportions of confused residents and which he found to contain residents of widely varying abilities, including some who were mentally handicapped. Meacher saw confusion as in quite large part a reaction to circumstances and felt that segregated homes were 'repositories for anti-social or aggressive behaviour', removal to which could be used as a threat by matrons in non-segregated homes. Noting among other things that residents in segregated homes were much less likely to have visitors, he argued strongly against segregation, feeling that it encouraged infantilising procedures, heavy sedation and other undesirable practices.

Despite Meacher's criticisms, both specialist and mixed care for the confused continues to be provided. The bulk of specialist provision for the confused is in the hospital sector,[101] although all sectors provide some specialist accommodation for this group. Equally, most homes (except perhaps some in the private sector) have some residents who are confused.

A major study of mixing in non-specialised homes was carried out by Evans and his colleagues.[79] They confirmed American research showing that the amount of nursing time required varies with disability. More precisely, they showed major variations in the time required to toilet, bath, dress and undress residents, depending on their degree of dependency. They also showed that in homes with heavy levels of disability, a preventive system of toileting would require 35 per cent of staff time. Staff in such homes could only manage to provide physical care by resorting to poor practice (for example, lining up residents before toileting, or failing to toilet incontinent residents at all). They recommended that the proportion of confused residents in a home should not exceed 30 per cent. However, in my opinion the consequences of mixing confused and lucid residents were less clear than the consequences of a low staff ratio relative to the level of dependency among residents.

For their part, residents in local authority homes seem to give a fairly high priority to segregating the confused,[78] as do the majority of staff.[44, 79] In practice, however, both staff and residents seem to object to the behaviour which goes with confusion rather than to confusion *per se*. Residents identified by staff as particularly difficult are more likely than others to be confused. However, staff also seem to prefer working with the confused as a category and to speak more warmly to them, possibly because this group are more malleable and gratify the staff's wish to care. For their part, residents may display mild irritation with the confused and exclude them from the 'best' chairs in lounges, while the level of rational conversation appears to drop in lounges with a high number of confused residents in them.[102] Short-stay residents are undoubtedly often depressed by the extent of confusion they observe in homes, and long-stay residents often comment disapprovingly on the difficulty of having a decent conversation. There is, however, no evidence that confusion *per se* ranks very highly in the residents' list of residential sins.

6 Buildings

Buildings have a pervasive effect on residential care. They influence the degree to which residents can control their environment (for example, open their windows or get to the WC), the proportion who can have rooms of their own, the ease with which the confused can find their way around, the degree to which life is lived in public or private space and the ease with which group living can be introduced. At the same time, the effects of a building depend on other factors—for example the number of staff and the rules. Possibly for this reason there has been a failure to find any 'relationships between the physical features of the building and the behaviour of the people in it'.[103]

In the public sector there has undoubtedly been a great improvement in buildings since Townsend's research, and on one index at least the fabric of local authority homes is generally much superior to that found in voluntary homes.[23] Proprietors in small private homes face particular problems over buildings. It seems that a number of them have problems in making ends meet and the cost of, for example, a lift in a small private home can be prohibitive. In one study, private homes were found to be deficient in terms of handrails, making it difficult for frail residents to get about. The proprietors' need to let as many bedrooms as possible had also led them to economise on public spaces such as dining rooms and lounges.[33] These difficulties are to some extent a consequence of the small size of homes and their difficulty in making economies of scale. Other consequences of size, while no doubt important, have not been unravelled in this review.

In the local authority sector, three important studies have looked at the design of homes.[78, 102, 104] They have come up with different recommendations, one for unit living, one for ensuring as far as possible that the staff are kept apart from residents, and another for providing residents with a residential flatlet, which is private and lockable.

7   Homes as Resource Centres

Aspirations towards community care have led local authority manage-
ments to look carefully at the resources locked up in residential homes
and to see if these could not be used for the benefit of their surrounding
communities. Homes have been used as a base for the meals on wheels
service, centres for sheltered housing complexes, and sources of day
and short-stay care. In the 1981 PSSRU survey[38] 81 per cent of local
authority homes provided one or more services of this kind. Voluntary
homes were less likely to provide such services, although they were
more likely than local authority ones to be associated with sheltered
housing (18 per cent as against 7 per cent providing this service).
Comparable information on the private homes is not available, but
almost certainly they concentrate on the provision of long-stay care.

I have not found evidence on the effects of associating meals on
wheels and sheltered housing with residential care. Disappointingly so,
since the association of sheltered housing with residential homes has
prima facie some advantages. There are, however, a number of studies
which bear on provision of short-stay care and day care in residential
homes.

In England the provision of short-stay care in local authority homes
is rising steadily and there are now more short-stay than long-stay
admissions. In this respect, there are wide variations between
authorities but in no authority are the short-stay admissions likely to
swamp long-stay ones or if spread evenly across the homes to amount
to more than one or two short-stays in a fifty-bedded home at any one
time.

Short-stay admissions occur for a variety of reasons—the most
common being to relieve carers by providing them with a holiday or a
break from caring or by taking over while the carer is in hospital. Other
reasons have to do with the elderly persons and are designed to give
them a holiday, to assess them, to let them convalesce after a period in
hospital or to give them an experience of a residential home prior to a
possible admission.[19] The breaks may be provided on a one-off basis,
for example, for a holiday (the most common method) or rotated so the
elderly person gets so many weeks in and so many weeks out.[18, 19]
Generally, short-stay beds are provided in homes catering for permanent residents but some are placed in specialist homes or occupy a
particular unit in a specialist home.

Short-stay admissions can be evaluated in terms of their effect on the
home, the elderly person themselves or the carer. In general, the proportion of short-stay residents at any one time is too low to impinge
greatly on other residents. Certainly, very few of the latter are prepared
to complain about the number of short-stay residents in an interview,[84]
although in the staff's view they do not always treat them kindly.[19] For

their part, heads of homes complain of the administrative inconvenience of short-stay admissions such as naming clothes or losing laundry,[19] and while hoping that residents will introduce a breath of fresh air are concerned that one or two very confused short-stay residents may prove the straw that breaks the camel's back.

Heads of homes are doubtful about the effects of short-stays on their recipients.[19] In general, staff seek to treat short-stay and long-stay residents alike. In Allen's study short-stay residents, particularly if they had been living alone, appreciated the good food and in some cases the company.[19] However, they rarely experienced a holiday atmosphere, were not assessed or given rehabilitation, and sometimes complained of the lack of activity in the homes and the depressing decrepitude of the other residents.[19, cf. 105, 106] By contrast old people who went to the specialist holiday home were apparently loud in its praises and Allen makes a strong case for providing this form of care in separate homes or units.

In contrast to the doubts about the effects of short-stays on old people, there is general agreement that they are appreciated by carers and in the view of many of them are underprovided. In Allen's study the heads of homes were convinced of the benefits of short-stay for carers.[19] Levin and her colleagues provided some statistical evidence that a combination of short-stay and day care was beneficial to the carers' mental health or at least reduced the deleterious effects on mental health of caring.[18]

Day care, like short-stay care, provides carers with a break and its provision in homes raises many of the same issues. Three methods of provision can be distinguished. A small number of day attenders may spend one or more days a week in a home, the home may provide a day centre which uses the same staff and premises as the home's residents, or there may be segregated provision, perhaps in the home's grounds which does not use the same staff although responsible to the same head.[107] In the PSSRU (1981) survey, 75 per cent of the local authority homes provided day care within the homes and 11 per cent had attached day centres. Overall, about two-thirds of the places were in the homes and about one third in the attached centres, although occupancy rates of the latter were somewhat higher.[38]

As in the case of short-stay care the evidence suggests that segregated day care is preferred by users and insofar as the issue impinges on them by residents.[82] One study found that day care was perceived by its users as being significantly better in free-standing provision than in residential homes.[108] Commenting on this, Allen[109] wrote:

> (These) findings on day care are very similar to the findings on short-stay
> care. Neither day nor short-stay care is easy to organise successfully in
> homes mainly occupied by long-stay residents. Far from being the 'breath

of fresh air' hopefully envisaged by those running the homes (and those in social services departments), the day care attenders are often regarded as intruders, particularly if they are seen as competing for territory or staff time or attention, and most especially if they are highly mentally or physically dependent. Fennel and his colleagues in East Anglia[110] and Bowl and his colleagues in Birmingham[111] found a similar pattern in their studies of day care provision. Willcocks and her colleagues[78] also highlighted the same problem, and these findings are reinforced in a PSI study[19] where day care was often thought to be even more difficult to cope with than short-stay care.[109]

8 Inspection and Regulation

Apparent variations in the quality of residential care suggest a need for regulation. Attention has been focussed on this by the growth of the private sector and the consequent concerns about caring for profit, and the use of public funds without public accountability. These have led to the Registered Homes Act 1984 and the associated code of practice embodied in Home Life.[112] The legal and administrative apparatus surrounding inspection and regulation includes distinctions between homes that provide nursing, those which provide personal care and those which provide both (difficult distinctions given the problems of defining nursing and the overlap in the disabilities of clients in nursing and rest homes). It also sets a ceiling for the amount of money from the supplementary benefit system which may finance old people in different types of home. There has also been discussion of the need to assess old people being enabled to enter or continue in private homes by means of public money.

These measures face the difficulty of simultaneously containing public expenditure and ensuring high quality of care. It is probable that very few private homes have no clients paid through the supplementary benefit system.[97] The danger is that the combination of a ceiling on payments and insistence on expensive standards could drive proprietors out of business, or conversely that fears of doing this will lead to lax regulation. Similarly, the development of assessments for prospective entrants to rest homes might prevent them from taking a step which was not in their best interest or lead proprietors of homes to seek registration as nursing homes. Certainly requirements to, for example, have night staff awake during the night or install lifts could dramatically alter the 'cottage industry' character of private homes, making certain sizes of home uneconomic, and increasing the capital required for successful operation.

So far little attention has been paid to attempts to regulate local authority homes which, as recent events have shown, are themselves not immune from scandal. However, the DHSS (1979) survey of London homes implied that the external control of local authority homes was defective in certain respects.[42] Heads of homes appeared to be unclear in some instances about whom they were accountable to, complaints procedures were generally unclear, and recording variable. Doubts were expressed about the effectiveness of some home advisors. Even building standards seem hard to control. In 1981, the PSSRU survey found that 79 per cent of local authority homes were below the DHSS 1973 building notes standards.[38]

If local authorities have some difficulty in controlling their own homes, they are likely to face even greater ones in regulating the private sector. As yet unpublished research by Diane Willcocks and her colleagues suggests that the authorities vary widely in commitment to the task of regulation (as measured by the number of staff engaged per number of homes to be inspected) and in the way they are approaching the task. Inspection requires them to develop working relationships with the health service over dual registration as well as with fire officers, building inspectors and environmental health officers. New staff have had to be recruited and given appropriate support. The development of private residential care raises political issues. So inevitably the approach to regulation appears hesitant, and the number of deregistrations appears to be miniscule compared to the number of homes.[33]

Given these difficulties, Challis[113] has urged the importance of other methods of controlling quality. These might include the provision of information to prospective residents so that they would be able to 'shop around' among homes, the attachment of social workers or others to homes, advice to enable dissatisfied residents to move, or provision of copies of *Home Life* to residents and their relatives. Weaver and his colleagues describe attempts by Norfolk SSD to improve the quality of private care, for example, by discouraging unsuitable people from becoming proprietors, and by encouraging training.[33]

9   Residential Care and Other Settings

An obvious question is whether people in residential care do 'better' or 'worse' than old people with similar levels of disability in other settings. This question has not been satisfactorily answered and probably never will be. Certain comparisons can, however, be made.

First, old people in residential care are probably 'unhappier' than elderly people over 65 in the community.[83] This, however, is to be expected given their greater disability, the likelihood that they have been bereaved, and the sad events which often lead up to an admission.[45] Although residents are often lonely, even Townsend—no friend of residential care—found that they were not more lonely than other old people in the community.[1] Similarly, frail old people in the community are often bored.[10] Undoubtedly, the level of care received by old people in local authority homes is higher than that which they would receive in the community, which in turn is often pitifully low,[65] and is generally appreciated by the residents.

To some extent these uncontrolled comparisons can be supplemented by more controlled studies. One important experimental study[70, 71, 72, 73] found that given a flexible and adequate package of services very frail old people can be maintained in the community with apparent benefit to their supporters, their own well-being and their life expectancy. A comparison group fared less well in all these respects and its members were more likely to enter residential care. The results of this study needs to be viewed with caution. The benefits to the experimental group may come from a 'Hawthorne effect', the control group may not have received a good standard of service, and the variables which influence admission to care (for example, the attitude of the old person's family) could not all be taken into account. Other studies looking at different criteria have failed to find that residential care has much effect on mortality or functioning of frail elderly people when compared with other settings.[114]

Paradoxically, the group that are most likely to benefit from residential care are not the old people themselves but their carers. The whole policy of community care has been criticised as an attempt to exploit unpaid female labour,[115, 116] and the strains on many carers are undoubtedly great.[117, 118] As described in the last section, they often instigate requests for residential care. Three studies have now suggested that the mental health of carers improves if a confused relative is removed to a residential setting.[18, 119, 120]

Despite these findings, most carers do not want their relatives to go into residential care. Similarly, even when interviewed in a home, many residents would prefer not to be there. In one study a third seemed to be content with their situation, a third were putting up with it, and a third definitely wanted to be elsewhere.[79, cf. 41] The truth is that residential care has advantages and disadvantages. It suits some people and not others. The problem is how to give relatives and dependent old people a reasonable choice between residential care and other options, taking into account the possibility that their interests may conflict.

Part 4   Conclusion

This review has suggested that:

1   The vast majority of elderly people do not want to go into residential care. Asked to consider the possibility that they cannot look after themselves at home, most are likely to opt for sheltered housing.

2 Despite the above, demand for residential care outruns provision and will be increased by demographic trends. Compared to some other European countries England and Wales have few residential places for the elderly.

3 Partly for this reason community care policies have not over the past ten years reduced the numbers in residential care either absolutely or per thousand over 75. Nor has there been a shift of resources in favour of community services for the elderly. These apparent failures in community care have to do with the difficulties of joint planning, the incentives given to residential as against community provision, and restrictions on the finance required to expand domiciliary services.

4 Private residential care has no doubt filled part of the gap left by public provision but has not been concentrated on areas of greatest need. It is subject to conflicting policy objectives concerned with controlling costs, ensuring adequate standards and preventing the financial collapse of homes. It is therefore vulnerable to changes of policy as different objectives are given different weight.

5 Despite community care policies, many, probably most, of those entering residential care do so reluctantly. Most are less disabled than many remaining in the community and have not been receiving heavy packages of care. Efforts to prevent reluctant admissions would need to pay attention to strains on relatives and the need to provide alternative accommodation for frail old people who are homeless or under pressure to move quickly from where they are (for example, a relative's home or a hospital ward).

6 From the resident's viewpoint residential life can probably be assessed according to the degree to which, and the way in which, it meets basic needs for physical and medical care, allows residents control over key aspects of their lives (security of tenure, privacy, finance, physical environment) and counteracts loneliness and boredom without imposing uncongenial company or activities. No overall assessment can be given of the degree to which residential care meets these needs. However, problems can occur in relation to:

   (a) Physical care when there are too few staff relative to the number of very dependent elderly people.

   (b) Medical care (management of drugs, management of incontinence, assessment of the deaf—issues inadequately covered in this review).

   (c) Lack of security, privacy and choice.

(d) Lack of interesting activities or failure to enable individual residents to pursue their own interests.

(e) Provision of day care or relief care within a home, causing problems for the staff and probably a low standard of service for outside users.

7 Methods of regulating homes have only recently been developed and seem to be hesitantly applied, at least in many places. Other methods of improving the quality of homes (for example, professional support) or giving greater influence to residents (for example, advice services, codes of residents' rights, tenure, clear complaints procedures) have been little researched and possibly little tried.

8 In most of these respects, those suffering from dementia are a special case. They are probably the only group for which the majority of the general public think residential care is appropriate. Almost certainly they usually put more strain on their carers and are more difficult to maintain on their own than physically dependent people, and they raise particular difficulties in residential homes.

The problems raised in 1–8 above are unlikely to be bypassed simply by transferring resources from residential services to community ones. The factors which finally lead to admission (for example, family attitudes) are not easily used to target services. A shift of resources would thus provide a better service to many people who would not enter institutions in any case. This may well be equitable. Why should the social security system allocate five to six times as much per head to relieving the relatives of old people who are supported by public funds in private care, as to supporting relatives who care for very dependent old people at a cost to their own mental health? Why for that matter does the system tend to support residential rather than domiciliary services? However, unless massive funds are available to deal with these apparent anomalies, the latent demand for residential care for the elderly is unlikely to be much reduced and will have to go unmet or be diverted at the point of expression.

In general the findings pose problems rather than suggest solutions. Research has shown that the main policies on residential care for the elderly have not worked out as intended. It has not shown how the policies can be made to work, or what policies would be 'better'. In making their recommendations, the committee must therefore, like the researchers, move beyond the evidence. Three related issues may concern it—how many residential places should there be; for whom should they be provided; and how should homes themselves be run?

In considering the size and clientele of the residential sector, the committee may note the evidence that additional residential places are likely to be filled but many of those who fill them will probably not want or in a sense 'need' to be there. Conversely a reduction in the number of places might be a rash step given the evidence of unmet demand and the predicted increase in 'need'. One possible policy would therefore seek a 'standstill' in the number of residential places for the elderly (a difficult policy to implement given the problems of controlling the growth of the private residential sector without reducing the sector itself), and a determined effort to ensure that old people do not enter the homes if they would prefer not to and alternative arrangements can be made for them. Given the determined implementation of such a policy, a more accurate assessment of need for places might be made.

In considering improvements in residential care itself Diane Willcocks and her colleagues[78] have argued for changing the balance of residential living in favour of the individual, for providing what residents want, ie the normal, the unexceptional, the non-institutional, and for embodying these changes in the form of a residential flatlet which can be locked and provides personal space. Evans and his colleagues[79] have emphasised the importance of staff—the head of home who sets the ethos, and the care staff who can perform their caring activities with sensitivity or otherwise. Much of the evidence suggests to me the need for sheltered housing complexes with additional facilities (ie more staff, close liaison with domiciliary nursing staff, short-term assessment flats with vacancies for emergencies, a day centre and perhaps a small residential unit for the 'confused', many of whom seem to try the patience of all providers of care). These suggestions like most of those made at the end of research reports outrun the evidence and await the test of experience.

Annexe 1

Table 1: Notes and Sources
This table is based on Henwood and Wicks[11] Table 7 and adjusted on the basis of the following information:

Enumerated population, OPCS (1971), Table 6.[121]

Usually resident population, OPCS (1981), Table 1.[122]

1981 based projection for home population—mid year, OPCS (1984), Appendix Table 1.[123]

The numbers of people living alone and unable to get out of bed were estimated by applying proportions in sex-age groups (65–69, 70–74, 75–79, 80–84, 85+) with these characteristics (as given by 1980 General Household Survey[124]) to the numbers in same sex-age groups living in private households for the relevant year. These numbers were taken from private households in the 1971 Census; 1981 Census; and estimated from the proportion of the total population (in sex-age group) living in private households in 1981 applied to projected populations for 1991 and 2001. The individual sex-age estimates thus derived were added to obtain estimates for all persons 65+.

The numbers suffering from dementia were estimated by applying proportions in sex-age groups (65–69, 70–74, 75–79, 80+) suffering from organic brain syndromes, ie excluding mild dementia (as given by Kay and Bergmann, 1980, Table 2–3[125]) to the same sex-age groups in the *total* population for the relevant year. These sex-age specific rates of dementia are based on pooled data including sample populations from non-private households. Given that mild dementia is excluded, these estimates are clearly conservative.

Notes and References

1 Townsend, P. (1962), *The Last Refuge: A Survey of Residential Institutions and Homes for the Aged in England and Wales*, Routledge & Kegan Paul.

2 Department of Health and Social Security, Scottish Office, Welsh Office, Northern Ireland Office, (1981), *Growing Older*, Cmnd 8173, HMSO.

3 Wistow, G. (forthcoming), 'Health and local authority collaboration: lessons and prospects' in Wistow, G. and Brooke, T. (eds), *Joint Planning and Joint Management*, Royal Institute of Public Adminstration.

4   Registered Homes Act 1984, HMSO.

5   Bevan, A. (1947), *Second Reading of the National Assistance Bill*, House of Commons Debate, 24 November 1947.

6   Means, R. and Smith, R. (1985), *The Development of Welfare Services for Elderly People*, Croom Helm.

7   Department of Health and Social Security (1977), *Residential Homes for the Elderly: Arrangements for Health Care*, A memorandum of guidance, DHSS.

8   Association of Directors of Social Services (1985), *Who Goes Where? A Profile of Elderly People who have Recently been Admitted to Residential Homes*, ADSS.

9   Hunt, A. (1978), *The Elderly at Home: A Study of People Aged 65 and Over Living in the Community in England in 1976*, HMSO.

10 Sinclair, I. A. C., Crosbie, D., O'Connor, P., Stanforth, L. and Vickery, A. (forthcoming), *Bridging Two Worlds: Services and Informal Care for the Elderly Living Alone*, Gower.

11 Henwood, M. and Wicks, M. (1984), *The Forgotten Army*, Family Policy Studies Centre.

12 Salvage, A. (1986), *Attitudes of the Over 75s to Health and Social Services: Final Report*, University of Wales College of Medicine: Research Team for the Care of the Elderly.

13 West, P. (1984), 'The family, the welfare state and community care: political rhetoric and public attitudes', *Journal of Social Policy*, 13, 4, pp. 417–446.

14 West, P., Illsley, R. and Kelman, A. (1984), 'Public preferences for the care of dependency groups', *Social Science and Medicine*, 18, 4, pp. 287–295.

15 Thompson, C. and West, P. (1984), 'The public appeal of sheltered housing', *Ageing and Society*, 4, pp. 305–326.

16 Abrams, M. (1978), *Beyond Three Score Years and Ten: A First Report of a Survey of the Elderly*, Age Concern.

17 Campbell, A., Mitchell, S. and Earwicker, J. (1981), *The Elderly at Home in Hammersmith and Fulham: Report of the Research Project on the Needs of the Elderly*, London Borough of Hammersmith and Fulham.

18 Levin, E., Sinclair, I. A. C. and Gorbach, P. (forthcoming), *Families, Services and Confusion in Old Age*, Gower.

19 Allen, I. (1983), *Short-Stay Residential Care for the Elderly*, Policy Studies Institute.

20 Vincent, J. A., Tibbenham, A. D. and Phillips, D. R. (1986), *Choice in Residential Care: Myths and Realities*, Evidence submitted to Wagner Committee, (unpublished).

21 Thomson, D. (1983), 'Residential care since 1980', *Ageing and Society*, 3, 1, pp. 43–69.

22 Moroney, R. M. (1976), *The Family and the State: Considerations for Social Policy*, Longman.

23 Bebbington, A. and Tong, M. (1986), 'Trends and changes in old people's home provision over twenty years' in Judge, K. and Sinclair, I. A. C. (eds), *Residential Care for Elderly People: Research Contributions to Policy and Pratice*, HMSO.

24 Laing, W. (1985), *Private Health Care*, Office of Health Economics.

25 Audit Commission (1986), *Making a Reality of Community Care*, HMSO.

26 Department of Health and Social Security (1984), *Personal Social Services Local Authority Statistics*, RA/84/1–2, DHSS.

27 OPCS (1977), *Population Estimates*, Series PP1, No 2, HMSO.

28 OPCS (1981), *Population Estimates*, Series PP1, No 5, HMSO.

29 OPCS (1986), *Population and Vital Statistics*, Series VS No 11/PP1, No 7, England and Wales 1984, HMSO.

30 Information extracted from DHSS statistical bulletins 2/84, 6/85 and 2/86 and DHSS (1986), *Health and Personal Social Services Statistics for England*, HMSO.

31 Challis, L. (1986), 'Robbing Peter to pay Paul—handsomely', *Social Services Insight*, 1, 33, August 16–23, pp. 12–14.

32 Larder, D., Day, P. and Klein, R. (1986), *Institutional Care for the Elderly: The Geographical Distribution of the Public/Private Mix in England*, University of Bath: Centre for the Analysis of Social Policy.

33 Weaver, T., Willcocks, D. and Kellaher, L. (1985), *The Business of Care: A Study of Private Residential Homes for Old People*, Report No 1, The Polytechnic of North London, Centre for Environmental and Social Studies in Ageing.

34 Phillips, D. R., Vincent, J. and Blacksell, S. (1986), *Spatial Concentration of Residential Homes for the Elderly: Planning Responses and Dilemmas*, Evidence submitted to the Wagner Committee, (unpublished).

35 Davies, B. P., Barton, A. J., McMillam, I. S. and Williamson, V. K. (1971), *Variations in Services for the Aged: A Causal Analysis*, Bell.

36 Gorbach, P. and Sinclair, I. A. C. (1981), *Pressure on Health and Social Services for the Elderly*, National Institute for Social Work.

37 Glennerster, H., with Korman, N. and Marsden-Wilson, F. (1983), *Planning for Priority Groups*, Martin Robertson.

38 Darton, R. A. (1986), PSSRU *Survey of Residential Accommodation for the Elderly, 1981: Characteristics of the Residents*, Discussion Paper 426, University of Kent, Canterbury: Personal Social Services Research Unit.

39 Wade, B., Sawyer, L. and Bell, J. (1983), *Dependency with Dignity: Different Care Provision for the Elderly*, NCVO: Bedford Square Press.

40 Bradshaw, J. and Gibbs, I. (forthcoming), *Needs and Changes: A Study of Public Support for Residential Care*, Studies in Cash and Care No 1, Gower.

41 Power, M., Clough, R., Gibson, P. and Kelly, S. (1983), *Helping Lively Minds*, University of Bristol: Social Care Research.

42 Department of Health and Social Security Social Work Service, London Region (1979), *Residential Care for the Elderly in London*, DHSS.

43 Booth, T. A., Barritt, S., Berry, S., Martin, D. N. and Melotte, C. (1983), 'Dependency in residential homes for the elderly', *Social Policy and Administration*, 17, 1, pp 46–62.

44 Bowling, A. and Bleathman, C. (1982), 'The need for nursing and other skilled care in local authority residential homes for the elderly: Research report No 5, overall findings and recommendations', *Clearing House for Local Authority Social Services Research*, Birmingham, 17, 9, pp. 1–65.

45 Neill, J. E., Sinclair, I. A. C., Gorbach, P. and Williams, J. (forthcoming), *A Need for Care: A Study of Elderly Applicants for Local Authority Residential Care*, Gower.

46 Charlesworth, A. and Wilkin, D. (1982), *Dependency Among Old People in Geriatric Wards, Psychogeriatric Wards and Residential Homes 1977–1981*. Research Report No 6, University of Manchester: Research Section, Psychogeriatric Unit.

47 Clarke, M. G., Hughes, A. and Dodd, K. (1979), 'The elderly in residential care: patterns of disability', *Health Trends*, 2, pp. 17–20.

48 Wilkin, D., Mashiah, T. and Jolley, D. J. (1978), 'Changes in behavioural characteristics of elderly populations of local authority homes and long-stay hospital wards 1976–77', *British Medical Journal*, 2, pp. 1274–1276.

49 Hughes, B. and Wilkin, D. (1980), *Residential Care of the Elderly: A Review of the Literature*. Research Report No 2, University of Manchester: Psychogeriatric Unit.

50 Willcocks, D. M., Cook, J. and Ring, A. J. (1981), *Consumer Study in Old People's Homes: First Findings Vol II, Appendices*, Polytechnic of North London: Survey Research Unit, Department of Applied Social Studies.

51 Mitchell, S. J. F. and Earwicker, J. (1982), *Getting People Placed*, London Borough of Hammersmith and Fulham.

52 MacLennan, W. J., Isles, F. E., McDougall, S. and Keddie, E. (1984), 'Medical and social factors influencing admission to residential care', *British Medical Journal*, 288, 6418, pp. 701–703.

53 Sinclair, I. A. C., Stanforth, L. and O'Connor, P. (forthcoming), 'Factors predicting admissions to local authority residential care: A study of a sample of old people living alone and in touch with home helps and social workers', *British Journal of Social Work*.

54 Kay, D. W. K., Beamish, P. and Roth, M. (1962), 'Some medical and social characteristics of elderly people under state care: a comparison of geriatric wards, mental hospitals and welfare homes', *Social Research Monograph*, 5, pp. 173–195.

55 Stapleton, B. (1976), *A Survey of the Waiting List for Places in Newham's Hostels for the Elderly*, London Borough of Newham Social Services Department: Applied Research Section.

56 Sheldon, J. H. (1948), *The Social Medicine of Old Age*, Nuffield Foundation.

57 Grad, J. and Sainsbury, P. (1968), 'The effects that patients have on their families in a community care and a control psychiatric service: a two year follow up', *British Journal of Psychiatry*, 114, pp. 225–278.

58 Issacs, B. (1971), 'Geriatric patients: do their families care?', *British Medical Journal*, 4, pp. 282–286.

59 Sanford, J. R. A. (1975), 'Tolerance of debility in elderly dependents by supporters at home: its significance for hospital practice', *British Medical Journal*, 3, pp. 471–473.

60 Bartlett, H. and Challis, L. (undated), *Private Nursing Homes for the Elderly: A Survey Conducted in the South of England*, University of Bath: Centre for the Analysis of Social Policy.

61 Wenger, G. C. (1984), *Care Networks Project. Surviving in the Community. Some Demographic and Social Factors*, Working Paper No. 33, University College of North Wales: Department of Social Theory and Institutions.

62 Harris, A. (1968), *The Social Welfare of the Elderly*, HMSO.

63 Avon (1980), *Admissions to Homes for the Elderly: A Survey of Alternatives*, Avon County Council, Social Services Department, (unpublished).

64 Barnes, C. D. (1980), *The Relentless Tide: A Study of Admission into Homes for the Elderly*, Surrey County Council, Social Services Department.

65 Plank, D, (1977), *Caring for the Elderly: Report of a Study of Caring for Dependent Elderly People in Eight London Boroughs*, Greater London Council.

66 Brocklehurst, J. C., Carty, M. H., Leeming, J. T. and Robinson, J. M. (1978), 'Medical screening of old people accepted for residential care', *Lancet*, 2, 8081, pp. 141–142.

67 Ovenstone, I. R. K. and Bean, P. (1981), 'A medical, social assessment of admissions to old people's homes in Nottingham', *British Journal of Psychiatry*, 139, pp. 226–229.

68 Cooper, M. (1981), *Needs Assessment of Elderly Clients: New Operational Procedures Briefing*, Essex County Council, Social Services Department: Research Section.

69 Golding, K. and Cooper, M. (1981), *Alternatives to Residential Provision for the Elderly: Final Report*, Essex County Council, Social Services Department.

70 Challis, D. J. and Davies, B. P. (1980), 'A new approach to community care of the elderly', *British Journal of Social Work*, 10, 1, pp. 1–18.

71 Challis, D. J. and Davies, B. P. (1985), 'Long-term care of the elderly: the community care scheme', *British Journal of Social Work*, 15, 6, pp. 563–579.

72 Davies, B. and Challis, D. (1986), *Matching Resources to Needs in Community Care*, Gower.

73 Challis, D. and Davies, B. (1986), *Case Management in Community Care*, Gower.

74 Latto, S. (1984), *Coventry Home Help Project*, Coventry Social Services Department.

75 Clough, R. (1981), *Old Age Homes*, Allen & Unwin.

76 Paterson, L. (1978), 'A suitable case for care: the selection of residents for old people's homes', *Health and Social Service Journal*, 188, 4850, pp. E1–E7.

77 Shaw, I. and Walton, R. (1979), 'Transition to residence in homes for the elderly', in Harris, D. and Hyland, J. (eds), *Rights in Residence*, Residential Care Association.

78 Willcocks, D. M., Peace, S. and Kellaher, L. with Ring, A. J. (1982), *The Residential Life of Old People: A Study in 100 Local Authority Old People's Homes, Volume I*, Research Report No 12, Polytechnic of North London: Survey Research Unit.

79 Evans, B., Hughes, B. and Wilkin, D, with Jolley, P. (1981), *The Management of Mental and Physical Impairment in Non-Specialist Residential Homes for the Elderly*, University of Manchester: Department of Psychiatry and Community Medicine.

80 Schulz, R. and Brenner, G. (1977), 'Relocation of the Aged: A Review and Theoretical Analysis', *Journal of Gerontology*, 32, pp. 323–333.

81 Thomas, N. (1981), 'Design, management and resident dependency in old peoples homes' in Goldberg, E. M. and Connelly, N. (eds), *Evaluative Research in Social Care*, Heinemann.

82 Booth, T. (1985), *Home Truths*, Gower.

83 Peace, S. M., Hall, J. F. and Hamblin, G. R. (1979), *The Quality of Life of the Elderly in Residential Care*, Polytechnic of North London.

84 Willcocks, D., Ring, J., Kellaher, L. and Peace, S. (1982), *The Residential Life of Old People: A Study in 100 Local Authority Homes. Volume II: Appendices*, Polytechnic of North London: Survey Research Unit.

85 Godlove, C., Richard, L. and Rodwell, G. (1982), *Time for Action: An Observation Study of Elderly People in Four Different Care Environments*, University of Sheffield: Joint Unit for Social Services Research.

86 Wade, B., Finlayson, J., Bell, J., Bowling, A., Bleathman, C., Gilleard, C., Morgan, K., Cole, P., Hammond, M. and Eastman, M. (1987), 'Drug use in residential settings' in Judge, K. and Sinclair, I. A. C. (eds), *Residential Care for Elderly People*, HMSO.

87 Bowling, A. and Bleathman, C. (1982), 'Beware of the nurses', *Nursing Mirror*, 29 September, pp. 54–58.

88 Clarke, M. G., William, A. J. and Jones, P. A. (1981), 'A psychogeriatric study of old people's homes', *British Medical Journal*, 283, 14 November, pp. 1–8.

89 Hitch, D. and Simpson, A. (1972), 'An attempt to assess a new design in residential homes for the elderly', *British Journal of Social Work*, 2, pp. 481–501.

90 Gupta, H. (1979), 'Can we deinstitutionalise an institution? Part 2', *Concord*, 13, pp. 47–57.

91 Peace, M. and Harding, D. (1980), *The Haringey Group-Living Evaluation Project*, Polytechnic of North London: Survey Research Unit.

92 Booth, T. and Phillips, D. (1987), 'Group living in homes for the elderly: a comparative study of the outcomes of care', *British Journal of Social Work*, 17, pp. 1–20.

93 Sinclair, I. A. C. (1971), *Hostels for Probationers*, HMSO.

94 Tizard, J., Sinclair, I. A. C. and Clarke, R. V. G. (1975), *Varieties of Residential Experience*, Routledge and Kegan Paul.

95 Martin, D. N. (1977), 'Disruptive behaviour and staff attitudes at the St Charles Youth Treatment Centre', *Child Psychology and Psychiatry*, 18, pp. 221–228.

96 Imber, V. (1977), *A Classification of Staff in Homes for the Elderly*, HMSO.

97 Phillips, D. R. and Vincent, J. A. assisted by Blackwell, S. (1986), 'Petit bourgeois care: private residential care for the elderly', *Policy and Politics*, 14, 2, pp. 189–208.

98 Knapp, M. R. J. (1979), 'On the determination of manpower requirements of old people's homes', *Social Policy and Administration*, 1313, pp. 219–236.

99 Clough, R. (1986), '**Staffing in residential homes**' in Judge, K. and Sinclair, I. A. C. (eds), *Residential Care for Elderly People*, HMSO.

100 Meacher, M. (1972), *Taken for a Ride*, Longman.

101 Norman, A. (1986), *Severe Dementia: Provision of Long-Stay Care*, Centre for Policy and Ageing (unpublished report).

102 Lipman, A. R. and Slater, R. (1975), *Architectural Design Implications of Residential Homes for Old People*, Final Report, Social Science Research Council.

103   Bland, R. and Bland, R. E. (1983), 'Recent research in old people's homes: a review of the literature', *Research Policy and Planning*, 1, 1, pp. 16–24.

104   Wyvern Partnership (1977), *Evaluation of the Group Unit Design for Old People's Homes*, University of Birmingham: Social Services Unit.

105   Kuh, D. and Bold, D. (1981), *The Evaluation of Short-Term Care for the Elderly Provided in Residential Homes*, University of Exeter: Institute of Biometry and Community Medicine.

106   Thornton, P. and Moore, J. (1980), *The Placement of Elderly People in Private Households: An Analysis of Current Provision*, Monograph, University of Leeds: Department of Social Policy and Administrtion.

107   Edwards, C. and Sinclair, I. A. C. (1980), 'Debate: segregation versus integration', *Social Work Today*, 11, 40, 24 June.

108   Edwards, C., Sinclair, I. A. C. and Gorbach, P. (1980), 'Day centres for the elderly: variations in type, provision and user response', *British Journal of Social Work*, 10, 4, pp. 419–430.

109   Allen, I. (1986), 'Short-stay residential care, day care and other uses of local authority homes for the elderly' in Judge, K. and Sinclair, I. A. C. (eds), *Residential Care for Elderly People*, HMSO.

110   Fennel, G., Emerson, A. R., Sidell, M. and Hague, A. (1981), *Day Centres for the Elderly in East Anglia*, University of East Anglia.

111   Bowl, R., Taylor, H., Taylor, M. and Thomas, N. (1978), *Day Care for the Elderly in Birmingham*, University of Birmingham: Social Services Unit.

112   Avebury, K. (1984), *Home Life: A Code of Practice for Residential Care*, Report of a working party sponsored by the Department of Health and Social Security and convened by the Centre for Policy on Ageing under the chairmanship of Kina, Lady Avebury.

113   Challis, L. (1987), 'The regulation of private social care', in Lewis, B. *et al*, *Care and Control: Personal Social Services in the Private Sector*, Policy Studies Institute.

114   Gilleard, C. J. and Pattie, A. H. (1978), 'The effect of location on the elderly mentally infirm: relationship to mortality and behavioural deterioration', *Age and Ageing*, 7, 1, pp. 1–6.

115   Land, H. (1978), 'Who cares for the family?', *Journal of Social Policy*, 7, 3, pp. 257–284.

116   Finch, J. and Groves, D. (1980), 'Community care and the family: a case for equal opportunities', *Journal of Social Policy*, 9, 4, pp. 487–511.

117   Equal Opportunities Commission (1982), *Caring for the Elderly and Handicapped: Community Care Policies and Women's Lives*, Manchester: Equal Opportunities Commission.

118   Nissel, M. and Bonnerjea, L. (1982), *Family Care of the Elderly: Who Pays?*, Policy Studies Institute.

119 Gibbins, R. (1986), *Oundle Community Care Unit: An Evaluation of an Initiative in the Care of the Elderly Mentally Infirm,* Northamptonshire Social Services Department, Joint Research Steering Group.

120 Whittick, J. (1985), 'The impact of psyochogeriatric day care on the supporters of the elderly mentally infirm, in *Dementia Research Innovation and Management,* Age Concern Scotland.

121 OPCS (1971), *Census 1971: GB Non Private Households,* HMSO.

122 OPCS (1981), *Census 1981: GB Sex, Age and Marital Condition,* HMSO

123 OPCS (1984), *Population Projections 1981–2021,* PP2 No 12, HMSO

124 OPCS (1982), *General Household Survey 1980,* HMSO.

125 Kay, D. W. K. and Bergmann, K. (1980), 'Epidemiology of mental disorders among the aged in the community' in Birren, J. E. and Sloane, R. B. (eds), *Handbook of Mental Health and Ageing,* pp. 34–56, New Jersey, Englewood Cliffs: Prentice Hall.

Costs and Residential Social Care

Bleddyn Davies and Martin Knapp

Personal Social Services Research Unit
University of Kent at Canterbury

CONTENTS

Costs and Residential Social Care

Part 1   Introduction

1   The New Economics of Social Care

Compared with a decade ago, it might seem to the cynical observer of our social care services that the word 'effective' has everywhere been replaced by 'cost-effective', and that 'efficient' has displaced 'efficacious'. The cynical observer would be wrong, but there can be no doubting the dramatic changes that have given us new ways of looking at what are often old issues. Few policy discussions take place without searching questions about the attempt to consider costs as well as non-material outcomes.

We applaud the new cost-consciousness as much as we deplore any hints at cost domination.

The demographic changes of the latter part of the 20th century, the exigencies of need, the realities of fiscal constraints—all exogenous to the social care sector—have only served to reinforce what has always been the case: so long as need (recognised or not) exceeds available supply it will always be necessary to recognise the cost implications of choosing one course of action over another. Those exogenous trends have been coupled with pervasive changes within social care: the post-war emphasis, recently considerably strengthened, on de-institutionalisation; the boom in private sector provision and third party payments out of social security budgets; the decentralisation of service administration and decision-making; the growing and welcome emphasis on quality assurance; and the impact of 'consumerism' in social care. These raise pressing questions about the targeting of resources and, inevitably, the cost effects.

Superimposed upon these various trends and shifts—and certainly not independent from them—are the trappings of the 'new managerialism'—the Financial Management Initiative, Körner and the NHS performance indicators, the now well-established but still young Audit Commission and Social Services Inspectorate—each with at least one eye on efficiency, effectiveness and economy. These are no Thatcherite

[297]

ephemera or ceremonial paraphernalia. They are already, and will surely remain, fundamental institutional reminders of the 'new economics of social care'.

The changing level of prosperity of many who, at an age at which they are at risk of needing long-term care, are granted the power simply to bypass some forms of state provision, the experiences of generations whose level and styles of living have allowed them a degree of personal autonomy unknown in the past, changes in women's employment and the attempts of many to define and assert rights may not be new, but we would be foolish not to recognise that our social institutions will require wise and energetic leadership if they are to adapt to their steady growth. The trappings of the new managerialism may already be aiding that adaptation.

What, then, is the role of cost information? What do we know about the costs and the cost-effectiveness of residential care and its alternatives? What are the cost incentives towards 'good' social care, and what are the disincentives?

2 Target Populations and the Balance of Care

i The Balance of Care Model

Our point of departure is the familiar balance of care 'model', the central premises of which can be summarised by Figure 1. This 'model' has been used to illustrate service allocation strategies on numerous occasions, usually with reference to elderly persons. In its earliest forms, as described by operations researchers in the 1960s, it was a simple, popular, but ultimately unsatisfactory planning tool. Subsequent discussions have elaborated and qualified it,[1-7] although it reappeared—and was temporarily quite influential—in its simplest and potentially most misleading form in the last three outputs from the now defunct Audit Inspectorate.[8-10] It is a useful didactic device. The basic elements of the model and figure are:

- *Care modes*, which are alternative combinations of services received by a particular client group, usually long-term care services and always assumed to be mutually exclusive.

- *Costs*, which were originally not defined with any precision, but latterly have come to mean comprehensive, opportunity costs. They may be opportunity costs to one or a combination of interest groups and/or to society as a whole. They are either marginal or average costs per client (or client week), depending on the context.

- *Characteristics*, such as dependency, degree of handicap, delinquency or behavioural difficulty, which are assumed to be correlated with the cost of care, often because of an almost tautological association. As we move from left to right along the horizontal axis of Figure 1 so the level of dependency, behavioural difficulty or delinquency increases.

Figure 1: Balance of Care

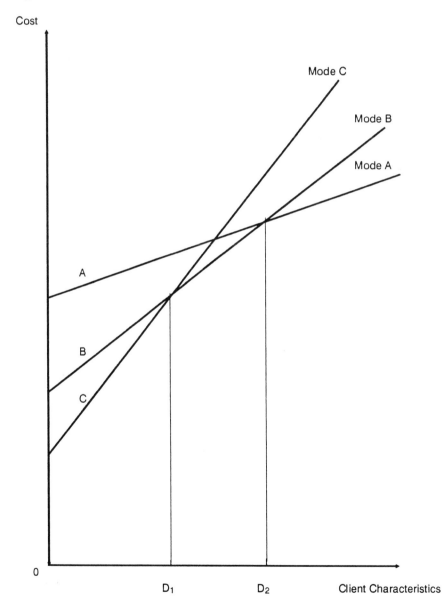

Cost

Mode C

Mode B

Mode A

A

B

C

0

D_1 D_2 Client Characteristics

The three lines on the figure represent the association between costs and characteristics for three different care modes (A, B and C). In discussions of costs of care for elderly persons these are usually hospital, residential and community care, respectively, and the lines represent the cost-dependency gradient. The cost is the amount of money that needs to be spent to assist an elderly client to carry out (or to have performed on their behalf) tasks which compensate for disability (etc) to achieve a satisfactory level of functioning. It is implicitly assumed that these costs allow the achievement of equally acceptable results in the three care modes. In discussions of costs of care for children these three care modes might be residential provision, a foster placement and 'home on trial', or for young offenders they could be a custodial sentence, a period in a community home with education and inter-mediate treatment (IT). In each case the cost of the care mode is (implicitly) assumed to measure the resources needed to achieve an equivalent level of effectiveness or placement success.

This is clearly a simple and appealing model. If it is the case that the expenditures indicated for the care services for clients of different degrees of dependency *are* achieving equally acceptable results, then the target allocation is quite straightforward:

> *Under the assumptions of the balance of care model*, the most cost-effective mode of care for a person with characteristics (say, dependency) between O and D_1 will be mode C; for a person with dependency between D_1 and D_2 the most cost-effective mode is B; and above D_2 it is mode A.

This balance of care model is a useful device provided that (a) we carefully interrogate and suitably adapt its assumptions, and (b) the empirical evidence with which we use it is appropriate.

In the remaining part of this section we set out the assumptions made in this 'model' (and our qualifications to them) and the issues requiring empirical evidence. We conclude the section by defining target criteria in the light of the logic of the balance of care model and its various qualifications. In Part 2 we present evidence for elderly persons, in Part 3, children and young persons, and—in much less detail—other client groups. It will quickly become clear that in both quantity and quality the evidence is rather different for the various client groups. There have been cost studies of services for *elderly persons* for many years, particularly since Wager's study in Essex[1]. When one of us embarked on a study of the costs of *child care* in 1982, following a limited exploratory study in 1977, we could find virtually no previous research (in any country) apart from work treating local authorities as units of analysis.[8, 11, 12] There is now at least a reasonable amount of evidence on most of the salient policy questions. This stands in contrast to what appears to be available by way of cost evidence on services for people with a learning difficulty (mental handicap), mental illness or physical handicap, although there is currently some very interesting work in progress.

ii Outputs
The equivalence of the outputs or outcomes of the modes of care was implicitly assumed in the argument described in Figure 1. Since the argument was first developed, a large repertoire of devices for the conceptualisation, definition and measurement of outputs has been developed. However, the connections between resources and outputs are often indirect, and it is rare to find clear evidence from British research which describes those connections. Some of the outputs from social care are *intermediate*: they reflect attainments of service-level objectives such as the provision of residential care, the delivery of midday meals, and so on. Of more relevance are the *final outputs*: attainment of client-level objectives, especially the enhancement of quality of life, and assessment of the impacts on informal carers and communities.

One task, then, is to be clear about the objectives and the dimensions of output for care services, and to examine the linkages between them and resources or costs. In this way we might be able to interpret Figure 1 as representing not just differences in *cost*, but differences in *cost-effectiveness*.

iii Modes of Care
The balance of care model was originally developed in the context of long-term care planning and the three modes of care were assumed to be discrete and mutually exclusive during any care period. For most elderly people the modes of hospital, residential home and community care satisfy this assumption. For many children their lengths of stay in the modes of residential care, foster care and with their natural family are probably sufficiently long for the model to have some validity. However, there is growing use of more complex packages of care involving residential and non-residential elements—the growth of short stay care in old people's homes, the establishment of 'family centres', the concept of residential IT—and this blurs the distinctions between modes. These considerations do not require the abandonment of Figure 1, but we do need to specify the alternative choices carefully, and recognise that in most cases there will be many more than three alternatives. Until such time as service managers are able to mix services in an infinite number of combinations to exactly match the diversity of need, this didactic device will be fine.

In discussing particular client groups we will often be comparing residential care with a 'more institutional' setting such as geriatric hospital, detention centre or secure unit, and with a form of community care which could include foster family provision, intermediate treatment, domiciliary and day care, and so on. At times, of course, our terminology will need clarification, as for example with the tendency in discussions of the rundown of long-stay hospitals to include residential care modes under the 'community care' banner.

iv Definitions of Cost

What are we measuring on the vertical axis of Figure 1? The common notion of cost is the figure produced by the finance officer at the end of the financial year for a complete service or a single unit of provision, weighted by the number of clients or client weeks. The annual publications from the Chartered Institute of Public Finance and Accountancy (CIPFA) have refined these 'costs' for a number of key social care services.[13] These are not adequate for our purposes, although they sometimes have relevance in modular calculations and we will sometimes have to rely on them for want of anything better.

Without going into great detail we will be looking for at least four forms of improvement to these routinely available cost statistics:

(a) We should aim to include as many as possible of the *hidden or indirect costs* of a care service, such as field social worker inputs into residential care for children, which are not costed on the residential budget, or the NHS resources that support group home settings for adults with a learning disability as an alternative to hospital.

(b) We should use *opportunity cost* concepts which recognise that what you pay for a resource need not reflect its true value to you or to society, and that some apparently free resources (volunteers, for example) do have an implicit social cost.

(c) We should be aware that there will usually be a great deal of *variability* around any quoted average cost figure. Some of that variability reflects differences in the characteristics of service users—as the balance of care model maintains as its central feature—and some of it reflects other factors such as regional location, scale of activity and ownership which are amenable to empirical examination (and therefore to statistical standardisation). The cost-raising properties of these factors are not mere 'nuisances', as some balance of care modellers would appear to suggest, but contain pressing policy data. Are there, for example, economies of scale or specialisation? Does high occupancy lower average cost? Is the public sector more or less cost-efficient than the voluntary or private?[6]

(d) Even after the inclusion of hidden costs, the use of opportunity costing and the standardisation for appropriate cost-influencing factors, the figures relate to the *present* context of care. Changing the balance of care will mean changing the costs. These changes will come about in at least three ways. First, the *efficiency* with which services are delivered is improving and this is likely to continue. This is partly because of the efficiency imperative which is permeating public policy, and partly (and more interestingly) because of the innovative supply responses of care agencies to the diversity of needs presented by populations.[14, 15] Second, we have the *Pandora effect*: the availability of services greater in quantity, better in quality, and more relevant to the needs of the population will generate additional demands. Third, changing the balance of care will *alter the 'typical' characteristics of users*. For example, increasing the boarding out proportion has raised the average age and average degree of 'difficulty' of children now in residential accommodation, and has had a corresponding inflationary effect on average cost.

Together these various 'add-ons' and 'take-aways' complicate the reckoning of the costs of care. We shall also see that they can be sufficient to reverse the ordering of costs as suggested by the routine accounting figures.

Over and above these amendments to the cost definition we have the choice between average and marginal cost. The former is the total cost of a service divided by the number of units of output during a specified time period; for example, the average cost per resident week or per day care attendance. The marginal cost is the amount expended on one additional unit of output, such as the cost of boarding out one more child. The choice of which cost measure to use will be dictated by the policy issue under consideration, and the likely scale of the resultant change in care practice.

v Client Characteristics

What are the relevant client characteristics against which to measure cost? What, in other words, are we plotting along the horizontal axis in Figure 1? The early balance of care models for elderly clients of social and health services looked at dependency, which they tended to define narrowly. For young offenders we might measure the seriousness of offence (the tariff), and for some children we might rely on some measures of 'difficulty' presented by behavioural and other problems. (We shall see that there is some circularity in the definition of dependency and other characteristics when used in a cost discussion.) We are first seeking a comprehensive, summary measure of those client characteristics and circumstances which influence the need for care. At the point at which a decision is made by the client or a carer about the most appropriate placement, these client characteristics are predetermined. The decision maker takes them as given in making a placement or when offering incentives to appropriately channel autonomous or semi-autonomous client demands. Thereafter, those characteristics may well alter—improvements being among the outputs of the care process. We are then, secondly, seeking to identify cost-raising properties of those client characteristics. The logic of the balance of care model is that cost—or rather cost-effectiveness—should influence the placement decision.

vi   Cost Variations between Areas

Inter-authority cost variations are legendary. Some of these variations reflect or are influenced by differences in the inheritances of relatively unadjustable capital stocks. Therefore target specifications for modes of care should vary between areas. Balance of care modellers build in 'second best options' in the event of physical constraints on the supply of what they consider the most appropriate mode for a client in given circumstances. Examples include different models of geriatric practice and supplies of (local) foster placements. Others argue that the causal mechanisms which underlie and amplify or diminish the inter-dependence of services within a system are anything but uniform or mechanistic. This makes it more difficult to derive decision rules for targeting resources at needs from local studies. A related issue is the influence of certain third party agents which constrain the allocative process and raise costs to care providers. Examples of such agents are magistrates, social security officers, general practitioners and planning authorities. Again, it tends to be differences rather than similarities between such agents and their influences on social care responsibilities which have more impact on targeting criteria and policy. We will have to be aware of these various supply and other constraints in trying to move a care system towards an 'optimum'.

vii   Inter-Sectoral Differences

It is sometimes claimed that voluntary or private care services are cheaper or more cost-effective than public services. There is surprisingly little reliable British evidence with which to confront these claims, and what there is supports them with a number of qualifications. The rapidly changing inter-sectoral balance within the residential care sector and elsewhere heightens the need for good evidence, not least because some of the changes have themselves been predicated on assumptions about relative cost-effectiveness differences between the sectors and the implications that any differences may have in both the short- and long-term.

Going hand in hand with the changing inter-sectoral balance of provision has been the growth of third-party financing, particularly from social security budgets. The extent of this can be over-estimated, for only a third of all publicly-funded adult residents of private and voluntary residential homes are supported from social security pay-ments. Nevertheless, an important corollary to the examination of inter-sectoral cost differences is due consideration of the charging strategy of non-public homes, the demands for their services, relations between the sectors, and incentives to good practice. Regulatory procedures are included here.

viii Inter-Modal Differences and a Targeting Criterion

Finally then, we come back to the basic balance of care diagram and its assumptions about the relative costs and cost-effectiveness of the different modes of care. Is it the case, for example, that community care for the elderly population is a cost-effective option at low levels of dependency, but not at high levels? Is hospitalisation the most cost-effective mode of care for adults with the most severe of psychiatric disorders? Some research has tended to assume affirmative answers to each of these questions and to focus only on the 'boundaries' or 'margins' between care modes.[3, 16] Fortunately, some of the community care experiments for elderly people, some of the demonstration projects aimed at rehabilitating long-stay hospital populations, and some of the foster placement campaigns for 'hard-to-place' children, have been prepared to make more than merely marginal changes to the balance of care. We must examine what these experiments, demonstration projects and campaigns have revealed about cost-effectiveness.

We need to go further than this, of course. We must also specify a targeting criterion which uses the cost-effectiveness information in the broader context of other objectives. The criterion we suggest is that persons should receive services in that care mode which:

minimises the disruption to their previous life style,

maximises their chances of a 'normal' life style,

is subject to the constraint of an adequate or socially acceptable standard of care,

is subject to the constraint that no more than an equitable burden should be borne by clients and informal carers,

and in which the costs to the public purse are the lowest.

This targeting criterion emphatically does *not* mean that the cheapest care mode is necessarily to be selected, although sometimes this may happen. It *does* mean that the relative, aggregate costs of alternative modes must be weighed against differences in the other components of the criterion—continuity, normalisation, effectiveness ('adequate' or 'socially acceptable' standards of care as adjudged by care agencies or clients), and equity or fairness. In the context of the 'new economics of social care', anything less comprehensive than this targeting criterion cannot be acceptable.

3 Routinely Available Cost Data

We cannot get very close to comparing present allocations of services with this targeting criterion by relying on routinely available data. There is no need to dwell on this inadequacy, but it is useful to note the sources of cost data and the orders of magnitude of the cost figures they produce. The obvious starting point is the annual CIPFA publications of *Personal Social Services Statistics* (estimates and actuals). In Table 1 we reproduce the mean value of the average cost per resident week in each of eight forms of local authority residential care, using the latest available figures (1985–86). These mean costs hide considerable inter- and intra-authority variations, exclude hidden and opportunity costs, and may anyway be subject to distortion as a result of differences in accounting practice between areas. This last problem is likely to be relatively minor. Of more fundamental importance is the variety of labels attached to ostensibly identical services. It is, for example, increasingly dangerous to assume that the label 'community home' describes the same form of care in any two authorities.

The CIPFA statistics also include average cost figures for most of the well-established non-residential services. These include day care for most client groups, sheltered employment and training centres, home

Table 1: Unit Costs per Resident Week in Local Authority Residential Care, 1985–86*

Service and Clients	Shire Counties	London Boroughs			Met Dist	All LAs
		Inner	Outer	All†		
	£	£	£	£	£	£
Elderly persons						
Old people's homes	109	172	139	149	117	115
Children						
Observation and assessment centres	378	726	776	747	282	399
Community homes with education	410	779	765	772	316	433
Other community homes and hostels	257	448	443	440	239	275
Children with Learning Disabilities						
Residential homes	280	629	505	541	329	324
Physically and Sensorily Handicapped						
Residential homes	185	290	291	290	187	197
Adults with Learning Disabilities						
Hostels	134	241	174	193	138	142
Mentally Ill Adults						
Hostels	136	155	165	161	136	143

* Some local authorities did not make returns to CIPFA for all services.
† Includes City of London not included in Inner or Outer London columns.
Source:[13]

help, meals on wheels, the so-called 'family centres', and others. These are useful data for some purposes, but any examination of the allocation of services would need to combine them in suitably defined community care packages, and there would still be many resources omitted, not least field social work inputs.

The other primary cost source—apart from local statistics—is the *Health Service Costing Return* which annually tabulates unit costs for geriatric, psychiatric and day hospitals, by Regional Health Authority, and community health services by district.

Part 2   Evidence: Elderly Persons

The balance of care model set out earlier was first developed in the context of services for elderly persons. We have already noted the comparative wealth of empirical costs evidence for this client group. Almost all of that evidence has included an assessment of *dependency* as well as cost. The basic model assumes that the cost of care achieving equally acceptable results (see *Outputs* below) is higher the greater is dependency. That is almost true by definition: if 'dependency' is measured by the resources required to achieve the compensation, and costs measure most of those resources, clearly one would expect a positive correlation. However, the assumption has real substance when for 'dependency' is substituted 'disability' or 'handicap'.

Because of data limitations and in the search for simplicity, most studies of the cost-dependency relationship have employed aggregated indicators of dependency-generating characteristics (such as mobility, continence, self-care capacity, confusion, wandering behaviour and health status). The results are informative and reliable. More recently there has been a move away from aggregated indicators. In community care contexts these indicators are less successful in predicting costs than (i) individual disability-related characteristics, and (ii) other factors like the extent and richness of social support networks, attitudes towards help and services.[7, 17] In some areas, variations in housing conditions also have a large influence.[3, 18, 19, 7] (The greater explanatory power of individual characteristics rather than scales illustrates that a statistical analysis of the effects of disabilities on costs is likely to provide the formula for an indicator of dependency which is better than a more arbitrarily weighted dependency indicator derived on some other premises. We should be cautious in employing summary dependency scales developed in a context very different from the area of application.)

1 Outputs

Ten years ago we embarked on what proved to be a major task of identifying the dimensions of outcome or effectiveness of residential care for elderly persons, reviewing the instrumentation available for their measurement, and specifying the causal linkages between resources, features of the social environment of homes, histories and characteristics of residents and these outcomes.[20] Our colleague David Challis conducted a review of the dimensionality of outputs in community settings.[21] The principal dimensions that need to be introduced when moving from a cost to a cost-effectiveness criterion are:

- nurturance,

- compensation for disability,

- independence,

- morale,

- social integration

- family relationships, and

- community development.

We will not discuss the interpretation and measurement of these any further in this Report. We will need to refer to them, however, in much of the ensuing.

2 Modes of Care

Given the Committee's focus on residential care the most appropriate modes to consider are: geriatric and other hospital provision, residential care, and community or domiciliary care packages. When discussed in balance of care models these are labelled A, B and C, respectively, in Figure 1. That is, it is assumed that community care is most cost-effective at low levels of dependency, hospital provision is most cost-effective for very highly dependent elderly people, and residential care comes somewhere in between.[3, 5] We will focus on the range and variety of community-based packages as the principal alternative to residential care. These packages may well include some short-term institutional care (hospital, nursing home or residential home) and will almost certainly involve services in the client's own home and some day care.

There are, of course, moves to rehabilitate some long-stay elderly hospital patients in residential or nursing homes, for example under the government's Care in the Community initiative,[22] and there are the NHS experimental nursing homes aiming to divert such persons in the first place. However, the proportion of all residents in residential homes for whom the principal alternative would be hospitalisation must be very small. Likewise, the numbers of elderly people presently in hospital who might conceivably be accommodated in old people's homes is also very small in relation to the total already thus accommodated. We shall briefly review the relevant evidence here, but concentrate on the (wide) margin between residential and community services. It should be noted, however, that there are system effects working through from the health sector. For instance, models of geriatric practice differ, and these differences affect the influence of health care inputs on whether someone will enter an old people's home. Equally the very existence of large numbers of hospital places may cause admissions to hospitals to be higher among the elderly, and so put more persons into a situation where their informal carers may be able to press and obtain authoritative support for discharge to an old people's home.[23] The variety in these causal mechanisms and their effects on system interdependence therefore make it difficult to derive decision rules about targeting of general applicability to all areas from case studies.[7]

3   Local Authority Residential Homes

i   Costs and Dependency

British evidence on costs and dependency in local authority residential homes is sparse and to some degree contradictory. Estimates for Cheshire showed the average operating cost to the social services department for the one resident in five rated as 'heavily dependent' to be 20 per cent higher than that of the two persons in five rated 'minimally dependent'.[24] The greater the rated dependency, the greater the costs. Wright and his colleagues, using data based on matrons' judgments about the needs for care time of individual residents in one authority, produced similar results.[5] Mooney, using slightly different definitions in his Scottish study also found the consistent cost gradient. He also found the costs of those on the margin of need for hospital care to be no less than 44 per cent greater than those on the margin between domiciliary and residential care.[3]

However, not all research has found such a consistent relationship. Knapp's analysis of 1970 data for homes run by county boroughs suggested that those rated 'heavily dependent' consumed less staff time than those rated 'moderately dependent'.[25] Darton and Knapp, working from the widest and most comprehensive of the British data collections to date, suggested that the costs of 'minimal dependency' might have been higher than those of 'limited dependency' among large homes: though the confidence intervals swamped the difference despite the large number (235) of homes studied. They did not find the inconsistency for homes of other sizes.[26] Figure 2 illustrates the relationships between costs and dependency and Table 2 reports estimates.

There are clearer signs of inconsistencies in the relationships between disability and costs in the American literature on nursing homes and rest homes. Various studies have found those of moderate disability to be more expensive than persons of medium disability, though not all relationships were well established statistically.[27, 28] But there were also important studies suggesting consistent relationships. Davies and Challis review the American literature in more detail.[7] It is there argued that studies may have underestimated the effects of

Figure 2. Average cost by home size by dependency, local authority old people's homes

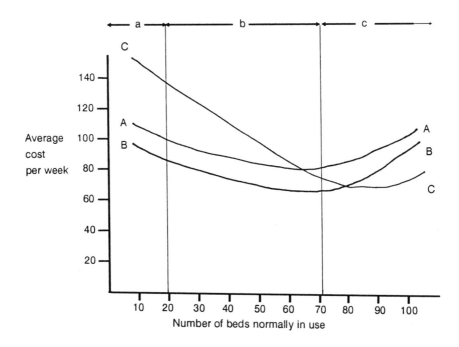

Plot of predicted average cost per resident week by home size by dependency category.

Key: a, 2% of homes (min. = 9); b, 93% of homes; c, 5% of homes (max. = 106); A-A, minimal dependency; B-B, limited dependency; C-C, appreciable or heavy dependency.

Reproduced from Robin Darton and Martin Knapp (1984), 'The cost of residential care for the elderly: the effects of dependency, design and social environment', *Ageing and Society*, 4, pp. 157-183.

disabilities on costs in both countries, first, because there is frequently a mismatch between the disability characteristics of residents and the nature and intensity of the services which the home can provide. Need judgements reflect supply constraints as well as the welfare shortfalls of residents, and dependency is a context-specific need judgment. So disabilities, handicaps and other functional deficits are only some of the predictors of dependency. The totality of care resources available to a home is just as much cost-determining as the service actually required by residents, Jensen and Birnbaum showing that services *offered* predicted costs better than services *delivered.*[29] The US studies do not control for variations in the quality of life and care. Second, studies are often based on samples of residents within homes. This has the effect of attenuating regression coefficients. The measurement of most disability characteristics is subject to error, errors in predictor terms attenuate regression coefficients, and the studies have not corrected for the resulting unreliability.

Table 2: Estimated Average Cost Function, Old People's Homes, 1981

The estimated cost function indicates that average expenditure on manpower and running expenses per bed normally in use per resident week is equal to:

−552.826*		
+1.743**	x	Labour cost index
−3.264**	x	Number of beds normally in use in group-living homes
−1.604**	x	Number of beds normally in use in non-group homes
+0.024*	x	Number of beds normally in use in group-living homes, squared
+0.014**	x	Number of beds normally in use in non-group homes, squared
+10.725*	x	Percentage occupancy level (at 31 October 1981)
−0.058*	x	Percentage occupancy level (at 31 October 1981) squared
+5.995*	if	staff of home have duties in sheltered housing
+4.358*	if	all laundry done within the home
+7.736*	x	Number of permanent admissions in 12 months to 31 October 1981 per number of beds normally in use
+3.188*	x	Number of short-stay discharges in 12 months to 31 October 1981 per number of beds normally in use
+4.927*	if	mixed-sex non-group-living home
+34.823**	if	single-sex group-living home
+63.294**	if	mixed-sex group-living home
−12.488**	x	Proportion of residents in limited dependency category
+51.714**	x	Proportion of residents in appreciable or heavy dependency categories
−0.814**	x	Number of beds normally in use weighted by proportion of residents in appreciable or heavy dependency categories

Significance levels: * $0.01 < P \leqslant 0.05$, ** $P \leqslant 0.01$. F value for equation: $F = 37.58$, $P \leqslant 0.0001$. $R^2 = 0.76$, adjusted $R^2 = 0.74$, $n = 218$.
Source: Robin Darton and Martin Knapp (1984), 'The cost of residential care for the elderly: the effects of dependency, design and social environment', *Ageing and Society*, 4, pp.157–183.

Perhaps, therefore, one should not overstate the inconsistency of the results of the British studies. However, neither must one forget that this is a new area of investigation with a small body of literature based on collections of data whose content if not scale has always forced the exclusion of such important data as final outputs (outcomes of importance in their own right) and evidence about the workings of the causal processes which determine the relationships between costs and outputs.

ii Costs, Outputs and Efficiency

We have already noted that the equivalence of the outputs of the modes of care was implicitly assumed in the balance of care model. We also noted that the connections between resources and outputs are often indirect. Unfortunately, we lack a study of the relationships between costs and direct measures of final outputs in local authority residential homes. The 1981–82 PSSRU survey of homes collected data about features of the social environment arguably associated with the quality of life and care. Analysis failed to find any marked correlation between costs and these characteristics.[26] The results are shown in Table 3.

Table 3: The Effects of Indicators of Social Environment on Average Cost, Local Authority Old People's Homes, 1981

Social environment dimensions	Mean values	Correlation with actual average cost	Effect on average cost per resident week[1]	
			Actual	Residual[2]
(Constant term)	—	—	103.65**[3]	0.40
Regime	0.31	0.14	9.79	2.25
Motor control	0.98	−0.24	−30.66**	−5.86
Privacy	0.51	0.01	4.35	4.93
Participation	0.65	0.01	3.31	−1.77
Interaction	0.78	−0.09	−6.80	−0.96
Homogeneity	0.16	0.10	23.26	−8.10
Continuity	0.94	0.07	4.00	5.57*
F value for equation			3.88**	2.57*
R^2			0.12	0.08
n			213	213

1 Regression of actual (observed) and residual average cost on the seven dimensions of social environment, including a constant term.

2 The residual average cost is the actual average operating cost *minus* the average operating cost predicted by the cost function shown in Table 2.

3 Significance levels are shown in the table as follows: * $0.01 < P \leqslant 0.05$; ** $P \leqslant 0.01$.

Source: Robin Darton and Martin Knapp (1984), The cost of residential care for the elderly: the effects of dependency, design and social environment, *Ageing and Society*, 4, pp.157–183.

Because we are without a study of the costs of final outputs for residents in homes in different need-related circumstances we are unable to estimate equations to yield the information required to plot precisely relationships of the kind postulated in Figure 1.

iii Reference Opportunity Costs to the Social Services Department

The data of the PSSRU survey of local authority homes make it possible to estimate the opportunity costs to social services departments of residential care. That is, given the emphasis on community care provisions as alternatives to residential care, it is possible to calculate from the survey data the spending maxima for community-based services for persons with different characteristics without making community-based care more expensive than residential care. Continuing to operate residential homes for elderly people imposes both operating and capital (land and construction) costs. Together these are usefully calculated as opportunity costs. If some or all of the present stock of local authority homes are to be closed down in favour of the development of community care services, these opportunity cost savings need to be accurately forecast. At a territorial level, residential care costs are sensitive to variations in three factors:

(a) the inheritance by authorities of homes with different cost-affecting characteristics;

(b) targeting strategies with respect to the dependency of residents; and

(c) targeting strategies with respect to the total number of long-stay residents in homes.[30]

The inheritances of authorities vary greatly. They are not equally able to convert old people's homes into flatlets, or respite care accommodation, or multi-purpose facilities. One of the more interesting developments in the elaboration of the balance of care approach, therefore, has been able to explore the implications of variations in the circumstances of authorities, including variations in their inheritances of capital stock.

The second factor to be examined was the set of target strategies with respect to the dependency of residents. The Audit Commission[31] argued (p.2) that

Some people are inappropriately placed in residential care. Where there is pressure upon places some of those that need residential care cannot secure it, and remain at risk in the community. In three of the seven authorities studied in detail, about half of the residents in the authorities' homes might be expected to be able to be supported in the community, if the necessary resources were available; in each case, the number of severely physically disabled residents (who would be expected to justify a residential place) was well below the average. . . . Often, however, the underlying cause is lack of effective management. . .

The Audit Commission argued that many of the severely disabled—more mobile than the bedfast, chairfast or those unable to feed themselves unaided, but unable to perform some important personal tasks (including one or more of bathing, combing hair, washing hands or face) or prepare light snacks—require residential care if they have little or no support from friends and relatives. They argued that few elderly people with only moderate physical disability and not requiring personal care needed residential care. They suggested that authorities should develop explicit statements of the factors which would normally warrant admission of a person with moderate disability (only) to residential care. So, they argued, the core group to be cared for in residential accommodation should comprise: some very severely physically disabled clients who are not cared for by the NHS, and those severely physically disabled who cannot be supported adequately elsewhere (by friends and relatives or a package of community care) including those with behaviour disorders not cared for by the NHS. Of course, targeting could never be reduced to formulae.

The Audit Commission and other commentators accept the massive substitution of community for residential care, and accept that homes will provide for the more disabled of their present populations. However, authorities will certainly consider and adopt targeting strategies which yield very different mixes of residents by dependency across the country. These will reflect local expectations and judgements, but also variations in the alternatives available.

Third, targeting strategies with respect to the total number of long-stay residents in homes will be of influence. Irrespective of the implications of targeting policies for the dependency mix in homes, they may require very different numbers of places. Most of those who are heavily dependent are cared for by friends and relatives. Even among recipients of the community services, those living with relatives receive far more of their assistance from informal carers than from social services. Targeting policies for residential care must take into account the relief of carers facing unacceptable burdens. Authorities will need to consider the implications of attaching differing priorities to doing so. Furthermore, changes in need-related circumstances—for instance, demographic profiles and the geographical movements of potential carers—will differ greatly between areas.

So it is important to consider the implications of variations in the number of places required for opportunity costs as a separate factor.

Different assumptions can be made about the second and third factors—targeting with respect to dependency, and with respect to the total number of residents—in the context of the different inheritances of homes. Four scenarios are acted out in the Davies *et al* study.[31]

1. In the first, the long-run opportunity costs are estimated under the assumption that the 1981–82 number and dependency mix of residents are maintained. This allows a description of the opportunity costs of 'current' provision. The results indicate substantial differences between areas, and that variations in land and construction costs compound the variations in operating costs. Overall, the expected opportunity cost exceeds the predicted operating cost by between 7 and 13 per cent, making it cost-effective to work with higher costs per case cared for in the community than would be inferred by looking only at average operating costs.

2. Under the second scenario, the number of residential places is reduced to that number required to accommodate those of heavy and appreciable dependency *in 1981–82* (there were four dependency categories—heavy, appreciable, limited and minimal—and 30 per cent of residents were in the first two categories), assuming that the homes closed were those which were *not* purpose-built during the 1970s and which did not satisfy building note requirements. It is also assumed that the more expensive homes are closed first. In this case—with the accommodation of only heavily and appreciably dependent residents—opportunity costs would have been substantially higher—up to 17 per cent—and higher still if residential sector vacancies were concentrated in the most expensive homes. Again, this is a *reference calculation*; it shows the potential for developing effective community care policies which could be somewhat more costly than today's residential care but still cheaper than the residential care sector under this projected scenario.

3. The third scenario differs from the second in its assumption that there would be no reduction in the total number of residential places. All places open in 1981–82 would be used to accommodate elderly persons of heavy or appreciable dependency. Even without any capital spending or adjustment of staffing levels made necessary by the change in targeting, opportunity costs would be up to 20 per cent higher, and higher still with a purposive concentration of vacancies in the most costly homes.

4. Finally, if new homes were opened to allow an expansion of residential accommodation, and if those new establishments had cost structures similar to those of the homes newly occupied just prior to the 1981–82 PSSRU survey, costs would again be substantially higher than a simple extrapolation of today's figures would suggest. This is true whether or not adjustments are made for dependency.

The estimates produced by Davies, Darton and Goddard are

provisional and work is continuing to refine them. The results suggest that, under quite reasonable conjectures about the future targeting of local authority residential care, more can be spent on *community* care without it becoming 'cost-ineffective' than a simple extrapolation of current national average costs in old people's homes might suggest.

iv 'Add-Ons' and 'Take-Aways'

If the horizon for the setting of targeting criteria is long—the exercise is to set some future level of capital stock and targeting criteria—we must make allowance for the effects of improved management on operating costs. This will reduce costs. At the same time we need to add on some missing cost elements. First, we have an addition to make for the slow adjustments of resources to greater dependency. The Darton-Knapp equations show the relations between costs and dependency as they are rather than as they would have been in a world in which resources are perfectly adjusted to needs.[26] Authorities have adjusted the resources of homes slowly and imperfectly to their average dependency mix.[31] Indeed, the dependency mix can change faster than resources can be adjusted, since some of the adjustments require substantial periods to implement. The effect is to overstate the cost effects of dependency, although by how much we cannot say. Improved resource management could bring these dependency effects down.

Second, we have not included those 'hidden costs' of residential care: the costs of resources and services provided for residents but not costed under the residential budget. These might include a local authority laundry service, various peripatetic NHS services, and the opportunity costs of volunteer inputs. We know of no evidence about these hidden costs.

4 Private Old People's Homes

i Fees and Dependency in 1981

The PSSRU survey of 1981 also covered private homes, there being information for 153 establishments in the twelve authorities. Data were collected about the dependency characteristics of residents in a form which permitted classification into the four-category DHSS dependency grouping which Darton and Knapp found to predict variations in the operating costs of local authority homes.[26] Additional data were collected for 51 of the 153 including registration officers' ratings of (a) the quality of physical care in the home, (b) the proprietor's involvement, (c) relations between the local authority and the home and (d) the atmosphere in the home. Also the PSSRU research team made subjective assessments of the homes in which they conducted interviews and collected the additional data. It was thus possible to study the relationship between the average charges of private homes and the proportion of residents appreciably or heavily dependent. Average fees or charges varied directly and consistently with this proportion: if the proportion appreciably or heavily dependent was greater by 10 per cent, average charges could be as much as £22 per week higher, at 1981 prices.[32, 33] The charges equation is reproduced in Table 4. The composite dependency indicator may have understated the influence of behavioural disturbance. Some equations suggested that a 10 per cent greater proportion with behaviour disturbance was correlated with a charge of some £18 per week higher. These gradients are substantial given a mean charge of £80.

Alternative models based on the data bases of 153 and 51 homes yielded dependency mix effects on charges which were consistent though varying in scale. The effects of the proportion heavily or appreciably dependent appeared to be smaller in equations based on all 153 homes.[32] The proportion of residents assessed by matrons to be a major nuisance also entered the equation predicting charges. This 'major nuisance' variable was significantly positively correlated with the variables measuring heavy and appreciable dependency, having an effect on the coefficients in both of the alternative models. The lines plotted in Figure 3 indicate how average weekly charges in the private old people's homes varied with both the dependency proportion and the nuisance variable. These are not estimates of the charges for persons at differing levels of dependency, because to estimate these requires the mathematical manipulation of the average charge function reported in Table 4 to obtain what we might call the 'marginal costs of dependency'. These particular calculations suggest that the effect on fees of accommodating an additional heavily or appreciably dependent resident (without changing the total number of residents) is approximately £2.20 per week (1981–82 prices) in a ten-bedded home and less in larger homes.

ii Changes in Fees and Dependency since 1981: the Impact of the Policy Environment

The Americans have long argued that structures and behaviour in their long-term care industry have been to a substantial extent the product of government policy. The comparative study of the nursing home industry across American states shows that reimbursement and regulative interventions were perhaps the largest influence on differences between states. Among other things, they had a large effect on resource structures, and so on costs and charges.[34, 35] The large and well publicised changes in social security and regulative arrangements in England and Wales, occurring at a time when the industry was growing fast and so was at its most adaptable, could well have transformed the relationships discovered in the PSSRU study of 1981. More interesting, the changes

Figure 3. Average charges in private homes and proportions of residents heavily or appreciably dependent or a 'major nuisance', 1981

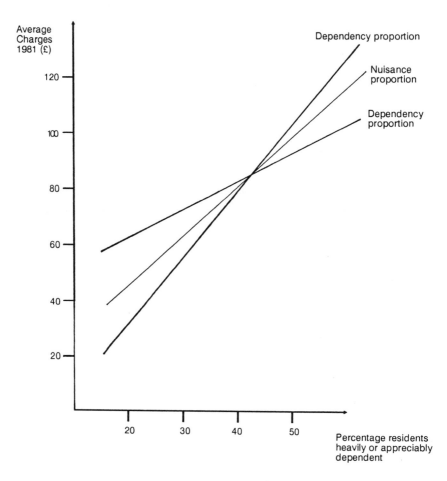

may have caused a permanent change in the behaviour of suppliers, making cost structures more responsive to the incentives provided by government interventions.

The changes are well known, and have been the subject of important analysis.[36-38] They are described in Ian Sinclair's chapter in this volume. The most important features were that large changes were made both to the levels and eligibility criteria for social security support for residents in homes in April 1985. New standards have been worked out and imposed and new regulative arrangements made, increasing the advantages enjoyed by larger homes.[39,40] These have substantially

Table 4: Estimated (constrained) Charges Function for Private Residential Homes for the Elderly, 1981

The estimated function indicates that average charge per resident week is equal to:

−5.1		
+0.074	x Average domestic rateable value per person, by local authority area	(2.4)
+13.35	x No. of single bedrooms as a proportion of all bedrooms	(3.7)
+6.02	x A dummy variable taking the value 1 if the home either has all bedrooms on the ground floor or has a lift to upper-storey bedrooms	(3.3)
−11.52	x The proportion of residents in the home on 31 October 1981 assessed as *not* being depressed	(−2.9)
+4.95	x No. of short-stay residents admitted to the home in the twelve months prior to 31 October 1981 as a proportion of beds normally occupied	(2.5)
+0.000843	x A regional index of the value of domestic house prices in 1980 obtained from *Economic Trends*	(2.4)
+4.13	x A dummy variable taking the value 1 if the home has men and women in residence	(2.0)
+26.31	x The number of supervisory staff in the home divided by the number of beds normally occupied	(2.5)
+6.61	x The proportion of residents in the home on 31 October 1981 categorised as having appreciable or heavy levels of dependency according to the DHSS four-category classification	(1.9)
+4.41	x The number of acres per person, by local authority area	(3.1)
+0.058	x The number of economically active women as a proportion of all women aged 16-plus, by local authority area, obtained from the 1981 Census	(2.4)
+0.275	x No. of beds normally occupied in the home	(2.3)
+12.14	x The proportion of staff in the home with a nursing qualification	(2.3)

Notes: t—statistics are shown in brackets.
$F = 17.0$
$R^2 = 0.64$
$\bar{R}^2 = 0.60$
$N = 138$

Source: Ken Judge, Martin Knapp and Jillian Smith (1986), 'The comparative costs of public and private residential homes for the elderly', in Ken Judge and Ian Sinclair (eds) *Residential Care for Elderly People,* HMSO.

affected the structure of incentives and constraints faced by home providers. The eligibility criteria and the regulatory changes obtained widespread publicity. The scale of the changes and the publicity given by them have probably increased the responsiveness of suppliers. Indeed, it is said that proprietors quickly brought their charges up to the ceilings when these were imposed by the DHSS. The speed of response may also have been increased by the rapid development of the residential home associations, associations with which many authorities work closely. The supply of places has thus grown fast, particularly in areas whose stock of places in the private sector was smallest.[41] The entrants are able to make their investments in buildings, staff and organisation in direct response to the new structure of incentives. There is evidence of the greater involvement of financial institutions in lending to finance the purchase and adaptation of homes. Loans again encourage fast response to incentives. Until the current research by the PSSRU/CHE team is complete, we shall be unable to reassess variations in charges.[42] Our first task is to report recent data about charges levels for people in homes.

The best known of the recent direct evidence about the average level of charges in private homes was collected and analysed by Ernst and Whinney.[43] Caveats must be entered to the reliability of the information collected since the study suffered certain technical difficulties, including a very low response rate. However, its estimate of mean gross costs in private residential homes for the elderly was £117, suggesting that the mean gross cost was higher in real terms than average charges in 1981. The Ernst and Whinney estimate led them to conclude that the mean gross cost was substantially higher in private than in voluntary residential homes; £117 compared with £90. These figures refer to 1985. The 1986 survey by the PSSRU/CHE team also established a significant difference between the two non-public sectors (a mean charge of £143 to residents of private old people's homes compared to a mean of £122 in voluntary homes).[44] The Audit Commission's illustrative examples assume that the costs of care in private (and the much smaller number of voluntary) homes are now substantially higher than in local authority homes. For 'a frail elderly person on a state pension and without substantial savings, qualifying for attendance allowance at the lower rate for a disability incurred after retirement age', the estimates are £133.25 in a local authority home and £138.55 in a private or voluntary home. This is based on a comparison of the Board and Lodging allowance, various benefits, and net revenue costs in local authority homes at 1985 prices.[45] Our extrapolations for 1985, based on the assumption that the ratio of the total operating and capital costs to gross revenue costs in 1985 was the same as for authorities in the PSSRU study in 1981, suggest that opportunity costs to the authority of local authority homes was in 1985 much the same as the mean cost in private homes estimated by Ernst and Whinney. However, these comparisons between the sectors are crude, based as they are on bare cost or fee averages, and thus neglecting differences between the sectors in the characteristics of homes (particularly the facilities offered), the characteristics—especially dependency—of residents and, of course, the quality of sevices and the final outputs for residents. The only cross-sector comparisons of old people's homes' costs and charges in Britain which have attempted to standardise for at least some of these exogenous (and endogenous) differences were based on data for 1981.[33,46,47] Their relevance today is not clear, given the dramatic changes in the intervening period. The US literature on cross-sector differences is interesting but also of limited utility to today's policy problems.[48]

How private and voluntary home charges *now* vary with dependency is uncertain. Ernst and Whinney[43] found no relationship between costs and dependency in what they called their 'limited statistical analysis', and the PSSRU/CHE study has yet to analyse charge-dependency relationships. Whatever emerges will depend upon market structures and responses, the subject to which we now turn.

The critical feature of the market for independent residential and nursing homes—at least on the demand side—is that the social security system is a third party payer which alters the price of care to zero for a large segment of the population of potential consumers. The social security system provides indefinite payment at set rates for all who obtain a place and are eligible because of low income and assets. This not only reduces the price of care to zero without test of disability unless the 'very dependent elderly' rate is claimed, but also reduces the price of private residential care compared with home care for those eligible for Supplementary Benefit. The effect is to create a perverse incentive which encourages residential not community-based care. This is particularly the case if persons are not eligible for the Attendance Allowance and if they are without a carer who can claim the Invalid Care Allowance because they have given up work to care for an invalid living in their own home for more than 35 hours a week and have earnings less than £12 per week.

For those ineligible for Supplementary Benefit, the social security system can presumably reduce the costs of private residential care for those receiving the lower level attendance allowance of £20 per week, though only to the extent that homes do not charge differentially for persons of varying dependency to an extent which removes the benefit. The social security system provides no subsidy to others ineligible for Supplementary Benefit.

So, for what Ernst and Whinney[43] estimate to be between 30 and 40 per cent of residents who depend on Board and Lodging Allowances, (para. 7) the level of demand for care is completely inelastic with respect to the price nursing homes wish to charge; that is, the number wanting to enter and remain does not change when homes alter the price of care when that price remains below the DHSS limits. However, almost all other potential consumers face a downward-sloping demand curve.

The effect of the social security on the demand curve for private residential home care is as shown in Figure 4. The downward-sloping demand curve for those ineligible for means-tested benefits has a kink at the Board and Lodging level, is displaced to the right at that level by the horizontal demand curve from those eligible for Supplementary Benefit. The demand curve is D-D1-D2-D3. The demand from private payers is probably very elastic. In Wisconsin a value of −10 was

Figure 4. The demand for private home beds

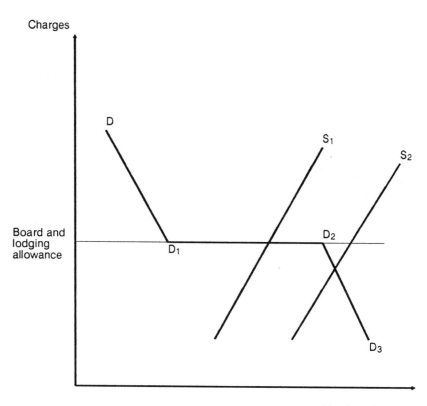

estimated for the demand elasticity.[35]

The social security Board and Lodging Allowance has been set at a rate which in 1986 appeared to be just above the average charge then made by private homes.[49]

On the supply side, if the owners of proprietary homes wish to maximise profits, they will attempt to charge privately-financed residents more. There is some evidence of this. For instance, whereas the Ernst and Whinney estimate of average costs was close to the DHSS limit of £120, the mean charges for Supplementary Benefit claimants admitted after April 1985 and accommodated in shared rooms was £118, close to the DHSS limit, while the mean charge for a shared room for non-claimants was estimated to be £125. However this evidence confounds effects due to higher quality care with price discrimination by source of payment. With our current market structure and an excess demand for beds, the private sector suppliers would have an incentive to concentrate competition through quality on the provision of better standards for private payers. (This is the explanation offered by Bishop for the negative correlation between the proportion of beds occupied by Medicaid beneficiaries and the Medicaid reimbursement rate for American facilities[50].) The profit-maximising strategy would be to make the income or marginal revenue from the last place filled equal to the marginal cost of providing the care. If the numbers of persons willing to pay the price charged to SB claimants exceeds the number of beds, it will be those dependent on Supplementary Benefit who will not obtain them. Thus, in areas with (and at times of) chronic excess demand, private proprietors will be more likely to discriminate against social security cases. The markets in the United States have proved volatile, partly because of clumsy policy interventions. We have had no evidence that the UK central government will always avoid exacerbating a situation of excess demand. Some local authorities could at times make changes causing even more volatility and greater excess demand. Indeed, as politically responsive organisations, one might envisage situations in which some social services departments would be under pressure to do so by some who could quite foresee the consequences.

The behaviour of voluntary homes would be similar if they sought to expand their provision 'to meet need' subject to the constraints that they did not make losses above the level of their income from sources other than charges, and that they were satisfied with the quality of the care they offered. They too would charge more to some private payers. Their behaviour would differ from profit maximisers only to the extent that they might operate at higher levels of both intermediate and final output; that is, offering more places (if faced with an identical level and structure of demand), a higher standard of care and greater levels of resident-specific effectiveness.

There are many ways open to the central government to influence supply and demand. Some are also open to local authorities. A 'trade and industry' policy for long-term care might develop means of directly influencing the supply of places in private homes by setting upper limits on the number of registrations, and operating a formula which relates these numbers to needs, perhaps integrating the treatment into a GREA methodology. (The Americans operated 'Certificate of Needs' policies in similar circumstances.) They may influence supply by other regulatory means; for example, by varying the standards that are acceptable according to the area's supply in relation to needs, or by varying general planning criteria between areas. Again, many fiscal instruments can be used; central and local tax exemptions and other subsidies to capital investment are prime examples. These are all supply-side policy instruments. Others could operate on demand.

Currently the most fashionable demand-side instrument is the development of assessment arrangements in the context of improved home care. This is a device which American experiments suggest has limited effectiveness when a large proportion of the market is not dependent on social security at the time of admission.[7] At the same time, there are serious reservations about limiting the constitutional rights of citizens to choose forms of residence for which they have the means to pay, at least initially. The potential effectiveness of what is crudely called 'assessment' depends greatly on its nature and its context in the effectiveness of the performance of the core tasks of case management. Realistic assessment of the circumstances of new admissions to homes would probably conclude that admission was as appropriate as any other alternative form of care available. However, a system which was highly effective in the performance of all the core tasks of case management, and in which the case management had greatly influenced the incentives faced by suppliers, would be expected to offer a greater variety of alternatives. As in the Kent community care project, the case managers could always arrange to fill gaps themselves and so directly increase the range of alternatives.[17] Also such a system would be expected to allow the circumstances of clients to deteriorate to the point at which residential care was the only feasible alternative. Again the community care experiments illustrate how this can be done directly or by securing the more effective use of other (particularly health) services for those entering from the community and those being discharged from hospitals after short stays.

Of course, the most powerful and readily available instrument for government to use is the level of Board and Lodging Allowances and related benefits. Indeed, if government attempts to handle the market by using only one or two instruments, it is almost inevitable that it will lean heavily on varying social security levels in the absence of a coherent policy using all these and other instruments. Figure 4 suggests the consequences of fixing it at different levels in relation to demand.

Fixed too low, there would always be excess demand for places. There is little incentive to improve standards for Supplementary Benefit payers, since the beds will anyhow be filled. Some of those eligible for Supplementary Benefit who satisfied the assessment criteria would be refused places. Indeed, it becomes worthwhile keeping some vacancies unfilled by SB payers in the hope that a private payer will appear. (In the United States, Bishop argued that homes tended to target at an occupancy rate of 95 per cent for this reason.[50]) Fixed too high, costs would escalate, more providers would make profits larger than the efficient would require to keep them in the industry. Ernst and Whinney suggested[43] over-supply in many areas with a vacancy rate nationally of approximately 9 per cent and regional variations in the rate between 3 and 12 per cent. The PSSRU/CHE survey of 1986 reveals similar figures: for the full (nationally representative) sample of residential homes for elderly people the vacancy level averaged 11 per cent in the private sector and 7 per cent in the voluntary. However, *median* vacancy levels were rather lower (4 and 5 per cent) and arguably are more pertinent. The over-supply of places relative to *demand* is thus small, though over-supply relative to *need* is probably rather larger.

However, perhaps the worst of all worlds is to allow the Board and Lodgings rate to fluctuate greatly through time. (Recall how hire purchase regulations were varied greatly and frequently during the 1950s because of the inadequacy of the range of instruments and futile attempts to smooth short-run fluctuations in aggregate demand in the economy.) Instability of demand not only inhibits long-run planning on which rising quality and efficiency depend, but creates periods when proprietors have severe cash-flow problems and so are tempted to press down costs on the most controllable items, many of which have immediate effects on the quality of resident care. This is frequently described in analyses of the regulative history of the American nursing home industry[34].

Reimbursement and quality assurance policies and arrangements can also affect the market powerfully. Such matters as the effects of reimbursement arrangements—prospective formulae not fixed with the particular facility in mind, retrospective facility-specific reimbursement, case-mix reimbursement, and outcome reimbursement—and the interdependence between these arrangements and other regulatory activity have been discussed elsewhere in the British literature[34, 35]. One of the lessons of that literature is that payment levels and differences must be designed around the most important of the policy objectives of the whole set of policy interventions, and that what these should be will differ in time and place (and so the precise payment formulae should vary). For instance, if the greatest danger is that the elderly people with characteristics and conditions requiring highest costs will not be taken, the payment formula might focus on compensating for resident characteristics. However, if a greater danger is induced dependency, the formula might attempt to reward successful rehabilitation. However, the incentives embodied in a payment system must be large, simple and stable; and so they must be complemented by other regulatory activity: subtlety of policy impact is achievable only when the elements of the policy are made to fit one another.

Instruments of a wide variety of kinds already exist in rudimentary form in this country. That the foundations for their further development exist is one of the two main reasons why it is superior to adopt as one's metaphor for guiding policy development a 'trade and industry policy' rather than a 'regulatory policy'. The other reason is that to fail to act proactively to anticipate and prevent market failure, but instead to wait for market failure to become a national political scandal, is to make the solution of policy problems almost impossibly costly in every way. On this the American evidence is particularly illuminating. There are many countries whose study illustrates how we can get into a mess in this area: for instance, Australia[51] and the Netherlands. The United States is particularly instructive because it has made the most determined attempt—indeed, perhaps the only really determined and largely successful attempt—to get out of it, and done so by a variety of experiments and big investment in policy arrangements and techniques.

However, if the industry settles into a pattern of immediate and large responses to changes in state social security and regulatory arrangements, the nature of the implicit policy questions will change. Instead of asking whether (i) charges made by private homes are less than the costs of local authority homes for equally acceptable types of care—the 'Select Committee' question to which the PSSRU papers on inter-sectoral differences were addressed—and (ii) benefit rates are adequate to cover charges—a question implicit in the discussion by Ernst and Whinney and the Ministerial statement which followed it—we should ask such questions as:

What financing and regulatory arrangements and levels would allow efficient operators to produce acceptable care for persons in different circumstances?

What would be the consequences of alternative arrangements for the behaviour of providers?

American analysis and experiments provide important leads for the development of British policy argument.

iii Charges and 'Quality'

Analysing the data from the 1981 PSSRU survey of private homes, Judge established a relationship between the average charges of homes and 'quality' ratings by the PSSRU visitors and by local authority registration officers[32]. Simple ordinal rating scales were employed for assessing 'quality'. There was a difference of about 12 per cent in charges between the homes in the first quintile (lowest 20 per cent) when ordered by quality and those in the fifth quintile (the top 20 per cent). In addition the difference between the best three-fifths and those homes (less than a tenth of the sample) rated 'poor' by registration officers in the quality of their physical care and social environment was associated with a difference in charges of five per cent. It would seem that there *was* a positive association between perceived 'quality of care' and fees charged. However, the standard errors were large. Also variables measuring the qualifications of staff, the number of supervisory staff, and physical standards like the proportion of beds in single rooms—all arguably indicators of high standards—were correlated with average charges.

iv **Opportunity Costs**

In principle, the assessment of the opportunity cost of a place in a private home should be based on a logic similar to our assessment for local authority homes (Section 3 *iii*). It would depend on two things: (i) the rate of change in demand and supply and the resulting composition of the stock of homes by standard of care and fees, and (ii) variations in the inheritance by areas of homes and 'firms', and the incidence on them of charge-affecting characteristics. We can make little progress at the moment on the first of these. We know of no British modelling analysis to predict demand and supply. Indeed, we suspect that it is premature to develop the argument on which such modelling should be based, since the policy environment and the supply responses of the industry are not yet stable enough to make predictions of a helpful degree of accuracy. We can get further with examining the second set of influences on opportunity costs. In the 1981 survey average charges in private old people's homes varied from £62 in one local authority area to £89 in another. Clearly the costs of those of moderate or heavy dependency would vary between areas with the changes in the number of places supplied. However, it does not seem worthwhile undertaking the type of analysis described in Section 3 *iii* of this part of the chapter, since the charging structure—indeed the costs structure—of private sector provision is likely to be heavily influenced by the policy and levels relating to state payments and related matters. These are likely to be altered substantially in the near future.

v **Regulation Costs**

The Social Services Inspectorate study of the costs incurred by local authorities in implementing the *Registered Homes Act, 1984* from January 1985 reported that authorities' assessments of their distribution of activity implied:

* the average cost of a new registration to be £501, allowance having been made for the separate assessment of managers and owners. Authorities did not generally opine that the effort involved in assessments varied greatly with the size of the home;

* an average expenditure on continuing regulatory activity of £13.65 per registered place[52].

The Report suggested several caveats about the estimates. First, procedures and practice for the continuing activity had not yet been fully implemented and costs were likely to increase. 'In many instances, authorities were still clarifying their policies and procedures and were only beginning to address a range of technical and professional issues raised by the new package. . . insufficient time was being devoted to "annual" work to ensure an adequate range of inspectorial, developmental and supportive activity in relation to registered homes'[52].

Second, the study was unable to collect information about the costs to other than the social services department and presented no findings about these costs, recommending that consideration should be paid to ways in which information about these costs could be collected.

Third, a statistical analysis suggested that it was necessary for authorities to spend a substantial amount of money on the maintenance of the technostructure for the activities irrespective of the scale of the activities undertaken. An alternative interpretation would be that there are substantial economies of scale in regulatory activity overheads, and maybe in all such activity. Fourth, the study did not report statistical analysis investigating variations in the costs of continuing regulatory activity with the scale, type and regulative histories of homes. American regulative experience has thrown up a wide variety of strategies which would yield quite different structures of variations in the costs of such activities.[35]

We would add just one further comment. The case for regulating the private sector is mirrored in the public sector. There is no room for complacency about quality of care in *any* sector, as the Social Work Service study of London homes revealed,[53] and as highlighted by events in Southwark during 1987. There is also no reason to believe that the costs of assuming quality and efficiency in the public sector would be very much less than the cost of regulating the private. No one has yet calculated the former.

5 Hospitals and Nursing Homes

The United Kingdom did not develop a large nursing sector for continuing nursing care. In this it is unlike countries such as Australia[54]; or the Federal Republic of Germany (where, in 1980, the proportion of the population aged 65 and over in nursing homes, 1.2 per cent, was about one half of the proportion in residential homes, but where the proportion in geriatric beds was about 0.15 per cent); or the Netherlands (where 2.5 per cent of the population aged 65 and over were in nursing homes in 1983 and 8.0 per cent were in old people's homes in 1981); or the United States (whose nursing homes in principle offer care at one or both of two levels, each of which is reimbursed at a different rate and is subject to different federal and state regulations, as too are residential homes—'adult care homes' or 'domiciliary care facilities').

Policy debates often consider the desirability of developing facilities which aim at the social environments of the best social care facilities but which are also designed, equipped and staffed to provide nursing as

well as personal care with adequate medical support in order to achieve
the substitution for places in the long-stay wards of hospitals. Our first
aim here is to present orders of magnitude of the costs of care in
hospitals.

We must distinguish between the costs of (a) long-term care in
geriatric wards, (b) long-term care in psychiatric wards, and (c) short-
term acute care in various specialisms, although we can provide
evidence only for the first of these. The costs of out-patient departments
in general and geriatric hospitals, psychiatric out-patient departments,
psychiatric day hospitals, and other hospitals will be included in the
discussion of community care packages.

In principle, the opportunity costs of a patient week in a geriatric or
psychiatric ward vary between areas and depend on the assumption
made about the number of beds required to implement targeting
policies. Studies of specialty costing suggest large variations in costs per
inpatient day. For instance, some computations by the Treasurer's
Department of Southmead Health Authority for geriatric ward costs in
1981–82 using the Magee method showed a mean cost per patient day
of £57. But there were variations between the eight hospitals in costs for
the geriatric speciality of between £37 and £76, the variation being only
partly due to differences in the length of patient stay. So the same
exercise should be performed as for local authority residential homes.
Adjusting for inflation yields a mean of approximately £512 per week for
running costs. A more recent calculation of the costs of *short-term*
hospitalisation among those elderly persons included in the PSSRU's
domiciliary care project included both running costs and capital costs,
the latter calculated from land, building and equipment elements. Cost
per week in 1984–85 ranged from £204 for a psychiatric bed in a long-
stay hospital in Yorkshire to almost £1,000 for a surgical bed in
London.[55] Wright *et al* estimated capital building costs for 1977 under
different scenarios.[5] Put with average running costs for a region,
Davies and Challis estimated opportunity costs at a five per cent discount rate under three Wright scenarios for capital costs. Adjusted to
1985 prices, the estimates are shown in Table 5.[7]

Anderson used a DHSS review of nursing skill mix in wards in long-
stay geriatric hospitals to yield variables for an analysis of nursing
costs.[56] The best predictors were an index of the standard of care, the
overall cost per inpatient day of the hospital, and the number of patients
on the ward. The *overall hospital cost* per inpatient day was positively
correlated with costs, as might be expected. However, standard of care
had a negative effect. The author tentatively attributed this to the calibre
of the ward sister: a good sister achieving both a high standard of care
and economy in the use of staff. The scale variables predicted considerable variations around the least cost scale of 26 patients. A
20-patient ward could be expected to have a cost disadvantage of 16 per

Table 5: Hospital Costs per Inpatient Day at 1985 prices

Hospital type and cost category	*Capital scenario and capital cost per bed*		
	New building *(£40,000 per bed)*	*Upgraded building* *(£25,000 per bed)*	*Improved building* *(£2,000 per bed)*
Acute			
revenue cost	83.50	83.50	83.50
capital cost	5.79	3.62	0.29
total cost	89.29	87.12	83.79
Geriatric			
revenue cost	37.60	37.60	37.60
capital cost	5.79	3.62	0.29
total cost	43.39	41.22	37.89
Psychiatric			
revenue cost	36.50	36.50	36.50
capital cost	5.79	3.62	0.29
total cost	42.29	40.12	36.79

Source: Calculated from Health Service Costing Returns, England, 1984–85, reflated
Wright estimates[7] of capital cost, 5 per cent discount rate and 60 year lifespan of
buildings.

cent and a 30-patient ward could be expected to have a cost disadvantage of 7 per cent. However, most important for our argument, the analysis did not find variations in dependency to be important, possibly because there was too little variation in the general indicators of aspects of dependency covered by the analysis, physical handicap and mental deterioration. Some features of physical dependency were more variable but were not used as regressors. We have noted that individual client characteristics explain cost variations better than composite scores which attach arbitrary weights to the characteristics. It cannot therefore be inferred that the proposition of Figure 1 is invalid.

6   Community-Based Care

British studies of cost and dependency in community care have established gradients, though they vary between studies. The gradients discovered by Mooney in Aberdeen and Wager in Essex were both shallow, a finding confirmed by Wright and colleagues, who showed a shallow gradient of less than a fifth between the third least and tenth most disabled recipients.[1, 3, 5] Plank found a steeper gradient in the London boroughs.[57] However, these studies were unable to control for outputs. It has long been argued that the home care services do not vary inputs sufficiently; they achieve only low levels of 'vertical target efficiency' (see below). For instance this was one aspect of Tilda Goldberg's critique of the services' 'budgerigar response' to need.[58] Davies[35] and the Audit Commission[31] suggested that too high a proportion of the resources were being consumed by those of low measurable need. Davies and Challis reviewed the literature showing how such allocations were likely to occur, and causal processes were analysed in the discussion of the evidence about the potential for improving the substitutability of the community-based care mode for long-term care in institutions.[7]

i Opportunity Costs to Social Services Departments: Observed Variation

The PSSRU's study of domiciliary and day care services yielded estimates of costs by type of need in each of twelve small-area social service systems.[59] Table 6 shows the predicted weekly opportunity costs for a particularly important group of recipients, households with one elderly person. The table classifies costs by a typology of cases which combines the Isaacs-Neville distinctions between 'critical', 'short' and 'long' interval needs for basic care (food, warmth, cleanliness and security). 'Long interval need' clients are those who require inputs less than daily. 'Short interval need' clients require help with tasks, such as meal preparation, occuring at intervals once or more daily. 'Critical interval need' clients require frequent intervention at short notice.

The table illustrates the following findings of the domiciliary care study:

- Among clients with low levels of social support, there is a clear gradient in the cost of support with the level of dependency of recipients. However, (i) that gradient is not steep, the costs of the

Table 6: Predicted average weekly opportunity costs for households with one elderly person living in an 'average' neighbourhood by area and typology class

Typology	Area							
	4	5	6	7A	7B	9A	9B	10
0	11.78	6.87	8.15	9.49	7.08	11.41	15.72	11.23
1	11.18	6.41	7.65	8.96	6.61	10.82	15.03	10.65
2	12.02	7.05	8.35	9.71	7.26	11.64	15.99	11.46
3	17.01	10.97	12.58	14.25	11.24	16.56	21.69	16.35
4	18.95	12.55	14.26	16.03	18.26	18.48	23.88	18.26
5	13.48	8.18	9.57	11.03	8.41	13.08	17.68	12.89
6	25.45	17.92	19.96	22.05	18.26	24.91	31.12	24.65

Source: Bebbington *et al* (1986)[59]

packages for persons of critical dependency being on average only between two and three times as great as those for users of long-interval dependency, and (ii) the gradient varies substantially between authorities.

- The cost of the packages received by users of critical dependency, but with substantial informal support, is in each authority intermediate between the cost of packages to short and long interval need recipients.

- For each broad client type, the cost to authorities of the packages varies greatly.

The same model also showed that couples received less than persons living alone. However, whether the neighbourhood in which the recipients lived was well-to-do compared with the average, poor compared with the average, or rural did not have a significant correlation with the opportunity cost of the care package.

These results are compatible with those of others.[5, 9, 31] They do not necessarily imply misallocation, since the need typology is only a crude indicator. Some clients of low dependency obtained substantial quantities because those who allocated services had goals additional to (or other than) meeting the basic needs summarised by the typology. Other clients of high dependency and low informal support received little because of substitution by other services (particularly community health services, the contributions of spouses, the aggregate contribution of a wider network of informal carers, or the consumption of services provided privately) and because of their will to remain independent.

The study also analysed the costs of outcomes. As is discussed below, the improvements in the quality of life and care which were the results of variations in service input—indeed, the consequences of input differences even for such straightforward outcomes as death or admission to an institution for long-term care—are not to be seen without the most thorough data analysis. Not all the effects which might have been predicted of an equitable and efficient system are visible; and of those that exist only some have so far been spotted. Table 7 shows the implications of some equations for persons living alone and receiving service over the whole of the evaluation period of the study.

Having searched diligently for almost every output needle in the service haystack, the study's results suggest, again using the Isaacs-Neville need distinctions, that:

- the costs of packages received by those of critical dependency are on average less than those of short interval need;

- the costs of those of long interval need are less than those of short interval need;

Table 7: Some welfare outcomes of the Thanet Community Care Project

Variable	Mean Change		Significance p
	Experimental	Control	
(a) Client quality of life			
Morale	2.99	−1.00	<.001
Depressed Mood	−0.68	−0.17	<.05
Anxiety	−0.39	−0.2	NS
Loneliness	−1.46	0.36	<.001
Felt capacity to cope	5.03	0.66	<.001
(b) Client quality of care			
Need for additional help night and morning	−0.58	0.13	<.05
Need for additional help with personal care	−9.47	−1.29	<.001
Need for additional help with domestic care	−6.68	−1.71	<.001
Increase in social contact	5.66	−0.77	<.001
Need for additional services	−2.44	0.69	<.001
(c) Quality of Life of Principal Informal Carer			
Level of subjective burden	−1.12	−.33	.03
Extent of strain	−1.24	−.5	.09
Mental health difficulties	−.82	−.25	.09
Difficulties in social life	−.71	−.67	NS
Difficulties in household routine	−.76	−.42	NS
Difficulties in employment	−.18	−.01	NS
Financial difficulties	−.12	−.25	NS

Note: NS indicates not significant
Source: Davies and Challis (1986)[7]

- the costs of those who remained in critical interval need may have been less than those whose needs diminished from critical to short interval;

- the costs of those whose needs diminished from critical to short interval were more than those whose needs diminished from short to long interval;

- the costs of those whose needs increased from long to short interval exceeded those whose needs remained long interval;

- the costs of those whose needs may have increased from short to critical interval exceeded those whose needs remained at short interval.

We would predict relationships such as these in an equitable and efficient system. However, there were other relationships which one would not expect to exist in an efficient and equitable system:

- the cost of someone whose needs fell from short to long interval were less than those of someone whose needs were throughout at short interval level;

- the costs of someone whose needs increased from short to critical interval were higher than for someone who was throughout at critical interval.

ii Costs, Area Labour Markets, and the Operating Characteristics of the Home Help Service

Goldberg and others argued that the costs of providing an hour of service to clients would depend on such operating characteristics of domiciliary services as the turnover of home helps and clients; the degree to which service was concentrated on a few or spread between many; the span of control of home help organisers; and the proportion of home helps employed for a number of hours which would make them ineligible for the guaranteed working week.[60] Davies and Coles hypothesised that factors such as these would reflect variations in the geographical characteristics of areas in other factors such as the demand for women's labour and the nature of the needs which the services might set out to meet.[61] They tested the arguments using data for one large authority. The analysis found that the turnover of home helps did have a significant effect on costs. However, the effects of client turnover were ambiguous. Costs were sensitive to the average number of hours of service delivered to each client. With the other characteristics taken into account, the span of control of home help organisers proved unimportant, though costs tend to diminish as spans of control increase. The rate of economic activity among married women had a substantial effect. Although the time spent travelling between cases was higher in sparsely populated rural areas, the effects on overall costs were not great. However, community-based care services are not as widely available in areas with sparse populations.

iii Potential for Improved Equity and Efficiency

Results derived from a wide range of studies so far suggest that the relationships between costs, needs-related circumstances and outputs do not fully exploit the potential of home care services. This conclusion has been drawn in several important reviews of the literature and studies based on the analysis of primary data.[7, 9, 31, 45, 58] However, if there is great inefficiency in the use of resources by the community-based services, such estimates as those quoted in the preceeding paragraphs lead to an understatement of the potential role of those services and so an overstatement of the need for institutional services, assuming that the 'new managerialists' in the social and health care services achieve success in improving efficiency.[62] Conversely, without such success, even the most vigorous pursuit of a well-funded strategy of substituting for institutional long-term care might be a failure. The signs of that failure would be that many dependants would have their needs met less adequately; that the proportion of the care inputs made by informal carers would increase and that higher proportions would be making sacrifices which would generally be regarded as unfair; higher probabilities of mortality; and a failure of community social care services to prevent the accidents and crises which so aggravate needs as to make more expensive modes of care essential.

Reanalysis of Hunt's data for 1976 had suggested that perhaps 30 per cent of recipients nationally did not obviously suffer the incapacities which would demonstrate obvious need, implying vertical target efficiency of 70 per cent.[63] Vertical target efficiency measures the degree to which available resources are targeted at those deemed to be in need. However, more sophisticated analysis suggested that the vertical target efficiency of the home help service might have been 75 per cent or higher in 1980, although there were substantial variations between types of authority, and so, presumably large variations between authorities.[64] The data most probably understates the true degree of vertical target efficiency because it does not allow adequate account to be taken of needs created by cognitive deficits, affective disorders and behaviour problems. It is in the other community social care services that the problem of vertical target inefficiency is greatest.

Service allocations attach excessive priority to those living alone and those without obvious support from women as spouses or other relatives. The effect is both to create an unfair burden and to cause the care system to break down. Applying the targeting criteria which best reflected authorities' allocation behaviour yielded a degree of 'horizontal' target efficiency—an estimate of the proportion of those in the target group actually receiving services—of only 35 per cent. Targeting criteria which gave higher priority to the relief of informal carers yielded lower degrees of horizontal target efficiency.[64] The research literature is replete with accounts of the inadequacy of help to informal carers and examples of the breakdown of care. The PSSRU domiciliary care study shows that the mean score on a malaise inventory for carers of a sample weighted with the most dependent is comparable to that of young mothers with normal children of pre-school age,[59] and so is much lower than (for instance) parents of people with learning difficulties. However, the tail is long, and so is the period of time during which many carry the burden.

There is some evidence that there is extensive unmet need for community-based services judged by the criteria reflecting authorities' allocation behaviour. We have quoted the Bebbington-Davies estimate of 35 per cent for horizontal target efficiency for the home help service in 1980, the proportion of persons in a target group receiving service.

Since the degree of vertical target efficiency—the proportion of home help resources consumed by members of the target group—is higher, 75 per cent, unmet need appears to be a larger problem quantitatively than consumption by those not in need.

In the past, the community social care services have been slow to make the changes needed to achieve substitution for instutional long-term care, more closely match resources to the needs of users, and find new and more efficient ways of meeting needs. Research literature suggests great inertia in service systems. However those in close touch with the agencies, and some earlier PSSRU research, have suggested accelerating change from the early 1980s, though many of the innovations were often narrow in their scope and coverage.[14,65] Some of the changes have directly focussed on the performance of the core tasks of case management.[66]

The PSSRU domiciliary care study was designed to ensure that the efficiency-improving innovations of the last five years would not be under-represented. However, the results suggest that the effects have not yet tapped the potential for substituting for institutional long-term care.

(a) Given recipient needs, increments of spending above the average appear to achieve only the narrowest measurable beneficial outcomes—a diminution in the numbers feeling that they would wish for more service inputs—and those for only a minority (those most handicapped) of the one in three recipients living alone and receiving services through the evaluation period of six months.

(b) Given factors influencing recipient needs, the evidence suggests that differences in the volume of the home care services do not affect client morale.

(c) Given such factors, differences in the volume of home care services received appear to have no impact on clients' opinions about the quality of the service with respect to housework, help with rising and retiring, and diet.

(d) More positively, given such factors, differences in the volume of home help inputs, personal care service inputs, and social work inputs all appear to increase the number of problems judged to be brought under control by the worker who is the most important performer of what core tasks of case management are performed. Their views may be slightly optimistic, since they are commenting on the success of the efforts of their sections or their own efforts. However it certainly cannot be discounted. Again, variations in inputs in *short-term institutional care* seem to have a positive effect. However inputs of social day care and meals do not.

(e) Most positively, given such factors, variations in the consumption of home help seem to reduce the probability of being admitted to an institution for long-term care. The average consumption among those continuing to live in the community was 2.5 hours per week. The average among those not doing so was 1.7. Variations in the inputs of meals likewise seemed to reduce the probability of admission to institutions for long-term care. However, the analyses have not yet allowed for some important recipient circumstances associated with the breakdown of community-based care. Moreover, significant positive relationships have not yet been found for day care, personal care, and social work.

So there are signs that variations in home help inputs in particular have effects on the probabilities of institutional entry, though (i) searching for positive effects of increasing inputs has been like looking for the proverbial needle in the haystack—there is little sign that many of the beneficial effects one might postulate are in fact there, and some of the others are not large; and (ii) we have not worked the data sufficiently to be certain that it is the variation in inputs which cause the varied outputs, not some mechanism almost or entirely unrelated to these variations.

The importance of such negative findings as (a) to (d) is that they suggest that the services generally lack the properties of Heineken lager: they reach only the most obvious parts of the anatomy of need. In particular, they fail to affect the anatomy of need pervasively enough to make us confident that a well-funded and energetically implemented policy of spending more on the services would necessarily be successful in achieving substitution for long-term care in institutions without a substantial loss of welfare to clients and informal carers; the proposition contained in the first paragraph of this section.

However, the most successful experiments suggest that the policy could achieve far more if the use of resources in general were as efficient as their use in the experiments.[7, 17] Indeed, the contrast with radical experiments is stark. For a group of whom one in three would have died within a year, one in three would have been admitted to a hospital or home for long-term care, and only one in three would have continued to live in their own homes, community care

(a) halved the probability of death, halved the probability of entering an institution, and doubled the probability of continuing to live in their own homes;

(b) improved the perceptions of surviving clients of their state of well-being (by the criterion of a dozen or so morale-related scales);

(c) improved the capacity of recipients to perform the activities of daily living independently;

(d) improved their quality of care (as rated by a score of criteria by the social work evaluator and the clients themselves);

(e) reduced average costs to the social services department without imposing additional costs on health services;

(f) relieved informal carers of some diswelfares and reduced the costs to them over the period during which the elderly client survived, though prolonging the period during which they provided support;

(g) appeared to reduce the social opportunity costs of care over that period of survival; and

(h) reduced the costs of improvements in the quality of life and care.

The consequences for the costs of outcomes valued in their own right are shown in Table 8. The Gateshead Community Care Project is yielding results which are in most respects no less favourable.[67] These experiments *do* seem to have some of the characteristics of Heineken lager.

It is important to understand why the same experiments achieve outcomes which are altogether more successful than standard community-based care. We understand the processes at work in the Kent community care project.[7, 68] The 'Heineken causal process' depended on the creation of confiding relationships achieving improvements in morale, and so a new feeling by clients (and others) that they could manage independent living, and, as a result, a great reduction in the probability of admission to institutions for long-term care. Confiding relationships and morale were substantially unaffected by simply leaving fewer functional deficits uncompensated by matching resources to needs more narrowly conceived. The Heineken processes depended on different assumptions as well as on changes in structures and resources. There are great gains to be made if the community social care services can generate Heineken processes. Another causal process of vital importance for the achievement of community-based services is the 'exchange process' which strengthened the cooperation between personnel from different occupational groups. Community care projects initiate and reinforce exchange processes by increasing the ability of the case managers to help others achieve mutual professional goals.

The implication is clear. The combination of:

- better targeting,

- increased levels of provision of home care services,

Table 8: Estimated costs to the social services department of combinations of subjective well-being and quality of care for recipients of community care and standard provision, £ at 1977 prices

Client type	No change		Some improvement (10% Morale; 20% Quality of care)		Substantial improvement (30% Morale; 60% Quality of care)	
	Community care £	Standard provision £	Community care £	Standard provision £	Community care £	Standard provision £
1. Extremely frail, mentally impaired, very poor health, reliant on spouse, otherwise isolated and lonely.	363	1,140	519	1,334	1,202	2,617
2. Physically frail, not mentally impaired, relies on spouse, doubts capacity to cope.	194	516	278	826	743	2,340
3. Mentally frail, depressed, lives with spouse, support from relatives, unrealistic about capacity to cope.	331	70	415	380	880	1,894
4. As type 3 but less depressed, lacks any social support.	725	214	809	524	1,274	2,038
5. Lonely, depressed, lives alone, mentally pressured, lacks social support, at risk of falling.	965	352	927	512	1,073	1,723
Dependency Group 1	367	174	357	369	563	1,651
Dependency Group 2	296	264	258	424	404	1,635
Dependency Group 3	510	156	594	466	1,059	1,980
Dependency Group 4	11	313	167	507	850	1,790

Source: Davies and Challis (1986)[7]

- a greater emphasis on creating the conditions in which the performance of the core tasks of case management can be more effective and which create incentives to achieve the progressive improvement in the equity and efficiency of the matching of resources to client and carer needs,

- more effective interagency cooperation at planning and field levels, and

- the sensitive but firm application of the practices of the new managerialism

could allow the community care services to substitute for long-term care in institutions.

7   The State of the Evidence

Great progress has been made during this last decade in providing appropriate evidence to allow quantitative argument about targeting policy. We have been unable to discuss all the topics important for the application of the economist's logic; far less glean every scrap of data to fill obvious gaps for that exercise. However it will be clear that there are some areas about which we already have substantial information. There are others (like the behaviour of private residential providers or the costs of outputs in community-based services) which research now in progress will illuminate greatly. There are others which have hardly been mentioned because so little has been done to quantify the most important influences; for instance what we have called the 'Pandora effect'. However we have seen how quickly evidence can date. We think that we see an accelerating rate of change in the social care of the elderly. If this has been the triennium of change in private residential care, the next five years may see rapid changes in community-based services in response to the infusion of new managerialist ideas and energy. If so, it will be difficult to monitor long-term care without such devices as long-term care data bases.

Part 3   Evidence: Children and Young Persons

1   Cost Awareness and Targeting Criteria

There is no explicit 'balance of care model' for children and families, nor is there a readily available aggregate indicator to summarise their needs for support like dependency. There is also rather less empirical evidence. The interest in—and concern about—the costs of child care services is a very recent phenomenon, probably dating from the period in the 1970s when public expenditure trends, and particularly social expenditure trends, looked set to take a new direction. That interest was provided with a natural focus by the District Auditors' study,[8] and received a significant spur when the House of Commons Social Services Committee posed some tricky costs questions to DHSS witnesses in November 1982.[69] Those questions, despite the District Auditors' evidence, revealed the dearth of relevant costs information.[70, 71] The cost issues raised by the Select Committee, by local authorities' auditors with their *Value for Money Handbooks*, and by elected members centre on the choice between different modes of care; these include

residential *or* foster family placements for children 'removed from their parents';

custody *or* residential accommodation *or* intermediate treatment (IT) *or* a supervision order (without IT) for juvenile offenders;

hospital *or* residential care *or* special family placements *or* natural family provision with respite care for children with learning difficulties; and

residential assessment *or* community-based assessment.

Superimposed on these choices—each with its own cost element—are related issues about the costs of residential care, for example

the relative costs and cost-effectiveness of public, voluntary and private residential provision, and the contracting-out of residential child care; and

variations in average cost (within a sector) between and within local authority areas.

In each case there is an implicit balance of care approach: for which children with what characteristics and with what family circumstances is care mode A 'better than' care mode B, where 'better than' is a criterion which includes one or more of the following elements: effectiveness (or final output), equitable burdens for informal carers, continuity, normalisation and cost? Because, as with services for elderly persons, we have some cost information but disappointingly little data on effectiveness defined with sufficient comprehensiveness to reflect the breadth of the practice objectives and dimensions of client well-being, we have to rely on the kind of targeting criterion specified in Part 1, Section 2.

2 Outputs

In reviewing the available evidence on costs of services for children and families we will have relatively little to say about the outputs of care. Those outputs would clearly be context-specific, but would probably span such dimensions as improvements in (or maintenance of, or lessened deterioration in): physical, psychological, emotional, and social well-being; educational progress; behaviour in school and at home; attachment to peers and to family and other adults; adaptability and adaptation to life after the episode in care; the child's and parents' perceptions, and general maturity. For young offenders, reduced likelihood of recidivism will be an important indicator of the success of the caring intervention. It will probably not be enough. It will be necessary to include the seriousness and speed of reoffending, as well as some of the 'softer' measures of impact listed above. There *are* studies of effectiveness, some of them with reasonably comprehensive dimensionalities and fairly penetrating causal explorations. However, as Roy Parker's chapter in this volume points out, we still lack in Britain a thorough study of the comparative effectiveness of different child care modes. A DHSS-sponsored working party is currently discussing these issues of outcome measurement and will report in 1988.

When we turn to cost-effectiveness analysis there are really no studies which measure up to the accepted criteria of such an approach. This is the case, both because outputs have been neglected and because cost measurement has often been so cavalier. Schofield reports findings from a study conducted in Leicester which was originally billed as a 'cost-benefit' analysis.[72, 73] It was actually no such thing, 'merely' a comparison of the costs of preventive social work with families, with alternative conjectures about the placements of children should such prevention fail, about the probability of failure and about the length of time spent in care. This is actually an interesting study with some unusually broad cost definitions (taking in health as well as social services, adding a casework cost element and so on), but it was not a 'cost-benefit' study: it had no information on the differential impact of care over 'no care' on children and their families. (A more recent conjectural study of the costs incurred and the costs saved by preventive social work is reported by Pinniger.[74])

An attempt was made in a study conducted in Suffolk by one of the authors to assess effectiveness alongside costs. It was not possible to directly assess child well-being using available instrumentation applied to the kinds of dimensions cited above, principally for funding reasons. But it *was* possible to ask case holders to specify the objectives at the point of admission of a child into care, and to review progress in achieving those objectives over a period of up to a year. A cohort of 93 children was used for the study and, in view of the very many need-generating characteristics found in the child care population, this number was too small for disaggregated and focussed analysis. For the record, no relationship was found between average cost of care and the degree of attainment of these initial objectives when looking at the full sample[75] (see section 4 *iii* below).

3 The Costs of Residential Care

We saw from Table 1 that the annual CIPFA statistical publications include average operating cost per child week in observation and assessment centres, community homes with education (CHEs), other community homes and hostels, and accommodation for children with learning disabilities (mental handicaps). (Residential nurseries disappeared from the statistics a couple of years ago, and CHEs may soon follow.)

These statistics are interesting but ultimately unsatisfactory for the reasons described in Sections 2 and 3 in Part 1 above. More useful costs data for residential provision will be disaggregated at least to the home level, will include all 'hidden' costs, and will allow qualification or standardisation for differences in achievement, quality of care, location, scale, and so on. The PSSRU survey conducted in 1983 was designed with these cost improvements in mind and, almost by accident, provided probably the most comprehensive picture of residential children's homes undertaken in England and Wales for at least 20 years. A total of 789 homes was covered by the survey (see Table 9). A 'census' was conducted on 2 March 1983, with questionnaires completed by heads of homes, and supplemented with financial and other data for the twelve month period ending 31 March 1983 provided by social services department headquarters staff or their voluntary organisation equivalents. Information was collected and processed in such a way as to provide a fine classification of the types of establishment.[76]

Operating costs for the financial year 1982–83 are given in Table 10 for all local authority homes and some voluntary homes, and weekly fees are given for some voluntary and all private homes. These figures reveal marked differences between sectors and between designations but conceal wide variations *within* sector-designation cells.

Table 9: PSSRU **Survey of Children's Homes, 1983. Sample Size by Designation and Sector**

Designation	Local Authority	Voluntary	Private	Total
Community Home	434	105	18	557
Adolescent Unit	20	5	1	26
Hostel	22	10	2	34
Community Home with Education	29	8	11	48
Home for MH or PH Children	36	23	5	64
Observation and Assessment Centre	57	0	0	57
Other	2	1	0	3
Total	600	152	37	789

Source: Knapp and Smith (1984)[76]

Table 10: **Children's Homes' Costs and Fees by Sector and Designation, March 1983**

Designation	Local Authority Cost	Voluntary		Private Fee
		Cost	Fee	
Community home	169	125	102	117
Adolescent unit	352	176	175	250
Hostel	184	140	233	163
Home with education	304	298	166	238
Mental/Physical handicap	274	215	173	159
Assessment centre	301	—	—	—

Note: Costs and fees in the voluntary sector are calculated for overlapping but not identical sets of homes.

Source: *ibid.*

i Cost Variations within Sectors

That there are marked variations in the cost of care between authorities is beyond doubt, but what do these variations *mean*? Why is it that costs and fees appear to vary between the three formal sectors—local authorities, voluntary organisations and private sector establishments? Averaged across authorities, operating cost per child week in *local authority* homes ranged from £106 in one shire county to £364 in an Outer London borough. The mean was £169 (1982–83 prices). These are costs for 'non-specialist' community homes and hostels. We sought to 'explain' these inter-home cost variations, and the estimated cost function from that study is given in Table 11. We discuss these results below.[77] The aim of the cost function is to tease out causal relationships between average cost per child week in a home and various characteristics of the home, its location, its services, and of course its child residents. These relationships are examined simultaneously with the aid of suitable multivariate statistical techniques.

Table 11: The Estimated Average Operating Cost Function for Local Authority Community Homes and Hostels

Variable	Coefficient	t-statistic
Constant term	−526.619	−6.247***
Labour cost index	8.518	12.895***
Average number of residents in the home during the year	3.317	4.938***
Reciprocal of average number of residents	324.528	9.419***
Occupancy rate (average no. residents/no. places)	−196.683	−13.949***
Proportion of bedroom places in single rooms	15.865	1.674*
DV (dummy variable): 1=Vehicle owned by home; 0=not	13.935	1.718*
DV: 1=Vehicle hired from commercial organisation: 0=not	9.414	1.984**
DV: 1=Home provides after-care and home-on-trial support as day care; 0=not	21.443	1.307
DV: 1=Home provides emergency day care; 0=not	32.743	2.053**
DV: 1=Home provides preventive/at risk day care; 0=not	56.372	2.829***
DV: 1=Staff have social work responsibilities outside home (for residents or non-residents); 0=not	13.733	3.390***
Average age of children resident on survey day	−17.029	−2.600***
Square of average age of children	0.757	2.824***
Proportion of residents who are girls	−62.250	−2.513**
Square of proportion of residents who are girls	54.761	2.237**
Proportion of residents who are mentally handicapped	−59.455	−1.796*
Square of proportion who are mentally handicapped	151.540	2.714***

$R^2 = 0.703$ Adjusted $R^2 = 0.691$
$F = 54.806***$
$n = 411$
Significance levels: $*0.10 > p > 0.05$; $**0.05 > p > 0.01$; $***0.01 > p$
Source: Knapp and Smith (1985)[77]

For the *private sector* we had no cost data, but information on fees charged in March 1983. The small number of homes covered by our survey (a common problem since the sector *appears* to be so small [78]) forced us to estimate a fee equation for all designations of home together. The results are given in Table 12, and are discussed briefly below.[79]

Table 12: Estimated Fee Equation for Private Children's Homes

Variable	Coefficient	t-statistic
Intercept term	60.13	2.28**
Percentage of residents receiving full-time education (or training) within the home	1.47	6.22***
Proportion of bedrooms with just one or two beds	41.90	1.77*
Dummy variable taking value 1 if home staff have 'outside care duties' (see text), and 0 otherwise	36.52	1.98*
Dummy variable taking value 1 if home has benefit of volunteer car service or similar, and 0 otherwise	−49.70	−1.95*
Mean number of previous placements in care for residents of the home	15.33	1.70*

$R^2 = 0.69$ Adjusted $R^2 = 0.64$ F = 12.59***   n = 34
Significance levels: *$0.10 > p > 0.05$; **$0.05 > p > 0.01$; ***$0.01 > p$
Source: Knapp (1987)[79]

Table 13: Estimated Cost Function for PSSRU Sample of Voluntary Community Homes and Hostels

Dependent variable = average operating cost per resident week, 1982–83.

Variable	Coefficient	t-statistic
Constant	111.058	1.13
Labour cost index	2.110	2.25**
Reciprocal of average number of residents	−281.522	−3.68***
Occupancy rate	−356.609	−4.28***
Square of occupancy rate	173.106	3.63***
Proportion of bedroom places in rooms with 2 beds	45.203	2.81***
Range of ages of residents	−4.310	−5.02***
Mean previous placements in care per child	5.520	2.42**
Proportion of residents spending most of day in the home	179.738	4.32***
Square of proportion of residents spending day in home	−151.168	−3.28***
Square of proportion of residents whose last residence was in a foster home	80.220	2.38**
Dummy variable for home providing any day care facilities	18.858	2.07**
Dummy variable for home with staff having after-care duties outside the home	−27.792	−2.433***
Dummy variable for home providing any other social work tasks outside the home	−13.390	−1.75*

$R^2 = 0.720$ Adjusted $R^2 = 0.653$
F = 10.679***   n = 68
Significance levels *$0.10 > p > 0.05$; **$0.05 > p > 0.01$: ***$0.01 > p$
Source: Knapp and Fenyo (1986)[80]

Table 14: Estimated Mark-up Function for PSSRU Sample of Community Homes and Hostels

Dependent Variable = $\dfrac{\text{Fee—Average Operating Cost}}{\text{Average Operating Cost}}$

Variable	Coefficient	t-statistic
Constant	1.808	3.32***
Labour cost index	−0.017	−3.27***
Reciprocal of number of places	−3.384	−4.90***
Occupancy rate	0.330	3.56***
Proportion of bedroom places in single rooms	−0.142	−1.72*
Dummy variable for assisted community homes	0.260	3.31***
Voluntary organisation size	0.009	4.52***
Ratio of home average operating cost to average operating and capital cost of local authority community homes and hostels in the 'planning area'	−0.608	−5.45***
Places in the home as a proportion of all voluntary home places in the planning area	−0.521	−1.90*

$R^2 = 0.771$ Adjusted $R^2 = 0.733$
F = 20.575   n = 58
Significance levels: *$0.10 > p > 0.05$; **$0.05 > p > 0.01$: ***$0.01 > p$
Source: *ibid.*

There was a richer data base for the *voluntary* sector with overlapping samples of homes for which we had information on both operating costs and fees. These allowed us to calculate a proportional mark-up between costs and fees. This was actually negative—a subsidy element—for 35 per cent of homes and anyway would be unlikely to cover capital and administrative costs. We were then able to examine four features of voluntary children's homes—their costs, fees and mark-ups, and their utilization by local authorities (see Tables 13 and 14).[80]

In order to understand these cost and fee functions we describe five issues of relevance.

Economies of scale. The Curtis Committee Report proposed that large institutions be abandoned in favour of small 'family group' homes with no more than 12 children under the charge of a married couple. This emphasis on small scale, particularly in the public sector, has characterised the post-war period. In 1983 the average size of these 'ordinary' public sector homes was almost exactly that recommended by the Curtis Committee. The estimated local authority cost function indicates that the cost-scale relationship is U-shaped. Operating costs are minimised at approximately 12 places (assuming 80 per cent occupancy), although there is relatively little cost variation around this cost minimising scale except at the extremes of the home size range. The cost-scale association for voluntary homes is very different. Average operating cost rises monotonically with scale but at a decreasing rate. In fact, from around 15 places, increases in scale make little difference to cost. Bringing in capital costs, either as depreciation figures or preferably as replacement cost annuities, does not significantly alter either scale relationship. Scale is directly associated with proportional mark-up in the voluntary sector. Thus, not only are average costs higher in larger voluntary homes, but fees charged to local authorities are also *proportionately* larger. There is no scale effect evident in the private sector.

Empirical studies are always going to be constrained by the characteristics of the available sample. It may be that nonspecialist establishments larger than the observed range can be more cost-effective, but in the public sector the scale of home recommended in policy statements is apparently consistent with a cost-effective scale of home. In the voluntary sector the scale diseconomies reflect the different staffing arrangements required by larger homes. Small homes are often run by highly motivated married couples with only part-time assistance (if any). Most would see themselves as little different from salaried foster parents providing a family environment. Larger scale brings organisational and perhaps also motivational complications which raise unit cost.

The London effect. The major resource in residential child care is labour—74 per cent of direct revenue expenditure during 1982–83 was on staff. Labour markets for residential home staff are likely to be localised; excess demand will generate competition among employers through internal and external labour markets, pushing up salaries and non-pecuniary advantages (such as accommodation or less disruptive hours), more paid overtime, the employment of lower quality staff and/or the regrading of posts. In the examinations of cost variations we used the Department of the Environment (DoE) labour cost index as a proxy for regional salary differences. The index values reflect the marked salary difference between London and the rest of the country, with few other differences noticeable.

If this labour cost index was behaving purely as an input price indicator we would expect a regression coefficient of unity (subject to measurement and estimation error) in the cost functions. If, as has been argued, this index under-values inter-authority variation in labour costs, particularly between London and the rest of the country, then a slightly larger coefficient would pick up the pure input price effect.[81] The coefficient in the local authority function, however, is substantially greater than unity and we could not find any home-level indicators (such as home size, child characteristics, non-residential service provision) which could explain the cost differences between London and the rest of the country over and above the salary differential. The absence of any satisfactory explanation of the London differential is interesting, for the estimated labour cost coefficient in the voluntary sector equation is substantially smaller than in the public equation, although again greater than unity. The differences between the two sectors could therefore reflect either missing variables (particularly indicators of the 'difficulty' of children, although we examined some), or organisational slack.

These interpretations must be seen against a backcloth of worsening relations between central government and the London boroughs and the less generous rate support grant settlements of recent years. To date there has been no evidence presented to support the first reason for the marked public-voluntary difference—missing child 'difficulty' effects. Even if this was the case it does not necessarily justify the reluctance of London boroughs to contract-out more residential care to the non-public sectors, for the voluntary sector appears to have a cost advantage at all levels of 'difficulty'. We return to this later.

The 'cost-difficulty gradient'. The PSSRU survey of 1983 included a number of questions designed to gather information on those characteristics of children which might have an influence on the cost of care, although it was not possible to gather information on all of them. Those covered by the questionnaire were age, sex, length of time in the home since last admission, place of previous residence, number of placements during present care episode, and the presence or otherwise of mental and physical handicap. Only three of the child characteristics entered the public sector cost function, and overall the cost-difficulty relationship appears *not* to be of importance. This conclusion must be qualified, first, because the data collection did not include indicators of some of the principal dimensions of difficulty, and second, because local authorities may not have increased the resources available to homes in line with the rising difficulty of residents. Anyway many of the more difficult children are accommodated in 'more specialised' residential establishments (CHEs, adolescent units, observation and assessment centres or homes for mentally or physically handicapped children) so that the cost-difficulty gradient can be properly seen only by examining all designations together.

However, these qualifications must *themselves* be qualified in the light of the results for private and voluntary homes. Voluntary sector costs are higher in homes with a narrower age range, where children have had more placements in care prior to admission to the home, where more children are in the home during the day, and where a larger proportion of children were admitted to the home following a foster placement breakdown. In the private sector the only significant child characteristic is the mean number of previous placements in care, which raises the average fee. Included in these functions for the two non-public sectors, therefore, are commonly cited 'difficulty' indicators. For example, whilst important in explaining cost variations in the voluntary sector, the proportion of children who last resided in a foster placement does not alter local authority cost. This can be interpreted as implying that local authorities do not adjust—or do not feel a need to adjust—the supply of resources to homes in response to change in child characteristics.

Service diversification. In recent years, children's homes have taken on a broader range of care functions than the provision of residential care. Many of the community homes and hostels in our 1983 sample provided day care, acted as centres for meals on wheels services, provided some education on the premises which might be taken up by nonresident children, and employed staff whose regular social work duties included very broad responsibilities for residents and their families, as well as social work tasks for nonresidents and their families. Staff costed on a residential budget will be providing services which benefit clients other than children resident in the home. This could result in an overestimate of the costs of residential care. On the other hand, it could be that staff of the home are expected to undertake these additional duties without the home receiving compensation. This will have a nonpecuniary cost in the short term, but possibly a marked pecuniary effect in the long term. These uncompensated nonresidential services will divert staff from their residential tasks and could lower the quality of care offered to residents. This is likely to have a long run impact on the wellbeing of clients; that is, on the final outputs of the home. It might also raise the staff turnover rate.

In all three sectors there are observable cost implications of service diversification. The provision of day care raises cost in both the public and voluntary sectors, suggesting that homes are compensated (though possibly not fully) for the service provision. The provision of day care in private homes is more common than in either of the other two sectors, but there is no expectation of an effect on *residential* fees (as opposed to day care fees) unless there is marked cross-subsidisation, and indeed no effect is found. There is an important cost-raising effect in the private sector, however, attributable to the provision of social work tasks *outside* the home by care staff employed *in* the home. About a half of the private homes provided some such services. These outside care tasks also raise costs in the public sector but, surprisingly perhaps, appear to depress costs in the voluntary sector (an effect which could suggest marked cross-subsidisation within organisations). The other statistically significant 'service effect' is in the private sector. Fee variations are dominated by the provision or otherwise of education within the home: each percentage increase in the proportion of residents educated or trained (full-time) leads to an increase in weekly fee of £1.47, and this variable alone accounts for more than 50 per cent of the observed fee variation.

Thus, the dominant (supply-side) charging strategy in the private sector is a fairly simple one. The provision of education is also associated with cost in the public and voluntary sectors but is not picked up by the modelling reported here because of the restriction of the samples to 'non-specialist' community homes, few of which provide education on the premises, and those that do often receive 'free' inputs from the local authority education department.

Market responsiveness. There are a number of ways in which the voluntary sector appears to respond to market pressures. The determinants of the mark-up in the voluntary sector fall into four groups: scale effects, relative price effects, pressure of demand effects and market penetration effects. These four do not represent the totality of associations between the sectors, partly because in common with all other empirical studies, we can never be sure that all possible influences have been included in the analysis, and partly because some of the links between the sectors are already appearing in the cost function. These include the difficulty of children and the provision of non-residential services, both of which will alter in response to local authority demands.

The size of a home, as measured by the number of places provided, and the size of an organization (as measured by the number of homes) are each positively associated with fees. The influence of the former works through two channels: larger homes incur higher costs (other things being equal) and add a proportionately larger mark-up. The effect of organisational scale may be mirroring the finding in other settings of a positive relation between firm size and profitability, and Ken Judge's work suggests that small business proprietors of old people's homes expect and extract a low return on capital, at least in the short run.[32] The lack of association between cost and organisational scale also conforms with American results.[82] Homes run by larger organisations may therefore be charging higher fees not because of a cost difference but because of an ability to add a larger mark-up (or an unwillingness to subsidise local authority provision).

A number of relative price and cost variables were examined for their effect on mark-up. The variable in the equation is the ratio of operating cost in the voluntary home (the baseline for the fee calculation by the supplier) to the average operating plus capital (depreciation) cost of local authority community homes and hostels (the baseline for the contracting-out decision by the demander) in the planning area in which the voluntary home is located. If voluntary costs are high relative to public costs there will be a lower proportional mark-up, suggesting that voluntary organisations are responding to relative costs. If their objective is to survive, and that means in almost all cases surviving by attracting sufficient numbers of contracted-out children, they must subsidise such placements (for example, out of charitable donations and capital sales). Few voluntary organisations are keen to use their non-fee income in this way, partly because administrative and capital expenditures have to be covered, partly because they feel no moral commitment to subsidising the public sector, and partly because the diversification of services (as a necessary response to the falling residential child care population) is rarely funded by public agencies until well-established and of proven effectiveness.

Finally, there are a number of influences on mark-up which might loosely be termed 'market pressure effects'. The proportion of available places in the home occupied over the year is directly related to mark-up. A home is less inclined to subsidise local authority responsibilities when it is successful in filling its available places. The ratio of places in the home to all voluntary home places in the area has a negative effect, which is at first counter-intuitive. However, this result mirrors similar findings in US health care studies of a positive association between price and supplier density. It can be explained in terms of the hidden costs (particularly associated with distance). It is 'full price' (fee plus hidden costs) rather than fee which determines demand, and a falling number of voluntary homes in an area will alter the demand from local authorities.[83]

The other two variables in the mark-up function possibly have both demand and supply interpretations. Voluntary homes are either *assisted* (integrated into the former regional community homes system) or *registered voluntary* (not integrated). Local authorities appeared to view the two types of voluntary home differently in 1982–83 (although this was denied—and we do not disbelieve it—in a series of interviews with local authority staff in 1986), and this carries through to a higher proportional mark-up, either because assisted homes tend to take the more difficult children or because they face a local authority demand which is less price-elastic. The other variable of interest here is the labour cost index. Costs are higher in London voluntary homes than in voluntary homes elsewhere. Organisations respond to this by forgoing some of their 'profit' (or accepting the burden of a larger subsidy to the public sector) in an attempt to maintain their competitiveness. There is probably some regional cross-subsidisation within organisations in order to achieve this, as well as to reduce the amount of fee variation.

These cost variations within the sectors have mainly focussed on non-specialist community homes. We have also examined cost variations between local authority observation and assessment centres (see Section 5 *iii*).

ii Cost Variations Between Sectors
We have recently been examining the cost differences *between* the sectors beyond the kind of comparisons described in the previous section. We have been looking at four questions:

What accounts for the marked cost differences between the sectors?

Do these cost differences represent efficiency or cost-effectiveness differences?

Do these cost differences influence local authority placement patterns? That is, do they encourage contracting-out?

Are these cost differences likely to persist?

Reasons for the cost differences. As we saw earlier, some of the cost differences are *beyond* the (immediate) control of local authorities, voluntary and private agencies. These could include location (and hence labour market pressures and property prices), scale of enterprise and home and the characteristics of children. Some of the cost differences will be *within* the control of providers and it would be relevant to call them efficiency (or inefficiency) factors. The level of staffing and some local decisions about wage levels could be examples. In our research we have been able to gather fairly comprehensive evidence on the first source of variation between the sectors, and on the basis of some evidence and opinions on quality of care differences we have attempted to determine the extent of any efficiency difference between the sectors. It is not yet possible to compare these cost differenceś with data on quality of care or quality of resident life.

Focussing on non-specialist community homes and hostels we were unable to find factors *beyond* the control of providers which accounted for very much of the cost difference, and this was after some extremely thorough statistical analysis.[84] Nor could we find circumstantial evidence to support the view that the cost difference reflected a quality of care difference. Ninety per cent of the children in voluntary and private homes are placed there by local authorities and remain on social worker caseloads with fairly regular contact. It seems most unlikely that major differences in quality of care would be tolerated, particularly at a time when there is no shortage of available residential places from which to choose. Many of the local authority middle and senior managers interviewed by us in 1986 were, in fact, of the opinion that the voluntary sector offered *better* quality care than the public, an important reason being the fact that few use a shift system for their care staff and most seem able to attract highly motivated individuals.

The sources of the 'efficiency' difference. What, then, accounts for the 'efficiency' or 'cost-effectiveness' difference? The following are among the reasons for this difference.

(a) EMPLOYMENT FLEXIBILITY: Voluntary and private homes do not employ staff on shifts to the same degree as local authorities. Those organisations and homes that do use a shift system expect staff to work unpaid overtime as and when necessary. Part-time and volunteer staff appear to be more easily accommodated outside the public sector. Small homes—in both the voluntary and private sectors—are often run almost as family businesses. Small voluntary homes (less than a dozen children) are cheaper to run than large homes. This employment flexibility generates lower costs because staff work longer hours even though most are paid on NJC rates; because of the free input of family members in some homes; and because these homes can more easily adapt their staffing (and thus their costs) to fluctuations in occupancy. It is, however, also the case that voluntary homes have a higher rate of care staff turnover than local authority homes.[85]

(b) LONDON EFFECT: As we have seen, the effect of a London location was much greater in the local authority sector than in either the voluntary or private sectors. Wage differences can explain only part of this effect. Most of the private and voluntary homes in London had vacant places at the time of our survey, so the boroughs had the *opportunity* to contract-out. Are some authorities hampered by political pressures or by a 'no redundancy policy' from placing children in homes which do *not* seem to offer inferior care but which *do* offer substantial savings?

(c) CHILD CHARACTERISTICS: We could not find variations between the sectors in the 'difficulty' of children, although there may be facets of behaviour which we were unable to measure and which do vary. Our results suggest that local authority staffing levels (and thus costs) do not adjust to changes in child difficulty, whereas there are observable responses in the voluntary and private sectors.

(d) SUBSIDIES: Many voluntary homes charge a fee to local authorities which is below average operating cost, and all voluntary homes appear to be charging below *full* cost. Voluntary organisations are subsidising local authority care out of their non-fee income. Private sector fees are low probably because proprietors accept low current remunerations in return for long term capital gains.

(e) COMPETITION: One reason for these subsidies is that voluntary (and private) homes are having to 'compete' for local authority placements. We have already reported our evidence to suggest that voluntary organisations adjust the degree of subsidy (or mark-up) to remain competitive with local authorities and with other organisations.

(f) TAX ADVANTAGES: Voluntary organisations which are charities will benefit from some central and local tax exemptions which may give them a cost edge over public providers of care, and (less so) over private sector providers. Our understanding is that these are of only limited impact in Britain, although some US evidence indicates how inter-State differences in tax laws and levels has an impact on the relative supply of voluntary and private sector services.[86]

(g) CAPITAL COSTS: The ACC and AMA guidelines for the negotiation of fees with voluntary organisations exclude an element to cover the capital costs of the homes. A local authority is likely to include a depreciation allowance in reckoning its own costs. This guideline thus institutionalises another form of subsidy to the public sector.

The influence of relative costs on contracting-out. The available evidence here is mixed. In our interviews with managers in the three sectors it was clear that many social workers and placement officers assume that high fees indicate 'specialist' provision and high quality care. There were also instances of local authorities which compared average costs for all homes run by the authority with the fee charged by a single 'specialist' voluntary or private home. This wrongly discourages the use of specialist establishments for children with special needs. (Of course, when local authority homes are below full occupancy, the *marginal* cost of use will be lower than average cost, and often lower than voluntary and private sector fees). A pointer to the future comes from some very recent analysis of the contracting-out of residential child care in relation to the needs of areas and the characteristics of supply. A cross-section analysis of placements in the voluntary sector indicates that a 10 per cent increase of voluntary home fees relative to local authority costs (*all* designations of home together) will generate a 6 per cent fall in the proportion of a local authority's residential child care population placed in voluntary sector establishments.[87] There *is*, it would appear, a price-responsiveness among authorities.

Will this cost (cost-effectiveness) difference persist? We would anticipate that the voluntary and private sectors will maintain a cost advantage over the public, but that it will be a rather smaller advantage than at present. This conjecture can be understood by reference to the above sources of inter-sectoral efficiency differences.

(a) EMPLOYMENT FLEXIBILITY: Staff turnover is higher in the voluntary than the public sector, and this may reflect the falling number of highly motivated persons prepared to work in the voluntary sector under less favourable conditions of employment. There are, for example, dwindling numbers of people joining religious orders. We expect a constraint on the supply of the sorts of people historically important in the voluntary sector to push up costs. The private sector homes are generally run by proprietor-managers. Will the dwindling use of private homes by local authorities deter such 'enterprise'?

(b) LONDON EFFECT: There may be no change here at all. If there *is* a change we would anticipate that the RSG penalties of recent years and the proddings of the Audit Commission would be reducing the difference between London and other authorities, and thus between London authorities' homes and the voluntary sector.

(c) CHILD DIFFICULTY: Voluntary and private homes are now accommodating children with a range of behavioural and other problems, making them 'more difficult' than the population of voluntary and private sector homes in years gone by. This trend is likely to continue. So, if some of the cost differences between sectors reflect chracteristics of children (difficulty, disturbance, delinquency) not adequately measured by our study, we then have a third reason for a diminishing cost advantage. Even without this assumption of a narrowing of the differences in child care populations between the sectors we can see how—relative to the voluntary and private sectors—the degree of organisational slack in the public sector (it does not respond to 'difficulty variations' by altering resource levels) gives it more flexibility to accept an increasingly difficult clientele at little extra cost. The private and voluntary sectors appear to have less scope for future efficiency gains than the public.

(d) SUBSIDIES: Voluntary organisations generally prefer to spend their non-fee incomes—mainly from legacies and donations—on services that fit their general organisational goals. They may not value the subsidising of local authority care responsibilities as consistent with those goals.

(e) COMPETITION: In so far as voluntary and private organisations are competing for local authority placements a cost advantage is likely to remain. This might be the only long term source of cost and efficiency differences.

(f) TAX ADVANTAGES: These are small, and we have no way of predicting future changes or their future relevance. The present government has generally extended tax advantages and deductibles, to the advantage of the voluntary sector at least, but at the same time has lowered tax *rates*.[88] What the overall effect has been is not clear.

(g) CAPITAL COSTS: As local authority capital stock—the homes themselves—gets older, so the proportion of current costs attributable to depreciation allowances falls. The difference between total public sector cost and the allowable fees charged by the voluntary sector has thus diminished, and this will continue until new local authority establishments are opened.

*The changing role of the voluntary sector.*We offer the briefest of evidence here. Martin Knapp and Andrew Fenyo have extracted data from the registers of 'assisted voluntary homes' and 'registered voluntary homes' held by DHSS, and have analysed the data for March 1983 and 1984. Homes were categorised by designation (non-specialist community homes, adolescent units, hostels, community homes with education, homes for children with learning difficulties or physical handicaps, and other) and changes were examined from one year to the next.

The results are given in Table 15. In just one year, 46 voluntary homes closed and 14 new homes opened. The net decrease in the size of the voluntary sector was 11 per cent in the number of homes and 12 per cent on the number of places. There was a disproportionately larger decrease amongst adolescent units (where both the number of homes and places had more than halved) and the non-specialist community homes. Despite the reduced provision occupancy levels declined over the year. The provision of CHEs and homes for physically handicapped children and children with learning difficulties rose slightly, but again occupancy fell.

iii The 'Hidden Costs' of Residential Care

The 'hidden' or indirect costs of residential care are associated with field social work support, the range of nonresidential services received by children in residential homes (psychiatry, intermediate treatment, child guidance, playgroups, occupational and speech therapy, and so on), and the variety of administrative and overhead costs. Many of these costs will fall to agencies other than the social services department.

Easily the most important of the hidden cost elements for the majority of children in care is the time spent by the child's field social worker. One recent study looked at the field social work input for *children in residential care.*[89] This fieldwork input averaged three hours per child per week, and included visits to the residential home and the child's natural family, contact and consultation with agencies and individuals with other responsibilities for the child, travelling time, and desk-based administration. Around this average there were marked variations, reflecting differences in the needs of children, characteristics of the homes, the extent to which other agencies were involved and the distance between the social worker's office and the residential placement. At the time of the study (June 1983) this field work input to residential care was costing at least £25 per child per week.

Similar cost calculations were made for other hidden elements of care—social services, education, NHS and probation inputs—and the sum expressed as a proportion of the directly observed residential costs, distinguishing the 'type' of home:

Table 15 The Changing Role of the Voluntary Sector, 1983 to 1984

	Non-specialist Community Home	Adolescent Unit	Hostel	Community Home with Education	Home for Children with Learning Difficulties or Physically Handicap	All[a]
Number of Homes						
1983	185	16	37	22	27	290
Closed	28	5	6	2	3	46
Net re-designation	-2	-4	+1	+3	+2	
New	5	0	3	2	3	14
1984	160	7	35	25	29	258
Number of Places[b]						
1983	3,651	190	356	1,027	555	5,742
Closed	383	52	54	64	40	648
New	73	0	27	34	38	176
1984	2,977	79	321	1,058	601	5,047
Number of Children[b]						
1983	2,918	159	339	928	692	5,092
Closed	281	27	34	50	40	470
New	28	0	22	22	32	105
1984	1,865	51	234	874	424	3,460
Mean Occupancy[c]						
1983	0.92	0.82	0.99	0.86	1.33	0.96
1984	0.69	0.63	0.70	0.76	0.76	0.70
Mean Weekly Fee						
1983	122	152	137	267	208	144
1984	131	196	140	302	223	159
Mean Fee Inflation	10%	20%	13%	18%	11%	

Notes: a. The totals include 2 homes with unknown designation each year, and 1 convalescent home in 1983.
b. These include estimates for homes with missing information.
c. These are means of individual home occupancies, and not the ratios of (total children)/(total places).

15 per cent for (non-specialist) community homes,

7 per cent for observation and assessment centres,

5 per cent for community homes with education, and

5 per cent for homes for mentally or physically handicapped children.

Two points should be noted. First, these figures are averages; child and social worker characteristics were correlated with these hidden cost 'multipliers'. Second, the calculations are all for children who have been in their residential placements for at least three months, and these children generally impose lower demands on the non-residential sector.[90]

4 Boarding Out Costs

There is little information on the costs of boarding out services in Britain, and certainly not enough to do more than make informed conjectures about the relative costs of boarding out and residential care. There is, in fact, very little information in the broader international literature to guide us; Culley, Settles and Van Name[91] and Fanshel and Shinn[92] offer some descriptive US data for foster family care and some alternatives, but even this is incomplete (Culley and colleagues look only at the costs of raising a child incurred by a family; Fanshel and Shinn look only at boarding out payments), is not cross-tabulated by client characteristics and is, of course, now rather dated. The major evaluative studies of the outcomes of boarding out in the UK have not included a cost element.

i Direct and Hidden Costs of Boarding Out
Until recently the annual CIPFA statistics included columns of expenditure on boarding out services and the average number of children so placed over the year. Those statistics allowed a crude cost per child figure to be calculated for each authority. It is no longer possible to obtain this figure from the CIPFA statistics—which tends to suggest that the earlier data was as unreliable as most people feared—and we are now left with no national data on these costs. The National Foster Care Association annually publishes boarding out payment *rates* for most local authorities in the UK and most voluntary organisations, presenting them in considerable detail by age, handicap, additional payments, and so on. This is a most interesting annual tabulation, but does not tell us how many children are placed nor what are the *actual* boarding out payments.

Even if the CIPFA statistics of past years had been reliable, or even if the NFCA tabulations had noted the frequencies with which different levels of boarding out rate had been paid, we would still have only an incomplete picture of the full costs of foster care. Two studies have attempted to calculate those full costs, one covering eight local authorities but relying on aggregate expenditures and assumptions about their allocation[8] and the other gathering detailed information for individual children but in only one local authority area and for a cohort of admissions to care.[93]

The District Auditors' study came in for some criticism—some of it gratuitous and distinctly disingenuous, some of it warranted. What was interesting and very useful about the report was its willingness to move beyond the direct costs of boarding out services (although it failed to do likewise with other services). The study distinguished three groups of children:

> young children for whom the alternatives are foster care and placement in a residential nursery,
>
> older children for whom the alternatives are foster care and a family group home, and
>
> older children exhibiting behavioural and other difficulties for whom the alternatives are foster care and a CHE.

They costed the processes of finding and supporting foster parents and added these to the boarding out allowances. They argued that field social worker costs did not differ between foster care and its alternatives, that overhead costs would be negligible and equivalent between alternatives, and other cost elements were ignored. These assumptions need to be challenged. The first is contradicted by other evidence (see below), the second is likely to be correct, and the third is a dangerous omission. There was also no explicit consideration of the characteristics of children, and other research has established a clear link between such characteristics and costs.

The PSSRU study was conducted in Suffolk with a cohort of new admissions to care. It was found that the hidden cost element for children boarded out is generally larger (both absolutely and proportionately) than for children in residential placements. Field social worker involvement is greater, and a larger number of other social services department staff and other agencies will be involved. The Suffolk data on these hidden costs of boarding out are not immediately comparable to the figures on the hidden costs of residential care given in Section 3 *iii* above, for the former refer to a cohort of children recently admitted into care, and who are not therefore as settled as the residential group.

The hidden costs of boarding out range from a very small proportion of the direct costs (the payments to foster parents) to a large multiple (see Table 16). Hidden costs are on average 176 per cent of the direct costs, and can be as much as 360 per cent for those children in care for only a few days. Not included in these costs of family placements are the full costs of recruiting, preparing, training, and matching foster parents with children in care, nor the costs of foster placement breakdown or foster parent turnover. These can often be considerable, as the District Auditors' study revealed.[8] Nor do they include hidden costs to foster families. The boarding out payment may or may not accurately reflect the amount that foster families require if they are to continue offering homes to children in care. If the payment is greater than the amount required, then there exists a potential for cost savings by local authorities. It is more likely, however, that the boarding out payment is below the (perceived) adequate compensation required by potential foster families. This can only be speculative, but it is supported by the excess demand for family placements in very many areas of the country. If the boarding out payment is 'insufficient' for some families already providing care they will eventually give up fostering. If more boarding out is planned, the level of payment will have to rise, so that even if it is the 'right' amount currently, it must understate the amount required if all children whom it is intended to board out are actually boarded out. (See Section 4 *iv* below)

Table 16: Direct and Hidden Costs of Boarding Out

Length of care period (days)	Direct placement cost (£)	Social Worker cost (£)	All other costs (£)	Cost per child per week (£)	Hidden cost as percentage of direct cost %
0–7	30	88	20	138	360
8–30	31	29	16	76	145
31–91	27	12	8	48	74
92–365	27	12	7	47	70
Total	29	37	14	80	176

ii The Relative Costs of Boarding Out and Residential Care

The seventh *Annual Report* of the Church of England Central Home for Waifs and Strays, 1887, included an appeal:

> The cost of maintaining a child under seven years of age, who would be boarded out, is calculated at £13 per annum; a child over that age who would be placed in one of the Homes, at £15 per annum.

We thus have early evidence—albeit anecdotal—of the relative costs of boarding out and residential accommodation, and evidence which suggests that costs were little different between the two settings at that time. In the intervening 101 years very little evidence of better quality has emerged. (Wagner quotes Thomas Barnardo's slightly earlier comparison of residential care costs—£16 per annum—and the cost of prison at £80.[94] His motive was also fund-raising.)

More recently, there have been local studies of the kind produced by the London Borough of Wandsworth which compared average (direct) resident care costs with an aggregated foster care cost (boarding out payment, field social work and set-up costs).[95] The calculations for adolescents revealed a fairly marked cost advantage for foster care, but client characteristics were not included and the cost measures were not comprehensive. Another study which drew conclusions about the relative cost of these two placement alternatives was Nancy Hazel's evaluation of the Kent Family Placement Service.[96] This, too, made strong assumptions—particularly that the (unmeasured) field work costs relevant to foster placements would be cancelled out by the (unmeasured) county treasurer's department costs going into residential care. On this basis, and without discussion of other cost elements or an examination of the association between costs and characteristics, she concluded that 'residential care is very much more expensive than any kind of foster care' (p. 154). Her study has much to commend it but the cost analysis is not adequate. A similar conclusion would have to be reached about the District Auditors' study.[8] The cost calculations were the best of their kind at the time they appeared, but were based on aggregates and glossed over the different circumstances and characteristics of clients. The conclusion of the study was certainly interesting, however, for it emphasised the relevance of marginal cost considerations:

> In the short term (and when looking at the placements of only a small number of children) there is likely to be little difference in the expense incurred to either place a child with foster parents or, for an authority with vacancies in a family group home, to place the child in the authority's own residential accommodation . . . For larger groups, and in the longer term, . . . fostering is the least expensive option (p. 20).

These and most other comparisons of the costs of residential care and boarding out fall into the trap of assuming that like is being compared with like. However, it is quite clear that—on average—the characteristics of children accommodated in residential homes are different from the characteristics of children boarded out. Children in residential care are typically more 'difficult' than children boarded out. The meaning of the term 'more difficult' is not easy to specify exactly, but it is clear that children with physical handicaps or learning disabilities, with delinquent tendencies or backgrounds, older children and those with certain emotional or behavioural characteristics (aggression, hyperactivity, propensity to self-mutilation, and so on) are much less likely to be boarded out than to be in residential care. There is evidence to support this.[97] Furthermore, there is enough evidence from the available research on the costs *within* the foster care sector (if only for the direct, boarding out payment, element of costs) for us to conclude that the average cost of care will be positively associated with the degree of difficulty displayed by children because of the greater demands that they make on staff and on the families in which they board. If both of these arguments are true—that more difficult children are likely to be found in residential care and, other things being equal, generate higher costs—then the resource implications of trying to board out a higher proportion of children will be very different from those suggested by a simple comparison of present average cost figures.

Figure 5. Cost-difficulty relationship for residential care and boarding out

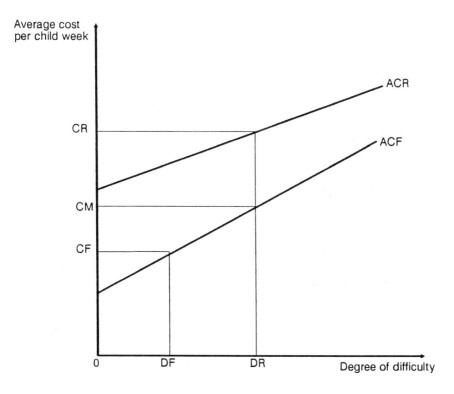

These two arguments can be summarised with the help of Figure 5 (a simplified version of the balance of care diagram) which demonstrates some of the cost implications of a shifting placement pattern. The two lines drawn in the figure represent the average costs of care in a residential setting (ACR) and a foster home (ACF) for each level of difficulty. Each line is drawn to represent average cost as an increasing function of difficulty. For simplicity it has been assumed that the cost of residential care is greater than the cost of foster care at all levels of difficulty, and indeed this seems a reasonable supposition to make on the basis of available evidence. The average degree of difficulty for the populations of children currently accommodated in residential and foster homes are denoted as DR and DF respectively. Associated with them will be two average cost figures (denoted CR and CF) that are offered in the studies reported above, although of course without including all of the hidden cost elements. If a child of difficulty DR (the average amongst the residential population) is successfully boarded out, the cost to the authority will not be the present average boarding out cost (CF), but will be the larger amount CM. The savings to a local authority of boarding out a larger proportion of children in care, therefore, will be exaggerated by the simple (mean) average cost figures prepared for children currently in care (even if these costs include the omitted services discussed earlier). Whenever a child of difficulty between DF and DR is moved from a residential to a boarding out placement, there will be an increase in the (mean) average cost of both services (although a fall in total care expenditure).

This may explain the real cost inflation experienced by both residential and boarding out services in the last few years. As an increasingly large proportion of children in the care of the local authorities has been boarded out (rising from 33 per cent in 1976/77 to more than 50 per cent today), so the average difficulty of these children has gone up, and so has the cost (by more than 30 per cent in real terms, for *both* placement options). Social services departments have had to pay higher boarding out allowances and provide a greater degree of support from fostering officers and field social workers. This means higher direct and hidden costs of foster care and higher recruitment and training costs. The alternative is a higher breakdown rate. Residential care is thus left with the more difficult children, raising its own average cost. Residential care will become more conspicuous to elected members in budget-conscious authorities and residential staff will face a harder residential task at the same time. This will in turn mean a higher rate of staff turnover from an already volatile sector.

This argument is not suggesting that the relative expansion of boarding out services is in any sense 'wrong'. What it suggests is that the comparative cost figures presently available exaggerate the savings to be achieved by family placements. The danger is not that too many children will be boarded out, on the contrary, but that local authorities' attempts to move towards higher boarding out proportions will inflate both the allowances and the fieldwork support. The implications for breakdown rates should be obvious.

iii Placement Combinations during Care Periods

Any measurement of cost must be based on a time interval, be it a week, year, care period or lifetime. This immediately introduces the complication that some children will experience *both* foster and residential placements during that interval. This greatly complicates the evaluation of services and the costing of care, especially if a large proportion of children change from one placement to another. This is particularly a (research) problem when studying children admitted into care, and was a factor which impinged upon the analysis of our own Suffolk cohort data. The solution was to look at a system of equations: how much time did a child spend in each of five broad types of placement (home on trial, foster home, community home, specialist residential resource like CHE or OAC, and hospital), and how do these time intervals influence cost? Children were included in the study for the whole of a care period or twelve months, whichever was the shorter. Of the 88 children included in the study, 51 spent the *whole* time and 20 spent *no* time in a foster placement. No child spent the *whole* of the study period in any other broad placement type.

In the analysis we examined a number of detailed hypotheses about the impact of child characteristics and family circumstances upon placement experiences and costs. One general hypothesis was that it was these characteristics and circumstances which dominated the explanation of cost variations between individual children rather than the placement type. This was rejected by the analysis. In other words, whilst these characteristics and circumstances are important in the prediction of where a child is placed and how much it costs, it is the broad placement type which still dominates cost calculations. A corollary of this is that the 'cost-difficulty lines' in Figure 5 do not cross. Residential care is (currently) more expensive than foster care for all children.[75]

iv The Foster Care Supply Response

Many local authorities appear to have hit a supply constraint on suitable foster families. Many authorities maintain that there are children in residential accommodation who would benefit from family placements, were there enough of the latter. The characteristics of children in the two settings overlap.[97] What role, then, is there for varying the boarding out rate to attract more foster families?

There has been no British research focussed on inter-authority variations in boarding out payments. It is, however, abundantly clear that a significant part of the variation cannot be explained by the characteristics of children. Certainly, most authorities have developed 'special' family placement services for 'hard-to-place' children, and paid enhanced boarding out rates. These enhanced payments are often described as payments to foster parents for the 'wear and tear' of fostering. It is at least as important to note that some authorities are paying higher amounts in order to stimulate a sufficient supply of family placements. Many of the London boroughs that we have worked with express the view that they cannot recruit any more families within the boundaries of the borough and so, against the 'localisation' recommendation of the Child Care Act 1980, board children out with families some miles from their home areas and natural parents. This has three implications. First, simplistic criticisms of local authorities for not boarding out 'enough' children are dangerous. Second, some of the variation in boarding out payments—and perhaps much of it—is beyond the control of local authorities. They simply face a supply constraint. This should be noted in the calculation of grant-related expenditure assessments and in discussions of the appropriate and the feasible balance of care. Third, some of the shire counties around London are losing their potential (and current) foster families to higher paying London boroughs.

There is a pressing need for a focussed examination of the family placement supply constraint and its impact on the achievement of what some would regard as 'best practice' child care. Such an examination would need to clearly set out the nature and determinants of the demand for foster care by local authorities (say), and the nature of determinants of the supply of placements by the population of an area. It is reasonable to postulate demand and supply relationships with respect to the boarding out rate as illustrated in Figure 6. The supply of families is probably an increasing function of boarding out payments. The available anecdotal and causal evidence would certainly bear this out. A study in the US found this, with price elasticities of perhaps 0.5 to 1.0.[98] That is, doubling the boarding out rate would increase the number of foster homes offered by between 50 and 100 per cent. (This was a very simple study, but its results are certainly a good basis for discussion.) What determines this supply schedule? Among the relevant factors would be the costs of raising a child, the state of local unemployment and of domiciliary employment opportunities (particularly that which might perhaps be a substitute—such as student accommodation), and so on.

On the demand side it would be possible to draw up a number of hypotheses concerning boarding-out payment levels, the available funds released by residential home closures, the characteristics of the child care population, and so on. For simplicity, assume that these rates are invariant with respect to the number of families that an authority wishes to find. The demand schedule is thus a horizontal line in Figure 6, at the boarding rate set by the authority. If this is the 'old demand' schedule, corresponding to a boarding out rate of £A per week, we can see that only C family placements will be forthcoming. If the authority is actually looking for rather more—say D placements—then it will need to raise the rate to an amount £B. Now, this is a highly simplified analysis which emphasises that local authorities in some areas need to pay

Figure 6. Demand and supply of foster families

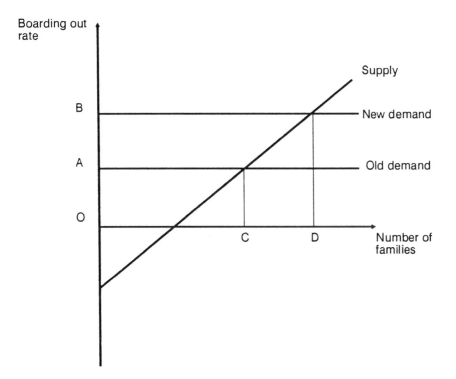

more (in boarding out rates and in support costs) if they are to find a greater supply of foster families. This is deserving of more study.

5 Services for Particular Child Care Needs

i Offenders

The balance of care model has applicability in the consideration of the role of residential care for young offenders. Although it is generally assumed that a community alternative such as intermediate treatment must be cheaper than residential care or a custodial sentence, in fact there has been little research to bear this out. Again we face the difficulty that it is not easy to be sure that like is being compared with like, and of course costs incurred by the courts, prison establishments, social services and probation, and other agencies, all need to be taken into account. Furthermore, sentence lengths vary a great deal. A detention centre sentence can be as short as 21 days, whereas intermediate treatment orders generally require attendance by a juvenile offender for 90 days, and a residential placement in a community home or CHE could last very much longer. There is as yet only limited and local evidence on the relative effectiveness of intermediate treatment and its alternatives. However, the DHSS is funding a major study of effectiveness by the Institute of Criminology, University of Cambridge, and an associated study of cost-effectiveness by the PSSRU.

Consider, then, the relative costs. The costs of custody can be calculated from the average weekly operating costs of youth custody and detention centres published by the Home Office. There is considerable variation between higher cost establishments, such as Feltham Youth Custody Centre (£468 per inmate week in 1984–85), and Campsfield Detention Centre (£553) which have lower than average numbers of trainees and those such as Stoke Heath Youth Custody Centre (£204) and Aldington Detention Centre (£242) which are much larger. On average, weekly costs were £268 for youth custody and £348 for detention centres in 1984–85. However, when the 'hidden extras' are taken into account, these raise the average cost of a detention centre sentence by more than a third to somewhere in the region of £455 a week.[99] (A similar 'hidden cost multiplier' is likely for youth custody sentences.)

Because official statistics do not give comparable data for intermediate treatment, we have to rely on the findings of local research projects which have attempted to compare the costs of intermediate treatment with other sentences. A Tameside study took four alternatives to intermediate treatment: community home with education, community home, supervision order, and detention centre—and compared the costs of each with intermediate treatment for a given individual. This was done by selecting four representative individuals each of whom would, in the absence of intermediate treatment, have received one of the four alternatives, and allowing for probable differences in length of sentence.[100] If we look first at crude cost per week figures, with the exception of a straightforward order with intermediate treatment, all the other sentences are more expensive (see Figure 7). The most expensive custodial option is a detention centre sentence at around £455 a week— the same individual could receive intermediate treatment for around £60 a week in 1984–85. When the costs of an average *sentence* were examined—rather than cost per week—the difference narrowed, but intermediate treatment still worked out cheaper than other options, apart from a supervision order without an intermediate treatment requirement. Thus while a detention centre sentence would cost over seven times as much as intermediate treatment on a cost-per-week basis, it would only cost just under twice as much taking length of sentence into account.

Figure 7. Relative costs of Intermediate Treatment and its alternatives

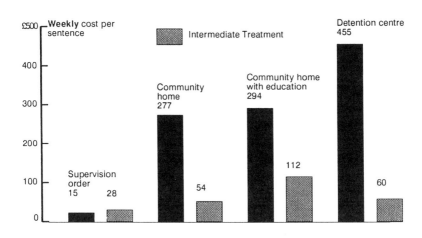

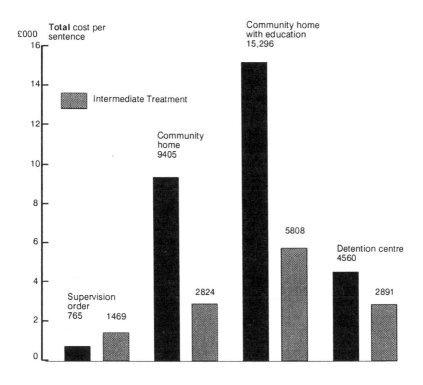

Source: Discussion Paper 374, Personal Social Services Research Unit, University of Kent at Canterbury

ii Services for Handicapped Children

Our comments here must be brief. We have been unable to find any British evidence which satisfactorily relates cost to client characteristics, or calculates cost consistently across two or more care modes, or examines variations in cost *within* a care mode. The evidence that is available is thus subject to the kinds of cautionary remarks made earlier and which do not need detailed repeating. Baldwin offers some comprehensive findings on the costs to a natural family caring for their handicapped child.[101] She did not cost health or social services inputs. Baldwin, Haycox and Godfrey costed all services and family inputs in a study of mentally handicapped children living at home.[102] Cost per child per week, at 1981 prices, totalled £138, of which 16 per cent was borne by the families themselves out of earned income and 33 per cent from social security benefits. This compared with a mean cost of £274 (1982–83 prices) in local authority homes for mentally or physically handicapped children (see Table 10) to which would be added a hidden cost element of some 5 per cent (see above). Wright and Haycox compared the costs of small community-based units for mentally handicapped children (run by the NHS) with hospital care.[103, 104] The former were on average 28 per cent more expensive in the long term, and 98 per cent more expensive when only marginal savings can be reaped by closing a children's ward within a hospital. These costs are comprehensively measured.

iii Assessment

In their Report on *Children in Care*, the House of Commons Social Services Committee recommended a 'greater sense of urgency in the development of non-residential assessment...There will always be a need for expensive residential observation and assessment for some children. It is not primarily financial considerations alone that lead us to seek a greater degree of urgency in moving towards forms of domiciliary assessment and observation'.[69] The government responded: 'The Committee's recommendation as a whole is essentially for local authorities to put into effect within their available resources.' It is therefore clear that although the motivation for a movement away from residential and towards community assessment is concerned with the validity of the resulting assessment and the impact on children and their families, financial considerations are of some import.

We are aware of no cost information on non-residential assessment (although a DHSS-funded study is underway and Fuller[105] has provided a very useful broader literature review) and only two, rather limited, studies of residential assessment.[106, 107] The earlier study was based on a sample of 140 observation and assessment centres in England and Wales but a very restricted data set. Mean cost was £109 per child week (1976–77). The study had three principal conclusions: economies of scale operated only up to a scale of between 10 and 20 places, marked (and expected) regional differences existed, and high occupancy generated lower average cost. The later study was based on the 1983 PSSRU survey, and the 45 observation and assessment centres with complete cost and other data. All were local authority establishments. Mean cost per child week was by then £312 (1982–83 prices). *Inter alia,* the study found a negative influence of length of stay upon average cost, that a secure unit or a separate staffed unit would raise costs, and that some child characteristics were associated with cost variations. This work continues.

6. Other Client Groups

We have focussed on the two client groups about which most has been written and for which there is most cost data. There is as yet relatively little cost information and research for the other client groups served by residential care which takes us beyond the bare financial indicators discussed in Part 1 Section 3. However, we see no reason for rejecting the relevance of the basic balance of care framework to the discussion of planning and targeting criteria, on the understanding, of course, that the underlying data bases and the policy arguments built upon them take cognizance of the issues raised in this chapter. The economic evaluations of services for adults and children with learning difficulties now underway at York[108], the evaluation of the Care in the Community initiative[22] and of psychiatric reprovision[109], and the 1986 national survey of voluntary and private residential and nursing homes for all adult client groups[42] are examples of work which will later feed into informed policy argument about the future roles of residential social care.

Notes and References

1. Wager, R. (1972), *Care of the Elderly*, Institute of Municipal Treasurers and Accountants.

2. Fanshel, S. (1975), 'The welfare of the elderly: a systems analysis viewpoint', *Policy Sciences*, 6, pp. 343–347.

3. Mooney, G. (1978), 'Planning for balance of care of the elderly', *Scottish Journal of Political Economy*, 25, pp. 149–164.

4. Knapp, M. (1980), 'Planning for balance of care of the elderly: a comment', *Scottish Journal of Political Economy*, 27, pp. 288–294.

5. Wright, K., Cairns, J. and Snell, M. (1981), *Costing Care*, Sheffield University: Joint Unit for Social Services Research.

6.   Knapp, M. (1984), *The Economics of Social Care*, Macmillan.

7.   Davies, B. and Challis, D. (1986), *Matching Resources to Needs in Community Care*, Gower.

8.   District Auditors (1981), *The Provision of Child Care: a Study at Eight Local Authorities in England and Wales.* Bristol: District Auditors.

9.   Audit Inspectorate (1983), *Social Services: Provision of Care to the Elderly*, HMSO for the Department of the Environment.

10. Audit Inspectorate (1983), *Social Services: Care of Mentally Handicapped People*, HMSO for the Department of the Environment.

11. Davies, B. (1968), *Social Needs and Resources in Local Services*, Michael Joseph.

12. Davies, B., Barton, A. and MacMillan, I. (1972). *Variations in Children's Services among British Urban Authorities*, Bell.

13. Chartered Institute of Public Finance and Accountancy (1987), *Personal Social Services Statistics, Actuals, 1985–86*, CIPFA.

14. Davies, B. and Ferlie, E. (1982), 'Efficiency-promoting innovation in social care: social services departments and the elderly', *Policy and Politics*, 10, pp. 181–203.

15. Ferlie, E., Challis, D. and Davies, B. (1984), 'Models of innovation in social care of the elderly', *Local Government Studies*, 10, pp. 67–82.

16. Department of Health and Social Security (1981), *Report of a Study on Community Care*, DHSS Information Division.

17. Challis, D. and Davies, B. (1986), *Case Management in Community Care*, Gower.

18. Draper, D. H. (1976). *The Allocation of Care to the Elderly*, University of Bradford: Department of Social Work.

19. Townsend, P. (1962), *The Last Refuge*, Routledge and Kegan Paul.

20. Davies, B. and Knapp, M. (1981), *Old People's Homes and the Production of Welfare*, Routledge and Kegan Paul.

21. Challis, D. (1981), 'The measurement of outcome in social care of the elderly', *Journal of Social Policy*, 10, pp. 179–208.

22. Renshaw, J., Hampson, R., Thomason, C., Darton, R., Judge, K. and Knapp, M. (1988), *Care in the Community: the First Steps*, Gower.

23. Gorbach, P. and Sinclair, I. (1981), *Pressure on Health and Social Services for the Elderly*, National Institute for Social Work.

24. Davies, B. and Knapp, M. (1978), 'Hotel and dependency costs of residents in old people's homes', *Journal of Social Policy*, 7, pp. 1–22.

25. Knapp, M. (1979), 'On the determination of the manpower requirements of old people's homes', *Social Policy and Administration*, 13, pp. 219–236.

26. Darton, R. and Knapp, M. (1984), 'The cost of residential care for the elderly: the effects of dependency, design and social environment', *Ageing and Society*, 4, pp. 157–183.

27. Skinner, D. E. and Yett, D. (1970), *Estimates of Cost Functions for Health Services: the nursing home case*, paper for the 40th Annual Conference of the Southern Economic Association.

28. Meiners, M. (1982), 'An econometric analysis of the major determinants of nursing home costs in the United States', *Social Science and Medicine*, 16, pp. 887–898.

29. Birnbaum, H., Lee, A. J., Bishop, C. and Jensen, G. (1981), *Public Pricing of Nursing Home Care*, Abt Books, Cambridge, Massachusetts.

30. Davies, B., Darton, R. and Goddard, M. (1986), *The Effects of Alternative Targeting Criteria and Demand Levels for the Opportunity Costs to the SSD of Care in Local Authority Homes*, Discussion Paper 484, University of Kent at Canterbury: Personal Social Services Research Unit.

31. Audit Commission (1985), *Managing Social Services for the Elderly More Effectively*, HMSO.

32. Judge, K. (1986), 'Value for money in the residential care industry', in Culyer, A. and Jönsson, B. (eds), *Public and Private Health Services*, Blackwell.

33. Judge, K., Knapp, M. and Smith, J. (1986), 'The comparative costs of public and private residential homes for the elderly', in Judge, K. and Sinclair, I. (eds), *Residential Care for Elderly People*, HMSO.

34. Davies, B. (1981), *A Policy Accident and the Regulatory Response: an historical study of the development of policy, procedures, tools and practice in the reimbursement and regulations of nursing and rest homes in the United States 1965–80*, Discussion Paper 165, University of Kent at Canterbury: Personal Social Services Research Unit.

35. Davies, B. (1986), 'American lessons for British policy and research on long-term care of the elderly', *Quarterly Journal of Social Affairs*, 2, pp. 321–55.

36. Brooke-Ross, R. (1985), 'Regulation of residential homes for the elderly in England and Wales', *Journal of Social Welfare Law*, March, pp. 85–94.

37. Day, P. and Klein, R. (1987), *Accountabilities: Five Public Services*, Tavistock.

38. Day, P. and Klein, R. (1987), 'Residential care for the elderly: a billion-pound experiment in policy-making', *Public Money*, 6, pp. 19–24.

39. Weaver, T., Willcocks, D. and Kellaher, L. (1985), *The Business of Care: a Study of Private Residential Homes for Old People*, Polytechnic of North London, Centre for Environmental and Social Studies in Ageing.

40. Weaver, T., Willcocks, D. and Kellaher, L. (1985), *The Pursuit of Profit and Care: patterns and process in private old people's homes for old people*, Polytechnic of North London, Centre for Environmental and Social Studies in Ageing.

41. Larder, D., Day, P. and Klein, R. (1986), *Institutional Care for the Elderly: the geographical distribution of the public/private mix in England*, Bath Social Policy Papers, no. 10, University of Bath.

42. Research led by Robin Darton (University of Kent at Canterbury) and Ken Wright (University of York) on private and voluntary residential and nursing homes is due for completion at the end of 1987.

43. Ernst and Whinney (1986), *Survey of Private and Voluntary Residential and Nursing Homes for the Department of Health and Social Security*, Ernst and Whinney.

44. Darton, R., Jefferson, S., Sutcliffe, E. and Wright, K. (1987), *PSSRU/CHE Survey of Residential and Nursing homes: descriptive statistical report*, Discussion Paper 523, University of Kent at Canterbury: PSSRU.

45. Audit Commission (1986), *Making a Reality of Community Care*, HMSO.

46. Judge, K. and Knapp, M. (1985), 'Efficiency in the production of welfare: the public and private sectors compared', in Klein, R. and O'Higgins, M. (eds), *The Future of Welfare*, Blackwell.

47. Knapp, M., Montserrat, J., Darton, R. and Fenyo, A. (1987), *Cross-sector, Cross-country Efficiency Comparisons: old people's homes in Catalunya and England and Wales*, Discussion Paper 513, University of Kent at Canterbury: Personal Social Services Research Unit.

48. Bishop, C. (1980), 'Nursing home cost studies and reimbursement issues', *Health Care Financing Review*, 14, pp. 47–64.

49. House of Commons Debates, 18th June 1986.

50. Bishop, C. (1979), *Nursing Home Behaviour under Cost-Related Reimbursements*, Brandeis University, Boston: University Health Consortium.

51. Parker, R. (1987), *The Elderly and Residential Care: Australian Lessons for Britain*, Gower.

52. Department of Health and Social Security Social Services Inspectorate (1985), *The Registered Homes Act, 1984: Study of Local Authority Costs*, DHSS.

53. Department of Health and Social Security Social Work Service (1979), *Residential Care for the Elderly in London*, DHSS.

54. Philips, T. (1981), *A Comparative Cost Evaluation of Alternative Modes of Care for the Aged*, University of New South Wales, Kensington: School of Health Administration.

55. Netten, A. (1987), *Costing Hospital Beds*, Discussion Paper 543, University of Kent at Canterbury: PSSRU.

56. Anderson, R. (1986), *Variation in the Cost of Care: long stay geriatric wards*, DHSS (unpublished paper).

57. Plank, D. (1977), *Caring for the Elderly*, Research Memorandum 512, Greater London Council.

58. Goldberg, M. and Connelly, N. (eds), *The Effectiveness of Social Care for the Elderly*, Allen and Unwin.

59. Bebbington, A., Charnley, H., Davies, B., Ferlie, E., Hughes, M. and Twigg, J. (1986), *The Domiciliary Care Project: meeting the needs of the elderly*, Discussion Paper 456, University of Kent at Canterbury: Personal Social Services Research Unit.

60. Goldberg, M. (1977), 'Reviewing services for the old', *Community Care*, 6th December, pp. 27–30.

61. Davies, B. and Coles, O. (1981), 'Towards a territorial cost function for the home help service', *Social Policy and Administration*, 15, pp. 30–40.

62. Davies, B. (1986), *Assuring Quality, Efficiency and Effectiveness in American Long-Term Care: a review of research, innovation and experiment*, Discussion Paper 420, University of Kent at Canterbury: Personal Social Services Research Unit.

63. Davies, B. (1981), 'Strategic goals and piecemeal innovations: adjusting to the new balance of needs and resources', in Goldberg, E. M. and Hatch, S. (eds), *A New Look at the Personal Social Services*, Policy Studies Institute.

64. Bebbington, A. and Davies, B. (1983), 'Equity and efficiency in the allocation of personal social services', *Journal of Social Policy*, 12, pp. 309–330.

65. Davies, B. and Ferlie, E. (1984), 'Patterns of efficiency-improving innovation: social care and the elderly', *Policy and Politics*, 12, pp. 281–295.

66. Ferlie, E., Challis, D. and Davies, B. (1987), *Efficiency-Improving Innovations in the Community Care of the Elderly*, Gower.

67. Challis, D., Chessum, R., Chesterman, J., Luckett, R. and Woods, R. (1988), 'Community care for the elderly: an urban experiment', *British Journal of Social Work*, 18, supplement, pp. 13–42.

68. Davies, B. and Missiakoulis, S. (1988), 'Heineken and matching processes in the Thanet community care project: an empirical test of their relative importance', *British Journal of Social Work*, 18, supplement, pp. 55–78.

69. House of Commons Social Services Committee (1984), *Children in Care*, HCP360 (Session 1983–84), HMSO.

70. Knapp, M. (1985), *Children in Care: Planning without Costs*, Nuffield/York Folio 7, Nuffield Provincial Hospitals Trust.

71. Knapp, M. (1987) 'Wrong numbers', *Social Services Insight*, 17 July, pp. 20–23.

72. Schofield, J. A. (1976), 'The economic return to preventive social work', *International Journal of Social Economics*, 3, pp. 167–178.

73. PA Management Consultants (1972), *Cost-Benefit Analysis in Social Services for the City of Leicester*, PA Management Consultants.

74. Pinniger, R. (1981), 'The estimated opportunity costs of preventive social work with children and families', *Clearing House for Local Authority Social Services Research*, Birmingham, 6, pp. 55–73.

75. Knapp, M. and Baines, B. (1986), *Explaining Variations in Cost per day and Cost per care period for Children Received into the Care of a Local Authority*, Discussion Paper 412, University of Kent at Canterbury: Personal Social Services Research Unit.

76. Knapp, M. and Smith, J. (1984), *The PSSRU National Survey of Children's Homes*, Discussion Paper 322, University of Kent at Canterbury: PSSRU.

77. Knapp, M. and Smith, J. (1985), 'The costs of residential child care: explaining variations in the public sector', *Policy and Politics*, 13, pp. 127–154.

78. Berridge, D. (1984), 'Private children's homes', *British Journal of Social Work*, 14, pp. 247–260.

79. Knapp, M. (1987), 'Private children's homes: an analysis of fee variations and a comparison with public sector costs', *Policy and Politics*, 15, pp. 221–234.

80. Knapp, M. and Fenyo, A. (1986), *Fee and Utilization Variations within the Voluntary Residential Child Care Sector*, Discussion Paper 378/2, University of Kent at Canterbury: Personal Social Services Research Unit.

81. Begg, I., Moore, B. and Rhodes, J. (1984), *The Measurement of Inter-Authority Input Cost Differences*, Cambridge Economic Consultants.

82. Young, D. and Finch, S. (1976), *Foster Care and Nonprofit Agencies*, Lexington: Heath.

83. Greenhut, M. L., Hung, C. S., Norman, G. and Smithson, C. W. (1985), 'An anomaly in the service industry: the effect of entry on fees', *Economic Journal*, 95, pp. 169–177.

84. Knapp, M. (1986), 'The relative cost-effectiveness of public, voluntary and private providers in residential child care', in Culyer, A. and Jönsson, B. (eds), *Public and Private Health Care*, Blackwell.

85. Knapp, M. (1985a), 'The turnover of care staff in children's homes', *Research Policy and Planning*, 3, pp. 19–25.

86. Hansmann, H. (1987), 'The effect of tax exemption and other factors on the market share of nonprofit versus forprofit firms', *National Tax Journal* (forthcoming).

87. Knapp, M., Baines, B., Fenyo, A. and Robertson E. (1988), *The Costs of Child Care*, ch.10, forthcoming.

88. Knapp, M., Robertson, E. and Thomason, C. (1987), *Public Money, Voluntary Action: whose welfare?*, Discussion Paper 514, University of Kent at Canterbury: Personal Social Services Research Unit.

89. Knapp, M. (1986), 'The field social work implications of residential child care', *British Journal of Social Work*, 16, pp. 25–48.

90. Knapp, M. and Baines, B. (1987), 'Hidden cost multipliers for residential child care', *Local Government Studies*, 13, pp. 53–73.

91. Culley, J., Settles, B. and Van Name, J. (1976), *Understanding and Measuring the Cost of Foster Family Care*, Newark: University of Delaware.

92. Fanshel, D. and Shinn, E. B. (1972), *Dollars and Sense in the Foster Care of Children*, New York: Child Welfare League of America.

93. Knapp, M., Bryson, D. and Lewis, J. (1984), *The Comprehensive Costing of Child Care: the Suffolk cohort study*, Discussion Paper 355, University of Kent at Canterbury: Personal Social Services Research Unit.

94. Wagner, G. (1982), *Children of the Empire*, Weidenfield and Nicolson.

95. London Borough of Wandsworth (1977), *Adolescent Boarding-Out Project: an evaluation report*, Wandsworth, Social Services Department.

96. Hazel, N. (1981) *A Bridge to Independence*, Blackwell.

97. Knapp, M., Fenyo, A. and Baines, B. (1988), 'Consistencies and inconsistencies in child care placements', *British Journal of Social Work*, 18 (supplement) (forthcoming).

98. Simon, J. (1975), 'The effect of foster-care payment levels on the number of foster children given homes', *Social Services Review*, 49, pp. 405–411.

99. Knapp, M. (1984), 'The relative costs of intermediate treatment and custody', *Home Office Research Bulletin*, 18, pp. 24–27.

100. Knapp, M. and Robertson, E. (1986), 'Has intermediate treatment proved cost-effective?' in Harrison, A. and Gretton, J. (eds), *Crime UK 1986*, Policy Journals.

101. Baldwin, S. (1985), *The Costs of Caring*, Routledge and Kegan Paul.

102. Baldwin, S., Haycox, A. and Godfrey, C. (Undated), *A Comparison of the Financial Costs of Caring for Mentally Handicapped Children in Three Settings*, University of York.

103. Wright, K. and Haycox, A. (1984), *Public Sector Costs of Caring for Mentally Handicapped Persons in a Large Hospital*, Discussion Paper 1, University of York: Centre for Health Economics.

104. Wright, K. and Haycox, A. (1985), *Costs of Alternative Forms of NHS Care for Mentally Handicapped Persons*, Discussion Paper 7, University of York: Centre for Health Economics.

105. Fuller, R. (1985). *Issues in the Assessment of Children in Care*, National Children's Bureau.

106. Knapp, M., Curtis, S. and Giziakis, E. (1979), 'Observation and assessment centres for children: a national study of the costs of care', *International Journal of Social Economics*, 6, pp. 128–150.

107. Baines, B. (1985), *The Operating Costs of Observation and Assessment Centres: a working note*, draft paper, University of Kent at Canterbury: Personal Social Services Research Unit.

108. A book is in preparation on the economics of services for people with learning difficulties, authored by Alan Haycox, Martin Knapp, Alan Shiell and Ken Wright. This will pull together a number of hitherto unpublished research studies.

109. Knapp, M., Beecham, J. and Renshaw, J. (1987), *The Cost-Effectiveness of Psychiatric Reprovision Services*, Discussion Paper 533/2, University of Kent at Canterbury: Personal Social Services Research Unit.

Index

Acts of Parliament will be found grouped together under Acts of Parliament

A

Abel-Smith, B, 20
Aberdeen, 330
absconding, 88, 108, 109
ACC, 355
Acts of Parliament:
  Child Care Act 1980, 104, 366
  Children Act 1984, 131
  Children and Young Persons Act
    1969, 74, 77, 79, 82
  Chronically Sick and Disabled Act
    1970, 205–6, 207, 210, 235
  County Asylums Act, 160
  Criminal Justice Act 1982, 79, 181
  Custody of Children Act 1891, 14
  Disabled Persons (Services,
    Consultation and
    Representation) Act 1986, 208
  Education Act 1981, 65
  Health and Social Services and
    Social Security Adjudications Act
    1983, 185
  Health Services and Public Health
    Act 1968, 166, 184
  Industrial Schools Acts, 28
  Local Government Act 1929, 21
  Lunatics Act, 160
  Mental Deficiency Act 1913, 128
  Mental Health Act 1959, 13, 128,
    166
  Mental Health Act 1983, 166–7
  National Assistance Act 1948, 166,
    204–5, 206, 244

National Health Service Act 1948,
  128
Nursing Homes Act 1975, 207
Poor Law Acts, 204
Reformatory and Industrial Schools
  Act, 14
Registered Homes Act 1984, 42,
  185, 207, 277, 327
Residential Homes Act 1980, 207
Unemployment Act 1934, 18
adopted children, 100, 104, 105
alcoholics, 186, 189
Aldgate, J, 90–1
Aldington Detention Centre, 368
Allen, I, 248, 259, 265, 276–7
All-Wales strategy, 131, 146
AMA, 355
Anderson, Arthur, 75
Anderson, D, 137
Anderson, M, 23, 24
Anderson, R, 329
Andover Union, 10
anti-psychiatry, 187
approved schools, 30, 50, 63–4, 75,
  79–80, 81, 87, 106, 109, 110, 111
Apte, R Z, 181, 182
Ashington, 133
Association of Directors of Social
  Services, 256
Atkinson, D, 138
Atkinson and Ward, 139, 144
attendance allowance, 231
attendant schemes, 234

[379]

Printed in the United Kingdom for Her Majesty's Stationery Office
(170/88) Dd289418 3/88 C25 G443 10170